THE TROUBLED LAND

McGRAW-HILL BOOK COMPANY

NEW YORK   SAN FRANCISCO   ST. LOUIS   DÜSSELDORF   JOHANNESBURG
KUALA LUMPUR   LONDON   MEXICO   MONTREAL   NEW DELHI
PANAMA   RIO DE JANEIRO   SINGAPORE   SYDNEY   TORONTO

ELBERT W. STEWART

CHAIRMAN, DEPARTMENT OF SOCIOLOGY AND ANTHROPOLOGY
BAKERSFIELD COLLEGE

THE TROUBLED LAND
SOCIAL PROBLEMS IN MODERN AMERICA

Library of Congress catalog card number: 76–38623

ISBN 07-061343-5

567890 HDBP 76543

This book was set in Trade Gothic by Applied Typographic Systems, printed by Halliday Lithograph Corporation, and bound by The Book Press. The designer was Janet Bollow; the drawings were done by Judith McCarty. The editors were Ronald D. Kissack and Eva Marie Strock. Charles A. Goehring supervised production. Cover photograph by Ernest Braun.

PICTURE CREDITS

Picture Editor: Helen Ansell, Photofind, San Francisco
Unless stated otherwise, pictures courtesy of Photofind, San Francisco

PART ONE   RESPONSE TO CHANGE   Ed Cooper   13

CHAPTER ONE   THE STRAINS OF THE CITY   Louis Goldman, Rapho-Guillumette   18   Helen Ansell   22   William M. Rosenthal   28   Baron Wolman   32   Klink   38   Michelle Vignes   40

CHAPTER TWO   CHALLENGE TO EARTH, SEA, AND SKY   Dave Bellak   44   NASA Photo via UPI   48   Gerhard Gscheidle   50, 54, 66   George Ballis   57

CHAPTER THREE   THE CONSUMER TRAP   Roger Lubin   78   Robert A. Issacs   85

CHAPTER FOUR   THE CREAKING CURRICULUM   Howard Harrison   94, 115   Nick Pavloff   97   Roger Lubin   106   Sahm Doherty, Camera 5   111

CHAPTER FIVE   WORK FOR THE NIGHT IS COMING   Robert A. Issacs   120   Currier & Ives, 1872, Library of Congress   123   Michelle Vignes   131   Ted Mahieu   135, 142

CHAPTER SIX   FAMILY: THE LOOSENING BONDS   Howard Harrison   146   Larry Keenan, Jr.   151   John Roone   160   Ernest Lowe   163   Michelle Vignes   167

TO MY WIFE, LILLIAN

PREFACE

The troubles that now plague America are particularly oppressive to a land that has long believed in its destiny and has seen its historical accomplishments as a mere prelude to the limitless progress of the future. The land is troubled by old problems that it had thought would be ended by now: poverty and slums, unwholesome labor conditions, educational inequality, and rising crime rates. It is troubled, too, by wars and riots and racial strife, by threats to the environment, by mounting population, and by cities devouring the green valleys that gave them birth. The land is troubled that its fantastic growth of scientific knowledge and industrial production should not automatically cause most of its social problems to wither away. It is as though a great dream had become clouded (as dreams often do) with its promise constantly receding into the distance.

We can always remind ourselves that other times have had their problems too, and that man has shown great resilience in surviving troubles and crises, but such a statement brings only slight consolation. A reminder of a dismal past does little to hearten the unemployed, the impoverished, the wornout coal miner dying of black lung, or the armless veteran returning from a futile war in southeast Asia. They, and a large segment of modern youth, take little comfort in knowing that other ages have suffered more and have been less acquainted with justice than our own. Their interest is not in the territory already traversed, but in the road ahead. In the past, perhaps, poverty and gross inequality were made necessary by scarcity of goods, and racial bigotry was made inevitable by ignorance. There is a difference today, a difference characterized by both frustration and hope. The frustration springs from the very wide gap between social desire and social reality. The hope springs from two great sources: the scientific and social knowledge that has removed many social ills from the realm of the inevitable, and the growing discontent with our failure to apply that knowledge more fully.

If social knowledge is to be applied more fully, greater attention must be devoted to the study of social problems. Sociology must avoid the temptation of aloof, olympian views of the world, of writing mainly for professionals, and of traveling mainly on safe, well-worn paths. Whether the sociologist knows the answer or not, he must at least examine the issues of the day in the light of his own discipline and in terms understandable to the layman.

The task of this book is to present social problems in such a manner as to stimulate involvement and to bring sociological explanations into the language of the everyday world. Sociological perspectives are used to analyze the sources of social problems and their interlocking nature, the consequences of technological normative change, and ways in which social orders lead inevitably to conflicts and dilemmas. Care has been taken, though, not to allow conceptual analyses to overshadow the facts on which they are based or to deaden the impact of gross inequities in the social order. From this approach, the student will come to realize that the problems of urbanism, racism, environment, crime, poverty, job insecurity, injustice, and war are his problems, and that they are amenable to improvement. He must be warned, however, that the rate of social improvement is so slow that many of these very problems will continue to haunt him throughout his life, unless, as Ramsay Clark has said, we can make the pursuit of justice the passion of America. This is possible only if social problems are seen as pertaining not to mere statistics, but to flesh and blood people, our kinsmen of all classes and colors.

The following pages attempt to produce a sense of urgency about social problems, to present tools for their analysis, and to make suggestions for what students themselves can do, individually or collectively. Every effort has been made to give clear explanations and to select problems that are close to home, problems that involve the lives of us all. Part and chapter openings are charged with a sense of inquiry to provoke student thought and serve to link each section to the basic ideas discussed in the Introduction. There are suggestions for further readings and for activities, and there are questions at the ends of chapters — hopefully not questions to write lengthy themes about, but questions to rouse concern and debate and to encourage further learning and genuine analysis. The solutions to social issues are never clear cut, so a social-problems book is and has to be controversial, more a stimulus to thought than a technical manual.

The materials of an ideational nature are in nearly all cases drawn from the writings of sociologists. Much of the illustrative material, for the sake of currency and relevance, has been taken from recent books, current magazines and newspapers, and from commission reports. The world we live in is the world reported on by the mass media and struggled over by politicians in state, local, and federal centers of government. It is this world that we must plunge into, not only for study, but for participation. The political decisions, so necessary for the amelioration of social problems, must be our decisions, based on a knowledge of our world and our times.

Several people have been helpful in the preparation of this book, sometimes by direct suggestions and sometimes by relating their experiences with student projects. I wish to thank particularly Mita Dhariwal, David Rhea, and James Glynn of the Sociology Department of Bakersfield College. My appreciations go also to Thomas Yale of the Biology Department for his careful critique of the environmental studies, and to Angel Campos for his suggestions on the subject of racial and ethnic groups. Karen and Fred Kearney were especially helpful in providing insights into the legal problems of the poor and the general problems of agricultural workers. I have profited particularly from the help of an outstanding editor, Ronald Kissack, whose concern for social problems and good teaching techniques matches his skill in editing. My thanks go also to Janet Bollow for the excellent design she created for the book. Finally, I am indebted to Otto Larsen of the University of Washington for his helpful suggestions on the plan and organization of this book and for his criticisms and encouragement.

ELBERT W. STEWART

THE TROUBLED LAND

INTRODUCTION

Twentieth-century America presents a strange paradox of scientific and technological achievement accompanied by mounting concern over social troubles. Sometimes the promises of a scientific age are obscured from sight by concern over increasingly deadly war potential, deterioration of the natural environment, urban dislocation, racial and intergenerational conflict, and overpopulation. Today's threats and uncertainties bring an unquestioned relevance to the study of social problems. The troubles of society must be faced and studied if they are ever to be ameliorated.

THE UNIQUE NATURE OF THE TROUBLED LAND

Trouble and strife have accompanied the human race through much of its history, but there is a difference between the problems of the present and those of the past. The differences are reassuring in some ways and threatening in others. When historians relate the record of earlier crises in human affairs, they are often speaking of problems that are no longer major worries. Wars and threats of wars remain, of course, and are even more menacing than in the past, but many of the problems have changed. Our fear of devastating plagues has nearly disappeared, and to a great degree so has our fear of flood and drought, of famine, of declining populations, and of the physical inability to supply the needs of the people. Gone are the high infant-mortality rates that made parents compulsive about having large families. No longer is poverty made inevitable by economic scarcity, and no longer need certain races and classes be submerged into peonage in order to support a leisure class.

Successive scientific triumphs of the last century or more have virtually freed us from such types of worry, but they have opened new problems. These problems have produced such strains and maladjustments in social systems that we can hardly keep abreast of technological change. Greater productivity and scientific knowledge have outmoded many old customs, folkways, and mores and have brought a demand for new values. The need to adjust to new conditions has complicated the problems of deviance and crime by adding new types of value conflict and new means of evading the law. The great industries that have promised an abundant life have also poured their poisons into the waters and the air. Finally, modern science has made the ancient custom of fighting wars so deadly that it could well bring the human race to an untimely end.

THE GENESIS OF SOCIAL STRIFE

Everyone but the totally unobservant is concerned with the types of problems developing in the new society, and nearly everyone is looking for explanations of their causes and possibilities for their solution. The politician, the minister, the reformer, the campus militant, the businessman, the farmer, the laborer — all have their points of view and their social concerns, depending on their training, interests, and conceptualizations of social reality.

Sociologists also have their special orientation to the field of social problems. They attempt to give careful attention to facts and trends, to develop explanations and concepts for analysis, and to avoid being swayed by vested interests. They conceptualize social systems in a way that shows their strains and suggests possible means of ameliorating problems. Sociology, along with other sciences, seeks method and system in its approach. Obviously the first step in a systematic approach to the study of social problems is that of defining the field.

DEFINITION: THE CRITERIA OF SOCIAL PROBLEMS

Although all the social concerns of the day are generally regarded as social problems, some are more important than others. Some problems belong only to a limited locality or period of time or only to a few individuals. Are they also social problems? Very often situations that are now regarded as social problems have existed for many years but were once considered so much the natural order of things as to be largely ignored. What, then, converts a particular situation or development into a social problem?

THREE COMMONLY USED CRITERIA Three commonly used criteria for defining social problems are: numbers of people involved, conflict with societal norms, and amenability to improvement. All are valid points but, as we shall see, are not quite sufficient. A problem is not considered social unless it affects a fairly large segment of society. One man's loss of a job is simply his own personal problem; mass unemployment is a social problem. Or, if a mere handful of women encounter unequal employment rights, their cases will probably be dismissed as exceptional; if such large numbers encounter inequalities that complaints and protests are common, then female inequality becomes a social problem. The only difficulty with this type of definition is that it omits certain cases involving rather few people, but cases that the knowledgeable public, nevertheless, regards as highly undesirable, such as the inhumane treatment formerly accorded the mentally ill or the inhumane treatment of many juvenile cases, recently uncovered by a Senate committee headed by Senator Bayh. Such cases do not involve large segments of the population or the possibility of mass protests, but can we refuse to call them social problems?

The second common criterion — a situation violating social norms — is definitely involved in both the examples just given. In other cases, though, we have to ask "whose norms?" Low wages are a social problem for labor unionists, but for some employers they might be desirable. And at the same time many people are complaining about the harshness of our laws against marijuana, some citizens are saying that the laws are not harsh enough. So rather than saying that social problems arise from situations conflicting with the social norms of the entire society, we must widen our category to say they conflict with the norms of large segments of the population. Not only is there disagreement about societal norms, but the normative definition of social problems is complicated in another way: sometimes the norms themselves have to change. In Chapter 10, the dictum of "multiply and replenish the earth" will be spoken of as an outmoded norm. The problems of ecology discussed in Chapter 2 will be seen partly as the result of a mastery-of-nature norm that has become a threat to the survival of man and many other species. Many modern-minded people consider the eye-for-an-eye definition of justice an idea that should have been discarded long ago. New conditions, new cultural habits, and additions to knowledge often change the norms. Our normative definition of a social problem should be stated as "a condition of normative violation, normative conflict, or a need for normative change."

The third common criterion—amenability to improvement through social effort—is clear in one respect but not in another. If astronomers predict the eventual death of the earth by the sun's turning into an exploding star, we can hardly apply the words "social problem" because there are no conceivable social solutions. There are marginal cases, however, where we might debate whether there are social solutions. At one time poverty was regarded as an inevitability that could be relieved slightly by charity, but not really ended. Now there is repeated talk of ending poverty, and there are economic possibilities for doing so. A problem still remains, though, regarding improvement. Not all elements of society will always agree on what constitutes improvement. Problems, therefore, are matters for lengthy debate until some kind of consensus is reached. Agreement to take action sometimes depends upon whether the problem looks threatening to the society.

SOCIAL PROBLEMS AS SOCIAL THREATS Many militant followers of various causes feel that social concern is often awakened only when social situations pose a threat to the system. Even the late Dr. Martin Luther King, Jr., noted for his nonviolent philosophy, wrote in his famous "Letter from a Birmingham Jail" of the need for creating a "situation that cannot be ignored." Frances F. Piven and Richard A. Cloward[1] make a strong case historically for saying poverty has generally been dealt with in an ameliorative manner only when it begins to pose a threat to the social order. The philosophy behind early English poor laws of the Tudor period and French poor laws of about the same era was to make almshouses capable of allaying violence, but miserable enough to drive people to work if there were any available jobs. A much more contemporary example is that of racial inequality. For the vast majority of whites, gross inequality of treatment of the black race was barely noticed until organized protest began to threaten business, urban areas, political alignments, and the nation's reputation abroad.

It can be argued that the matter of threat is not part of the social problem itself but, rather, an indication of whether anything will be done about it. The reason for calling it an actual part of the problem is that the criterion of normative strain is not met until there is a strong awareness of normative strain. Situations are not necessarily definable as problems until they are brought to public consciousness. The sociologist, however, should be more aware of potentially threatening developments than the layman and also of the possible consequences of trying to solve problems. In trying to perform his role in this respect, he will often think in terms of "latent functions."

LATENT FUNCTION AND PROBLEM DEFINITION Occasionally a social problem exists partly because it is a natural consequence of something the society strongly desires. This idea was originally developed by Robert K. Merton[2] and is termed "latent function." Various customs and institutions of society have their "manifest" or intended consequences, as well as certain unexpected, and often undesired, consequences known as "latent" functions. The institutions of courtship and romantic love in our society, for example, have the manifest function of ensuring that most people get married, even though marriages are not arranged as in some cultures. Romantic love is glorified, and the freedom of people to choose their own partners is considered a natural, inalienable right. Implied in the right of choice, however, is the right to individual happiness, which may or may not be attained in the marriage. If the individuals are not happy, then they will probably get a divorce. Thus the loudly acclaimed belief in individual freedom has the latent function of a high divorce rate, which the society regards as a social problem.

Some types of crime are analyzed by Merton as the latent consequence of the generally approved American requirement that everyone be judged on the basis of how well he succeeds. Since people do not all have equal access to success goals (for such reasons as deprived background or discrimination), some find success possible only through illegal means. Hence, the "good norm" of success striving can lead to an unusually high incidence of larceny, graft, and embezzlement. This problem will be discussed more fully in Part 3.

Merton's idea can be used for visualizing the possible consequences of solutions to problems. The problem of crime could probably be greatly reduced by giving police and other investigative authorities vastly greater powers than they now have, but such a policy could have the latent function of eliminating many of our civil liberties. It could in the long run, perhaps, have the latent consequence of public outrage against law enforcement and an increasing number of acts of defiance.

6   [2]Robert K. Merton, *Social Theory and Social Structure*, The Free Press, New York, 1949, pp. 71–81.

SOCIAL PROBLEMS AND THE FUTURE Finally, a definition and delineation of social problems should attempt to take the future into consideration. Often the problems of public concern are essentially problems about the future — e.g., population growth, pollution, education, and automation. Sometimes the future results of the problems are less obvious. A childhood of malnourishment might cause cerebral damage throughout life; if it exists in all the poorest parts of a county it could seriously impede any later attempts at self-improvement. Chemical contaminants and atomic radiation might cause genetic damage to future generations. The likelihood may be slight, but any possibility must be viewed as a social problem.

Most problems discussed in this book have their implications for the future and are thus of particular concern. Much of the younger generation is idealistic enough to be concerned not only with their own survival, but also with the problems of racial and ethnic equality, humane treatment of the poor and sick and deviant, and the quality of justice. They are worried about pollution, the future availability of jobs, and the quality of education and its relevance to the future. They are particularly concerned about the horrendous possibility of nuclear destruction and the need for a better type of international order. Most problems of this type meet all the criteria suggested above: societal concern, normative strain, and amenability to improvement. If not handled correctly, these problems are a threat to the total society and in some cases to the entire human race. In many cases the problems themselves are the latent consequences of what was once seen as desirable change. For this and other reasons, problems do not appear suddenly and in isolation, but are of an interlocking nature.

THE INTERLOCKING NATURE OF SOCIAL PROBLEMS

In thinking of the modern problems that concern us most it is helpful to visualize them as arising in various ways. Some are most clearly understood as the consequences of invention and social change; others are best understood as a consequence of normative strain, a gap between ideal and reality. A third type of social problem arises out of the inability or unwillingness of people to conform to the roles expected of them by society — a type encompassing health and mental health problems as well as crime and delinquency. Finally, there are problems that arise out of the nature of societies and their interaction with others — aggression and war. These types of problems are all interrelated, however. One cannot think of war without thinking of normative breakdown, terrifying inventions, and social change. Problems can hardly be seen in isolation.

There are many examples of the interlocking nature of social problems. In the case of modern urban problems, for example, good automobiles and roads (technical change) have led to the feeling of a need to move about easily and at will (normative change) and have contributed to a pattern of suburban growth. Suburban populations have made the location of industry in the suburbs profitable (technical change), and this change has dried up employment opportunities in the central slum areas (normative strain). Idleness and unemployment have led in turn to resentment, higher crime rates (deviant behavior), and to quarrels over police treatment (normative conflict). All these problems have led to demands for urban renewal (technical and social change) and for public transportation systems (technical change) that will bring benefits especially to the urban poor (redress of normative strain). As another example, family problems involve an interplay of the type of social change that separates parents from their children during work and school hours, changing norms about the roles of women and children, and even deviance in cases where the family is unable to perform its role of properly socializing the young. And social problems are interrelated in that often the solution of one creates another. Ending the problem of premature death has led to the problem of population explosion. Solving the problem of population increase leads to normative conflict over contraception and abortion and may even downgrade the traditional role of woman as housewife and mother.

THE SOCIAL CHANGE PERSPECTIVE The first set of problems discussed in this text refer to technological change and the resulting strains in the social system. The industrial-urban revolution of the last centuries has brought new types of urban and environmental problems, problems of industrial labor, distribution of wealth, economic cycles, the shrinkage of agricultural employment and rural life, greater interdependence, and greater potentials for both the enrichment of life and the destruction of life. Industrial change has its ramifications in all the other types of problems we shall discuss. As one billiard ball strikes another, and that one in turn strikes a third, technological change sets off a chain reaction, changing first the means of livelihood, and then affecting the normative system, possibly leading to new types and degrees of deviant behavior. As progressive change is brought about in the world's potential for destruction in warfare, the problems of human organization and of survival also become more acute.

William Fielding Ogburn[3] used the concept of "cultural lag" to explain how scientific and technical change begin to exert their influence on all elements of a culture. Since a culture includes both material traits (cars, factories, airplanes) and nonmaterial traits (values, ideals, regulations), the various parts of a culture can develop inconsistencies. Ogburn's idea was that some elements of a culture become antiquated relative to the rest of it, are no longer appropriate, and constitute strains or disjunctures. He termed these out-of-date elements, and the time required for them to catch up with societal needs, as cultural lags. One of his examples was that of the size of counties made small so they could be traversed by horse and buggy in one day. Such boundary lines are cultural lags in an age of rapid transportation. Other examples include a wasteful, exploitative attitude toward natural resources, outdated as resources are depleted (although it might have served fairly well when rapid development was the primary aim), and the continued use of forms of city gov-

[3]William Fielding Ogburn, *Social Change*, The Viking Press, Inc., New York, 1950, pp. 200–220.

ernment that were intended for small towns and do not fit modern organizational needs. In these cases, norms are involved, but the strain is described primarily as a need for adjustment to technological and other forms of change.

NORMATIVE STRAIN AND INCONGRUITY All societies are based upon normative systems, rules of right and wrong, enforced by custom and tradition and sometimes by law. Changing technologies, living habits, and educational requirements often interfere with long-established behavioral rules of this type. Consequently, although social change may be involved in the genesis of social problems, many problems can be seen primarily in the light of normative strain. All societies have their incongruities between social practice and stated belief, but they often find means for rationalizing them away, or they manage to keep them out of their consciousness.

In an age of considerable education and sophistication, however, incongruities are often laid bare. Why should racial inequality exist in a society whose norms speak of a dedication "to the proposition that all men are created equal?" Why should a society that claims to believe in peace be so frequently at war? Why should there be a strong reproductive norm in a world worried about overpopulation? Why must some segments of the population be relegated to poverty? Such questions become more insistent as greater awareness dawns and as means are developed for making protests effective.

ROLE FAILURE AND DEVIANCE In all societies there are problems of failure of conformity to the norms and to proper role behavior. The failures are sometimes the results of inability to perform required roles, as in the case of the physically or mentally handicapped. More frequently the problem is one of unwillingness to abide by the rules and to perform as expected. Occasionally people deviate from the rules as a matter of principle, like the civil rights leaders who deliberately challenged Jim Crow laws or peace demonstrators. More common types of crime will be given considerable attention—white- and blue-collar crimes, crimes for money, crimes of revenge and violence, crimes with victims, and crimes without victims—certain types of sex "crimes," for example, and the use of various drugs.

Drugs of all types, including legal alcohol, are included in the section on role failure and deviance. In a search for excitation or relief from boredom, people often find outlets that lead to excess. Sometimes social traditions are able to prescribe limits on the use of alcohol or drugs so that they are little or no problem. When it becomes possible to use various forms of alcohol, marijuana, drugs, and tranquilizers in excessive amounts, however, many problems are created for society. They interfere seriously, even tragically, with the performance of socially prescribed roles, and they lead the society to ask if its drug problem is symptomatic of some chronic illness.

The treatment of those who deviate from the law is as much a social problem as deviance itself. It constitutes a normative problem for a society that believes in due process and equality of treatment and in the possibility of rehabilitation. What is possible in the name of justice, and what happens to the men behind bars?

9

THE ULTIMATE PROBLEM: SOCIAL NATURE AND SURVIVAL

The final group of problems we shall consider has to do with the immediate survival of the species, rather than merely the forces that are disruptive to social systems. These problems could also be said to arise from the nature of man and be characteristics of human organization. Recently, with an increasing interest in the writings of animal ethnologists and physical anthropologists, we have begun to wonder whether the problems of war and violence are something rooted in the nature of man. Or are they simply the consequence of certain types of social organization and competition?

The problem of "the killer ape" is ancient. In the imagery of older times it might have been called the problem of the devil within. The term "killer ape" might be a misnomer, for the other apes are not killers of their own kind, and any characterization of human nature is open to controversy. There is a school of thought, however, that sees man as the descendant of a killer ape and therefore a vicious creature, not perfectable, and in need of constant watching. This point of view and its refutations are presented in Chapter 15. Sociologists tend to shy away from attempts at defining just what human nature is, but they are very much aware of what human beings do. The history of man is a bloody one. The record of recent and present wars, research among living primitives, evidence from comparative animal studies, and evidence from archaeology all tell the same story of a fighting creature. At the same time, much research has been done on the resolution of conflict and methods of conflict avoidance. We must look at both the historical warnings and the indications of hope for the future.

CONCEPTS AND SOCIETAL MODEL

In the discussion of Merton's analysis of latent function, we were examining one well-known concept in the field of sociology. A concept is an idea about a class of events or phenomena. For example, in Merton's concept of latent function the idea applies to latent or unintended results of romance, individual choice of marriage partners, and of success striving. The idea of latent function is applicable to a class of phenomena (unanticipated results) whether we are talking about marriage, deviant behavior, religion, education, or any other social institutions or traits.

Sociology deals in concepts of this type and helps to explain the social order with them. We have already looked at a second example—Ogburn's idea of cultural lag. Cultural lag can refer to the failure of highways to keep up with the production of automobiles, the failure of contraception customs to keep up with the problem of population explosion, or any of the other consequences of the gap between technical possibilities and social realities. There has already been a reference to role expectations. Actually, all society can be analyzed as a system of positions and roles, and most of its problems can be seen as failures in the definition or performance of social roles.

Such concepts are helpful in organizing our thoughts about society and about social problems. The concepts mentioned are discussed in the introductions to various sections of this book. In the part dealing with incongruities, the idea of normative strain and value conflict will be discussed further. In the section on deviant behavior the very important concept of anomie is explained, as well as the concept of learned patterns of deviance. In the final section, the concept of culture—the greatly varying patterns of living devised by the various peoples of the world—is inquired into as a possible explanation for patterns of war or peace. Subcultural differences within a society are prominent in the investigation into the nature of racial and ethnic problems in Chapter 7. All such concepts are important tools of analysis for sociological inquiry. Equally important is the model of society perceived by the sociologist.

SOCIETAL MODEL A model is a simplified pattern with which a difficult system can be compared. A very common sociological model of society is sometimes referred to as "organismic," meaning that society is seen almost as a great living organism, with each member resembling a cell, making a contribution to the whole. There are two troubles with such a model. First, it makes society seem even more prescriptive than it is and turns the human being into a creature without individual will. Secondly, all organisms die, and an organismic analogy can make it seem that all societies are doomed to eventual extinction. Sociology likes to think of systems as undergoing change but not going through birth, maturity, and death.

A much more common sociological perspective is to view society as an ongoing system of interaction between individuals and the total culture, always subject to change and minor dislocations, but with a tendency to restore a balance between its parts. The latter perspective is generally favored by implication in this book, but with certain reservations. It must not be assumed that all problems are always and inevitably solved or that periods of strain and crisis are necessarily of short duration. There is, too, the possibility that a social system might have to make fairly drastic changes, not merely minor adjustments. In this respect the book's viewpoint is somewhere between an easy reassurance that all will be well and a gloomy prediction of doom. Whether tomorrow's society is less troubled than today's depends upon public awareness, study, and action. An involved generation can make the difference.

PART ONE

RESPONSE TO CHANGE

The following six chapters will examine city, environmental, consumer, educational, occupational, and family problems. These topics are all united by a common thread. All contain many elements of cultural lag, being unable to keep pace with the challenges presented by modern science and technology. Normative change is involved too, of course, and sometimes even deviant behavior, but social change is the theme that links the topics together most clearly. All these areas of study have drawn attention before, but in the rapidly changing modern world they present new complications, and some, especially urban and environmental problems, are reaching the stage of crisis.

WHAT IS NEW

In each of the areas under consideration in this section, long-existent problems appear in new forms. City problems are new in their vastness, their heterogeneity, and their governmental and social chaos. Modern transportation, productivity, disease control, and displacement of rural workers have caused urbanization and suburbanization on a scale never before achieved. The environmental pollution problem results partly from the very growth of the city, but even more from modern industry and transportation. Environmental pollution is not entirely new, but its scale is such as to dwarf all previous contamination problems.

The consumer has been bilked before and has some legal protections today that he did not have in the past, but the techniques of deception have grown. It is now possible to use the findings of chemical science in a manner inimical to the public welfare and to use all the techniques of modern psychology and sociology to develop ways of trapping the consumer. Education and its costs and failures have always been problems of public concern, but now the educational system has to take on a greater burden than ever before. It has to train and retrain and relegate people to the innumerable and changing occupational roles required by society. The nature of work has changed drastically as hours decline, automation renders many skills obsolete, and doubts arise as to what jobs still have a future. Finally, the family becomes an embattled institution, unable to perform many of its older educational, protective, and integrative functions as other institutions expand at its expense.

MEETING THE SOCIAL PROBLEMS CRITERIA

The topics of Part One are social problems in that they meet the criteria discussed in the Introduction. They involve large – tremendously large – numbers of people; there are always strains between what society perceives as desirable and what is actually accomplished. All the problems included are amenable to improvement – of being brought closer to societal ideals. On the other hand, if not improved they are all threats to the social order and to future generations. Reform attempts, however, must be studied with care. Many proposed solutions could result in unforeseen (latent) consequences of an undesirable type. Already we have witnessed the development of certain detergents and fuels that solve one problem only by creating an even more serious one.

INTERRELATIONSHIPS

The problems of the city, it will be pointed out, are a combination of many other social problems. The urban industrial changes and the general technological inventiveness of the society have solved many of the problems of want and created many of the problems of abundance: crowding, disposal of wastes, and air and water pollution. Inventions, however, are adopted readily by societies whose customs and needs have prepared them for more and more inventions. Inventions change the way of life of a people, but the people in turn develop the habits of thought and action that call for even more inventions. Transportation can never be fast and efficient enough to suit the people, and products cannot be sufficiently packaged, loaded with preservatives and "cosmetic" effects, and made sufficiently disposable and convenient. There is a two-way interaction between invention and demand for invention.

Similarly, there is a two-way relationship between inventive change and social norms. What was once the luxury of a college education turns into a necessity and a right as the technical society finds room only for the educated. Education, in turn, accelerates inventiveness and social change. High productivity makes poverty much more of a normative strain than in the past, and education is looked upon as one means of alleviating poverty.

The rapid pace of social change also has its effects upon role problems and deviance. The residents of slum areas are left in the backwash of social change; their self-image suffers and they become alienated. Deprived conditions in a relatively affluent society create the resentments that are one of the correlates of high delinquency rates. Finally, technological change results in a potential for more destructive wars, and modern economic needs concentrate populations into highly vulnerable, congested urban areas. The problems are all interrelated.

THE SOCIAL CHANGE PERSPECTIVE

The social change perspective emphasized in this section is largely an elaboration of the ideas of Ogburn. Important inventions lead to a need for shifts in all segments of social systems. The development of efficient agriculture not only replaces farm workers but also demands their urbanization. Once in the city they can become welfare cases unless new opportunities are developed for them. The internal combustion engine has not only led to new means of transportation, but it has resulted in new problems of air pollution and a demand for new laws for safety in auto design. It concentrates industry and jobs. It leads to greater mobility of families, new dating customs, and drive-in theaters, banks, and even churches. The need to keep pace with industrial change and to regulate industries in the public interest increases the power of government, but as will become clear in the discussion of the food industry, regulated businesses try to thwart too much regulation.

Families are wrenched by the economic changes that have ended most farms and other small family enterprises and have employed the father and often the mother away from home. Educational systems find a gap between their institutional ways and the demands for training personnel for the industrial-scientific society. Technological changes occur so rapidly that the importance of a man's work is lessened, and sometimes his job is made obsolete. For young people, the problem of occupational choice becomes difficult not because the new type of society lacks a variety of jobs, but because many of the jobs are not rewarding and others face possible obsolescence. These and many others of the problems of city, environment, family, education, and labor can be seen, then, as the direct or indirect consequences of technological change. The following chapters will examine these problems in more detail.

1 *Judging by their size and rapid growth, American cities could be listed among our most spectacular successes. Why, then, do we speak of urban crisis and dislocation? Does the very technical change that has made modern cities so gigantic also threaten to undermine them; if so, can science and technology reverse the process? Why, after a century of campaigns to clean up the slums, do slums remain an integral part of all large American cities? Why is urban renewal often looked upon as an enemy by the poor and by racial and ethnic minorities? And why do ghetto developments and housing segregation continue unabated in a society that speaks so loudly of racial equality?*

The problems of urban growth and of vulnerability of the city to economic and political forces will be discussed in this chapter, and also the problems of slums and social segregation. We shall look, too, at the contention that there is something about city life, or at least parts of city life, that has a strong effect on one's mental and emotional development. Finally, we shall look at the governmental and ecological problems of urban sprawl and ask what better suggestions can be made. Despite the problems of the great city, it is a place of interest and growth, economically necessary. Are there ways of managing city and suburbs in a pattern of harmony? What have other countries done? What can we do?

THE STRAINS OF THE CITY

URBAN COSTS In the morning the traffic begins to increase along all the highways that are engineering miracles in themselves but never adequate for the rush hours. It seems that whoever lives at one end of the city works on the other side, and each driver, alone in his car, contributes to the dangerous rush and level of noise and congestion that fray the nerves of even the most hearty. If a visitor to the city should decide to take public transportation, in most cases he will find it grossly inadequate, poorly maintained, and given little financial support or attention. City residents would not even know how to direct him. Public transportation is generally not adequate; the automobile is used out of necessity.

Near the core of the city are the old tenement buildings, some being torn out for the sake of urban renewal, others still standing, decadent, but the only places with rent low enough for poor families. Children grow up here, learning the ways of the street, outwitting the police and the school, surviving in their gangs, defending their turf, both loving and hating the city, scarred and toughened by it, and often embittered by it. Some may later set fire to it.

Meanwhile the well-to-do escape farther and farther from the urban centers, spilling over old villages, building new suburbs, and agitating for better freeways and transportation to travel back to the city. The city finds its tax base shrinking as the rich exit and the poor enter. Crime rates are high in the slums and the costs of police and fire protection mount, as do the costs of garbage disposal, sanitation, transportation, parks and recreation, welfare, and education. On a national average, per capita taxes are nearly $25 higher in the city than in the surrounding areas, and the cities receive less per capita in governmental aid for education and other purposes than do the surrounding suburbs.[1] In the period from 1950 to 1966, local government revenues increased by 29.8 billion dollars, but expenses increased by 43.7 billion and debts by 58.7 billion.[2] Some people would question calling the cities sick; few would question calling them financially starved.

URBAN VULNERABILITY In the Northwestern United States is a prosperous area centering around a great aircraft industry, generally kept prosperous by the demands of the airlines, but always supplemented by the demands of the federal government for bombers.[3] Since the warplanes of last year are now obsolete, new types must be put into production, and prosperity seems endless. Occasionally, however, there is a change of government policy; the pace of spending slows down, and contracts are canceled. There is an uneasy realization that much of the prosperity of a whole section of the country depends upon international conflicts. What if conflict should slow down too much? Local workmen shudder at the possibility, as do local politicians.

[1]Alan K. Campbell and Philip Meranto, "The Metropolitan Education Dilemma: Matching Resources to Needs," *Urban Affairs Quarterly*, vol. II, p. 57, September 1966.
[2]The President's Commission on Civil Disorders, *Report of the National Advisory Committee on Civil Disorders* (The Kerner Report), Bantam Books, Inc., New York, 1968, p. 392.
[3]"Appalachia in Seattle?" *Newsweek*, pp. 56–57, August 17, 1970.

How does a man vote if he is laid off just after making a down payment on a new house and just before paying the doctor bill for the new baby?

Small towns have been known to die as a consequence of the very industrial change that has created the big cities. Recently the people of the little town of Bay St. Louis, Mississippi, experienced the ordeal of industrial life and death. After encouraging its development as a testing center for NASA, the government changed policies, making deep cuts in the NASA budget and ending the town's boom. The government announced that the space center would be closed at the end of 1970. Meantime local residents had bonded themselves for millions of dollars for water, power, schools, airport, and other facilities, looking forward to growth and prosperity, with solid promises from well-known leaders of the space program. Then the government ax fell, leaving the town to atrophy or to find some new ways for the government to restore it to life. Homes that were built for rental are now tenantless, and the villagers who had invested their savings are now thousands of dollars deeper in debt.[4]

Even the big city is not immune to recession by governmental decision. Seattle depends overwhelmingly on the aircraft industry, and Los Angeles finds the same industry to be a vital part of its economic diet. A major shift to public transportation and a corresponding decline in private automobiles could be a blow to Detroit. Many seaports would find a large portion of their spending money cut were it not for generous government subsidies to ship lines — 50 million dollars in 1969.

In some respects the city is a giant with feet of clay. Arthur J. Vidich and Joseph Bensman, in *Small Town in Mass Society*, show the pattern of economic dependence of the small town. In their study, small-town residents liked to think of themselves as independent of the mass society, but in fact they were controlled by industries and institutions located elsewhere. The same is often true of the city.

There are, of course, other types of urban vulnerability. New York experienced a prolonged blackout because of a power shortage. Debilitating smog alerts have occurred in Los Angeles, New York, London, and Tokyo. All cities depend upon rapid transport and are vulnerable to strikes called by national unions.

The city is covered over with a pall of smog and soot for much of the year, even if it is built on a wind-swept coastal plain. Its problem of disposal of sewage, garbage, and industrial waste is just as serious, tending to contaminate rivers, coastlines, and underground aquifers, threatening the health of the residents of all surrounding areas.

THE DIVISIONS WITHIN

A major difficulty of cities is that of the divisions within. There always have been, and have had to be, various sectors of the city serving diverse purposes, but there has usually been a sense of unity underlying the diversity. The ancient city-states had a quality of unity about them, holding, as they did, first claim on the loyalties of their

4"Boom Town Deeply Hurt by Space Cuts," *Los Angeles Times*, April 22, 1970, Part I, pp. 1, 15.

people. Occupation and social class were varied, but the city was the governor and protector, and the bond that held people together. The city, in this sense of the word, is a thing of the past. It is the great mass society, if anything, that gives the people a sense of commonality, and the city is a thing of fragments — of business centers and high-rise apartments, ghettos, and a wide belt of suburbs, with a confusion of names, shopping centers, school districts, zoning areas, governmental agencies, and associations.

There are divisions between social classes, races, and ethnic groups. There are divisions between inner city and outer city, divisions of economic interest, of party and policy, and of those who belong and those who do not. There is also an important division between those who believe in the city and those who do not; and even for those who believe, there are differences. To some it is a place of culture, enjoyment, and civic pride; to others it is disagreeable, but a living; to yet others it is a place for economic exploitation. The city copes with all types, or there would be no city. If, however, it is important that more people believe in the city or that cities be developed in such a way that more people *can* believe in them and take pride in them, it is important to study the implications of the divisions within.

SLUM AND SUBURB   Within the city there is a general segregation of social classes that helps to keep poverty hidden. The very poor live close to the inner circle of the city or they may be strung out along railroad tracks, but they tend to be separated from the middle class. Occasionally urban renewal will complicate the pattern by bringing high-rise apartments to the areas surrounded by urban blight, and poverty will become more obvious and its bite will be felt more keenly. Value of residence usually declines by slow degrees, however, and a cartographer could map class elevation almost as surely as he plots contour lines. Among the lower valleys in this pseudo-relief map are the slums, a place of stagnation. Just how deteriorated they should be before being designated slums, and how ruthlessly they should be torn out, are matters for debate.

CONFLICTING VIEWS OF URBAN RENEWAL   For generations Americans have worried about slums. There have been numerous efforts at slum clearance by individual cities and in recent decades increasing efforts on the part of the federal government.

> **Make a study of at least one specific physical need of your community, such as public transportation, parks and playgrounds, improved zoning or building codes. Draw up a plan of what could be done and submit it to a councilman for his study and response.**

At present the major federal agency for slum clearance is the Urban Renewal Administration, which has made possible the development of large acreages by exercising the right of eminent domain, that is, forcing the sale of property for the public good.[5] Once the property is acquired, it is usually developed by private enterprise with generous federal assistance.

There are really two types of interests at stake in the process of urban renewal: human and economic. Urban renewal was once urged primarily by social reformers, who saw slums as a menace to human values and felt it would be possible to bring all slum dwellers into the common, middle-class value system of a home in the suburbs or its equivalent. Now, many of the very people who were once the supporters of urban renewal are often its critics. Such books as Jane Jacobs's *The Death and Life of Great American Cities* and Martin Anderson's *The Federal Bulldozer* have been highly critical of urban-renewal projects. Jacobs stresses the breakup of neighborhoods and community feeling, the loss of small shops that were once the meeting places of old friends and the centers of neighborhood news and small talk. Anderson questions whether the value of urban renewal is worth the cost and whether its benefits fall equitably. The problem is that it has been hard to get renewal projects to serve two conflicting interests: those of the businessmen, who are trying to prop up the values of the central city and increase its economic yield, and those of the poor people, who see the cheap rents in the run-down central areas as an economic necessity. Furthermore, until rather recently, central location of housing for people who cannot afford cars has been an advantage in getting to work. With a present trend toward business development in the suburbs, this benefit is changing to a detriment in most cities.

Little by little, attempts have been made to reconcile the two types of interests. What is needed is a more consistent enforcement of the policy of relocating people who are moved out of old tenements by urban plans. However, the problem is complicated by the fact that those moved out are blacks in about 70 percent of the cases—people who already feel bitterly deprived. The Urban Renewal Administration demands attempts at relocation of displaced persons and generally builds public housing more or less the equivalent in capacity to the housing units that are demolished.[6] But this policy has not worked. The new housing is not finished in time or is not in a convenient place; both white and black residents resent its institutional quality and complain that it draws too many problem families. The consequence is that only 20 percent of the displaced people actually end up in public-housing developments. Presently more work is being done to hire social workers to help in the relocation of people, but the funds for improvements in urban renewal have been hard to wring out of the government in times of war, inflation, and complaints over high taxes.

[5]Nathan Glazer, "The Renewal of Cities," *Scientific American*, vol. 213, pp. 194–204, September 1965.
[6]*Ibid.*

A CASE STUDY OF AN ETHNIC COMMUNITY   Ethnic areas in the city often develop a real sense of community. In earlier America, at a time when people believed in the picture of the American city as a great melting pot, there were many heart-warming tales of the immigrant making a success in the new land. Ethnic neighborhoods were largely poor, but they usually represented gains for people who had known greater poverty abroad.

Often urban renewal has dislocated old ethnic communities, and Italians, Poles, Czechs, Greeks, and other groups have become intermingled with older American types. In view of the cultural ideal of Americanization and the melting pot, this change would seem favorable. There are cases, though, where it has worked very great hardship and brought feelings of bitterness. It has also interfered with another important American value—the right of people to live where they wish.

Herbert J. Gans has done a study of the effects of urban renewal on an Italian-American community in Boston.[7] Although the West End area he describes was popularly called a slum, Gans objects to the word in this particular case. The area had the type of community feeling and cohesion that is better described by the term "urban village"—an area in which new immigrants "try to adapt their non-urban institutions and cultures to the urban milieu."[8] The term is applicable to many Puerto Rican and Negro areas of American cities. Skid row is usually near such areas, even in contact with them, but it is an "urban jungle," a place of transience, "depressed if not brutal." In the case of the residential West End of Boston, the homes were poor, the majority of incomes low, there was a problem of dirt and garbage, but the apartments were large and kept neat and livable. Best of all the apartments were cheap, a point too often overlooked by urban planners. Children reared in the neighborhood got used to it; although small children loved a chance to get out into the country, as they grew older they found the country rather distressing; they needed people and activity around them. They placed little status importance on the type of housing, and resented having their area called a slum.

Gans suggests that areas be defined as slums only if they are harmful to their residents—firetraps, structurally unsafe, infested with rats or disease, or unquestionably inclined to draw children into illegal activities. They must not be called slums simply because they do not meet the standards of taste of the middle-class suburbanite. Gans charges that the West End was not a harmful place; it was redeveloped because it was a place in which developers could foresee a large profit. Much worse areas were passed up for renewal. The Italian-American community organized "Save the West End" committees, but to no avail.

There were old people who had lived in the community all their lives, or ever since leaving Italy, and knew only their friends and relatives in the area. They were

[7]Herbert J. Gans, *The Urban Villagers*, The Free Press, New York, 1965.
[8]Gans, *op. cit.*, p. 4.

A likely casualty of urban renewal.

to spend an old age in exile. There were small grocers who had managed to eke out a living, but could not afford to relocate in a city that already had too many small stores. There were the teenagers who found the new suburban areas boring and empty. All the families had less money to spend on groceries and doctor bills and shoes for the children. The redevelopment commission had promised that 60 percent of the people would be relocated in public housing; only 10 percent actually were. Eventually nearly all the families had to find houses on their own, in most cases less satisfactory from their point of view than the houses they had left.

This is but one story of redevelopment of an ethnic community. Many projects have been similar, and some have been better planned. It does, however, illustrate the problems that must be looked for, and the superficiality of assuming that all clearance of "slums" will bring immediate benefits to their residents. Scott Greer once summarized the problem with the statement "At a cost of more than three billion dollars, the Urban Renewal Agency has succeeded in materially reducing the supply of low cost housing in American cities."[9]

BLACK AND WHITE Today the poorest residential area is occupied to a large degree by blacks who have migrated from rural areas the last few decades. The creation of more and more suburbs has done little for the feeling of neighborliness and community that they were once expected to restore, but they have, by accident or design, served the purposes of segregation, both social and racial. Indeed, the most significant division that has been going on in American cities for the past few decades is the division between black and white. So great has been the influx of blacks into the central city that Washington, D.C., and Newark, New Jersey, are already more than half Negro, with New Orleans and Richmond at approximately the 50 percent mark, and Baltimore, Jacksonville, Gary, and Cleveland nearing the halfway point.[10] The significance of this development is that blacks occupy the most congested neighborhoods, the black ghetto—an area usually characterized by economic stagnation, but of high costs to the city. The per pupil-day cost of education, for example, has been increasing at an annual rate of 6.7 percent for the last two decades, but local taxes have not kept pace.[11]

The white exodus to the suburbs is even more rapid than the black entry into the central city. Thus future years may see the central city decline in political influence relative to the suburbs. Although there has been an increase in the number of blacks attaining middle-class status, they have not followed the trend of earlier European immigrant groups of moving out of the central city, nor do they seem likely to do so, because of white attitudes and real estate practices. Actually, there was a net in-migration of blacks from urban fringe areas to central cities from 1960 to 1966.

[9]Daniel P. Moynihan, "Urban Conditions," *The Annals of the American Academy of Political and Social Science*, vol. 371, p. 161, May 1971.
[10]The President's Commission on Civil Disorders, *op. cit.*, p. 390.
[11]*Loc. cit.*, p. 392.

In the twenty worst urban slums, the nonwhite unemployment rate varies from 50 to 300 percent higher than white unemployment.[12] A study of Los Angeles shows that employment in the predominantly black Watts area fell by 61 percent between 1965 and 1970. There had been a major race riot in the Watts area in 1965, still remembered by Californians as the worst riot the state has ever had. Millions of dollars have been spent to fight poverty in the area since the riot. Actually, some good has been accomplished in occupational training of some of the residents, but they have often moved out after receiving better jobs. For those left behind the sex ratio has grown increasingly lopsided, with the number of women exceeding the number of men by 44 percent. This helps to explain the unemployment problem, but it documents a major concern: those left behind, those unable to afford rents in other areas, seem to be involved in a vicious circle of poverty. Poverty forces them to live in jobless areas, which in turn leads to greater poverty.[13] White unemployment in Los Angeles has also increased slightly because of recession conditions. Negroes in Watts, however, show 16.2 percent unemployment compared to 4.3 percent for the Los Angeles area as a whole. Such conditions of unemployment are common in the nation's ghettos.

The urban center is becoming a poor place to find a job for either black or white. New industry, in 80 percent of the cases, locates outside the central city in places hard to reach by public transportation. Racial discrimination in employment adds to the problem. The result is a high incidence of dependency. In the urban slums six nonwhite children out of ten are supported by Aid to Families with Dependent Children (AFDC) payments during at least part of their childhood.[14] On the other hand, a Cleveland study showed no such conditions for those black families living outside the slums. Although the incidence of poverty increased in the slum area, the median family income rose by more than $1,000 per year for those families who had moved away.

Other ethnic groups have lived in separate enclaves of their own, but the word "ghetto" has not always been appropriate for other groups. Irish, Poles, and Italians lived in their own areas by choice and usually for one or two generations. If an area remained persistently ethnic, its people usually became the owners of their own businesses and had economic and possibly political control of their own sectors. Robert Blauner compares the Negro situation, on the other hand, with that of colonialism, administered from without by "foreigners." "The educators, policemen, social workers, politicians, and others who administer the affairs of the ghetto residents are typically whites who live outside the black community."[15]

There are now a few black mayors and some progress toward political control of black areas by blacks, but this is so belated and uncertain that the colonial com-

[12]Moynihan, *op. cit.*, p. 165.
[13]"Watts Jobless Rate Up," *Los Angeles Times*, August 7, 1970, Part I, p. 3.
[14]Moynihan, *op. cit.*, p. 169.
[15]Robert Blauner, "Internal Colonialism and Ghetto Revolt," *Social Problems*, vol. 16, Spring 1969.

parison still seems apt. The several black mayors of the nation's cities have faced almost insurmountable problems because they have been elected only after the central city has deteriorated financially almost beyond hope. Mayor Richard Hatcher of Gary, Indiana, has run a very clean government, has accomplished a little by way of housing in poverty areas, but has not had the funds or the power to reduce smog or crime. Mayor Carl Stokes of Cleveland is in a similar position. The Negro mayor of Newark, Kenneth Gibson, has inherited a city from a political crowd recently convicted of extorting $253,000 from city contracts, and allegedly connected with the Mafia. Gibson can hardly help but run a cleaner government, but he is having to take over a city on the verge of bankruptcy.[16]

POLICIES FOR THE GHETTO   The President's Commission on Civil Disorders suggested three possible policies for the ghetto, and three probable consequences: (1) present policies choice; (2) enrichment choice; and (3) integration choice.

As the commission points out, the present policies are leading in the direction of an increasingly divided country. A small segment of the black population is achieving a degree of prosperity, but even they are concentrated in the central city, not far from poorer black neighborhoods. For the majority, the conditions do not improve. Because of a high birth rate during the 1950s, the black population will have an increasingly large percentage of young men in the age group of 16 to 24 years in the immediate future. It is in this very group that unemployment and discontent is highest and explosive potential is a constant threat. Present policies call for federal investment in central cities, but the appropriations are small, partly because of war costs.

By enrichment choice the commission refers to trying to improve existing black communities with more job opportunities, encouragement to black business and a measure of economic independence, better education and training, and self-help programs. Such programs would cost much more than is now being spent. They would probably have the beneficial effect of creating a little more atmosphere of hope, but they would not solve the problems of a divided society; in fact, they might even further divide the middle class from the lower-class black communities. The enrichment program could aid the black separatist movement — a movement that advocates separate but equal status. Past experience has seen only failure in separate but equal

---

Make a racial and ethnic map of your community. Is there a clear pattern of de facto segregation? Is the segregation purely a result of economics? If not, find out what policies, official and unofficial, keep segregation going.

---

[16]"The Black Mayors," *Newsweek*, pp. 16–18, August 3, 1970.

The integration choice: black participation in the city.

policies. It is even possible that the idea of enrichment could end in a type of American apartheid, or intensified racism.

The commission finally turns to the integration choice as the recommended solution. Since jobs are being created primarily in the suburbs, there must be a determined effort to make it possible for Negroes to live there and to be equal competitors for the jobs. The problem of educating ghetto children could be met best in this manner, avoiding the shortcoming of lack of experience in the outside world for ghetto children, and also the economic costs and the hard feelings of extensive busing. Finally, in the opinion of the commission, integration is the only way to avoid dividing the society. This, we might add, is the only way the black could learn to believe in the city as a center of promise and therefore as a place demanding his loyalty and participation.

THE SUBURBS AND "ANTIURBS" The suburbs are not all of one type. Some have been created as the city spills out into surrounding village areas, remaking rural villages in the image of suburbia. Others have been planned in large tracts; the Levittowns, new communities, suddenly springing into existence. In social-class level they range from an aristocratic old suburbia to monotonous rows of cheaply built "little boxes." Although the suburbs are usually characterized as middle class, as though they were all on a common economic level, there is much social-class structuring about them. With the passing of time they begin to resemble the older parts of the city. The great growth of the last two decades has been suburban. Of the largest twenty-five cities in the United States, thirteen lost population between 1960 and 1970, but there was always growth in surrounding suburban areas. The 1970 census was the first to show suburban population outnumbering combined central city and rural population.

Often the suburbs lie outside the city limits, so the residents do not have to pay city taxes and do not have a voice in the city government. Although the residents are economically dependent upon the city, working there and buying there, they have an emotional dislike for it. Their aim is to find a quiet suburb, although the quiet suburb of today is often the noise center of tomorrow's growing metropolis. The poor resident of the slum is often a person who does not like the city either, but he lives there because of economic necessity.

Sometimes in old suburbia or in the "gold coasts" of the great cities there are urbanites who work to promote art and music centers, colleges, and museums. Mayors and other city politicians, along with business leaders, like to see redevelopment, and ordinary citizens call for greater expenditures for schools and playgrounds and transportation. There are not too many leaders, however, of the type of Pericles or Lorenzo the Magnificent, whose devotion is to city beautification. Prevailingly the American intellectual has not been an urbanite in truly loving and promoting the city; he has displayed a nostalgia for the rural past. In fact, he has questioned the city's democracy, its intelligence, its "Americanism," its heart, and its mind.[17]

THE MIND OF THE CITY

Old stories about the "country rube" and the "city slicker" point to a belief in strong personality differences between urban and rural types. Certainly in an age of extreme mobility and rapid communication the differences could be expected to decline, but there is still evidence of a difference. The city, whatever its problems, does have certain intellectual advantages. The urbanite is relatively free of the narrow confinement of the mind that is the function of neighborhood gossip in the small town. There are enlightening opportunities—more informative newspapers, radio and television stations, libraries, colleges, theaters, and book stores; however, these advantages are not used by all. The pace of life is faster, the nervous tensions greater, and the levels of noise and congestion more shattering. Do these characteristics lead to more mental problems for the city?

NEUROSIS, PSYCHOSIS, AND THE CITY In *The Intellectual Versus the City*, the Whites[18] present a long history of American opinion and the conclusions that there is something wrong with urbanism. To some extent the opinions represent nostalgia for a

[17]Morton White and Lucia White (eds.), *The Intellectual Versus the City*, Mentor Books, New American Library, Inc., New York, 1962.
[18]*Ibid.*

simpler way of life, but the criticisms come from many of America's leading intellectuals, among them such pioneers in education and sociology as John Dewey and Robert Park. There are charges of the creation of a thoughtless rabble, of rising class awareness that threatens democracy, of nervous tensions, of "homogenized" sameness, and of urban neurosis and crime. Is this mere opinion, or does it have its element of fact?

Leo Srole[19] and others did a lengthy study of midtown Manhattan, including the busiest and most congested parts of New York City. They concluded that midtown Manhattan is a place of serious psychological impairment for nearly one-third of its inhabitants, and that only 18.3 percent are free of any type of neurotic or psychotic disturbance. The situation is far worse for those with incomes of less than 6,000 dollars per year than for those with higher incomes.

Rates of violent crime have been positively correlated with density of population in urban centers, and some research indicates that perpetrators of violent crime have a lower than normal tolerance of crowding. Ulcers, coronary disease, and high blood pressure are also more prevalent in the city than in rural areas.[20] Professor P. G. Zimbardo[21] of Stanford did an interesting study to try to ascertain whether the level of violence and vandalism is greater in the city or small town. He had cars abandoned in the small town of Palo Alto and in New York City and secretly watched. In New York the car was vandalized by twenty-three separate persons or groups in a period of one week; in Palo Alto the car was left unmolested for the same period of time.

In many cases the evidence is to some extent against the city, but one needs to ask what part of the city, and at what levels of poverty and neglect? Srole's statistics would argue that adequate income could be a partial solution to the problems of urban life and neurosis. It should also be added that urban life does not have to be endured in the most congested areas of the city. Various studies constitute an indictment of living conditions in the areas of greatest urban rush, but no conclusions can be drawn from them about more inviting parts of the city.

MENTAL VERSUS EMOTIONAL LIFE   The early German sociologist Georg Simmel wrote on the topic of mental life and the metropolis. His conclusion was that urban life has a tendency to heighten one's intelligence in some respects because he must live in a more totally competitive world and a world in which more stimuli constantly impinge upon him. At the same time, said Simmel, there is a diminution of his emotional responses. He does not respond to situations of tragedy, pathos, and love with adequate emotion. He has become rather blasé, taking everything in stride with little emotional perturbation, with a blank countenance, an unconcern.

---

[19]Leo Srole et al., *Mental Health in the Metropolis*, McGraw-Hill Book Company, New York, 1962, chaps. 7 and 8.
[20]Paul R. Ehrlich and Anne H. Ehrlich, *Population, Resources, Environment*, W. H. Freeman and Company, San Francisco, 1970, p. 142.
[21]P. G. Zimbardo, paper presented to the Nebraska Symposium on Motivation, 1969.

Several recent research papers have been written on subjects related to Simmel's hypothesis. One question approached by such a study is whether people in large conglomerates become less sensitive to the feelings of others and less inclined to help in an emergency. A widely quoted series of experiments demonstrated that where a critical emergency develops (for example, heart attack or epileptic seizure), the larger the group of observers, the less likely anyone is to take immediate action to help. One person alone lends help because he knows he must. When others are present, subjects of the experiment fear overreacting or doing something that others could do better. Each tends to wait for the expert. Of several variables tested in the experiment, the only important one was the number of people in the group witnessing the tragedy. There was only one other correlation—a slight negative correlation between the willingness to respond and the size of the community in which the subject was reared.[22]

The urban person, of course, is likely to be in association with more people more of the time than the rural person. It is possible that the conditioning of the city resident to the presence of large numbers of people and his habitual dependence on someone whose specific duty is that of handling the emergency make him slightly less responsive to emergencies than the country person. Rather than grabbing a hose to put out the fire, he may be more inclined to ask why the fire department is so slow. There is also a rule of urban life of respecting the other person's privacy, possibly carried too far.

Stanley Milgram has examined Simmel's idea about the blasé attitude and the erosion of the emotions in the city.[23] He agrees with Simmel's description of the manifest phenomena and has new approaches to their explanation. We can think of our emotional lives and our total sensory receptivity, he says, in terms of inputs and outputs. There is a limit to the possibilities of each, and anything exceeding this limit is an overload on the nervous system. To avoid the neurotic anxiety that would develop from a concern about everyone we meet, we must select and restrict inputs by such devices as unlisted phone numbers, an unfriendly countenance, or the distant stare. The sense of moral responsibility is shifted by setting up special institutions to handle poverty, neglected children, and the needy blind. In this way it is

---

Is it really true that urbanization results in a tendency to ignore other people? Discuss instances from your own community that support or refute Simmel's ideas about the urban personality.

---

[22]John M. Darley and Bibb Latané, "Bystander Intervention in Emergencies: Diffusion of Responsibility," *Journal of Personality and Social Psychology*, vol. 8, no. 4, pp. 377–383, 1968.
[23]Stanley Milgram, "The Experience of Living in Cities," *Science*, pp. 1461–1468, March 13, 1970.

possible to overlook and wall out the poverty-stricken, the panhandler, the skid-row alcoholic, members of other races, and residents of the wrong side of the tracks. There are too many accidents and tragedies in the city for any one man to handle; he would collapse emotionally. The conscientious citizen, perhaps, takes an interest in certain charitable causes, but he cannot possibly participate in all. Milgram's conclusion is that the restriction of emotional inputs is a matter of response to urban conditions, rather than the response of a particular personality type, although he does not rule out the possibility that there can be something habit forming about the "walling out" type of response.

Evidence that the handling of emotional inputs is not determined purely by city life as such is the observable difference in this respect between one city and another. In some cities, visitors are treated with more politeness than in others; observers describe cities as having differences in atmosphere, from cold and aloof to warm and friendly. Milgram explains these differences as resulting partly from (1) differences in densities, the less crowded cities being less aloof; (2) the rural populations from which the cities are drawn; and (3) specific historical circumstances of the growth of the city. Paris and Vienna, for example, have preserved aristocratic attitudes toward the arts and entertainment, based on their historical positions, and will be congenial to the visitor of similar tastes. Such European cities, and also the American city of Boston, with a sense of history, are highly cognitive of historical sights and of tourists visiting them. They are not necessarily aware of their poverty areas. Cities seem to be as selective as individuals in their inputs and outputs. The evidence, however, would suggest that there is no need to be fatalistic about the urban personality type. It can change to some extent and need not be a serious problem in the city that controls crowding and has pride in its traditions and cultural attractions.

THE PROBLEMS OF GOVERNMENT

As cities grow, so do their administrative complexities, their interrelationships with other cities and other levels of government, and the number of ecological problems that are beyond their individual control. Old city governments become cultural lags in a megalopolis that extends far beyond their jurisdictional areas. New York City and its vicinity are served by 1,400 governmental and administrative districts; the San Francisco Bay Area is an urban concentration of similar governmental confusion. San Francisco employs the residents of a dozen communities strung over the Bay Area, providing their city services, paying them for their labor, but unable to tax them or to demand their participation. Precisely the same is true of most great American cities. San Francisco is an unusually good example because political decisions of a century ago restricted the City and County of San Francisco to a tiny dot of land at the northern end of the San Francisco peninsula. Many other cities as well are small incorporated islands foundering in a sea of suburbia.

THE INTERURBAN ENTANGLEMENT As cities spill over their boundaries and inundate the rural lands that once separated them from neighboring cities, new problems arise that are beyond the competence of any particular city government. If several cities are polluting the same river or bay, the one city that attempts environmental control is doomed to failure. Broad thoroughfares that end in narrow lanes as they enter the jurisdiction of the county or the next city become useless. Air pollution emanating from the uncontrolled industries of one city spreads over the entire urban complex and well out into the countryside. Urban problems of this type have become superurban, not merely metropolitan but "megalopolitan."

The highway problem is the first of the interurban problems to be attacked with great energy, although more in some states than in others. Much of the highway construction program is aided by state and federal governments, and the freeway systems become a matter of large-scale planning. Eventually the freeway problems escalate, however, with more people driving more cars for greater distances as roads improve. There is no permanent solution to the traffic problem, but in some states it can be said that the battle is progressing according to plan. Federal aid prevents the total collapse of a highway system in states unable to bear their own costs.

Highways, whatever their defects, are used here as an example of one possible solution to interurban problems—turn the matter over to higher levels of government. Undoubtedly this will have to be done—and to a certain extent already is being done—for problems of smog and pollution, urban renewal, and critical housing shortages. The question is, though, whether the rising curve of state and federal intervention in urban affairs should be extrapolated into the indefinite future until city functions vanish. Traditional American values favor local control over a number of decisions and yet, as we have seen, complete localization is no longer possible.

Possible intermediate solutions lie in the direction of interurban cooperation through new agencies. Such agencies are created for cities sharing a harbor or river. Through cooperation with county government, common building codes are developed and common planning commissions activated. Montreal is attempting a parliamentary system in which all outlying communities are represented in a common government. Experiments of this sort have been suggested for cities in the United States as well.

The great city of today seems to have little autonomy and almost no sense of genuine popular control over the direction of government.[24] In an address to the Seventy-Fifth National Conference on Government at Philadelphia in November 1969, Professor Victor Jones made several proposals aimed at solving both these problems. There should be neighborhood boards carrying government within the city to local levels, taking the place of the old ward bosses of the days of city political machines, but doing so in a legitimate way. Such recommendations have been made by charter-revision commissions for both Los Angeles and Sacramento and are

[24]Victor Jones, "Representative Local Government from Neighborhood to Region," *Public Affairs Report*, vol. 11, pp. 1–6, April 1970.

Local planning: Philadelphia's
restoration without demolition.

advocated by many authorities on city government. On the higher level, there is a need for more structural means of ensuring cooperation of areas beyond city limits or for close linkage of city governments, as in the Twin City Region in Minnesota. Plans could be adapted to the special needs of local regions but generally should provide for representation of the city governments included and also for direct representation of the people. Special provisions for minority representation could be made in a regional governing body.

Regional systems would permit planning in a way that would provide a proper balance between housing and commercial uses of newly developing areas, preserve needed open spaces, and link new areas together in an orderly transportation system. At the same time, the organizational level would stop short of complete federal control that might stifle such local plans as city improvement in St. Louis, the Los Angeles Music Center, the ethnic cultural centers of San Francisco, and the restoration of historic buildings in Philadelphia.

CITY STRUCTURE AND INNOVATION A very thorough study of one measure of a city's ability to face its problems was made recently by Michael Aiken and Robert R. Alford.[25] The rapidity with which a city drew up plans and appealed for federal urban renewal funds for which it was eligible was used as a measure of innovation. The study included 582 cities. There was no evidence that cities with high proportions of middle-class, well-educated citizens were particularly good with respect to innovation. Governments with power concentrated in strong mayors or city managers (once regarded as reform structures) were slower at such decisions than others.

To a great extent the innovation decision was made by older cities. Those with large ethnic minorities, low levels of education, and high rates of unemployment were the most likely to appeal for urban renewal funds. Part of the explanation is obvious: the greater the need, the more likely the plan for action. The authors hypothesize, however, that other factors are involved. The older communities had larger numbers of interorganizational networks, more organizations such as redevelopment agencies, welfare councils, and other community-decision organizations. When plans were made by such organizations, and general public opinion was not roused, innovation proceeded most smoothly. The experience of such cities lends support to Jones's idea of the need for more local boards to carry government to local levels and promote decision making by those most involved.

ROADS FROM MEGALOPOLIS

Although much has been said in criticism of the city, and more will be said about its environmental problems, there is no suggestion that the city be abandoned. Urbanism is the way of life for a majority of people living in industrial societies, and for increasing numbers of people in underdeveloped regions of the world as well. For America, the trend toward city and suburb continues to accelerate. This does not mean, however, that the city has to be an unplanned megalopolis, heedless of environmental destruction and of the urban blight and decay of areas left behind.

CITY SIZE For years Lewis Mumford has spoken of the possibility of building smaller cities that will leave green belts between themselves and neighboring cities. At first glance, such an idea does not seem feasible. During his long life Mumford has seen many new cities grow to approximately the desired size and then continue to expand beyond that size. There is a kind of American tradition of growth that leads us to expect all communities to expand or die, and there is an excitement about being where things are happening. Naturally the rapid growth of our cities has depended upon much more than values; growth takes place in response to economic opportunity. So far the economic opportunities seem to have called for the growth of many urban areas into gigantic size.

The solution envisaged by Mumford is to plan in such a way that essential industries will be spread out. An age of ready transportation and communication,

[25]Michael Aiken and Robert R. Alford, "Community Structure and Innovation: The Case of Urban Renewal," *American Sociological Review,* vol. 35, pp. 650–663, August 1970.

Alternatives of megalopolis: orderly, integrated development.

when central offices can provide organizational control over plants located in a dozen states, would seem to make such a development feasible. The Department of Housing and Urban Development is looking into possibilities for discouraging gigantic growth of cities and helping smaller areas. There is usually a wide gap between "looking into possibilities," however, and actually implementing policy. The federal government is such an enormous customer for industry and has so many economic favors to dispense that with determination it could probably promote small or intermediate-sized cities and slow the growth of the giants.

DISPERSAL There are other roads from megalopolis. One such road would be that of the dispersal of the ghetto. Charles Abrams[26] has suggested simply building large amounts of cheap public housing in surrounding areas, which would attract the present ghetto residents and cause the abandonment of the old tenements. Most social planners would not be that drastic but would call for ways of making housing available in new suburban areas without de facto racial restrictions and, as a minimum, would make sure that no one is expelled from his home by urban renewal unless suitable alternative housing is provided.

[26]Glazer, *op. cit.*

A temporary road from the metropolitan area could be provided by a great improvement in public transportation, making it easier for the urban poor to find jobs in new areas or to visit the country. In an age of protest over smog and highway congestion it would seem that public transportation would be easily promoted, but such is not the case. In the summer of 1970 the National Governors' Council rebuffed a proposal to spend part of the federal highway funds on public transportation, turning down the idea by a majority of twenty-three to twelve. Apparently they thought the voters who really count would prefer more highways for private cars.

ORDERLY DEVELOPMENT   Even within the great metropolitan area there are roads from megalopolis, for the word "megalopolis" implies not only size but ugly, confused, hodge-podge development. The regional governmental agencies, with orderly plans for development and redevelopment, could prevent much of what is most unpleasant about megalopolis. Parks and green belts could be left within, making possible an internal road from megalopolis.

Reformers in the Department of Housing and Urban Development hope to promote more uniform building and zoning codes across the country and better legislation for acquiring land for orderly housing development and other uses. The problem of rising building costs, which has created the greatest housing shortage since World War II, might be solved by a rapid increase in factory production of houses — one of the few industries to have largely resisted assembly line techniques until very recently. If cheap and efficient houses and transportation are not provided, the future of American housing might be more in the direction of apartment living — a noticeable trend of the past ten years.[27]

There are cities in today's world that do not present a picture of disorganized sprawl, blight, and dangerous social-class division. Some are wealthy, exclusive developments, but some are the cities of ordinary people — such cities as Stockholm, which has had city planning for 300 years.[28] In Stockholm many people are apartment dwellers, but the apartments are surrounded with gardens and playgrounds, are convenient to shopping, and have public transportation available. Many other European countries are concentrating on the development of garden suburbs, with careful planning and balance of human needs. No two nations can solve problems in precisely the same way, but it is good to know that countries whose per capita income

---

Get acquainted with the policies of your planning commission. Visit their office or meetings or invite a member to answer questions for the class. Is there a zoning adjustments board to hear complaints?

---

[27]"The Great Housing Crisis," *Newsweek*, pp. 69, 71, 74, June 22, 1970.
[28]Goran Sidenbladh, "Stockholm: A Planned City," *Scientific American*, vol. 213, pp. 195–205, September 1965.

is less than our own are able to build cities free of blight and with an atmosphere of well-being. The challenge of the cities is a challenge for architectural, ecological, and human engineering. The future of the cities depends upon new applications of science to solve some of the very problems that have resulted from a scientific-industrial age.

SUGGESTED READINGS

Dull, Leonard J., and John Powell (eds.): *The Urban Condition: People and Policy in the Metropolis,* Clarion Books, Simon and Schuster, Inc., New York, 1969.

A book of readings, centering on the urban environment and its effects on man, the problems of renewal and relocation, community action, and improved social planning.

Gans, Herbert J.: *The Urban Villagers,* The Free Press, New York, 1965.

This book, referred to at length in the preceding pages, is excellent sociology, describing all aspects of an ethnic community and the social consequences of its dislocation.

Goodman, Jay S. (ed.): *Perspectives on Urban Politics,* Allyn and Bacon, Inc., Boston, 1970.

Goodman's collection is essentially a study of political power and powerlessness in the city, including reviews of several community improvement projects, political attitude surveys, racial problems, and urban-suburban differences.

The President's Commission on Civil Disorders, *Report of the National Advisory Commission on Civil Disorders* (The Kerner Report), Bantam Books, Inc., New York, 1968.

The Commission Report, mainly a study of riots and racial problems, is also a study of the American city—housing, police policies, educational facilities, unemployment, segregation, inadequacy of recreational facilities and programs, and lack of political responsiveness.

Von Eckardt, Wolf: *A Place to Live: The Crisis of the Cities,* Dell Publishing Co., Inc., New York, 1967.

A well-illustrated book, emphasizing the need for beauty, expression, and individuality in building and planning. Von Eckardt's book has the merit of presenting visions of what the future could hold.

White, Morton, and Lucia White (eds.): *The Intellectual Versus the City,* Mentor Books, New American Library, Inc., New York, 1964.

Reviews the attitudes and writings of many American intellectuals, past and present, with misgivings about the city. Although some of the thinking is romantic and nostalgic, the book presents many thoughtful views of urban problems and the urban direction.

 **QUESTIONS**

1. Today's city is referred to as a "vulnerable giant." What are some of the social, economic, and technical crises to which it is vulnerable?

2. Why are there often strong differences of opinion between upper- and lower-income groups as to the desirability of urban renewal projects?

3. Evaluate the three possible choices for the ghetto described by the President's Commission on Civil Disorders.

4. What are the conclusions of studies cited about the effects of urban life on the personality? Do the conclusions apply to all types of urbanization or mainly to certain types of urban areas?

5. Discuss possible ways of dealing with the governmental, ecological, and human relations problems of the modern metropolis.

2 *Various kinds of poisons are entering the blood stream, and possibly the chromosomes, of many of the earth's species. Land, sea, and sky are threatened. What is the source of the threat? Our ancestors seem to have regarded the earth as a sacred being, not to be defiled or exploited. How did we come to think of ourselves as the masters of nature, capable of defying her laws? What are the contaminants? Are the contaminants confined to certain areas, or do they spread over the entire earth? Is the threat to the sea and the atmosphere real, or is the ecology talk something on the order of a fad? What are the policies of industry and government relative to ecological problems? Why has it taken us so long to become concerned about pollution?*

There are certain products that produce pollution but are nevertheless greatly desired by the public. Automobiles are one of the best examples. Are there alternatives to the internal combustion engine, or can a pollutant-free gasoline really be developed? Can we increase our use of electric power without threat to the environment? What about pesticides? Is there a way of controlling the insect pests that bedevil us without poisoning useful species and, perhaps, even ourselves? Can science find ways to solve the very problems it has helped to create? What policies are needed? How can the individual help?

CHALLENGE TO EARTH, SEA, AND SKY

An awareness of the environment, of ecology, of balance in nature, and of how man has upset that balance has dawned with dramatic suddenness upon the consciousness of urban-industrial societies. Naturalists have worried for decades about the disappearance of species, deforestation of the land, erosion of soil, and pollution of the rivers and lakes. But these have seemed to the public like rather isolated cases—a river here, a forest there, and the disappearance of condors or whooping cranes. Now the truth is beginning to dawn: all these problems are related. Homo sapiens is just one of the thousands of species that inhabit or have inhabited the planet and he, too, could disappear in the very process of ecological destruction that he has embarked upon with such zest and pride. His most advanced civilizations are the source of his greatest danger. As biologist Barry Commoner[1] states the problem:

> We have come to a turning point in the human habitation of the earth. The environment is a complex, subtly balanced system, and it is this integrated whole which receives the impact of all the separate insults inflicted by pollution. Never before in the history of the planet has its thin life-supporting surface been subject to such diverse, novel, and potent agents. I believe that the cumulative effects of these pollutants, their interaction and amplification, can be fatal to the complex fabric of the biosphere. And, because man is, after all, a dependent part of this system, I believe that continued pollution of the earth, if unchecked, will eventually destroy the fitness of this planet as a place for human life.

MAN AS MASTER

Environmental difficulties are the result of both the accomplishments of man and the philosophy of mastery that has developed from those accomplishments. It may be that early man as a primitive hunter was a humble creature, fearful of the world around him, wondering in the course of his hunting whether he would find a meal or be a meal. Today, whatever his anxieties, Homo sapiens sees himself as the master species. Even his religion is one of mastery over nature, and nature is largely omitted from his thought patterns. With all his sophistication, he can barely imagine, much less enter, the sacred world of his forebears.

THE SACRED WORLD Judging by cave painting and sacred objects of the remote past and by the study of living primitives, we can conclude that man once tended to see his world of nature as a sacred place, full of spirits that must be appeased and regarded with awe. Animals were hunted, but they were nevertheless thought of as kindred spirits, sometimes even as totemic ancestors. No Darwin was needed to convince primitive man that he was part of the animal world. Although man was a hunter and had to kill his prey, the prey deserved ritual respect. Even in recent years Eskimo have poured a libation to the spirit of the whale and the Ainu have treated a sacrificial bear with the highest ritual respect.

[1]Barry Commoner, *Science and Survival*, The Viking Press, Inc., New York, 1966, p. 122.

There has been not only a feeling of spiritual relationship between man and the animal world, but also between man and the land itself. The Cheyenne, for example, saw the relationship between man and the land as so close that an evil act on the part of man could contaminate the land and all its inhabitants. Elaborate rituals were necessary to purge the land of evil. The Pueblo Indians of the Southwest, gardeners rather than hunters, had the same feeling for the sacredness of the earth and sky. The duty of man was to live in harmony with nature, never to disturb her sacred spirits in any way. The attitude is not too different from that of Lao Tse in ancient China or, for that matter, of contemporary peasant people in much of the world, eating the good products of the wholesome earth, and in return loving her and caring for her.

THE MASTERY PHILOSOPHY   It would not be easy to name any particular period in history when the view of nature changed. Probably the change was gradual, as man began to feel sure of his potential to produce an agricultural abundance. The god of science replaced the gods of nature very slowly. Ancient Greece toyed with science, and the men of the Renaissance reawakened the interest. In England and America the early Puritan interest in science was stimulated by the pious thought that the study of nature was the study of the handiwork of God. There was also a strongly practical spirit about the Puritans, and this practical interest was pursued by many men following in their footsteps. No longer was nature seen as something to look upon with reverence, but rather as a barrier to be overcome for human good.

Nowhere was the dream of the conquest of nature pursued more diligently than in America, where the problem of conquering a wilderness lay before men. The wilderness was conquered, and out of the problems of such a conquest came an intensification of the view of man as master. Other countries have experienced such a sense of mastery—Russia pushing eastward across the vastness of Siberia, and Canada gradually subduing her endless taiga and tundra. Nowhere, however, was the success as spectacular as in the United States, nor the pace of development so rapid throughout the nineteenth century. The spirit of conquest had served man well. It is true that he had run roughshod over magnificent forests, and that the home of the deer and the bear, the beaver, and the quail and pheasant had fallen under the ax, or been burned, eroded, gullied, and washed away. A fantastic productivity had been achieved, a productivity of which man had never before dreamed, but at the cost of alienating man from the world of nature.

Man's abandonment of nature is eloquently described by anthropologist Loren Eisley.[2] Urban man "drew back from nature. His animal confreres slunk soulless from his presence." Man looked objectively upon the world, its animal life, and finally upon himself:

Man's whole face grew distorted. One bulging eye—the technological, scientific eye—was willing to count man, as well as nature's creatures, in terms of megadeaths. Its objectivity

[2]Loren Eisley, *The Invisible Pyramid*, Charles Scribner's Sons, New York, 1970, p. 144.

Invading the moon while earth's environment decays — the final irony of the mastery philosophy.

had become so great as to endanger its master, who was mining his own brains as ruthlessly as a seam of coal.

In Eisley's figure of speech, nature is man's first world, and his second world is the world of science, "drawn from his own brain." Man's task today is to consciously reenter his primary world of nature and preserve it for the sake of all terrestrial life. With billions of people now taking the place of the scanty populations of old, productivity can no longer be purchased at the price of the desecration of nature. Man can no longer see nature, as his forebears did, as a thousand sacred spirits to be appeased by offerings and taboos, but he still longs for the clear waters of uncontaminated lakes and streams. Perhaps he would still thrill to the sight of the stars if he could see them through the smog. City resident though he is, he moves to the green suburbs if he can afford it, rather than staying in the concrete city.

Along with changes in outlook, other changes must come about. A restoration of the environment may result in higher priced goods, a squeeze in profits as industries convert to noncontaminating types of production, and much greater regulation to make sure that standards are enforced. There may even be conveniences that the public will have to learn to forego.

THE CONTAMINANTS

Reform movements have some of the qualities of other forms of collective behavior, arriving with a degree of spontaneity and being much less predictable than established institutions. Enthusiasm waxes high at one time and wanes as new issues take the limelight. Recently the movement for purification of the environment has encountered an outpouring of enthusiasm. Its leaders have excited many people with dire warnings of impending catastrophe and have attracted attention and public support. The question is whether the movement can be transformed into action or whether procrastination and discouragement will set in, and the levels of pollution will continue their accelerating rise.

Some of the leaders of environmental movements have taken such strong positions as to make themselves subject to the charge of alarmism. Such is the case with Dr. Paul Ehrlich, probably the best-known lecturer and writer on the subject of increasing population. Perhaps, though, an alarmist is exactly what we need. We are reminded of Sir Winston Churchill's famous quip about Clement Atlee — "a modest man, with much to be modest about." Ehrlich is an alarmed man, with much to be alarmed about.

In the summer of 1970 NBC produced a television program entitled "1985." The production sequence was similar to that of an old dramatization by Orson Welles of an invasion from Mars, War of the Worlds. Reporters from various cities described the lack of oxygen and the high levels of carbon dioxide, ozone, lead, and other pollutants in the air. In several cases the reports were followed by coughing spells, and then silence. The commentator explained during breaks in the broadcasts of news how the victory over nature had turned into a rout of the human species. Pesticides contaminated the land, and the insects for which they were intended built up immunities. The upper levels of the atmosphere were so filled with carbon dioxide and contaminants as to turn the earth into a hothouse. Finally, the last voice fell silent and the end of the human race was implied.

Probably the producers of the NBC program would admit some exaggeration of the time element. Even the most dour prophets of doom expect the world to die a more lingering death than was represented, but they do consider death a real possibility. An examination of the facts will indicate why.

CONTAMINATING THE EARTH   It is hard to separate the land contaminants from those of the water and the air, since many of them spread from one element to the other. Some start primarily as pollutants of the land; these will be examined first. Every year the United States disposes of 55 billion cans, 26 billion bottles, 7 million automobiles, and 150 million tons of junk and garbage.[3] About one-third of the American population is not served by sewers, but dumps its sewage into cesspools and septic tanks

---

[3]Paul R. Ehrlich and Anne H. Ehrlich, *Population, Resources, Environment*, W. H. Freeman and Company, San Francisco, 1970, p. 128.

High productivity and rapid
obsolescence of equipment
contributes the waste
equivalent of 100 billion people.

that can contaminate underground sediments and groundwater. Another third of the population has sewers but dumps sewage without adequate treatment.

The disposal of wastes is vastly increased by the demands of industry for disposal of chemicals and slag. Although the United States makes up only 6 percent of the earth's population, it consumes 40 percent of the world's resources, and all this consumption results in more wastes for disposal. Because of the great number of "mechanical slaves" used in the United States, the total waste disposal, including all industry—extractive, manufacturing, and automotive—becomes the equivalent of the human wastes of 102.3 billion people.[4]

The amount of our solid wastes doubles every ten years, according to Richard D. Vaughn, Director of Solid Waste Management of the Environmental Health Service.[5] The national bill for disposal of solid wastes is presently 4.5 billion dollars per year. Collection methods are unsatisfactory, with only 6 percent going to sanitary landfills and most of the remainder into unsanitary dumps, except for 8 to 10 percent converted into air pollution by incineration. Approximately 60 million tons of solid wastes are abandoned or dumped illegally per year in New York City alone, along with 50,000 automobiles abandoned on the streets.

The land absorbs pesticides in incredible amounts, along with lead, mercury, fluorides, and atomic wastes, although many of these materials become problems mainly as they are absorbed into water supplies. Atomic wastes, however, do not have to be absorbed in water to become dangerous. At Grand Junction, Colorado, and nearby communities, tailings (leftovers from the refining of uranium ore) were used as fill in the construction of at least 4,000 homes. Later tests by the Public Health Service indicated that radiation levels had passed the danger mark in sixty-five of the homes, and residents are worried about all of them, fearing increased risk of cancer and leukemia for themselves and their children. In the opinion of Dr. Arthur Tamplin of the Atomic Energy Commission's (AEC) Lawrence Radiation Laboratory in California, there is no safety except in moving out all the houses.

The trouble with an increase in the amount of atomic radiation is that no amount is safe, in spite of governmental decrees as to how much is tolerable. The fallout created for America so far is only about 1 percent of the "normal" background radiation from cosmic rays, "but even this tiny increase may have been responsible for up to 12,000 genetically defective babies and 100,000 cases of leukemia and bone tumors."[6]

The use of atomic power plants, although they do not throw the same types of pollutants into the air as coal or oil, can nevertheless lead to problems. The present policy is to store such pollutants in empty salt mines. At the rate of development of

[4]James P. Lodge, Jr., of the National Center for Atmospheric Research, quoted by S. L. Benglesdorf, "U.S. Waste: A National Headache," Los Angeles Times, August 16, 1970, Sec. F, p. 1.
[5]Associated Press, "Pollution Experts Say No 'Quick Fix' Exists," Los Angeles Times, September 19, 1970, Part 1B, p. 2.
[6]Ehrlich and Ehrlich, op. cit., p. 137.

Dead birds today, dead seas tomorrow,
as off-shore drilling continues,
leakages occur, and tanker tonnage grows.

miles of water. Later the same phenomenon occurred in the Gulf of Mexico. In 1967 the ship Torrey Canyon sank off the coast of England, filling the waters with 166,000 tons of oil. In 1969 the Marpessa, the Mactam, and the King Haakon VII all exploded mysteriously and sank off the coast of Africa, pouring their black cargo into the ocean. The damage to sea life is incalculable. In one case 170,000 gallons of oil from a wrecked tanker killed 93 percent of marine life in the area of the wreck, and ten months later the area was still not repopulated. Little is known of deeper areas, but Dr. Howard Sanders of the Massachusetts Oceanographic Institute believes pollution at great depths is even more disastrous than surface pollution and does more damage to marine life food chains.[11]

The size of oil tankers increases year by year because profits can be increased and costs reduced by massive shipments. The latest tanker under construction will be $1/4$ mile in length and displace 477,000 tons.[12] (By comparison, the big Missouri class of American battleships — the largest American battleship ever built — displaced 57,900 tons). Danger mounts as tanker size increases. Danger mounts, also, as off-shore drilling increases. Small wonder that when Thor Heyerdahl first tried to cross the Atlantic by papyrus raft he found nearly all its surface filthy with oil and other pollution.

The oceans seem to be regarded as the universal sewer. Each year the United States alone dumps 48.2 million tons of waste into them. Conservationists here and abroad were horrified in the summer of 1970 when the Army decided to dump 3,000 tons of obsolete nerve gas into the ocean near the Bahamas, over the strong protests of Great Britain. Army experts assured the world that even if the gas leaked out of its containers, chemical reaction with salt water would destroy it within a day or two. The public has become a little uncertain about official assurances, however, and there was not even any assurance as to what might happen to sea life during those days. Fish live as deep as the 16,000-foot trench into which the gas was dumped. It is believed that some fish make seasonal migrations from deep to shallow waters. We do not know for sure that poisons laid to rest in the oceans will never reappear.[13]

Jacques-Yves Cousteau,[14] the greatest of underwater explorers, has traveled 155,000 miles over and under the sea during his long career in oceanography. Recently he summarized what he has seen; "The oceans are in danger of dying. The pollution is general." Cousteau continued, "Fish have diminished by 40 percent in 20 years." Besides decrying the use of the oceans as the great refuse dumps of the earth, Cousteau deplored modern fishing techniques — electric shocks to force shrimp from their holes, destruction of eggs and larvae, and the search for marine species in their once impenetrable retreats.

[11]"Warning Issued on Offshore Oil Drilling," *Bakersfield Californian*, August 14, 1970, p. 6.
[12]"Oil Supertankers," *Los Angeles Times*, August 6, 1970, Part III, p. 18.
[13]Rudy Abramson, "Environmental Council Report to Urge Ban on Ocean Dumping," *Los Angeles Times*, August 17, 1970, Part I, p. 1.
[14]"The Dying Oceans," *Time*, vol. 96, p. 64, September 28, 1970.

It is not just the oceans that are being poisoned, but streams and lakes as well. Lake Erie and the Hudson River are virtually beyond recovery. Pesticides, detergents (some containing arsenic), mercury, lead, fluorides, nitrogen compounds, phosphates, and various other agricultural and industrial wastes enter the streams and filter down into groundwater reservoirs. According to the United States Public Health Service, several million Americans are drinking water that is potentially hazardous to the health. Especially in systems serving communities of 100,000 or less, samples are often unsatisfactory, containing fecal bacteria, lead, copper, iron, manganese, nitrate, and in some cases, arsenic.[15]

One of the most recent hazards to attract attention in the United States (although Sweden has been aware of its dangers for ten years and Japan for fifteen years) is mercury poisoning in water and fish. Mercury-containing sludge from factories is dumped into streams and lakes, and it is now suspected that fish from such waters are unsafe for human consumption. Japan has experienced 100 deaths from the eating of mercury-poisoned fish; Sweden forbids the sale of fish from certain lakes that might be contaminated. Lake St. Clair in Canada is heavily contaminated, and so are Lake Erie and the Detroit River. For years people have been eating fish from such sources, and possibly undergoing mild forms of mercury poisoning — muscle tremors, depression, nervousness, and nausea.[16]

In the spring of 1971 the Food and Drug Administration took drastic action by withdrawing from the market the most contaminated type of fish commonly eaten by the American public — swordfish. For reasons only partly understood, some types of marine life absorb much more mercury than others.[17]

CONTAMINATING THE SKY   It is air pollution that is most likely to concern the average citizen, especially the urbanite. Although the word "smog" was coined by an English physician in 1905 and was long associated primarily with Los Angeles, it is now a phenomenon of virtually all cities, so much so that some doctors believe no urbanite past the age of 12 has entirely healthy lungs. Air pollution is one possible reason why life expectancy is no longer rising for the American male and rising very little for the American female. As mentioned in Chapter 1, air pollution is a problem that spills over the jurisdictional boundaries of cities; in fact, it crosses national boundaries and mountains and oceans. All the world shares a common sea of air that constantly circulates, and the smog of one locality, considerably diluted, is carried on to other parts of the globe. Air pollution even reaches the upper levels of the atmosphere and may be reducing penetration of the sun's rays. Its effects on weather are not clear, but the possibilities are worrisome. The words of Omar Khayyam take on a new significance:

[15]Rudy Abramson, "Millions Drink Contaminated Water," *Los Angeles Times*, August 18, 1970, Part I, pp. 1, 13.
[16]Daniel Swedling, "And Now Mercury," *New Republic*, pp. 17–18, August 1, 1970.
[17]Leonard J. Goldwater, "Mercury in the Environment," *Scientific American*, vol. 224, pp. 15–21, May 1971.

Smog, a menacing by-product of the motoring way of life and a growing cause of death in all cities. Scene of East Los Angeles.

And that inverted bowl they call the sky,
Whereunder crawling, coop'd, we live and die. . . .

We are cooped under the same sky, and we can all suffer a common fate if it is polluted to the point that it can no longer support life. A nightmare for the future is the development of more and more supersonic transport planes, operating at altitudes of 50,000 to 70,000 feet. Since such heights are in the stratosphere — above the circulating envelope of air that surrounds the earth — water, carbon dioxide, and particulates could remain there almost indefinitely, forming a permanent cloud cover at certain altitudes. Some meteorologists believe that the contamination of the upper atmosphere could create a "greenhouse" effect, locking in heat and raising the earth's temperatures.

57

Air pollution has existed in cities for many years. As long ago as 1661 John Evelyn complained that the "aer and smoak" over London made it resemble the "suburbs of Hell" rather than a civilized city. Pollution in those days came largely from coal and industry. The first American cities to take action to clean the air were also primarily concerned with coal and industrial smoke—St. Louis and Pittsburgh.

In Los Angeles, however, another type of pollution was developing, characterized by nitrogen oxides and unburned hydrocarbons and ozone, along with high levels of carbon dioxide. Los Angeles, with an abundance of sunlight, had just the catalyst for changing hydrocarbons into a complex chain of chemicals, including poisonous and plant-damaging ozone, and this city had the vast amounts of automobile travel to produce more than her share of hydrocarbons.[18] Los Angeles also is so situated as to make a perfect smog trap, with mountains to the north and east preventing the escape of air, and with other conditions that cause frequent temperature inversions, especially in the summer.

For a long time the smog conditions of Los Angeles were thought of as a subject of merriment for comedians and the boosters of rival cities, but now Los Angeles has worldwide company in her smog problem. Death rates rise during smog alerts in most of the major cities of the world. In Tokyo people sometimes wear gauze over their faces to keep out the dirt or even resort to gas masks. In Los Angeles, 10,000 people per year are warned by their doctors to move away, and children are kept from strenuous play and exercise on smog alert days because of oxygen shortage. New York City produces almost two pounds of soot and noxious gases per person per day. A medical examiner commented regarding lung cases, "On the autopsy table it's unmistakable; the person who spent his life in the Adirondacks has pink lungs. The city dweller's are black as coal.[19] Fortunately for New York, the air mass is seldom trapped as it is in Los Angeles, and temperature inversions are rare. There have been days, however, when stagnant air has resulted in sharp increases in deaths.

In one respect pollution is the same all over the world, whether in city or isolated village: the carbon dioxide level is constantly on the increase. Between 1860 and 1960 the carbon dioxide content of the air increased by 14 percent. It has been increasing more rapidly since 1960.[20]

Does your school have courses in environmental studies? If not, petition for such programs. They are becoming a part of the college curriculum in many schools.

---

[18]A. J. Haagen-Smit, "The Control of Air Pollution," *Scientific American*, vol. 210, pp. 31–38, January 1964.
[19]John C. Esposito, *Vanishing Air*, Grossman Publishers, New York, 1970, p. 204.
[20]Commoner, *op. cit.*, p. 10.

THE CONTAMINATORS

All living creatures exert their influence on the environment, breathing air, eating the food they need, and leaving their wastes. Until man discovered the use of fire he was no worse a contaminator than any other animal of his size and, even with the first use of fire, he was no real menace. The development of agriculture increased man's ability to contaminate, to burn and deforest the land and deplete the soil; but it was the industrial revolution that made him a real menace. With factories came smoke and soot, mines and slag piles, sump holes, industrial wastes in waters, and eventually oil slicks, exhaust fumes, smog, detergents, lead, mercury, radioactivity, poison gases, and other lethal agents.

Obviously some segments of the human race have become worse polluters than others. The few remaining unwashed Australian aborigines, ironically, are the purest of men in respect to environmental pollution, and no one is dirtier than the wealthy, daily bathed American, with his high-powered, premium-fuel cars, his motorboats, his thousands of throwaway containers, his indestructible plastics, and his generally sterile surroundings — rendered so by his deadly powders and sprays.

There is no question that the average citizen is one of the polluters, and various environmental organizations and women's groups have suggested rules for improvement — reducing miles driven, avoiding such things as overpackaging, too many plastics, throwaway bottles, etc. At the same time, blaming the average citizen has a certain danger: it can result in mere preaching, moralizing, and wishing everyone would be good. Sociology usually looks upon change from a different perspective, that of institutional change through law and regulation. If we wait for over 200 million people to solemnly resolve to be "righteous" about environmental matters, we may have to wait until the earth is completely destroyed. The institutional approach requires merely winning over a determined segment of the public that will keep up the pressure on government and industry until proper laws are instituted. Neither approach is easy, but the latter is more apt to succeed than the former. Presently a majority of people seem to be concerned about the environment, but some are not. A Harris poll in 1970 showed 2 percent of the people suggesting that the first way to save money in government would be to cut out all expenses on cleaning up the environment. The Daughters of the American Revolution, at their 1970 convention in Washington, D.C., adopted a resolution stating that the environment problem is being "distorted and exaggerated" by propaganda and warned the government against adopting an "unnecessary and harmful control program." Some DAR members implied that the environmental movement is subversive. "It's unbelievable the far-out people involved in the environment movement," one said. One lady whose husband is a scientist argued the case for environmental control but was cut off abruptly with the statement, "Scientists are a dime a dozen!"[21]

---

[21]"DAR Debate," *Los Angeles Times*, April 24, 1970, Part I, p. 4.

GOVERNMENTAL CONFUSION As air and water pollution problems become more complex, new agencies become necessary for handling the problems. Intercity, inter-county, and interstate cooperation is needed but hard to achieve, partly because of intergovernmental jealousy. On the federal level, a similar type of governmental paralysis takes place, according to Theodore H. White.[22] Various presidents have created a confusion of agencies for handling such previous environmental problems as reforestation, water conservation, and soil depletion, but no agency for the general supervision of the environmental efforts of today. As the present environmental crisis developed, almost nothing was done. "Cities draped their towers in acrid shawls of smog, lakes bobbed with organic sewage and plastic refuse . . . [and] scientists packaged chemicals in foods and poisons in spray cans."[23]

When President Nixon got around to trying to establish a master plan, he found five departments and forty-four major agencies involved in the "Who has the environment?" game. The antirat program alone is handled by the Fish and Wildlife Service; Agricultural Research; Health, Education and Welfare; Office of Economic Opportunity; and six other agencies. Other problems are tied to no agencies whatever. For thirty years government scientists watched the biological death of Lake Erie, but no branch of government was responsible, and none responded. In attempting improvement, various government agencies are found to be warring on each other, and congressional committees representing farm, business, and manufacturing interests are pulled in different directions. Several new agencies are now being set up, eventually to come under an Environmental Protection Agency with powers torn from existing departments.

THE PROBLEMS OF NAPCA At present the National Air Pollution Control Administration in the Department of Health, Education and Welfare (HEW) is charged with federal responsibility for air pollution control. The job is a vast one that calls for control of the entire auto and petroleum industries, the development of electric power (except hydroelectric), the burning of coal, and most activities of the chemical and refining industries. The control problem properly belongs to HEW, because air pollution has become a major threat to health. Besides causing rising death rates from respiratory diseases, pollution is now suspected of producing mutagenic effects, possibly causing genetic damage. Increase in particulate matter is associated with increase in the amount of stomach cancer, and carbon monoxide levels are high enough to account for some types of anemia and to put greater strain on the heart.[24] Emphysema, the nation's fastest-growing cause of death, is aggravated by smog and sulfur dioxide.

[22]Theodore H. White, "How Did We Get from Here to There?" *Life*, vol. 68, pp. 36–40, June 26, 1970.
[23]*Ibid.*, p. 37.
[24]Esposito, *op. cit.*, pp. 11–15.

DELAY IN THE AUTO INDUSTRY   It is estimated that 60 percent of all air pollution results from the internal combustion engine, to which the auto industry is firmly committed. Esposito, a member of Nader's investigative group, describes the response of the auto industry to the need for cleaning the air as "twenty years in low gear." He presents a mass of evidence from good authorities (among them Dr. Richard S. Morse of MIT) showing a steam car to be both feasible and economical and to virtually eliminate pollution. It is ignored by Detroit. So close is the relationship between autos and the petroleum industry that auto producers have remained blind to other possibilities, says Esposito. Henry Ford II is quoted as saying of oil and autos, "Like flowers and bees, where you find one the other is sure to be near."[25]

In the 1950s spokesmen for the auto industry maintained that smog was no serious problem, that the vapors dissipated too rapidly to cause damage. In the next four years they tried to picture air pollution as something confined to Los Angeles. Eventually the issue of air pollution led to a suit against the Automobile Manufacturers' Association for conspiracy to restrain improvements in the production of antismog devices, pushed especially by Los Angeles County Supervisor Kenneth Hahn. A weak compromise was worked out with the Justice Department in September, 1969.

Eventually clean air requirements were enacted, by California in 1966 and by the rest of the country in 1968, but enforcement is extremely weak. Although automobiles account for a majority of pollution, the program for control of automotive emissions accounts for only about 5 percent of NAPCA's budget. Even a high official of NAPCA had to admit that he would call the program "farcical."[26] Only two emissions are included: carbon monoxide and hydrocarbons. Nitrogen oxides were left out of consideration until 1973.

In 1969 NAPCA's checks consisted of testing twelve cars out of 2½ million, all carefully hand picked and specially produced. If they failed, all that was necessary was to take them back and work them over until they could pass. Later tests showed that cars that had traveled 11,000 miles failed either the carbon dioxide or hydrocarbon tests in 53 percent of the cases. For 307-cubic-inch engines of General Motors cars, the failure rate was 83 percent.[27]

STEEL   Chicago has long been plagued by serious pollution from the steel industry, but the city also depends very heavily on steel for economic livelihood. Consequently, Chicago revised and strengthened a 1963 auto pollution ordinance but gave U.S. Steel and Republic Steel several years to meet full compliance. In spite of annual progress reports, by 1969 the two companies had actually increased their dust out-

[25]*Ibid.*, p. 35.
[26]*Ibid.*, p. 52.
[27]*Ibid.*, p. 59.

put by 2,000 tons, although Wisconsin and Interlake companies had lived up to their agreement.[28]

COAL AND SULFUR DIOXIDE A leading killer among air pollutants is sulfur dioxide; it also corrodes buildings and does billions of dollars worth of property damage each year. New Jersey was one of the first states to attempt by law to control sulfur dioxide. The coal industry brought suit against the New Jersey law, which proposed to regulate the sulfur content of acceptable coal. The suit, which failed, was probably only a delaying action; if so, it was successful in allowing companies to sell below-standard coal for another year and adding greatly to the sulfur dioxide content of New Jersey's air. Unfortunately for the cause of clean air, many such delaying legal actions have been used.

ELECTRIC POWER Electric power, admittedly, faced serious problems. Hydroelectric potential is severely limited and already almost completely developed. Atomic energy has the defect of producing dangerous radioactive byproducts and of heating the water cycled for cooling purposes—a danger to marine life. Consequently, the burning of coal and oil becomes the means for producing much of our electric power. Chicago annually burns 6 million tons of bituminous coal of high sulfur content, emitting 420,000 tons of sulfur oxides into the air. In 1969 a period of thermal inversion resulted in 100 deaths there in two or three days. Although the electric industry must rely partly on unsatisfactory means of producing electricity, it could burn coal of lower sulfur content. This costs more, however, and would increase the price of electricity, which would in turn reduce the sales of electric appliances. Thus the industry, pushing its appliances, helps to create additional need for a commodity that can be produced cheaply only by polluting heavily.[29]

What about using only low-sulfur coal? This has, of course, been the goal of environmentalists. Esposito contends that power interests have waged a long campaign to convince Congress that such resources are virtually unavailable. The Geologic Survey concluded years ago that only 10 percent of the low-sulfur coal in the United States is located east of the Mississippi. Nevertheless, coal is just about the most abundant of minerals. If the 10 percent figure is correct, and if only half of that type of coal can be economically mined, there would still be enough coal to meet the nation's needs for forty or fifty years.[30]

STATE AND LOCAL CONTROLS Esposito concludes that federal controls under NAPCA are very weak and that local and state controls, with few exceptions, are just as inadequate. In Houston he found the controls so weak that they would be laughable if the

[28]*Ibid.,* p. 83.
[29]*Ibid.,* p. 94.
[30]*Ibid.,* p. 109.

pollution problem were not so tragic. In Texas, the regulation of pollution seemed to be left up to the major polluters themselves. New York City, in spite of remaining one of the most contaminated cities on earth, has made some progress, especially with sulfur dioxide. Washington, D.C., has made much less headway than New York. It may eventually become the pollution capital as well as the political and crime capital of the nation! The state of New Jersey offers some encouragement. There, pollution control was placed under the state health department and was supported by strong legal regulations and no reluctance to bring convictions. New Jersey was able to reduce particulate emissions by 80 percent in two or three years. On the opposite coast, Los Angeles, seeing the situation as desperate, has made vigorous efforts to do something about smog, but with little effect. Although the smog level per individual is somewhat reduced, population has grown so greatly as to leave the city no better off than before.

REASONS FOR DELAY Generally the progress in environmental improvement has been very slow. The reasons amount to a summation of nearly all the usual resistances to change. The first reason is vested interest. Vested interests not only oppose change, but in most cases they wield very powerful political influence. Not only the major industrial polluters, but the general public as well develop a vested interest in the old ways of doing things. The average American is used to the internal combustion engine, to using products extravagantly, and to using large numbers of electric appliances that are operated only by adding to pollution.

Ignorance of need is always a source of resistance to social change. Until recently, environmental problems did not seem acute enough to get excited about. Even now some people see the environmental movement as much ado about nothing.

Change often results in heavy financial cost. The costs of environmental control will be very cheap compared to the cataclysmic costs of doing nothing, but they nevertheless create financial problems. There are costs to industry and to the individual. Governmental regulatory powers and costs will also increase. There is also the other problem of costs: who is to pay? Many individuals and corporations will resist doing anything expensive until they are assured that the law will be enforced equally on all.

There is a type of resistance to change based on psychological adjustment to a creeping menace. The atmosphere becomes worse in small degrees, almost imperceptibly. "Surely another slight increase can be tolerated before we need do anything drastic" is a common reaction to the creeping menace.

What is your regional agency for environmental problems? Who selects the staff? What powers does it have over industry and the public? Information should be available at the county court house.

Finally, we have had to delay because we do not always know what to do. It is easy to dispense with one pollutant by adding another, as in the case of detergents, now made biodegradable, but containing too many phosphates. Many solutions still await scientific knowledge.

CAN SCIENCE SAVE ITSELF?

Most of the previous pages have been extremely grim—a natural characteristic of social problems texts. Grim facts must not be glossed over, but neither must the problem they pose be looked upon as insoluble. In an age of disillusionment it is easy to damn the human species as too blind or inept to solve its most urgent problems, but man has had a dramatic record of overcoming the hazards of the past. Now, of course, man is faced with new types of problems, this time problems of his own making and of the scientific genie that serves him. Can science, which has saved man from famine and pestilence, now save him from itself?

FREEDOM FROM THE SMOG MACHINE Solutions—or at least partial solutions—are possible in regards to the internal combustion engine, the biggest air pollutant. It could be cleaned much more than at present, but it will take legislative insistence and much stronger laws. Better yet, it is feasible to build steam cars that would eliminate nearly all pollutants. The Japanese Nissan Company (manufacturer of the Datsun) has signed a contract for rights to a pollution-free engine. Models are being produced in both Sweden and Japan.[31] Such a development could give the impetus to make the American automotive industry move more rapidly in the direction of pollution elimination. Congressional acts now call for elimination of 90 percent of automobile pollution by 1975.

There are, of course, political rather than scientific solutions to the problem of auto emissions—eliminate a large part of the autos from the road by such devices as rationing gasoline or greatly increasing public transportation.

ELECTRIC POWER The electric industry is a difficult case. High dams flood useful lands and hydroelectric potential is nearly exhausted already. As we have seen, atomic energy has great dangers, although these might be reduced in the future by new scientific breakthroughs. Pollution from burning fossil fuels can be reduced but by no means eliminated. Two scientists from the University of California at Riverside have suggested tapping geothermal fields. They estimate the power potential from steam and hot water wells in the Imperial Valley to be twenty times as great as that of Hoover Dam. The researchers, Robert Rex and Tsvi Meidas, think that many other geothermal fields could be found. The Metropolitan Water District of Southern California and several private firms are providing money for investigation.[32]

[31]"Plans Revealed for 1973 Car with Pollution Free Engine," *Los Angeles Times*, August 19, 1970, Part I, p. 1.
[32]George Getze, "Use of Steam Wells for Power," *Los Angeles Times*, August 8, 1970, Part I, p. 1.

WASTE For many of the problems of waste materials mentioned previously, there are solutions. Sewage treatment will have to be greatly improved, and at a higher cost than at present. Garbage removal could be greatly improved by more sanitary land-fills, but this would not constitute an adequate solution. More effort must be made to reduce the amount of garbage and trash by making more materials of easily de-gradable substances and by recycling. The vast piles of debris left from autos, washers, and other household appliances could be salvaged for reuse. Presently the price of such scrap materials is not sufficient to encourage their collection, a problem that might have to be solved by a certain amount of subsidization. In poorer countries nothing of the kind goes to waste.

PESTICIDES Among the most serious problems are agricultural fertilizers and pesti-cides. Robert van den Bosch[33] reports that after years of use of pesticides, we have more species of insect pests than ever before and that over 200 of these have devel-oped a resistance to chemicals. The situation reminds one of a comment by Ehrlich to the effect that man need not worry about being eliminated from the earth. A much more able and adaptable creature is ready to take over—the cockroach!

One trouble in the area of pesticides is that chemical agents are developed by people in the agriculture business, people who are interested only in the immediate control of certain insect pests, not in the total picture of ecology. Their salesmen are out to sell the product, not to worry about the environment. The best product from the commercial point of view is one with wide applicability to a number of pests, saving both time and money. DDT was once the answer to everyone's need. Now that its lethal and lingering effects are known, it is being replaced by organophosphates which, van den Bosch says, are even more lethal, although shortlived. The difficulty is that they kill too wide a range of insects. Often, too, there is rapid resurgence of the insect pests, with evolutionary mutations making them immune to the spray.

What you can do:
Walk or ride a bicycle
Cut down on wastes
Return items that can be recycled
Avoid pesticides as much as possible
Avoid unnecessary electrical appliances
Study voting records of local politicians
Join environmental organizations, such as Friends of the Earth, 30 E. 42d St., New York, N.Y., 10017.

---

[33]Robert van den Bosch, "The Insects are Beating Us," *California Monthly*, pp. 23–27, April 1970.

Losing the battle of the pests: while
contamination spreads, insects develop
full resistance to pesticides.

The insect problem is not easy to solve with chemicals; it will require a sophisticated, discreet approach to each type of pest—a more expensive method than that used today. Pest-control programs must be supervised by entomologists, not salesmen. In some cases, natural enemies can be used against insect pests, or it is possible to develop entirely sterile males so that the pest population eventually dies out.

Similar steps will probably have to be taken to restore the fertility of the soil and to avoid too complete a dependence on chemical fertilizers. Indications are that the ingenuity of modern science can rise to the task of ensuring agricultural production, provided world population does not increase to such a level as to make all efforts futile.

IMPLEMENTING SCIENTIFIC KNOWLEDGE Whether scientific knowledge will be applied is, of course, heavily dependent upon political decisions. Many impressive political speeches are being made on the subject of environment, but it must not be assumed that political speeches and committee reports are automatically translated into action. Some local and state governments have made a creditable record, and others have done nothing. There is no doubt that at present pollution levels are continuing to rise. Esposito concludes that the Air Quality Act of 1967, given the blessing of President Johnson, has not served the purpose of bringing pollution under control. He doubts that Nixon's proposals will be much more effective, partly because the burden of proof of contamination is still on the public, and possibilities for legal delay are endless. The new federal agency for the environment (Environmental Protection Agency) is weakened by being faced with the burden of proof.

Regardless of how many laws and enforcement agencies there are, much will depend upon whether strong pressures are brought upon governments and whether determined men hold office on environmental boards. Too often polluters rather than environmentalists are appointed to local control boards.

The public must always beware of false promises or statements to the effect that "at last we have pollution on the run."[34] The struggle will be long and difficult and, in a sense, can never be won entirely. As solutions to existing problems are found, new problems will arise. There is always the danger that air pollutant X will be eliminated only by increasing air pollutant Y.

A number of politicians are sincerely interested in the environment, but even the best are constantly being approached by pressure groups. There is always a temptation to yield to the side that promises the most in votes and campaign contributions. The pressures, however, will be on the side of the environment if millions of Americans join conservationist and environmentalist groups, keeping themselves informed and making their voices heard at the centers of political power.

[34]"Pollution: Puffery or Progress," *Newsweek*, pp. 49–51, December 28, 1970.

SUGGESTED READINGS

Chase, Stuart: *The Most Probable World*, Penguin Books, Inc., Baltimore, 1969.

> *The first half of Chase's brief glance at the future is largely on environment, cities, and population; the second half is on economic, political, and international problems. He correctly sees scientific advance as the root of the problems and also the hope for solution.*

Commoner Barry: *The Closing Circle*, Alfred A. Knopf, Inc., New York, 1971.

> *This book effectively condemns technology for what it has done to our ecology and our chance of survival. Commoner, one of the world's most respected biologists, gives us twenty to fifty years to survive under present conditions.*

Dasmann, Raymond S.: *The Destruction of California*, Collier Books, The Macmillan Company, New York, 1968.

> *This book deals with the conservation crisis in California — destruction of lands and forests, mistaken water policies, threats to the remaining giant redwoods. The book describes what is happening everywhere, but with particularly dramatic suddenness in California.*

DeBell, Garrett (ed.): *The Environmental Handbook*, Ballantine Books, Inc., New York, 1970.

> *Prepared for the first national environmental teach-in, the first half of* The Environmental Handbook *contains a wide variety of essays on environmental problems, and the second half deals with ecotactics — what can be done, individually and politically. The handbook also lists all the leading environmental organizations in the country.*

Ehrlich, Paul R., and Anne H. Ehrlich: *Population, Resources, Environment*, W. H. Freeman and Company, San Francisco, 1970.

> *A comprehensive book that should be in all libraries. The Ehrlichs are experts at gathering the information and making a dramatic presentation. A good resource book for the three interrelated problems included in the title. (The only book on this list not available in paperback.)*

Esposito, John C.: *Vanishing Air*, Grossman Publishers, New York, 1970.

> *Esposito, a member of Ralph Nader's team, presents a study of the atmospheric crisis, with strong condemnations of policies of delay. Governmental agencies and the auto and power industries come in for some harsh criticism.*

QUESTIONS

1. Contrast the "sacred philosophy" and the "mastery philosophy," and try to explain what developments led to the mastery philosophy.

2. Give some instances showing how the entire earth is interrelated in problems of ocean and air pollution.

3. Contrast the moralizing approach and the political-institutional approach to environmental control.

4. What are some of the reasons for delay in pollution control?

5. The chapter on pollution has suggested that all our environmental problems are subject to fairly effective control. Do you agree? What changes will be needed to bring about such control?

3 *How successful have seventy years of pure food and drug acts been in protecting the consumer? Obviously, they have helped in eliminating some of the most flagrant conditions described in the meat-packing industry at the turn of the century, but have new deceptions entered the food business? Is the new inventiveness of chemistry turned to enriching our foods, or is it simply serving us a dangerous "chemical feast?" Are other types of products designed mainly for safety, utility, and durability, or are they designed with little regard for any of these qualities? What new perils does the consumer face in an age that is just as inventive in merchandizing techniques as it is in gadgetry? Finally, what organizations, publications, and types of legislation exist to try to help the consumer?*

We shall find the answers to some of these questions far from reassuring. From infancy on, the consumer is met with many hazards to health and longevity, including baby foods, nutritionally deficient "unfoods," and potentially dangerous chemicals. His pocketbook is threatened by all kinds of deceptions—in insurance, on the grocery shelf, in time payments, and in the buying of goods that will quickly become obsolete. Bureaus have been created to aid the consumer, but there is always danger that regulator and regulated will grow too close together in association and attitude.

THE CONSUMER TRAP

A trap is a device for catching prey by stealth and deception, whether the prey be an animal, an enemy, or a suspected criminal. Most traps of this type, however, are regarded as too cruel or unfair and are forbidden by law. On the other hand, most traps set for catching the consumer by deception are still permitted; there are often legal regulations, but they are easily evaded. Generally speaking, the consumer is fair game. He finds traps in the grocery store, in loan offices, in real estate and insurance agencies, and in all kinds of televised advertisements. The foul food traps are still carefully baited, with the odor disguised by chemicals. There are other kinds of consumer traps that employ hidden timing devices, so that the products are timed to wear out rapidly or to become obsolete, as styles and models change with lightning speed.

The struggle to help the consumer is one with a long history, strewn with the wreckage of martyrs. As in the case of environmental pollution, some progress is being made, but new problems arise. New traps are set and, as the author of a book in the 1930s stated, one must learn to "eat, drink, and be wary."

THE PERSISTENCE OF THE JUNGLE

A sensation was created in 1906 when Upton Sinclair published his famous book, *The Jungle*. Sinclair's intent was to portray a junglelike society of crushing poverty and despair for its industrial workers and of types of corruption, craftiness, backstabbing, and disregard for human life that belong more to a jungle than to a civilized society. The whole story is viewed through the eyes of Jurgis Rudkus and his family, non-English-speaking immigrants from Lithuania, who are exploited and cheated at every turn. The search for jobs takes them to the slaughterhouses of Chicago, an area the book calls Packingtown. It was the description of the meat-packing industry that created the sensation, and in the public mind "the jungle" meant specifically Packingtown. Thousands of people became so nauseated at reading the book that they quit eating meat and meat sales declined drastically. The meat-packing industry claimed that the book was libelous and that the public was being alarmed over nothing. What were the real facts about the jungle in 1906 and what are they now?

THE JUNGLE IN 1906 So horrible was the story of the jungle that many doubted Sinclair's veracity. Major magazines ran articles written by members of the packing industry to discredit it, and threats of libel suits were made—but not carried out. President Theodore Roosevelt read the book, took immediate alarm, and appointed investigators to learn the true facts in the case. His investigators returned to tell him that there was no falsehood whatever in the book. Sinclair had accurately described the jungle. The entire industry crawled with filth, but the worst was the sausage-packing operation:

> There was never the least attention paid to what was cut up for sausage; there would come all the way back from Europe old sausage that had been rejected, and that was

mouldy and white—it would be dosed with borax and glycerine, and dumped into the hoppers, and made over again for home consumption. There would be meat that had tumbled on the floor, in the dirt and sawdust, where the workers had trampled and spit uncounted billions of consumption germs. There would be meat stored in great piles. . . . It was too dark in these storage places to see well, but a man could run his hand over these piles of meat and sweep off handfulls of dried dung of rats. These rats were nuisances, and the packers would put poisoned bread out for them, they would die, and then rats, bread, and meat would go into the hoppers together.[1]

As is generally known, pure food and drug acts were passed in 1907, and a Food and Drug Administration was created to make sure the public would never again face the risk of contaminated meat or other kinds of contaminated or chemically unsafe foods. In the intervening years the rats have diminished, but there are areas in which federal inspection does not take place, and there are many more miracles of chemistry than the glycerine and borax of 1906. A familiar old jingle was parodied in those days:

Mary had a little lamb,
And when she saw it sicken,
She shipped it off to Packingtown,
And now it's labeled "chicken."[2]

Whether lamb becomes chicken today we are not sure, but things still have a way of ending up with labels assuring the public that they are what they are not.

TODAY'S JUNGLE AND THE FOUR D'S   There is still a jungle today, partly because the Food and Drug Administration is not as alert as it should be, but mainly because some packing plants do not come under federal control. Meat processors who do not ship their meat across state lines are immune to federal laws. Consequently, they may be tempted to dispose of 4-D meat (dead, dying, disabled, or diseased). In 1966, 250 million pounds of meat were destroyed by federal inspectors because of disease, spoilage, and contamination. There is no way of knowing how much bad meat has escaped federal inspection. There has been an increase, however, in the amount of meat processed in nonfederally inspected plants.[3]

Consumers Union recently tested samples of pork sausage and found that 30 to 40 percent of the samples failed their absence-of-filth tests. One-eighth of federally inspected sausage and one-fifth of that not federally inspected contained insect larvae, rodent hairs, and other kinds of filth. Consumers Union also found much to be desired in the quality of fish sold on the market. Every month shipments of fish are ordered destroyed because of decomposition, positive staphylococci (bacterial

[1]Upton Sinclair, *The Jungle*, New American Library, Inc., New York, 1960, p. 136.
[2]*Ibid.*, p. 348.
[3]Ralph Nader, "Watch that Hamburger," in David Sanford (ed.), *Hot War on the Consumer*, Pitman Publishing Corporation, New York, 1969, pp. 45–47.

parasites on skin and/or mucous membranes), coagulase (an enzyme causing coagulation), or parasitic cysts. Imported dried fish have been found to contain maggots.[4] Water from sewage and industrial waste can easily contaminate shellfish and other marine products. Frozen salmon from the Great Lakes had to be destroyed because of high levels of pesticides.[5]

In recent years there has been a large increase in infectious hepatitis and salmonella, and a connection between these diseases and food contamination is suspected, although difficult to prove. Oysters, clams, and mussels are often eaten raw or only partially cooked, in spite of the floods of industrial and domestic sewage that pour into the waters in which they live.[6]

There are other details of today's jungle that are almost as nauseating as those related by Sinclair. Consumers have found dozens of offensive items in soft drinks, including decomposing mice, maggots, and cigarette butts.[7] It must not be denied, though, that in the years since 1906 progress has been made. Most impurities are now killed by chemicals. Most food does not spoil—it is too full of chemical preservatives. A question remains, however, as to whether the progress has been aimed at helping the consumer or primarily at fooling him.

FROM THE JUNGLE TO THE CHEMISTS Altogether, 485 chemicals and other additives can now be used in foods *without being mentioned on the labels*.[8] Turner, a member of one of Nader's investigative teams, leads one to wonder about the safety of many of these chemicals. In his book *The Chemical Feast*, Turner savagely attacks the Food and Drug Administration, picturing its attitude toward the major food producers as friendly enough to border on collusion. He also gives a long recitation of bureaucratic rigidity, stubborness, and "group-think" that reminds one of the caricatures of bureaucracy presented in *Parkinson's Law*, or of the idea of Laurence J. Peter that "incompetence rules the world." In Turner's opinion, the FDA neither holds, nor in any way deserves, the confidence of the American public. To one who has not read his book, the point of view may seem extreme, but a glance at some of the evidence he presents will make it clear why his title implies that we are eating chemicals rather than food.

In 1969, in a dramatic action taken by then Secretary of Health, Education and Welfare Robert Finch, cyclamates were recalled from the market because studies had indicated that they cause cancer in experimental animals. What the public did not know was that there had been very good evidence of this for many years before the removal of the cyclamates. As early as 1954 the Food and Nutrition Board of the National Academy of Sciences had warned against cyclamates. Eight years later the

[4]Nader, "What are We Made Of?" in Sanford, *op. cit.*, pp. 3–9.
[5]*Ibid.*, p. 6.
[6]Nader, "Something Fishy," in Sanford, *op. cit.*, pp. 37–39.
[7]James S. Turner, *The Chemical Feast*, Grossman Publishers, New York, 1970, p. 74.
[8]Turner, *op. cit.*, p. 236.

stand was reaffirmed, with the added conclusion that they do not even help in controlling weight, as they are supposed to do. Two Japanese scientists demonstrated in 1966 that cyclamates contain extremely dangerous carcinogenic ingredients. In 1968, Dr. J. Verrett found that cyclamates can cause deformation in chicken embryos. The FDA was supposed to adhere to the rule that drugs harmful to test animals should be removed from use. In spite of this ruling, cyclamates continued their twenty-year position on the Generally Regarded as Safe (GRAS) list. The public eventually learned that diet drinks contained cyclamates and that cyclamates were under suspicion. It was not generally known, however, that cyclamates were added to many other kinds of products, such as jams and jellies and canned fruit, and that even children's vitamins were coated with cyclamates. Since cyclamates were on the GRAS list, no mention of them had to be made on labels.

While the FDA remained inactive on the issue, the Harvard School of Public Health made a study showing that experimental rats fed cyclamates gained more weight than control rats without cyclamates. More importantly, an investigation of diabetics, who had generally been taking both cyclamates and saccharin, revealed that diabetics have six to ten times as many grossly deformed children as the normal population. At about the same time, another doctor found that cyclamates break chromosomes in experimental rats and could be mutagenic. None of these bits of information moved the FDA to take action. It was only when NBC, the *Washington Post*, and *Newsweek* began to publicize the story told them by Verrett that the FDA and the Secretary of HEW were forced to act.[9]

The story of cyclamates would be ancient history except that attitudes and policies of the Food and Drug Administration keep it alive, with the public wondering when a similar discovery will be made—possibly another one that has been kept under cover for years. The earlier thalidomide case had resulted in favorable publicity for the FDA, but even it was more a matter of good luck than of design. Had it not been for the determined efforts of Dr. Frances Kelsey, there would have been hundreds of cases of deformed babies born as a result of the drug having been prescribed for expectant mothers. The first word of the cruel effects of thalidomide came in the form of a dispatch from Germany to our Department of State, telling of 150 babies born without arms or legs because of the drug. The head of the FDA was informed by the Secretary of State but did not bother to mention the German information to Kelsey, who was responsible for making a decision on the drug.[10] Afterward the department boasted of having completely protected the public. Actually, more than 2½ million pills had been distributed, supposedly for experimental tests. Ten deformed babies were born in the United States; the deformities were probably caused by thalidomide.

In his attack on the FDA, Turner leaves one with no assurance that other cases of this kind will not arise. His well-documented contention is that the FDA has several

[9]*Ibid.*, pp. 3–29.
[10]*Ibid.*, pp. 221–227.

prominent blind spots having to do with chemicals, nutrition, food poisoning, and heart disease. After the cyclamate matter, the FDA took 64 other drugs off the GRAS list, admitting by implication that they had never been properly investigated. The bureau is still slow in investigating warnings about the possibility that saccharin can cause cancer, and it ignores warnings about monosodium glutamate in baby foods. The agency seems as little concerned about genetic damage caused by some chemical additives to experimental rats and chick embryos as it was years ago about cyclamates.

One of the other blind spots of the agency is that it continues to assert that nutrition in America is excellent, even as congressional investigations are reporting cases of malnutrition, not only among the poor, but among much of the chemically fed American public. It also ignores or minimizes the problems of food-borne diseases, such as salmonella and infectious hepatitis, which have been sharply on the increase in recent years. Finally, the FDA seems to take no interest in saturated fats and heart disease, in spite of warnings from the National Academy of Sciences, the American Heart Association, and the American Medical Association. The fat content of hot dogs and other kinds of meat is allowed to increase without mention, and manufacturers of polyunsaturated fats cannot advertise their products as such. Some industries are given marked preference over others.[11] Recently some doubt has been cast on the connection between fats, blood cholesterol, and heart disease as the result of a study done by the National Heart and Lung Institute;[12] but it is still hard to justify a position that will not allow honest labeling of saturated and unsaturated fats.

STAYING ALIVE

It would seem that the problem of staying alive, barring war or other disaster, should be less serious than in earlier times. Throughout most of America's history, life expectancy has increased as childhood diseases, diphtheria, smallpox, tuberculosis, and various other ancient plagues have been virtually eliminated. Other problems have replaced the old ones, however. Cancer and heart disease increase markedly, influenced, no doubt, by foul air, chemical additives, and nervous strain, as well

---

> Examine bottled drinks, fruit juices, and baby foods to see what you can learn about chemical additives. Check with *Consumer Reports* magazine. Report misbranded or contaminated foods to FDA, Department of Health, Education and Welfare, Washington, D.C.

---

[11]*Ibid.*, pp. 68–71.

[12]Harry Nelson, "Doubt Cast on Link between Fats in Diet and Cholesterol," *Los Angeles Times*, September 9, 1970, Part I, p. 1.

as by the cigarettes that are still advertised in lyrical tones as bringing the freshness of country living and all the ruggedness of manhood. Modern man also faces the need for rapid transportation, and his means of transportation are far from safe. These dangers, and other tensions of modern life, make him nervous, and he lights up more cigarettes, drinks more bourbon, and takes more preparations to calm him down, or pep him up, or ease his stomach, or put iron in his blood, or restore his vigor, or stop his headache, or allow him to sleep. With all these marvelous inventions, his life expectancy has ceased to lengthen.

UNITED STATES HEALTH AND LONGEVITY   Whatever the reasons, the people of the United States are no longer making strides in health or remaining at the forefront of the world in life expectancy. In thirty-six foreign countries the twenty-year-old man has a greater life expectancy than he has in the United States, and twenty-one countries give greater life expectancy to the twenty-year-old woman. In 1950 we were fifth in freedom from infant mortality; in 1968 we were thirteenth. There has been almost no increase in life expectancy since 1960. Black men actually die a little younger now than they did in 1959. The American diet has become worse instead of better in recent years, according to a study done for the *Journal of Nutrition Education*. The authors of the study expected to present a rather routine report showing our dietary improvements; they were shocked to learn that their report was just the reverse of what was expected. They concluded that infants of higher-income families were not as well nourished as those of lower-income families, and they also concluded that the greatest change for the worse had taken place since 1960.[13]

INTO THE MOUTHS OF BABES   There are suspicions that some of the additives put into foods can cause deformities, but assuming a normal baby is born, with a good appetite, what risk does he run? The baby first nurses from his mother who, as noted in Chapter 2, might produce milk contaminated with DDT. Next he is placed on a formula, sweetened by chemical additives. As he grows a little older he learns to ingest baby foods, which were once mainly fruit, vegetable, or meat. As the costs of these ingredients rose, the baby food companies began to add more and more starch and sugar — less nutritious, but cheaper.[14]

Since mothers sometimes taste baby food to see that it is good, and since starch makes the food taste too bland for an adult, the companies added a bit of salt and monosodium glutamate. Because the starches tend to become watery, companies developed new types that would not break down in a baby's saliva and that, in all likelihood, cannot be digested at all. Sugar is also added to make the food seem acceptable when tasted by mothers. The results of the additions are probably all harmful. The mother will have to start the constant battle against excessive candy eating because the infant has been conditioned to like sugar. An early taste for too much

[13]Turner, *op. cit.*, pp. 1–2.
[14]*Ibid.*, p. 85.

Into the mouths of babes — food or chemicals?

salt can also be acquired and may be retained for life. In many cases high salt intake is associated with hypertension. The starch and sugar help to make babies fat, but fat babies are not as healthy as those of moderate weight. Finally, there is the problem of monosodium glutamate. In 1969, Dr. John Olney of Washington University in St. Louis reported that injections of monosodium glutamate into mice caused specific brain damage. Following this revelation, Dr. Jean Mayer, nutrition advisor to the President, denounced the use of monosodium glutamate in baby foods. It is still being used, however,[15] but in fewer foods because of public outcry.

OUR DAILY BREAD As the baby grows into childhood he will, if he listens to the advertisements, learn to eat breakfast cereals, which claim to give him vigor and vitality. In the summer of 1970 the FDA issued a report stating that nearly all breakfast cereals are pure calories, with almost no food value. The typical American child will, in all likelihood, learn the blessings of pure, white bread, vitamin enriched. What he and his parents will not know is that in the refining process twenty-four ingredients are removed from wheat and only four are added.[16] He will drink a substitute for or-

[15]*Ibid.*, pp. 88–89.
[16]*Ibid.*, p. 111.

ange juice that is tangy but is really just a collection of chemicals with no fruit juice content whatever. He will, in fact, come across a large number of "unfoods."

An ingenious example of an "unfood" is one company's product called "beef stroganoff." Since meat is supposedly involved, the product comes under the regulations of the Agriculture Department, which says the package must contain 45 percent meat. The loophole in the law is that only the inner container—the one actually containing the meat—must tell the true story. The problem is solved for the producer by putting four packages inside the one the housewife buys. Only one of those four must contain 45 percent meat. Others contain noodles, breadcrumbs, and sauce.[17] The whole deal is neat and legal, and the inner package that is allegedly meat is actually part meat and part soybeans.

As he grows older a man may tend to put on weight. He can be sold various drugs for reducing purposes, but most of the drugs cause dehydration, thus producing only a temporary illusion of weight loss. Those that are effective appetite depressants are too dangerous to try, without medical advice.[18] A man may also hear that caffeine is bad for him, or he may be one of the few for whom it undoubtedly is bad. He resolves to stop drinking coffee, struggles hard with his resolution, and wins. What he doesn't know is that the colas he has become almost addicted to also contain caffeine, but the company does not have to mention the matter.[19]

In the process of growing up, our man will have gone through the stage of wanting to do the "in" thing. The in thing might be marijuana, which is discussed in a later chapter, but for more people it is simply tobacco. The young man looks over the brands and finds that all advertise special qualities. Some are for thinking men, some are worth fighting for, some are associated with the rugged outdoor life, and some are positively romantic. He becomes hooked on his own favorite and helps to make money for the tobacco company. He also, incidentally, erases a few years from his life expectancy. He hardly needs to be sent to the psychiatrist if he feels there is a plot afoot to kill him.

DRIVING A CAR In his late teens the young man decides to ride a motorcycle. His parents are appalled because motorcycles, they fear, are too dangerous. Finally, as a means of dissuading him, they buy him a car. Whatever car he selects will have the potential to kill him and many others as well. As Marshall McLuhan has said, the car gives the common man all the haughty insolence of a medieval knight, but changes his destructive potential from that of a mere lance to that of a guided missile. The man must have the car, however, for it has become "the protective and aggressive shell of urban and suburban man."[20]

[17]Sanford, "Unfoods: Do You Know What You're Eating?" in Sanford, *op. cit.*, pp. 53–57.
[18]Fred Trump, *Buyer Beware*, Abingdon Press, Nashville, Tenn., 1965, pp. 106–109.
[19]Turner, *op. cit.*, p. 112.
[20]Marshall McLuhan, *Understanding the Media: The Extensions of Man*, McGraw-Hill Book Company, New York, 1964.

Crumbling cars, built for speed, style, and power—anything but safety.

He will be operating a device that kills about 50,000 people per year at an average age of thirty-eight years. Each year 4 percent of the people who die in the United States die as a result of traffic accidents. Trains and buses also kill, but in relatively tiny numbers. For every 10 billion miles of travel there are 5 train fatalities, 13 bus fatalities, 14 airplane fatalities, and 570 auto fatalities.[21] It would seem only natural to assume, then, that society bend every effort to make sure that automobiles are as safe as engineering skill can possibly make them. Such is not the case.

Nader documents many instances of extremely dangerous cars, his initial case concerning the sporty Corvair.[22] His major theme is that Detroit should have been much more responsible in its attitude, emphasizing safety rather than power and style. There were cries of outrage and quackery against Nader, and many auto-loving people were willing to admit a certain amount of guilt on the part of the public for having shopped more for style and power than for safety. However, public support for Nader increased as it became known that General Motors had hired private detectives to follow him, to search his record for scandals, and to snoop into his private life, views, and associates.[23] In the summer of 1970 General Motors paid Nader $420,000 in settlement of a suit brought against the company for their harassing activities.

More important, however, than the argument with American automobile manufacturers—all are taken to task by Nader, and the manufacturers of small foreign cars even more so—is Nader's charge against the "Safety Establishment." Just as it was argued in Chapter 2 that preaching endlessly to the individual offender does little good, so does Nader contend that preaching safety to the driver does little good. The point is that if a man has an accident, he must have been violating a law. "Manslaughter charges are hurled routinely against drivers; there is yet to be any similar charge against the manufacturer for vehicle defects."[24] Incidentally, the year following publication of Nader's book, General Motors lost three judgments involving accidents with Corvairs.[25]

The Automotive Safety Foundation (ASF), established in 1937 by the Auto Manufacturers Association, gives grants for research work in driver training, laws, and

---

Before buying a car, check car safety. Write to Ralph Nader, Center for Study of Responsive Law, 1908 Q St., NW, Washington D.C. Also check *Consumer Reports.*

---

[21] Joseph Kelner, "Highway Murder," in Sanford, *op. cit.*, p. 220.
[22] Ralph Nader, *Unsafe at Any Speed*, Grossman Publishers, New York, 1965, chap. 1.
[23] David Hawkins, "The Safety of the American Automobile," *Science, Conflict, and Society: Readings from Scientific American*, W. H. Freeman and Company, San Francisco, 1969, pp. 252–256.
[24] Nader, *op. cit.*, p. 237.
[25] Sanford, *op. cit.*, p. 206.

highways, but never a cent for research on the safety of autos themselves.[26] Briefly, the Nader charge is that much of the safety effort has had the intended effect of taking pressure off the manufacturers and assigning the entire guilt to the driver. His book evoked a storm of protest but also awakened people and legislators. If interest does not die, the auto should become a less lethal device in the future, with killing not rising as fast as passenger miles.

Several states are now discussing proposals for no-fault insurance to relieve the present problems of auto insurance costs. The proponents of no-fault insurance contend that nearly half the insurance dollar is spent in court cases and that if insurance companies paid the costs of accidents to their insured, there would be a net saving in costs. The injustices suffered by drivers who are innocent but unable to prove their cases would also be relieved. At least part of the insurance industry is favorable to trying no-fault insurance as a possible means of ending dissatisfaction with present automobile insurance policies.

INSURANCE This discussion has made it sound as though premature death is the only thing to worry about, but there are other calamities to be faced. Nader gave estimates of property damages from traffic accidents for the year he wrote his book (1964) as 8.3 billion dollars. Surely the insurance companies must not enjoy paying vast sums of money and must be at the forefront of the fight for safe autos. Not so, says Nader. The Insurance Institute for Highway Safety (IIHS) is the tax-exempt insurance equivalent of the Automotive Safety Foundation. Its pronouncements parallel those of ASF—the public is careless, officials are not enforcing the law, and more traffic regulations are needed—but not one word about cars.

Even the Automobile Association of America (AAA) has been less effective than one might suppose. However, in 1963 and 1964 two officials of the Massachusetts AAA made attempts at imposing safety regulations on cars, but they found themselves defeated by clever legislative lobbying. One of the officials, Robert Kretschmar, spoke in the same words as Nader, accusing the auto industry of obfuscation of all attempts at safety and reminding them of earlier resistance to stop lights, directional signals, windshield wipers, and safety glass.[27]

THE LICENSE Not all the fault is with the automobile manufacturers, of course, although recently they have been getting the lion's share of unfavorable publicity. There is no denying the carelessness, insobriety, or lack of training of many drivers. The defensive driver, wishing to stay alive, must look upon the other driver's license as a license to kill. It is shocking to read the estimate of a Cincinnati neurosurgeon, Dr. F. H. Mayfield, that 6 million of the nation's drivers are subject to convulsive diseases. In thirty states licenses are renewed by mail, with no eye tests required,

[26]Nader, *op. cit.*, p. 247.
[27]*Ibid.*, p. 259.

providing one passed a test years ago. An aged motorist in Pennsylvania crashed into a tree and was killed; it was revealed that the man was totally blind but was being directed by an eight-year-old boy sitting beside him. Most state laws are lax enough to allow a man to drive even though his reflexes and vision are impaired by too much drinking. If he is thoroughly drunk he is usually taken off the road by his friends or by the police. The half-drunk driver is the real danger, and he is often allowed to go on his way.[28]

Some state driving laws are almost as generous in their definition of drunkenness as the old rhyme:

> Not drunk is he who from the floor
> Can rise again and drink some more,
> But he is drunk who prostrate lies
> Without the power to drink or rise.

THE PRICE PAID

Inflated prices are a matter of serious concern to the consumer, and they are, of course, sometimes made unavoidable by the economic pressures of a large buying public competing for scarce goods. Federal fiscal and monetary policies and escalating interest rates can have strong effects on prices, and so can the presently threatening tendency to increase international trade restrictions. A full-length book on consumer economics could not leave out these problems for the consumer or hundreds of others — real estate swindles, false guarantees, insurance policies that are canceled whenever a calamity befalls, get-rich-quick schemes for raising chinchillas, sweepstakes, chain letters, and many other possibilities listed in Trump's *Buyer Beware*. Many of these traps are avoided by the more wary. Our discussion has focused mainly on the types of consumer problems that are difficult for even the informed citizen to avoid: the problems of the grocery shelf and planned obsolescence, for example. To a degree the thousands of little advertising lies trap all people, even the sales resistant, with their tendency to make habitual thought patterns of their slogans.

THE GROCERY SHELF The food industry in recent decades has become a good example of oligopoly — control of almost the entire product by very few producers. Four firms prepare 85 percent of the nation's breakfast cereals. Most are bulky enough to look like a bargain, but in actual weight and nutritional value most represent a poor investment. Campbell Soup produces 95 percent of all prepared soups. Borden and National Dairy (Kraft) produce more than half the cheese on the American market. Processed foods, featuring food additives and a minimum of home preparation, exceeded sales of all other foods for the first time in 1969. The large firms making

---

[28]Kelner, *op. cit.*, pp. 221–222.

up oligopolistic control of much of the food market are very difficult for the FDA to regulate.[29]

Most of the food marketing is done by chain stores, which are fond of boasting that they work for a very low margin of profit. Based on food sales, it is true that the margin of profit is very low compared to that of many industries. Based on total investment, however, the story is quite different. Chain store profits on investment amounted to 12.5 percent in 1965.[30] In 1965 and 1966 there were consumer strikes in a number of stores, and it was amazing to see that prices could actually be reduced in response to housewife threat. The very fact that the markets invest so heavily in many kinds of trading stamps and games indicates that there must be a margin of profit greater than they like to admit.

The grocery shelf is loaded with several trick devices. Big, generous-looking packages are only partially filled. Some items are given favored treatment in a conspicuous spot at the end of the shelf, perhaps because the item is overpriced or otherwise hard to sell. Or it might be an item that people do not put on shopping lists but that might attract the housewife as an item for impulse buying. Another possible explanation is that the food brokers have worked their miracles to make sure a product is placed in a conspicuous location. Much of the food-brokerage business is done on the basis of proven sales records of goods, but when two competitors are close together in sales records, the broker might use a little "entertainment grease" to help push his product. "It can be anything from a pen with the company name on it to a broad for a week in the Caribbean,"[31] explained one very frank broker. Although the amount of entertainment grease is on the decline, it is still a sizable item that somehow has to be supported. As with the costs of other promotional schemes, the price is passed along to the consumer.

Packaging techniques become more refined with the passing of time, adding not only to the trash-pollution problems but to the deception of the consumer as well. Packages not only look as though they hold much more than they do, but they are priced in a confusing manner. Which is cheaper, the 13-ounce package for 73 cents, or the 15-ounce package for 85 cents? It would take an hour of extra shopping to make all the decisions properly. Even college-educated women failed a test in picking the best items for the money. A study in Washington, D.C. revealed that stores in

---

Check your grocery shelf for deceptive packaging, especially for empty space. Write a protest to the manufacturer about the air in your food.

---

[29]Turner, *op. cit.*, pp. 82–85.
[30]Sanford, "Gamesmanship in the Supermarkets," in Sanford, *op. cit.*, pp. 21–27.
[31]David Shaw, "Grocery Shelf Psychology—It Aims to Please," *Los Angeles Times*, August 18, 1970, pp. 1, 20, 21.

Bewilderment for the consumer, visual contamination, the hard sell, and no way of knowing the truth.

the same chain charged higher prices for food in the poorer sections of town, whether for white or black poor, and that the quality of perishable items declined.[32] The pattern of differential prices is generally true throughout the United States, although often the reason is higher costs in small, independent groceries in the poorer areas.

PLANNED OBSOLESCENCE The consumer, trapped by many small tricks of the grocery business, falls into a much more expensive trap in the obsolescence business. Women cannot help but complain about the obsolescence of fashions. Hemlines must rise and fall in order to make last year's clothes look odd so that more can be

[32]James Ridgeway, "Segregated Food at the Supermarket," in Sanders, *op. cit.*, pp. 26–29. (See also "What's Happened to Truth in Packaging?" *Consumer Reports* vol. 34, pp. 40–43, January 1969.

spent on consumer goods. At the time of writing, it seems that the fashion designers have decreed that skirts must lengthen, although a recent questionnaire indicated that only people over the age of seventy wanted this style. What used to be a problem mainly for women is becoming almost as much of a problem for men. Older styles of ties, shoes, sport coats, and various items that some men still prefer completely disappear from the market. The unseen hand of some czar of fashion seems to have signed a ukase that all must obey or face the living death of being passé.

Vance Packard wrote a book on obsolescence and similar problems, entitled *The Waste Makers*.[33] It was written before the environmentalist movement was as prominent as it is today, but some of its points are very similar to those of the environmentalists. In order to keep production humming, prosperity rolling, and profits gushing in, everyone must be induced to spend more and more. Otherwise the market would be glutted. Economists frequently comment on this particular dilemma of modern production; John Kenneth Galbraith is especially condemnatory of that characteristic of our productive system. It is Packard's book, however, that most boldly accuses much of industry of something approaching a deliberate plot against the consumer by making completely unneeded items seem like necessities of life. Their philosophy, Packard says, can be stated as "The way to end glut is to produce gluttons." Accordingly, more color matching is promoted to broaden sales of wardrobe items and matching items for the house. A one-car family is made to feel poverty-stricken, and a man pushing a lawnmower by hand is a disgrace to his middle-class neighborhood.

Another way to increase consumption is to increase the size of the items produced. Over a thirty-year period cars grew by four or five feet in length and increased fivefold in horsepower. They consume not only more gasoline, but also much more expensive gasoline. Increases in size and quantity were not enough, however. Packard quotes one writer for an industrial publication as saying, regretfully, "The more durable the item the more slowly it will be consumed." His suggestion was to make items *look* obsolete whether they were or not.[34] Other solutions to the problem were also found, such as making appliances with sealed units so that the handyman could not repair his own. A prominent journal for product designers presented an article suggesting "death dates" for all products—a way of speeding up replacement. Although many engineers and producers were outraged, quite a few thought it a commendable idea or at least "realistic" in terms of marketing needs. In a chapter entitled "The Short, Sweet Life of Home Products," Packard makes it sound as though the "death date" idea is pretty well implemented and that it would be wise never to buy a home appliance without first looking up its record in *Consumer Reports*. The problem of durables that are not very durable becomes more acute with the passing of time, the exhaustion of resources, the increasing numbers of people, and the ever-mounting piles of junk for which there is no satisfactory means of disposal.

[33]Vance Packard, *The Waste Makers*, Pocket Books, Inc., New York, 1963, p. 23.
[34]*Ibid.*, p. 55.

THOSE LITTLE LIES   The Justice Department filed a 1 million dollar suit against Geritol in the spring of 1970. For a decade the product had been advertised for people with "tired blood." Old people especially had been led to believe that Geritol was the last great medicine-man cure-all and restorer. A multimillion dollar business had flourished, making claims that the Justice Department calls deceptive and misleading.[35] The preceding year the Federal Trade Commission filed complaints against Allerest and Dristan, contending that neither completely relieves allergy as they had claimed. Both companies stopped the particular advertisements. Another famous little lie on television showed a rapid shave preparation so marvelous at softening beards that it was spread on sandpaper, and then the sandpaper was shaved clean. What actually happened was that sand was shaved off a glass surface.[36] Libbey-Owens-Ford auto glass was demonstrated to give fantastic clarity. One reason was that the glass was rolled down when the picture was taken.

Although in all the above cases FTC action was taken, there are numerous cases in which action cannot be taken. Many detergent advertisements stretch credibility. One merely shows a blood-stained shirt dipped into water containing the detergent and seconds later it comes out spotless. Clothes can come out whiter than white, cleaner than clean, purer than purity itself. There is no legal requirement that possible damage must be mentioned. Some types of toothpastes clean very well, but contain abrasives that are harmful to tooth enamel. Arthur Godfrey refused to advertise Axion until he was permitted to warn that it contained phosphates that could be water pollutants.[37] Generally such truths do not have to be admitted. Many of the little lies of advertising are lies of omission rather than commission.

Most people are fed other little lies. In spite of truth-in-lending laws, there are special carrying "fees" that run up interest rates. A group of Philadelphia loan companies was found to be holding second mortgages on homes in New Jersey, with special hidden charges that made the effective interest rates as high as 58 percent.[38]

Nearly every householder is met at the door occasionally by a personable young man or lady selling magazine subscriptions. A charming girl with a British accent says she is trying to make enough money to stay in the country and not lose her visa; please help. She is really from Chicago. A sales crew in Virginia threatened to burn a

---

Have you bought a faulty appliance or been unable to get satisfaction on a guarantee? Write to Mrs. Virginia Knauer, Presidential Advisor on Consumer Affairs, Washington, D.C.

---

[35]Daniel Henninger, "The One-Eyed Slicker," *The New Republic*, vol. 162, pp. 17–19, May 2, 1970.
[36]*Ibid.*
[37]*Ibid.*
[38]Jonathan Kwitny, "The Money Lenders," in Sanford, *op. cit.*, pp. 141–145.

woman's house if she wouldn't buy a subscription. She dropped dead of a heart attack. Sometimes the salesmen are as much victims as the customers. Deputy Attorney General Herschel T. Elkins of California reports cases in which young people were recruited in the East for magazine saleswork in California. They were given high promises of good pay, but no provision for transportation home. They had to sell or be stranded. They also found that they were being charged for food, travel, lodging, and other expenses, and often ended their sales tour owing the company money.[39]

The lies go on and on. Some are big; some are little. Attempts are made to deal with some of the consumer's problems, but others are fairly well ignored. The many examples given so far have included cases in which something effective is done, and some in which nothing is done. It is time to look at some of the basic causes of consumer traps and suggestions for remedies.

HELPING THE CONSUMER

There are several possible approaches to consumer problems, some calling for major institutional change, some for minor institutional change, and others for further use of the agencies now available. Regardless of the approach, the consumer must make himself heard politically and economically; without organization and effort he will continue to be misfed and overcharged.

THE ANTIESTABLISHMENT APPROACH   Sinclair was a socialist, thinking that the only solution to social problems lay in taking away the profit motive from industry. He was a gradualist, not calling for sudden and violent overturns, and at times, such as when he ran for governor of California, seeming to believe in working within the system. Nevertheless, when he wrote *The Jungle* his conclusion was that the only solution for the ills of the working man and the corruption of American society lay with socialism. In the uncompromising opinion expressed in *The Jungle*, all other attempts at reform would be mere palliatives. Sinclair believed that as long as people could make money by turning out bad products and mistreating labor, they would do so.

USING THE PRESENT SYSTEM   Trump takes a completely opposite approach. To a great extent his previously mentioned book *Buyer Beware* is practical advice to the individual consumer, warning him of the frauds to avoid. There is no condemnation of a great industry, such as the auto or food industry. There are many comments on petty swindlers, dishonest practices and dishonest practitioners, but these comments are always of evils begotten by evil people—not by an essentially evil or unworkable system.

Trump's book is very much worth reading because it is full of practical advice and has a list of the agencies and organizations to whom the consumer can turn for

[39]Alexander Auerbach, "Complaints Rise on Door-to-Door Magazine Sales," *Los Angeles Times*, August 28, 1970, Part I, pp. 24, 25.

help. Such agencies include the Federal Trade Commission, the Post Office, Consumer Advocates in some states, Better Business Bureaus, and the very Food and Drug Administration that Turner criticizes so strongly.

Consumer Reports, the publication of Consumers Union, also gives much practical advice on the rating of products and publicizes governmental actions against the food industry and various products. Its position is more critical of major industries than those books that concentrate mainly on swindlers. Most issues of *Consumer Reports* have a section entitled "The Docket" that gives a rundown of federal and state actions against false advertising, real estate and insurance swindles, and violations of truth-in-lending laws. Typical items from 1969 issues included reports of the finding of intolerable amounts of DDT in lettuce, insect parts and cat hair in butter, shipments of contaminated seafood, and insect filth in packaged rice.

Consumer Reports and its rival magazine, *Consumer Bulletin*, are of great help in trying to beat the "consumer trap." Ratings of nearly all conceivable products are given — automobiles, furniture, household appliances, washing detergents, shaving soap, toothpaste, over-the-counter medicines, tools and hardware, and so forth.

THE ESTABLISHMENT MODIFICATION APPROACH   Packard, Sanford, and Turner attack subsystems within modern American capitalism without attempting to attack the capitalistic system as a whole. Packard's *Waste Makers* is an appeal for industry reform, to prevent the production of shoddy goods and cheating the consumer. There is also an expression of concern with a system that will have to depend on constantly growing demand, even at the cost of waste and planned obsolescence.

Turner turns more explicitly to criticism of government and industry, but unlike Sinclair's, his criticisms are aimed at modification of the present system, rather than scuttling capitalism. Some of his criticisms pertain to the Food and Drug Administration: the policy of assigning too many products to the GRAS list without adequate investigation, denying that there are malnutrition problems, and looking upon nearly all food producers as "good guys." He recommends a system that will represent consumer organizations to speak before the FDA, rather than the present situation in which almost all consultations are with food and drug producers. He also suggests stricter use of antitrust legislation to break up oligopoly in the food industry. An even more important theme of his book is that of being sure that government regulators honestly regulate.

THE REGULATORS AND THE REGULATED   The problem approached by Turner has wide-ranging implications for the consumer, whether the Food and Drug Administration or any other regulatory commission is under consideration. The first efforts of regulated industries are aimed at getting their friends onto commissions. If they fail, the next attempt is to make friends with existing members of the commission, helping them to understand and be "reasonable." Only one important director of the FDA was caught in actual, provable conflict of interest, but there has been a tendency to develop an official attitude of implicit trust of the entire food and drug industry, whose bad actions were the original cause for creating the FDA.[40] It is difficult to have long conferences with the representatives of a regulated industry without becoming somewhat sympathetic. The industry's representatives, naturally, make every effort to be ingratiating, which no one can claim is either illegal or unethical. The trouble is that over a period of years too many representatives of industry become looked upon as old friends, but the consumers, whose interests are the reason for existence of the agency, are never seen. Head commissioners attempt to reform the system but find themselves enmeshed in a rigid, self-perpetuating system of thought and action, including listening to scientists friendly to department views and dismissing others as eccentric. Turner alleges that defense mechanisms are developed for congressional investigating committees, hiding much information on the grounds of protecting "trade secrets," justifying previous records, and covering up what cannot be justified.

There are bureaus and legislative acts to protect the consumer, but they can fall into relative disuse unless public pressure is placed on them. When the alarm bells are rung, as in the days of *The Jungle*, or as in the recent case of cyclamates, action is taken. What is needed is a more permanent, ongoing system for making sure that the consumer is represented. A suggestion to this effect would be a much larger representation of consumer organizations in meetings with the FDA, the Federal Trade Commission, and other agencies directly concerned with consumer problems. Such a policy would give the consumers countervailing power relative to the food and drug interests.

The current age of alarms has caused legislators and congressmen to push for more safety regulations on cars than we have had in the past. There is a tide of legislative talk and a trickle of legislative action on environmental problems. The danger is that the public may resume its usual pendulum swing from panic to complacency, and the pressure will be off. This is why it is important that new institutional means are developed for representing the consumer. Some states now have consumer advocates. Representation of consumer groups on regulatory commissions is a hopeful possibility. For reasons of consumer complaints and various other complaints against government, an office of ombudsman would be very much in order.

The ombudsman is an official in Scandinavian governments; his duty it is to hear complaints from the citizens against governmental bureaucracy. The only state with a strong office of ombudsman is Hawaii. There the first ombudsman, Herman S. Doi, is empowered to investigate all bureaus and commissions, with power to subpoena and publicize findings, to the great discomfort of agencies and bureaus. There is always the fear, of course, that the ombudsman will simply become another bureaucrat, but from a structural point of view he has a degree of independence from other bureaus and has no direct tie-in with the interests that they regulate.

[40]Turner, *op. cit.,* p. 218.

No system is immune to corruption or stagnation, be it bureau, consumer advocate, or ombudsman's office. Along with legislative and institutional reform, public action groups and alarmists are needed to trouble the placid waters of institutionalization. Sinclair would have thought of even these solutions as mere palliatives to a system that is fundamentally sick. Like many socialists of his time, he greatly underestimated the amount of improvement that would come about in working conditions and pay, but he properly criticized a system easily given to the production of shoddy goods, deceptive goods, and even dangerous goods. The only way to avoid solutions that would shatter the free enterprise system is to work out better means for correcting such abuses.

SUGGESTED READINGS

Margolis, Sidney: *The Innocent Consumer versus the Exploiters*, Pocket Books, Inc., New York, 1967.

> *Particularly good on such consumer problems as unfair credit practices, garnishment and repossession, home-improvement traps, and waste of money through brand names rather than generic names of pharmaceuticals. The book also has a useful final chapter on where to get help and advice.*

Nader, Ralph: *Unsafe at Any Speed*, Grossman Publishers, New York, 1965.

> *This is the book that finally roused the sleeping public to the realization that their autos are unnecessarily dangerous. A little bit of safety action has resulted; more will result if more of the public learns the facts presented by Nader.*

Sanford, David (ed.): *Hot War on the Consumer*, Pitman Publishing Corporation, New York, 1969.

> *This book contains such a wealth of information that it should be in all libraries. Excellent articles on four major topics: "A Closer Look at Food and Drugs," "Big Business Malpractices," "Your Safety Is at Stake," and "Insurance—Asset or Liability." (Not available in paperback.)*

Turner, James S.: *The Chemical Feast*, Grossman Publishers, New York, 1970.

> *As indicated by references in the previous pages, Turner's book is a well-aimed attack at the food industry, chemical additives, and the public agency responsible for pure food and drugs in America. Time magazine said ". . . it may well be the most devastating critique of a U.S. Government agency ever issued."*

Magazines: be sure to look over copies of *Consumer Reports* and/or *Consumer Bulletin*, especially if you are going to make an important purchase.

 **QUESTIONS**

1. How do modern chemical techniques tend to parallel the older problem of contamination of meat as described by Upton Sinclair in *The Jungle*?

2. Starting with infancy, describe the hazards to long life and health that confront a person as part of the consuming public.

3. The driver was once considered the sole reason for high death rates from automobiles. Where else does much of the fault lie?

4. In what ways is planned obsolesence related to the total economy and American way of life?

5. Discuss the problems involved in trying to set up regulatory commissions to protect the consumer.

4 *Why is there so much criticism of the educational system, in spite of the enormous amount of money spent on it, and in spite of its quantitative success in training manpower for the technological society? Does the education process become too routinized and depersonalized? Is there any end to the lengthening of the educational process? Are the schools assigned too many tasks to perform, including some that have passed their usefulness? Is the pace of education too fast? What are the reasons for campus unrest and for the growth of new types of student subcultures and countercultures? What means can be developed for increasing student participation in a manner consistent with legal process?*

The questions asked and the analysis to be presented in the next pages suggest a kind of malaise in the educational field for at least a part of the student generation. An unpopular war is part of the explanation, but by no means the total explanation. Even with its heavy burden of work, the educational system seems unable to keep pace with changing demands and changing perspectives of the young. Condemnation of the young is certainly no solution; the alternative suggested is for channeling student ideas and energy in a manner both innovative and constructive.

THE CREAKING CURRICULUM

Probably no other area of life exemplifies the theme of adjustment to rapid change as thoroughly as education. All societies must educate their people. In earlier agrarian societies education was primarily a family affair and not carried on through the formal institution of schools. In early civilizations, and even until fairly recently, formal education was generally for the select few. In some cases, as in certain Moslem countries and in early Puritan America, religious motives impelled a degree of literacy among common men so that they could read their Holy Scriptures; but for most societies even Holy Writ was a monopoly of an elite.

As the requirements of education in modern societies began to broaden, it still seemed that all but the most elementary education could continue to be a monopoly of the upper classes. The old priestly, legal, and medical professions were being joined by an increasing number of businessmen, scientists and researchers, and many other professions. They were admitted, grudgingly, into the closed circle of the learned and, as is often true of unwelcome guests, began to take over. For a long time the business courses seemed to set the pace of a new collegiate education, but by the middle of the twentieth century the new high priests were the scientists and the technical-managerial class. These groups were not a majority in higher education, but they had become the pacesetters, and they exemplified the brave new world of tomorrow. The brave new world had many attractions: rising standards of living, mechanical marvels, the conquest of hunger and disease, positions for far more college graduates, and a rational system of management of plants, products, and people. By accident more than by design, the management of people became a primary function of the educational system.

THE COLLEGE DREAM

If education could be measured purely in quantitative terms, there would be no question that the greatest period of educational enlightenment in the history of the United States (and the same applied to much of the rest of the world) began in the decades after World War II. People who had always thought of college as the privilege of a small elite now began to speak of college for a majority of people—at least two years of a community college. The prevalent view was that there would be no place in the new societies for the uneducated and that perhaps the new societies of the future would be hard put to provide as much educated talent as would be needed for their operation. Studies of social-class differences in attitudes toward education indicate that many poor people are less hopeful of advanced education as a goal for their children than are middle-class people, but to at least a limited degree the drive toward education penetrates all segments of society. To get to college, one must have the right attitudes, skills, and training. The indoctrination in these traits begins in kindergarten.

Graduation: achievement and shades
of doubt.

"BOOT CAMP" Harry L. Gracey[1] characterizes kindergarten as "academic boot camp." In the typical case he relates, a letter from the school prepared for parents stresses the idea that the most important achievement for their children will be learning to live with others and share in a small community. What the statement really means is that they will learn the routines imposed by the school. The routine in the school Gracey describes (in New York State, but typical of kindergarten in most states) is very tightly structured. Each day is divided into six parts: serious time, sharing time, play time, work time, clean-up time, and rest time. Some segments of the day are structured in such a way as to seem to give the children freedom, but always within the limits of school and teacher interest. When the children discuss a previous trip to the zoo, they seem most fascinated by the "spooky house," which the teacher is unable to identify. She carefully steers them back to a discussion of what they are *supposed* to learn and avoids petty distractions by childish interests. When child interest does not agree with school interest, it is ignored.

There is, of course, play time, when the children can follow their own direction to some degree, and which Gracey compares with the "informal groups" adults later

[1]Harry L. Gracey, "Learning the Student Role: Kindergarten as Academic Boot Camp," in Dennis H. Wrong and Harry L. Gracey, *Readings in Introductory Sociology*, The Macmillan Company, New York, 1967, pp. 288–299.

create on the job. What he could have added about the school "boot camp," however, is that even the play activity must be fitted into a mold. After so long a time children can no longer make up their own games but must learn to play the games of the adult world—baseball, soccer, football, and the like. Pleasures that arise spontaneously are hard to deal with under the system. Left to their own devices, children might play or roughhouse in a disorganized way. Even violence must be organized!

To return to Gracey's analysis, categorization sets in by the end of kindergarten. Most of the children are no longer difficult for the teachers; they are not only house-broken, they are schoolbroken. The best students both conform to the rules and identify with the school. A second group does not really identify, but submits. Finally there are the "problem children" who do not learn the routines of boot camp. The school might even employ a clinical psychologist to help teachers with such children. All three groups persist.

THE ACADEMIC CADET   As the child leaves his childhood status and becomes an adolescent of junior high school or high school age, he passes through many more forms of the routinization of life. He is quite likely to be "tracked," that is, placed in high, middle, or low academic-potential classes. A formidable amount of evidence shows that many of those placed on the lower tracks simply give up. Not only is their self-confidence crushed, but experimental evidence shows that many teachers are unable to believe in their capacity to improve and therefore reinforce the negative image and the propensity to fail.[2] Especially if he is in a lower track, the student is not likely to have challenging teachers. In nearly any track he will probably learn, just as he did in kindergarten, that it is not polite to ask "Why do we have to learn this?" He also will learn that, if he is to be "well adjusted," his recreations will center around the school expectation—school sports, dances, music, the peer group, and school politics.

In many respects the school policies tend to preserve immaturity, in spite of the fact that studies in both England and the United States indicate that physical maturity—the age of puberty—is three or four years younger now than a century ago,[3] indicating that high school students should be treated as politically mature, or nearly

---

Mass education often has too little time for the individual who needs help. Join a tutorial program and help a child. Contact local schools to see what can be done.

---

[2]See, for example, Walter E. Schafer et al., "Programmed for Social Class: Tracking in High School," *Transaction*, vol. 7, pp. 39–46, October 1970. See also, Robert Rosenthal and Lenore F. Jacobson, "Teacher Expectation and the Disadvantaged," *Scientific American*, vol. 218, pp. 19–23, April 1968.

[3]"Early Puberty," *Los Angeles Times*, October 16, 1970, Part 1A, p. 14.

so. Nevertheless, in such serious matters as government, the high school student is still treated as a rather small child. It would be possible for him to learn politics as a conflict of interest, with differing points of view advocated. It would be possible for him to see patriotism as a dedication to the historical ideals symbolized by his country, and therefore a good criticism of its present courses of action, or he could even see it as a dedication to the human race rather than to a nation. He could think of his teacher as a challenging critic, or as a person to be challenged in good-natured interchange. Unfortunately, this is seldom the case. The major pressures of politics and patriotism are toward narrow conformism, as taught in most high schools, rather than toward independent, critical thought.[4] The simplistic view of history and politics taught in high school is likely to be so drastically challenged in college that much of the earlier learning will be viewed as a hoax. The sudden realization that all is not perfect sometimes turns the student too far toward the counterpoint, nihilistic notion that all is false.

In the meantime, for the student whose life seems to be circumscribed by the school there must, of course, be other interests. When he was little, his family occupied a large part of his life. As he grew older, the peer group began to occupy his attention increasingly and to set patterns for him to follow. Peer groups have always been important, but they grow ever more important in a society in which people are reared to a great extent by their own age mates, where contact with family is minimized compared with the past, and where contact with teachers is too impersonal and socially distant to fill an important emotional need. The habit of dependence upon the peer group grows in various respects—entertainment and music, dress and hair styles, and many other fads, slang expressions and neologisms, and styles of thought and speech. Above all, the music becomes a medium of interaction within the youth subculture, the generational imperative, something written for the youth market, not promoted by school or other adult authority, and therefore having an air of freedom about it. Another separate and secret world develops in illicit activities: in sex, alcohol, and, increasingly, marijuana.

THE PUSH TOWARD COLLEGE   Although the entertainment world of the peer group and occasional work experience will provide some variation in the routine of school, school is expected to be the occupation and preoccupation of life for those who are going to succeed. Life is measured off in promotions from grade to grade and ticked off in increments of time until completion.

During the years of academic cadethood there will be constant pressure toward college. Teachers are college graduates; practically all think that they did the right thing by going to college and that they should encourage all their students to do likewise, unless they are of very low academic ability. To choose a good course in auto

[4]David Spits, "Politics, Patriotism, and the Teacher," *The National Elementary Principal*, vol. 43, pp. 17–22, January 1964.

mechanics, welding, mill work, or other necessary crafts is viewed almost as a confession of incompetence. A society that has long stressed the dignity of labor is almost uniquely scornful of a whole range of needed jobs and makes little provision to train for them or to encourage competent people to enter them. The result is that many students struggle with college in spite of no strong commitment to learning.

CREAKING UNDER THE STRAIN   The educational system of the United States groans under a heavy burden. It could be called a creaking system because of a slowness to adjust to the learning needed for today and tomorrow, and there is considerable truth in such a description. The idea of "the creaking curriculum" is being applied here, however, to refer mainly to the weight of the burden placed upon it. The burden is not only one of training the personnel needed for the social system, but of training them in a manner consistent with a belief in maximum opportunity for the individual and equality of opportunity. The latter goals are expected to be accomplished for students drawn from widely varying backgrounds and abilities, often but vaguely understood by the teachers in the educational system. The public interprets failures of the student as failures of the school system, and those teachers with the most highly developed superegos are inclined to see things in the same manner.

Meantime, against a background of a school system whose goals are almost impossible to achieve, new forces arise, new anxieties and concerns that must be met. In 1957, just after Russia launched her first Sputnik, the schools were accused of not having produced enough scientists. Immediately the average school began to dedicate itself to turning out scientific geniuses. As sex liberty increases in American society, and the rate of premarital pregnancy is popularly believed (mistakenly) to be almost entirely a problem of teenagers, the schools are condemned for not presenting sex education, or for teaching it, or for teaching it wrong, or for being too silent, or too puritanical, or too permissive. As a rising tide of drug abuse occurs, a demand is made for stretching the curriculum to include good, solid information on drugs. Often such courses are expected to teach both the truth and the attitudes of the older generation, even though the two fail to get together.

Finally, the curriculum creaks because it is faced with an unusual phenomenon in the younger generation, especially the college generation. College students have seldom been quiescent. A number of European and Latin American countries have long been accustomed to student radicalism. In the United States, however, much of the steam of youth has escaped through innocuous safety valves, planned and instituted by the college system — football, fraternities, homecoming queens, proms, and a number of rather repetitive fads. Today, whether the change be seen as a great new philosophy or as utter madness, it cannot be dismissed as frivolous in intent or consequence. Something new is afoot in reasons for protests, the defiance of the system, the style of life, and the rejection of the establishment; and the trend is bewildering to old-fashioned liberals as well as to old-fashioned conservatives.

THE ROOTS OF PROTEST

There is considerable disagreement as to the underlying causes of student protest. Those most condemnatory of student activists can call them the spawn of permissive child rearing or the dupes of clever propaganda; but permissive child rearing and subversive propaganda are certainly not new. Why should they account for such a radical change in the student generation? Why doesn't the "spoiled" child simply enjoy his advantages and become a rather innocuous playboy? Why should an indulged generation listen to propaganda against the very system that has permitted its easy life, relatively free from fear of poverty and want?

Perfectly competent analysts have suggested that changes in child-rearing practices may have wakened the spirit of the present college generation, but other elements were necessary to give it expression and direction. Some other elements in the life experience of the present college generation might, indeed, lead to an argument as to whether their rearing patterns have been as permissive as is commonly assumed.

TOO MUCH COLLEGE? The child born into middle-class America has very few tasks to perform around the house, and in his early life he is usually at the very center of the family circle. It soon develops, though, that he really does have a task to perform, and that is the task of going to school and preparing for a future that seems infinitely distant. There is every reason to believe that for the majority of students, and especially for those who are not stongly inclined toward scholarship, the tasks of school are more difficult than the old tasks of helping with the family farm and shop. The shadow of the schoolhouse lengthens interminably.

Half a century ago, for the majority of people, school continued until the growing boys and girls had reached what they and their families considered their level of need or ability. Then they dropped out, with the boys getting jobs and the girls becoming housewives. Those with great interest, parental push, and financial means remained in school, finally graduating from college. The system was unequal, but relatively uncomplicated.

The picture changed drastically over a period of two generations. Now all must stay in school—the lame, the halt, and the blind, the rich and poor, the conformist and the delinquent, the socially popular and the outcasts, male and female, athlete and uncoordinated, the bright and the dull alike—all are made to fit into the system. Some protest, some resist the confines, some even go to juvenile hall instead, but escape becomes virtually impossible. It would be grossly unfair to say that the schools are harsh or dominated by the lash. Almost the opposite is the case, with even the students sometimes complaining that not enough is accomplished. Nevertheless, there is a confinement, an inevitability, and a lengthening of the sentence. Furthermore, there is less freedom to explore the world on one's own, as was so important to earlier American youth—the woods, the rivers, the mountains, or even the alleys.

The unusual are gently guided to the right path. If they are hyperactive, they may be given pills; if they are introverted dreamers, they may be given a psychiatrist. Always, though, they are gently directed in a line that will prepare them for their future and fit them into the system.

Protests against fitting the growing child into a system are as ancient as Lao Tse and have been repeated by Wordsworth and Rousseau, among others. In American literature Mark Twain's best known writings are protests against growing up into an adult world through the prison of the school, but the spirit of the writing was different from today's; Huck Finn could escape. About thirty years ago Stephen Leacock, the Canadian humorist, took up the argument in a more serious vein in a book entitled *Too Much College.*[5] Since then Paul Goodman has written much more widely on similar themes, but Leacock's earlier book deserves reexamination. Leacock's humor is usually whimsical, sometimes even silly; but in *Too Much College* he uses it as a weapon.

Leacock compares the educational system with Aesop's fable of the toad that tried to puff itself up to become an ox. As the public clamors for new courses and duties of the school, the system grows bigger and bigger. Departments in colleges gain vested interests in courses; many are added, few are dropped. Everyone must halfway learn a foreign language, but never to the point where he can really use it fluently. In Leacock's opinion, departments of education devote half their time to teaching what is really unteachable—how to be an inspiring teacher. People with unacceptable English usages must be remade by the school. Those with little intellectual interest or ability must chalk up infinite hours in lecture halls. Those who aspire to medical degrees or other higher degrees find their preparations lengthening out, leaving only a brief interlude between mature competence and senility. Life is absorbed, not in living, but in preparation for the next stage, says Leacock:

> How strange it is, our little procession of life! The child says, "When I am a big boy." But what is that? The big boy says, "When I grow up." And then, grown up, he says, "When I get married." But to be married, what is that after all? The thought changes to "When I'm able to retire." And then, when retirement comes, he looks back over the landscape traversed; a cold wind seems to sweep over it; somehow he has missed it all, and it is gone. Life, we learn too late, is in the living, in the tissue of every day and hour. So it should be with education.
>
> But so it is not; a false view discolors it all. For the vastly great part of it the student's one aim is to get done with it . . . . [At last] he steps out of college a free man, without a stain on his character—and not much on his mind.[6]

Unlike many critics, Leacock even makes some practical suggestions for improvement: Change the absurd spelling of our language to make reading and writing

---

[5]Stephen Leacock, *Too Much College, or Education Eating Up Life*, Dodd, Mead & Company, Inc., New York, 1940.

[6]*Ibid.*, p. 19.

quick and easy; either learn foreign languages thoroughly or save the effort; learn basic mathematics, but not mere puzzles in numbers; even whittle away a little at hallowed literature and history, except for those who really treasure them.

TOO MUCH SYSTEM The very word "college" sounds old-fashioned today; even "university" is becoming outdated. This is the age of the "multiversity." Not only have the school years become preoccupied with an increasingly distant future, but they also have become a preview of the mass bureaucracies that lie in that future. Jacques Barzun speaks of World War II as the great divide between the old university and the new. Before World War II the administration of Columbia by a single president was possible; now, although there is a president, he can no longer function, except through a mounting hierarchy of intermediaries, to administer scores of departments, hundreds of faculty, and tens of thousands of students.[7]

The increase in student body in the great university is well known, but this is only part of the problem of school size. The university must now turn out scientists and engineers, contribute to medical research, war research, psychological research, sociological research, economic research, and provide a home for the arts and theater. The degree of specialization increases. The individual of broad interests is an anachronism. Once a renowned scholar might teach a variety of related subjects; now he teaches a subdivision of a subdivision of a discipline. The result is that the proliferation of staff outpaces the proliferation of students. "What one man would have taught in 1880 required three in 1920 and from ten to thirty in 1960."[8]

The specialization is, of course, a result of several kinds of social change. As the society becomes more scientifically oriented, it must spend more time on new research, which calls for high levels of specialization. The schools are also increasingly enmeshed in projects for the Defense Department and for private industry. Although the research work performs the traditional educational function of adding to knowledge, it is too practically involved with government and big business to meet the traditional criterion of pure science — knowledge for the sake of knowledge.[9]

Specialization does not result in better teaching. In fact, better teaching is discouraged by some characteristics of the educational system, one of which is bureaucratic rigidity. The bureaucratic system starts early in life. Goodman gives an ugly description of the New York school system, with 750 schools, 1 million children, and an annual budget of close to 1 billion dollars. As is so frequently the case with bureaucracies, goals are lost in the scramble to keep the organization running. For example, until recently it was impossible to get bilingual teachers because the bureaucratic rules said that no one with a foreign accent could be hired, in spite of

[7]Jacques Barzun, *The American University*, Harper & Row, Publishers, Incorporated, New York, 1968, pp. 6–8.
[8]*Ibid.*, p. 18.
[9]James Ridgeway, *The Closed Corporation: American Universities in Crisis*, Ballantine Books, Inc., New York, 1968, pp. 73–110.

the fact that 35 percent of the students were Puerto Ricans, speaking little or no English![10]

THE DECLINE OF TEACHING In college the bureaucratic system takes forms hardly credible to the uninitiated. The question "Is Professor Schwartkranz an interesting lecturer?" proves the questioner to be naïve. The "right" question should be "Is Professor Schwartkranz eminent in his field?" Nothing is so damaging to one's academic reputation as to be known as a good teacher but a poor research man. The fear of such reputational damage has "led to many a naturally good teacher deliberately hiding this particular light under a bushel lest he thereby be thought of as without promise as a research man."[11] One clever assistant professor is quoted as saying he is careful not to get tagged as "good with undergraduates," for fear all promotions will cease.

To the ordinary student, the ability to teach is much more important than the ability to do research. In answer to the question "In what ways would you bring about improvement in your school?" 46 percent of all students questioned in the college poll asked first for better teachers. Typical comments were "What good are degrees or academic reputations to me? I need a teacher." One student complained that his best teacher had been fired because he didn't want to do research.[12]

This is not to say that professors shirk their duties. A recent study of the campuses of the University of California indicates that the work week has actually lengthened, but the amount of time devoted to undergraduate students has declined. The additional hours go to graduate students and research work.[13] The ideal system becomes one that is economically productive—one professor with a student assistant, lecturing to an auditorium-sized class, and giving examinations that will be read only by an assistant or, better yet, a computer. The total impact reinforces an image of the withering individual in the mass society.

Another frequent student complaint concerns a grading system that has no court of appeal. Of the 10,000 students interviewed by the College Poll, 54 percent complained about the grading system. There were also strong complaints of over-

---

Make a survey of college opinion at your school as to what improvements are most needed—smaller classes, remedial courses, more vocational counseling? Present results to the administration.

---

[10]Paul Goodman, *People or Personnel*, Vintage Books, Random House, Inc., New York, 1968, chap. 3.
[11]Robert A. Nisbet, "Sociology in the Academy," in *Sociology and Contemporary Education*, Random House, Inc., New York, 1964, pp. 63–64.
[12]James A. Foley and Robert K. Foley, *The College Scene*, Cowles Book Company, New York, 1969, pp. 78–79.
[13]Daryl Lembke, "UC Professors Fire Back at Work Critics," *Los Angeles Times*, October 5, 1970, pp. 1, 22.

burdening the curriculum with courses that are irrelevant or whose relevance is not made clear to the student. Other strong complaints were voiced about red tape, cumbersome communication systems, and the slow pace of reform.[14]

REALITY AND IDEAL In the educational system there are other roots of protest that have existed for a very long time but have remained latent until recent years. One of the sources of protest is that of disparity between societal ideals and societal accomplishments. The present college generation has been more aware than earlier ones of such disparities, partly because frustration over the long, bureaucratic course they must pursue leaves them ready to vent their wrath on a handy target. The society has been more than obliging in presenting the targets. The first boldly marked target was racism and inequality; the next equally clear target was the Vietnam War. Other targets are not quite so clear, ranging from student rights and free speech to such vast, formless things as "the establishment," "the system," or the "military-industrial complex."

FROM PROTEST TO COUNTERCULTURE

In the days of the Kennedy administration many liberal students on college campuses saw a leader who appealed to them. They had already started a movement of protest against racism in the United States. Various freedom marches were formed, with Northern students going to the South to aid in demonstrations from Montgomery to Birmingham. Several lost their lives in the struggle for racial equality in Mississippi. Dedications to their memory were held on hundreds of campuses, and the strains of "We Shall Overcome" became well known to everyone. Liberal adults were torn between praise for the student's effort and concern for their safety. There was also concern that the young idealists would become martyrs to the cause in the sense of giving up education (in the narrow sense of the word) to pursue the cause of equality. Racists, of course, were outraged, but the general reaction was one of praise for the civil rights leaders.

Even when President Kennedy was replaced by President Johnson, a man far less congenial to the students, praise for their efforts continued. In calling upon Congress for a strong civil rights law, Johnson repeated some of the slogans of the civil rights movement. "We shall overcome" was given the meaning of the black overcoming his outcast status and of the white overcoming his bigotry and racism. In the same speech, however, a warning was issued against violence, for violence was beginning to occur—not only the violence of Mississippi sheriffs, but the counter-violence of the movement for equality. The latter was more disturbing to "the system" than the former.

[14]Foley and Foley, *op. cit.*, pp. 79–80.

Student activism: protest against war
and symbols of the establishment.

THE RISING TIDE In Berkeley in 1964, Mario Savio led a protest movement in favor of student freedom, which came to be known as the Free Speech Movement and featured disruption of classes by sit-in strikes. The strike was started by the administration's invoking an old rule against political recruitment and the collecting of funds on the campus. The immediate cause was unique among the protest movements, but the methods of fiery demonstration, verbal attack, rejection of compromise, and refusal to work within the system became part of the method of protest everywhere. The system always seemed too slow, cumbersome, and indirect for the student militants.

In the next few years Columbia, San Francisco State, and the University of California at Santa Barbara became major storm centers. At both Columbia and San Francisco State a strong alliance with black students over equal rights was vitally important. At Santa Barbara the protests were against the Vietnam War and against symbols of the establishment, especially the Bank of America and the police. From 1967 on, so many protests centered on the Vietnam War that some people began to think of the war as "the" cause of student protests. It must be remembered, however, that protests had started over other issues.

THE ACTIVISTS Kenneth Keniston,[15] in summarizing a considerable number of studies done on student protests and student subcultures, concludes that the students should be divided into two groups: a subculture of activists and a counterculture of the alienated. For the student activists he takes exception to part of the above analysis of the tedious path through school and the poor quality of instruction. He stresses strongly, however, the comment on the gap between real and ideal culture. The activist student typically comes from a middle- or upper-middle-class home, with liberal parents who are strongly aware of and concerned about such problems as poverty, racial inequality, and war. The activists are not very numerous and come to the fore mainly in some of the best academic centers of the nation, seldom in the worst. Although they attend academically superior universities, they may feel some relative deprivation—relative to their high aspirations regarding education. Their leaders are often graduate assistants, well acquainted with the system, generally of liberal convictions, and often frustrated by the long and difficult road to course completion and higher degrees. Generally, the activist leaders are superior students. Keniston concludes that student demonstrations depend upon protest-prone personalities, institutional settings, and historical situations. The personalities arise in liberal home backgrounds, where criticism is admired and where there is no great awe of authority. The institutional settings are those of large, impersonal universities with a reputation for drawing politically engaged students and faculty and where a large, heterogeneous grouping can collect readily. There is a slight change in backgrounds of students involved, depending on the cause of protest. In the case of the

[15]Kenneth Keniston, *The Young Radicals: Notes on Committed Youth*, Harcourt Brace Jovanovich, Inc., 1968, pp. 297–325.

antiwar movement, there is no relationship between socioeconomic background and active support. Many supporters of the War Moratorium of 1969 were working their way through college.[16]

In the chaotic, intercommunicative, modern world, occasions for protest are to be expected, with a likely rise and fall in the amount and type of protest over the years. Keniston contends that the protesters are generally intelligent and are likely to continue with protest movements only if they can reasonably expect to achieve desired goals. Long frustration may cause a decline in the possibility for protest, or a conservative backlash may discourage further attempts by undermining the causes for which protests have been staged. Several factors seem to work for continued protest; one or two against. Meanwhile, a quarrel arises over who is more guilty of campus violence, the students or the police and militia. The argument will be examined relative to recommendations of the Scranton Commission. Another very important aspect of the student protest subcultures must also be examined, however, and that is what Keniston designates as the alienated or what Theodore Roszak calls the counterculture.

THE STUDENT COUNTERCULTURE The aims of the student activists—race equality, free speech, peace, opportunities for the poor—could hardly be called countercultural. It could even be argued that the methods are not too foreign to American tradition, which has seen violent labor disputes, racist disputes, and even violent antiliquor and women's rights movements. There are, however, many student groups on some of today's campuses that could be characterized as countercultural. The line of distinction between them and the activists is made clearly by Keniston; it is a blurred line as seen by Roszak, although he, too, makes a distinction.

Theodore Roszak[17] sees a definite counterculture, weary of political methods and parties and movements, disillusioned by the "technocratic totalitarianism" of modern society. The prophets of the counterculture are those who are disillusioned with the search for freedom and meaning in the present way of the world. They represent a revulsion against the coldness and calculability of modern science, the physical and psychological manipulation of the individual, and the doctrine of expertise to fit everyone and everything into the proper niche. Their search for the new freedom has led from the discredited Timothy Leary and his LSD through Zen Buddhism, Ginsberg poetry, the Marxist-Freudian philosophies of Herbert Marcuse and Norman Brown, and the antiestablishment humanism of Paul Goodman. A grouping together of all these names makes it obvious, of course, that there is overlap between activists and counterculture, and yet they are analytically distinguishable. It might be said that the slogan of the conservative is "America, love it or leave it"; the slogan of

[16]Mark A. Tessler and Ronald D. Hedlund, "Students Aren't Crazies," *New Republic*, pp. 17–18, September 12, 1970.
[17]Theodore Roszak, *The Making of a Counter Culture*, Anchor Books, Doubleday & Company, Inc., Garden City, N.Y., 1969.

the activist is "America, change it or lose it." The counterculture, if it had an equivalent slogan, could very well say, "America, forget it!" The fate of the technological society is seen as so grim that it must be escaped, either into a rootless bohemia or a commune, or possibly it can be tolerated with enough drugs. One must never involve himself in the system; to do so is slavery and loss of independent identity.

In some ways the counterculture seems quiescent and relatively harmless. Since its votaries defy conventions in dress and appearance and in sex, and also often show an interest in the occult, they win no praise from "straight" society. At the same time, they are not as great a source of fear and worry as are the activists. Seen from another point of view, however, they may be a symptom of something much more pathological than mere activism. A society, like it or not, can profit from movements that demand reform and may ultimately be thankful for the generation of protests against its shortcomings. But when a society produces an increasing number of "dropouts," there must be a deeper malaise than the specific issues over which the activists demonstrate. There seems to be a disenchantment with aspects of the scientific society, and the disenchantment is not confined merely to a tiny subculture. Dr. Harold Brown, president of California Institute of Technology, complains of a lack of funds for research, brought on by a public disillusionment with science and an unwillingness to buy new programs. Symptoms of disillusionment seem to spread beyond the college campus.

THE REACTION

The preceding discussion of activism and counterculture leaves a number of questions. Do the activists and the alienated tend to merge increasingly with the passage of time and the growth of common hostilities? Just what is meant by activism? To many members of the public the very word conjures up images of closing classrooms, raging mobs, and burning buildings; to others it means legitimate involvement in politics and programs to help the underprivileged. Do student leaders worry about the possibility of producing a backlash that will go hard on the public financial support of colleges and universities? Finally, how extensive are public reactions against student demonstrations?

THE NUMBERS INVOLVED   Keniston stressed the idea that student activism is a phenomenon of only a few schools and of a minority of students. Keniston is a scholar who is careful with his facts; however, his cited work covers events only to the beginning of 1968. Since then there have been times when the number of students involved in strikes and demonstrations has increased. The Center for Research and Development in Higher Education at Berkeley completed a survey of ten universities in the summer of 1970. The Center found that 99 percent of the students quizzed considered activism effective, and 28 percent were willing to carry protest to the point of disruption of classes. More than half opposed suspension of students who disrupt normal functioning of the school by protest activities. More than half considered nonviolent mass protests and demonstrations necessary, and only 19 percent agreed that peaceful petitioning is apt to be more effective in the long run. Nine percent felt that physical confrontation and violence must at times be used.[18] Such statistics would make it seem that when confrontations actually arise, the distinction between the activists and the alienated becomes less important than in theoretical analysis. The same study indicates that one of the most immediate causes of demonstrations is the issue of student rights.

Although these statistics do not indicate a quiescent attitude on the part of students, it should be emphasized that only 9 percent seem to believe in violence even as a last resort, although the excitement of confrontations might cause additional students to support the militants at times. It should also be noted that there is a tendency for extremist groups to become divisive, quarrel among themselves, and disintegrate. Partly for this reason, Clark Kerr, former chancellor of the University of California, is mildly optimistic about the future.

THE PRESIDENT'S COMMISSION ON CAMPUS UNREST The President's Commission on Campus Unrest (also called the Scranton Commission) issued its report in September 1970. Like many such reports, it has become a center of controversy, but an attempt was made to appoint a well-balanced committee, headed by the moderate William Scranton. The burning issues of student violence and official violence were examined, and both types of violence were thoroughly condemned. Surveys showed that a great majority of adult opinion considered all the violence to have been the fault of the students. The commission severely denounced both sides for violence, and termed the shootings of students at Jackson State a result of police racism and the shootings at Kent State "uncalled for and inexcusable." Considerable credence was given to the student charge that suppression of peaceful demonstrations had often generated the violence that was so loudly decried. At the same time the commission found disturbing evidence against a number of student firebrands. "A small minority of politically extreme students and faculty members and a small group of dedicated agitators are bent on the destruction of the university in order to gain their own political ends."[19]

The commission recommended a softening of the official rhetoric against students, better training of police and national guardsmen, not just for repression, but also to prevent trigger-happy reactions and to open channels of communication with the students. "A nation driven to use the weapons of war upon its youth," said the commission, "is a nation on the edge of chaos."[20] Continued support for education

---

[18]Jeff Perlman, "Study Shows Students Favor Confrontation," *Los Angeles Times*, September 21, 1970, Part I, p. 3.
[19]Jack Nelson and Ronald J. Ostrow, "Campus Unrest Panel," *Los Angeles Times*, September 27, 1970, Part I, p. 1.
[20]*Ibid.*, p. 3.

**Counterviolence: mass arrest at
antiwar demonstration, Washington,
D.C., May 3, 1971.**

was called for, as well as a great increase in support for minority-group students and their colleges.

In its description of the new college subculture, the commission agreed very much with Roszak's previously stated views. The subculture stresses the importance of expressiveness in styles of dress and music, of great individuality, of hatred for war and racial inequality, and of turning one's back on a society that practices such offenses. It states that a majority of the students are not part of such a subculture, except for its music, and that there are wide differences in the degree to which the alienative subculture is followed.

IN DUBIOUS BATTLE   If no more than 8 to 9 percent of students believe there are situations in which violence is necessary, then why have there been such a large number of violent demonstrations? Part of the answer, no doubt, is merely what sociologists have long noted about collective behavior—the tendency for excitement to spread, escalate, and involve more and more people. Basically, the overwhelming majority of students are opposed to violence; 65 percent have never participated in any type of demonstration, and only about 5 percent admit to any violence.[21] Nevertheless, situations can occur in which demonstrations escalate into violence.

John Steinbeck used Milton's phrase "In Dubious Battle" as the title for one of his early books, which describes a technique of revolution. The technique was to provoke the police into acts of brutality that would antagonize the entire working class and bring them into a revolutionary frame of mind. Deliberately in some cases, and accidentally in many others, the revolutionary technique has worked on college campuses. The arrests of Berkeley students and mere passersby in 1968 inflamed the entire campus. Isla Vista, the student residential area of the University of California at Santa Barbara, gradually developed an atmosphere in which police and national guardsmen were hated by practically all students, even those who had once thought of themselves as conservatives. There were similar student reactions at Kent State, where four students were shot.

In a number of cases overreaction on the part of officialdom has played into the hands of the most radical student groups. There are also cases, according to the Scranton Commission, of politicians making inflammatory speeches against the students in order to court popular support. Such speeches have tended to unite the more moderate students behind the militants rather than to soften their attitude. Such escalation of the conflict tends to play into the hands of what can hardly be designated as anything but the "lunatic fringe" of radicals. (The Weathermen, an organization with almost no actual students in it, is the most prominent of the lunatic fringe organizations at the time of this writing.)

If the more radical student militants expected to arouse support from the workers, they have been badly disappointed. "Hard hats" have been vehemently anti-

[21] Foley and Foley, *op. cit.*, pp. 50–51.

student militant. In Santa Barbara, striking workers appealing for aid refused any help when it was offered by university students.

In certain other respects the battle has been dubious. There have been gains for black students and a number of cases of revision of rules to give students more voice in colleges, but a reaction against the institutions of higher education has set in. All the academic world has been asking itself what went wrong; activist students in particular cannot understand why a majority of the public thought the killings at Kent State were purely the fault of the students themselves, a point about which the President's commission agrees with the students. Of the many attempted explanations of public attitudes, an analysis by Andrew M. Greeley,[22] sociologist and Director of the National Opinion Research Center, is particularly apt. One of the basic problems arises from an isolation of the campus from the rest of society.

THE ISOLATED CAMPUS   The basic difficulty, says Greeley, is that the university is too inclined to form a closed community of its own, rather contemptuous of the "barbarians" outside its gates. Academic arrogance is resented by outsiders and communication is at a minimum. Hence many students and faculty members are amazed that the public is unwilling to vote more funds for education and views higher education with suspicion. To many of the poor, especially the poor white ethnic groups, there is no understanding of what students mean by "the establishment." To poorer people looking up from the bottom, Harvard, Berkeley, and Stanford students *are* the establishment in a sense that such a person as Spiro T. Agnew is not. The students are seen as sons of old Americans, no longer ethnic or poor—a definitely privileged class. There is no understanding of student protest against the entire system. Perhaps the white ethnic groups could understand opposition to the war if it were presented as a war "contrary to the noble tradition of our great country"; but if the war is presented as a conflict fought by the United States for the sake of our own "grasping, brutal, imperialistic establishment," the argument makes no sense to the white ethnics.

There are what might be called personality contributions to the problem, as well as institutional and ideological sources of communication failure. Greeley's studies indicate a large percentage of university professors are from unhappy home backgrounds, are iconoclasts who no longer follow the religion of their youth, and are also far removed from cultural averages in reading and artistic tastes and even

---

Help to bring the campus closer to the community. Participate in community self-help programs; work with scouts or YMCA or other youth groups; also do political party work.

---

[22]Andrew M. Greeley, "Turning Off the People," *New Republic*, vol. 162, pp. 14–16, June 1970.

in political and moral philosophies. These traits help to make them interesting and stimulating to college students, but they also help to isolate them from the nonacademic world. The young academics are closer in years and emotional identification to the student activists than to the total society; hence they defend students through thick and thin, even in cases where their action has been undeniably hotheaded and shown an arrogant unconcern for conventional ideas of law and order. In such cases, in the mind of the general public, the issues of battle are indeed dubious. Greeley even fears that the conflict could result in a resurgence of the venomous anti-intellectualism of the Joseph McCarthy era in the early 1950s.

TOWARD SOLUTIONS

There is no certainty that the activist trend of recent years will continue into the indefinite future. A change from war to peace could have a major impact on American campuses, and a possible reaction against extremism or a threatening wave of repression could also have a quieting effect. However, the problems that have caused protest to take disruptive and violent form will not suddenly melt away. A society valuing liberty must allow protest, but it can insist that protest take nonviolent forms and avoid long interruptions in education. There are presently disquieting murmurs against public support for colleges and threats of a new anti-intellectualism. To avoid such trends, educators must do a better job in the difficult region where education and political issues intersect. The extension to eighteen-year-olds of the right to vote presents a new challenge in political education.

REALISTIC POLITICS Political interest on the part of students must be encouraged, not deadened, and it must be clearly legitimatized rather than given an aura of subversion. One difficulty in the way of this objective is that childish pictures of political realities are long perpetuated. The facts of political life — pressure groups, secret committees, smoke-filled rooms, the merchandising of candidates, lobbying, and the techniques of exerting influence — are ignored too long. When they suddenly dawn on the consciousness of the young, they are seen as things of unmitigated evil, spoiling a system that was once believed to be perfect. David Easton[23] of the University of Chicago found that eighth graders were naïve enough to say that the average man has just as much political influence as large corporations or the wealthy! Easton also found that the students changed their minds very little in the years of high school.

The college student emerges as a sophisticated individual in most respects, and aware of the facts of political life to a degree. He is still unduly shocked by his sudden initiation into realities, however, and as yet has had no experience in either practical politics or protest. Protest movements are most common in situations where there

[23]David Easton, quoted by Muriel Beadle, "How We Have Created Young Radicals," *Los Angeles Times*, September 27, 1970, Sec. G, p. 3.

The way of persuasion and negotiation as an alternative to both violence and noninvolvement.

are no institutionalized means for making complaints heard or where there is no knowledge of such means. The student's inexperience and lack of training leads him to the protest movement as a means of expression.

Kenneth E. Boulding, in developing a theory of protest, says that a protest movement is likely to succeed only if it expresses a view that is widespread but not yet called to public attention. Such was the case with the early days of the civil rights movement, and it has been true to a considerable degree of the struggle against the Vietnam War. However, if the society is sharply divided, protest movements might raise even stronger counterprotests. An educational movement, seeking to educate people in a new direction, must be especially "chary of arousing counterprotest." It must be "low keyed and respectful of existing legitimacies, tying into them wherever possible." Even when the time is ripe for a protest movement it might run into trouble if it takes inappropriate form or if the object of protest is not clear.[24]

Although Boulding's article was not written for student demonstrators, his conclusions are worth their consideration. The problem of protest object and method

[24]Kenneth E. Boulding, "Toward a Theory of Protest," in Walt Anderson (ed.), *The Age of Protest*, Goodyear Publishing Company, Pacific Palisades, California, 1969.

cannot be solved entirely by students, however. When the protest is for student rights on campus, there should be better channels of negotiation than usually exist. When the protest is against political trends in the country, government compliance may not be possible. No government can submit to every protest that arises without collapsing into anarchy. There should, however, as the Scranton Commission states so strongly, be an attempt at communication and an abandonment of inflammatory rhetoric. Only in such an atmosphere could there be negotiation of such problems as ROTC training and military research on the campus.

STUDENT LEADERSHIP Whatever the worries of the older generation, the present college generation is already making itself felt in the social and political spheres. While still in college, members of the present generation have done much to help ghetto children and to push for opportunities for those with low incomes. They have taken an active part in agitation for preservation of the environment, and several active student leaders upon graduation have assumed important positions in governmental departments and foundations working for environmental improvement. They have promoted an interest in student rights, and reminded college administrations that the major function of a college or university is education of students, rather than merely research work for the Defense Department.

Students on many campuses have devised their own systems for rating professors and have tried to establish systems of student appeal to help make grading fair. It seems logical to surmise that a stronger sense of student participation could do much to prevent the sense of alienation that has become a definite part of the youth subculture. Perhaps it could even give a desired sense of living one's life along the way, rather than merely seeing college as "something to be done with."

UNFINISHED BUSINESS Although the United States has boasted of the efficiency of its educational system, much remains to be done. The level of illiteracy remains surprisingly high for a country with such an enormous and expensive school system. Although the United States Department of Education figures show that 86.2 percent of our 15- to 17-year-olds are in school, the situation for those who drop out becomes worse. Attempts at compensatory education for disadvantaged children have been poorly financed and need more effort. Of those Americans over 16 years of age, 18.5 million (13 percent) "lack the reading ability needed to survive in a paper work soci-

---

What facilities has your school for student participation? The best way to make student government effective is through full participation.

ety," according to a study done by Louis Harris for the National Reading Council.[25] The disabilities are most severe for children of the rural poor and the urban ghetto.

Another remaining problem is that the educational system fails to encourage women to achieve the positions for which they are capable. Students of middle ability can in some respects be regarded as another overlooked group in education. Not enough information is available about jobs for people taking only two years of college. Despite the enormous effort devoted to courses in education, not many teachers are rated highly by their students.

The list of unfinished business could go on and on, and it will remain the unfinished business of the college generations to come — generations deeply concerned with such problems as the need for peace and an uncontaminated environment. Higher education has more jobs to do than the mere programming of students to fill the right niches in the social system. It must invite ideas and criticism, and it must produce minds able to cope with the technological future in a manner that will not shatter society into a thousand alienated fragments.

SUGGESTED READINGS

Clark, Burton R.: *Educating the Expert Society*, Chandler Publishing Company, San Francisco, 1962.

> *A sound sociological analysis of education in the technological age — effects of modern technology on the status functions and cultural transmission functions of education. Also includes problems of organization and control, student subcultures, and, finally, an indictment of what the author sees as a trend toward "technical barbarism."*

Foley, James A., and Robert K. Foley: *The College Scene: Students Tell It Like It Is*, McGraw-Hill Book Company, New York, 1971.

> *Student attitudes and opinions based on polls and interviews — race, sex, riots, drugs, God, the faculty, business, and war are all included. The authors appeal also for the parental generation to read it, "for it is possible that the generation gap can be closed with greater ease than either side imagines."*

Page, Charles H. (ed.): *Sociology and Contemporary Education*, Random House, Inc., New York, 1963.

> *Selections by such prominent sociologists as Bierstedt, Bressler, Chinoy, Nisbet, and Page. Relationship between sociology and education, broadening aspects of sociology, challenges to the conventional wisdom, and popular sociology in contrast to academic research.*

[25] Morton Mintz, "18.5 Million Seen with Low Reading Skill," *Los Angeles Times*, September 13, 1970, Sec. A, p. 10.

Ridgeway, James: *The Closed Corporation: American Universities in Crisis*, Ballantine Books, Inc., New York, 1968.

A powerful indictment of the universities for too close collusion with business, government, and the defense department. Also protests the use of "graduate students as a pool of cheap labor."

Roszak, Theodore: *The Making of a Counter Culture*, Anchor Books, Doubleday & Company, Inc., Garden City, N.Y., 1969.

An outstandingly clear commentary on the intellectual currents affecting youth, from a modern nihilism to marxism and the philosophy of Marcuse.

QUESTIONS

1. Describe and give reasons for the processes that attempt to fit all students into a mold.

2. What are the pressures that cause the curriculum to "creak under the strain?"

3. The text contends that there is too much rush through college. Do you agree? If so, what are the reasons for a sense of rush?

4. Contrast student activists and the student counterculture.

5. Although the President's Commission on Campus Unrest was highly critical of police and national guard actions in many cases, they found the public blaming everything on the students. What seems to be the explanation?

6. What means may be developed for increasing the effectiveness of student movements both in college and in politics?

5 *What has happened to the old ethic of hard work? Has it defeated itself by turning out too many goods, or by making types of work for which only a minority of people have the required talents? Is there truth to the charge made by Goodman that many jobs facing youth are meaningless and unrewarding?*

Whatever the case about replacement of certain types of unskilled and semiskilled work, much blue-collar labor still remains. Have the problems of alienation of labor been solved? What about the practical problems of mine safety, adequate workmen's compensation laws, and attempts to lessen occupational diseases and health hazards? What is automation doing to jobs, and what will it do in the future? Is job security for the educated likely to be increasingly threatened by economic slowdowns and shifts in governmental policies? Are there any jobs to prepare for that are absolutely safe against declining need and layoff?

Finally, what are some views of the consequences of the changing nature of work in increasingly technological, bureaucratic societies? Will there be more work satisfaction or less? Can leisure activities give purpose to life if the amount of human labor needed continues to decline? How will leisure be used?

WORK FOR THE NIGHT IS COMING

One reason the educational system is overburdened with responsibilities is that such intensive training is now needed to meet the nation's work requirements. It is frequently said that there are no longer any jobs whatever for the uneducated and unskilled. The statement is a little exaggerated, but it is certainly in line with the trends that have been observable for several generations. In colonial America and through the first half of our independent existence as a nation, the majority of people simply inherited their occupations from their parents. The occupation was usually farming, a type of job that called for hard work and frugal living but was uncomplicated by the specialties of botany, zoology, entomology, soil chemistry, farm management, and marketing. The majority of nonfarm work was also manual labor that called for no advanced training or specialization.

Today the problem of occupational choice is one of the most trying of life, although it is seldom given the consideration it deserves in school curricula. Students going to college are worried about occupational choice, frequently change majors, and dread the possibility of preparing for blind alleys or overcrowded fields. From their high school days they are told how only a college education can guarantee them jobs that pay well and are personally rewarding. Many skeptical students wonder, not so much about the self-realization value of an education, but whether the modern, computerized society is producing the types of jobs that give a sense of fulfillment. Will occupational life be a useful, creative process, or will it consist mainly of developing salesmanship for unloading surplus goods on an unwilling public?

THE WORK ETHIC CYCLE

In a thought-provoking documentary film presented by NET in the early 1960s, the main musical theme in the background was the old American hymn "Work for the Night is Coming." The theme was used, the commentary said, because no other country had made hard work so much of a national ethos as had the United States. There may possibly be exceptions to the statement, but there is no doubt that we are products of what Max Weber called the Protestant ethic — an ethic of hard work, frugality, and striving. It can be said with little fear of contradiction that we have long since abandoned much of the frugality of which Weber spoke, but to a great degree the ethos of hard work continues. Even the wealthy people of America have not been idle; they have busied themselves at becoming wealthier than before. There has also been an unusually strong tendency (as will be explained further in Chapter 10) to view poverty as almost entirely the product of laziness and evil. For generations we have repeated Poor Richard's admonitions: "waste neither time nor money; an hour lost is money lost." Our homespun philosophers and poets have told us "procrastination is the thief of time," and "Act, act in the living present, heart within and God o'erhead!" And we have made heroes of the giants of production, so much so that Aldous Huxley imagined a *Brave New World* in which all events would be dated from "The Year of Our Ford."

The work ethic and conquest of a
continent.

THE NEMESIS OF THE WORK ETHIC   The work ethic consisted not only of hard work, but also of frugality. When such an ethic is applied to an entire society, and especially one with a rich domain to exploit, the time comes when there seems little point in being frugal. In fact, the work ethic and the frugality ethic become mutually incompatible. Unless people spend their money freely, there will be no market for the mountain of products ground out by an efficient technology and a work ethic. More attention must be turned, then, to consumer goods and to salesmanship and services. Nowhere else in the world is such a large part of the population engaged in the processes of producing services as in the United States, and this has a pronounced effect on the types of jobs available. The production ethic has nearly defeated itself.

THE NEMESIS OF THE COMPETITION ETHIC   Competition has been a major force moving the American economy toward greater productive efficiency, but competition eventually begins to defeat itself. The most efficient competitors run the less efficient out of business or make merger arrangements with them. Eventually the overwhelming amount of business is concentrated in the hands of a few giant corporations in each field of production, a condition referred to as "oligopoly." The result of the change in the competitive economy is that more and more people must be hired to work for gigantic concerns. Many years ago the gigantic concerns were opposed by the labor unions, but now union labor finds it more convenient to bargain with large concerns than with small ones. Now a new type of criticism arises, this time from higher echelons. It is feared that the human being is dominated by the organization for which he works—a condition described in such books as *The Organization Man*[1] and *Up the Organization*.[2] Large numbers of people, and especially college graduates, become organization men of the type described in these books—well treated in many respects, but having their lives, thoughts, aims, and values circumscribed by the organization. Only an insignificant number work for small concerns or for themselves.

ENSURING PERPETUAL MOTION   It has long been assumed that with vastly increasing productivity and with the growth of large organizations able to produce the goods and, to quite a degree, regulate the market, the need for workers would decline drastically. Sometimes it seems to do so, especially during economic recessions, but much of the time employment remains high. Techniques have been developed for keeping up a fairly frantic pace of production regardless of how glutted the market would have seemed to people of an earlier age.

One of the techniques for maintaining production has already been mentioned—planned obsolescence. Another technique for keeping consumption going is good advertising that will cause people to feel a need for previously unheard of commodities. By one means or another, a technique is developed for increasing consumer demand sufficiently so that all products will be sold. The result is what two genera-

[1]William H. Whyte, *The Organization Man*, Simon and Schuster, Inc., New York, 1956.
[2]Robert Townsend, *Up the Organization*, Alfred A. Knopf, Inc., New York, 1970.

tions of beatniks and hippies have called "the rat race." Many of the most talented men in society devote their lives to making people realize they need something they have never heard of before.

THE GREAT SUPERVISOR Even with great effort devoted to keeping the perpetual-motion machine running, there is always a feeling of danger. What if Mr. Smith should decide not to try to keep up with the Joneses? What if a million Mr. Smiths decided not to keep up with a million Joneses? There could be a major depression. To avoid the possibility of such a disaster, many people are employed by the government, analyzing the economy, deciding whether to give it a shot in the arm by deficit spending, or to slow it down by raising rediscount rates. Or should there be price and wage controls? Or should the government step in with makeshift jobs? Decisions of this kind, and the public knowledge that the government has to wrestle with such problems, gives a permanent atmosphere of uneasiness about the whole world of work. In earlier times man's work was much harder and often from sunup to sundown. Today the hours are shorter and the rewards higher, but the uncertainties are greater.

Besides regulating the economy through money supply and government spending, the government may act as an employer of last resort in times of recession or for the unskilled. Even in good times the government is the largest single employer of manpower, and the individual may find that his best area of employment is in a government job. His opportunities might be in private industry, but a type of private industry that is mainly geared to meeting governmental requirements—supplying the war machine, building airports and government edifices, designing bridges, highways, and aqueducts. Or he might be the representative of industry, working to get the contracts that ensure financial survival and affluence. Whatever his job, he will increasingly perceive it as part of a giant, interlocking organism of public and private sectors. The ethic of hard work has not only rendered frugality obsolete, but has subordinated individual enterprise to a mighty enterprise in governmental-industrial cooperation.

In the old hymn "Work for the Night is Coming," "night" symbolized the end of life and the path to one's heavenly reward. Now the "night" seems to symbolize the end of the individual's effort on his own plot of ground or in his own shop. Rather than reaching the heaven of traditional Western theology, we have evolved a system reminiscent of Eastern philosophy, in which the individual must merge with the oversoul. The oversoul in this case is a bureaucratic society, increasingly planned, dominating, and inescapable.

RELUCTANT YOUTH AND THE BUREAUCRATIC SOCIETY

The emerging society is called by various names: the technical society, the bureaucratic state, the administrative state, or even "technological totalitarianism." Whatever the emerging form of society might be called, it is one that promises abundance for people who plunge wholeheartedly into its mainstream. For the foreseeable future, however, not all people can enter the mainstream, but some will be swept into little side channels and into scum-laden pools of poverty. Moreover, the main course often shifts, and one can end in a backwash that will dry up unless fed again by waters of life in the form of federal money. Such is the occasional fate of much of the aeronautics industry. The shipping industry has always depended on subsidization for survival, and for years the same has been true for the agricultural field.

THE ENCIRCLING SYSTEM Years ago school reading books had stories in which boys grew to young manhood and then went out to "seek their fortune." The work world had a spirit of adventure. The talented and lucky individual could have innumerable experiences of life, from factory worker to typesetter to railroad brakeman, and he could eventually work his way up. Now there is something called "the break in the skill hierarchy," the point beyond which the man lacking special training can never go. There is also, as noted in the last chapter, a compulsion to train for a particular job from an early age.

The possibility of having various vocational experiences still exists, but on a diminishing scale. Employment for the young is not encouraged. Labor laws make such jobs difficult, and there are also other biases against youth. In a time of job shortages, there is a feeling that all available jobs should be given to the heads of households. There is also uncertainty as to how steady an employee a young person will make, although a recent Labor Department study shows them doing about as well as adults. Especially if he seems capable and ambitious, the young worker will be thought likely to look for "greener pastures" as soon as possible or for a return to school. There is also the possibility that he will be drafted and taken away from the job.

The net result of the employment bias against youth is an unemployment rate of 17.5 percent for 18- and 19-year-olds with one to three years of high school. Ironically, those with only an eighth-grade education show a slightly lower unemployment rate of 15.7 percent.[3] The probable explanation is that the eighth graders are seen as the stable lower class, not likely to change to better jobs.

The personal future of employment, then, becomes a curious contradiction for a freedom-loving society. One should be free to investigate a great variety of interests and viewpoints. He should investigate philosophies, political ideologies, and religious experiences. Also, before marrying he should date a number of girls, gaining experience before making decisions. But in the field of employment, he should take a battery of intelligence tests and occupational preference tests, go to a vocational counselor, then set his course without deviation and definitely without experience!

THE UNCERTAINTIES For many years people have been advised to get all the education possible and, generally speaking, the advice has been sound. In 1967, for those 25

[3]William Deuterman, "Educational Attainment of Workers, March 1969 and 1970," *Monthly Labor Review*, pp. 12–13, October 1970.

to 34 years of age, average incomes varied from $4,600 for persons with less than eight years of schooling to $8,850 for those with a college education. For those in the maximum income years of life (45 to 54 years) the variation was much greater, from $7,600 for the less-than-eighth-grade group to $12,500 for the college graduates.[4] In the same year over 1 million people lost their jobs. On the average, the job losers were one and a half years below the national norms in education. From the period 1950 to 1962, unemployment rates for the college educated averaged less than 2 percent and showed a steady decline. Unemployment rates for those with less than eight years of education increased from 8.4 to 9.5 percent. Figures of this type have been familiar for many years and have been encouraging to college students. The accompanying chart from the Department of Labor shows job distribution for 1970 in relation to education achievement (see p. 129).

In spite of generally better employment prospects for the educated, uncertainties have crept into the occupational picture. In November 1970, the Department of Labor said officially what was already apparent: there were more people with teaching credentials than jobs for teachers. One can argue that if a really excellent educational program were to be made available, all the extra teachers could easily be absorbed; but in terms of actual jobs available, the figures are discouraging. Education has been a greatly preferred field for women; the work hours can be made to correspond with the school hours of their children. Two-thirds of women graduating from college in recent years have prepared for teaching jobs.[5]

At the same time, it was becoming apparent that certain technical fields were, at least temporarily, oversubscribed. Not many years ago there had been speculation as to whether we could train enough talent to fill all the technical positions needed, and the United States was creating a "brain drain" by hiring too many experts from other countries. Now, suddenly, many thousands of aerospace workers are unemployed, including highly trained engineers. Some are reversing the "brain drain" and returning to their own countries. "Each time we go through one of these convulsions, the image of the industry as a good place to work tarnishes a little," said one Lockheed official, "and enrollment in engineering schools goes down."[6]

The implication of the official's comment is that the aerospace industry is simply going through temporary hard times, and this seems very likely; but can anyone wonder why enrollments in engineering schools go down? The situation is by no

---

In the *Monthly Labor Review* **or in the annual bulletins of the Department of Labor, look up the prospects for your own chosen area of employment.**

---

[4]Elizabeth Waldman, "Education Attainment of Workers," *Monthly Labor Review*, p. 20, February 1969.
[5]U.S. Department of Labor, *U.S. Manpower in the 1970s*, November 1970.
[6]Robert A. Rosenblatt, "New Jobless," *Los Angeles Times*, March 19, 1970, pp. 1, 32.

means isolated but is simply one of many cases of jobs strongly dependent upon the whim of the federal government. Many jobs in scientific research depend upon what policies happen to dominate thinking in Washington. Enthusiasts over the future of oceanography foresee one of man's greatest frontiers beneath the sea, but that frontier, and the employment of men trained in the field, depend upon federal policy. Such examples lead to concern about where the markets for technicians of the future will be.

LABOR DEPARTMENT REPORTS   All estimates of future employment conditions are partly guesswork, but some of the best-informed guesses are from the Department of Labor. As of 1970 the Department predicted that jobs in the engineering and scientific fields would show renewed upturns in the future. No comment was made about aeronautical engineering, but the reports specifically mentioned growth in the fields of environmental protection and restoration, fighting of terrestrial and marine contamination, and search for new deposits of needed minerals. The report admitted, however, that growth in the scientific and engineering fields will be slower than had been anticipated in an earlier national goals study.[7]

[7]U.S. Department of Labor, *Manpower Report of the President*, submitted to Congress, March 1970, pp. 169–170.

Actual and projected demand for new elementary and secondary school teachers compared with number of college graduates, 1963 to 1978 (numbers in thousands) Manpower Report of the President, Department of Labor Transmitted to Congress March 1970

YEAR	TOTAL TEACHERS EMPLOYED	NUMBER REQUIRED FOR GROWTH AND REPLACEMENT	NEW TEACHERS REQUIRED*	TOTAL NUMBER OF COLLEGE GRADUATES†	NEW TEACHERS REQUIRED AS PERCENT OF GRADUATES
1963	1,806	209	157	444	35
1965	1,951	208	156	530	29
1967	2,097	222	166	591	28
1968	2,178	239	179	667	27
1969	2,225	209	157	755	21
1970	2,245	190	142–190	772	18–25
1973	2,286	189	142–189	859	17–22
1975	2,304	183	137–183	928	15–20
1978	2,334	187	140–187	1,029	14–18

*Figures for 1963-1969 represent 75 percent of the total number required for growth and replacement, with a conservative allowance for the numbers of teachers who returned to the profession. Since the return flow of experienced teachers may possibly decline during the 1970s, the ranges shown indicate the numbers and percents of new teachers that would be required with a return flow ranging from 0 to 25 percent.
†Includes bachelor's and first professional degrees awarded.
SOURCE: Based on data from the Department of Health, Education, and Welfare, Office of Education.

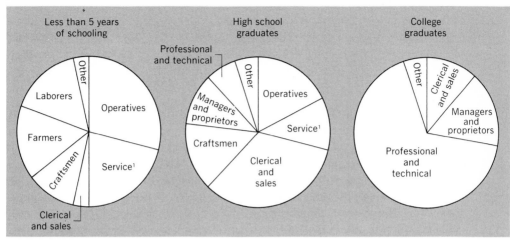

Less than 5 years of schooling

High school graduates

College graduates

¹Includes private household workers

The report is not particularly optimistic in its predictions about teaching jobs (see table). A declining percentage of college graduates can be absorbed in elementary and secondary teaching. Elementary school enrollment will decline until 1976 and show only a slight upturn after that. Another Department of Labor report gives similar information. Employment opportunities, it says, will continue to be good for those with the very highest qualifications and those seeking teaching positions in ghetto areas. There will also be jobs "in rural districts and in all geographical areas where teaching salaries are low and better paying positions are available in other fields in the community."[8] The statement is reminiscent of the teaching situation of the 1930s! The Department of Labor also predicts a continuation of the long decline in agricultural jobs and mining.

There will be large employment gains in other fields. Services and professions will absorb 40 percent more people in 1980 than they do today, and the growth will be particularly great in the field of medicine. State and local governments will employ 52 percent more people and the federal government 10 percent more, according to the forecast. Insurance, real estate, and trade will gain about one-quarter, and construction about 35 percent. Manufacturing, transportation, communication, and public utilities will all show employment gains of about 10 percent. A 10-percent gain, however, will barely keep up with population increase. Such figures are only in very general categories. The predictions are given in considerable detail in the *Occupational Outlook Handbooks* of the Department of Labor and are worth examining by a

[8]U.S. Department of Labor, *Occupational Outlook Handbook, 1970–71*, Bulletin No. 1650, p. 198.

person trying to make decisions for the future. The trouble is, though, that there is no real certainty about predictions which assume steady rates of economic growth in an economy that tends to spurt and falter rather than maintain a constant equilibrium.

Another important question is about the types of jobs and conditions of employment that will exist in fields that are subject to rapid technological change. Such fields of employment tend to hit the blue-collar worker first, but they are eventually of concern to the white-collar worker and the technician.

CHRONIC PROBLEMS OF INDUSTRIAL LABOR

The society that is moving in the direction of greater rationalization of production, closer linkage between government and industry, and greater giantism and efficiency in its techniques of production is even less reassuring to the common laboring man than to the college graduate. The increases in automated processes have been an incessant worry to labor union leaders and workers. There have been predictions of doom for the laborer, and there have also been predictions of shorter hours and improved wages, working conditions, and other benefits. The actual fact seems to be that automation has not taken away as many jobs as had been feared, but neither has it produced a generally happy, contented worker.

THE MIDDLE-CLASS LABOR MYTH   It is often said that the worker of today is so well paid that he no longer identifies with the working class, but regards himself as middle-class, happy, and immune from industrial alienation. The statement cannot be refuted in all cases because conditions of labor differ greatly from industry to industry. To weight the scales badly, one could start with a study of migratory agricultural labor, which is so depressed and so little changed over a period of time that its discussion must be left instead to a later chapter on poverty. Factory work is not nearly so depressed as agricultural labor, but studies of factory workers do not indicate a high level of satisfaction with the jobs. The authors of *Man on the Assembly Line* found that 90 percent of the workers hated their jobs, largely because of pace, noise, and inability to communicate with fellow workers.[9] Although workers were paid better than on their previous jobs, they generally disliked the assembly line jobs more. Harvey Swados expresses the assembly line worker's view succinctly when he says that although the working man possibly desires all the same commodities as the middle class:

> He works like a worker. The steel mill puddler does not yet sort memos, the coal miner does not yet sit in conferences, the cotton millhand does not yet sip martinis. The worker's attitude toward his work is generally compounded of hatred and resignation.[10]

[9]Charles Walker and Robert H. Guest, *Man on the Assembly Line*, Harvard University Press, Cambridge, Mass., 1952.
[10]Harvey Swados, "The Myth of the Happy Worker," in Eric and Mary Josephson, *Man Alone*, Dell Publishing Co., Inc., New York, 1962, pp. 105–113.

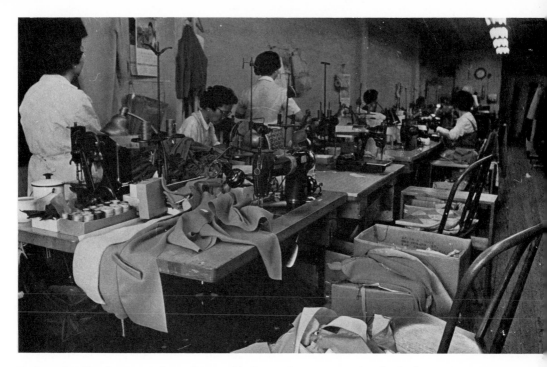

Far from the office in status and pay, the assembly line worker resents not just the drudgery, but the dehumanized role as well.

Swados continues to comment on the sense of being outside the system, of not counting, of not being quite human as long as one is a common laborer. Another commentator makes almost precisely the same contrast between laborer and white-collar worker. The white-collar worker, sitting in an office, identifies with the company, almost feels like part of management, even though his wages may be lower than those of the skilled laborer. Patricia Sexton[11] comments on her experiences of three years

Make an informal survey of worker satisfaction, interviewing blue-collar and white-collar workers and professionals.

[11]Patricia Cayo Sexton, "The Auto Assembly Line: an Inside View," *Harper's*, vol. 224, pp. 54–57, June 1962.

on the assembly line. The average person who has not faced assembly line work, she says, finds it hard to imagine some of the causes of strikes, but they often boil down to a denial of human dignity. "Comes lunch time, there's a good cafeteria for the office staff, but it's too far away for the plant workers." Anyway, plant workers just don't belong there. The pace of the line is so antagonizing, she says, that many workers try to get on as sweepers, even though the job doesn't pay as well. She also mentions such little indignities as being timed for a trip to the restroom, and "no doors on the johns." With the work pace as wearing as it is, anger can mount over a slight speed up, or refusal of a coffee break, or the decision to no longer have coffee carts on the factory floors. In spite of complaints about the union, workers rally around the union when a strike is called, and a strike—hardship though it entails—has certain excitement about it, since it is a way of striking back at the high and mighty.

S. M. Miller and Frank Riessman[12] summarize some differences between the position of the laborer and the middle class. For one thing, although many unionized jobs today pay well, not all jobs are unionized and some pay very poorly. Although hours of labor approach a standard forty per week, they are often much longer. Overtime is just about necessary for supporting a family. Another problem is that income is less predictable than it is for white-collar work; there are frequent temporary layoffs or reductions in work days per week. The possibility of strikes is greater, and the chance of promotion is almost nonexistent.

HEALTH AND HAZARD   Studies of social class differences have consistently revealed a difference in life expectancy between classes. One reason concerns differences in working conditions. Much of the current interest in problems of the poor has centered on those without jobs, as though a person with any type of fairly regular employment has no serious problems. As a matter of fact, many Americans still work at jobs that are lethal. During the twentieth century, 100,000 men have been killed in mines, and 1.5 million serious accidents have been reported since 1930. The deaths do not stop. In 1968, seventy eight were killed in a single mine disaster at Farmington, West Virginia. In the 1940s Harry Truman called on Congress to improve mine safety legislation. Nothing was done, and more than 200,000 miners have been killed or injured since then.

Another killer that awaits the coal miner is much slower than cave-ins and explosions but is just as sure, and that is black lung. The lung tissue becomes increasingly scarred and useless, until the miner is laid off for being unable to do a full day's work; later he begins to gasp for breath. The Surgeon General of the United States estimates that we have 100,000 cases of black lung among miners.[13] In 1969 a new safety law was passed for miners that should eventually bring improvement, although the first year the law was in effect the accident rate was higher than the year before.[14]

[12]S. M. Miller and Frank Riessman, "Are Workers Middle Class?" *Dissent*, vol. 8, pp. 507–513, Fall 1961.
[13]Robert Coles and Harry Huge, "Black Lung: Mining as a Way of Death," *New Republic*, January 1, 1969.
[14]Ward Sinclair, "Confusion in the Coalfields," *New Republic*, pp. 17–18, July 18, 1970.

Unfortunately, there are many other unsafe industries in the United States, and many seem to be growing more dangerous. The Bureau of Labor Statistics shows increasing accident rates during the last decade in ten industries. Each year there are 14,000 deaths and 2 million injuries in industrial accidents, and 500,000 workers are disabled by industrial diseases.[15]

Many accidents are caused by moving vehicles; some would be difficult to stop, but too many are the result of indifference. One foundry in Michigan has only 1,000 employees, but is faced with suits from 350 of them—all over silicosis, a crippling disease of the lungs caused by inhaling the fine silicon dust from sand used in casting. The foundry is old and not in line with modern standards. The lawyer representing the plaintiffs contends that since the maximum liability per worker is only $12,500 plus medical care and funeral expenses, the company has been unconcerned. Similar types of lung diseases result from work with asbestos, but New York City is the only place with safety standards regarding its use. A condition called "brown lung" has developed among 100,000 textile-mill workers as a result of breathing fine cotton dust.

Most of the types of accidents and diseases discussed are far from inevitable. Several plants have worked hard for safety, and the work has paid off. Labor unions are agitating for strengthening of safety regulations, but so far nothing substantial has happened. In spite of the quadrupling of the appropriation for mine-safety inspections, Nader charged recently that the Bureau of Mines was conducting only one-eighteenth as many inspections in 1970 as it did in 1969.[16] The health problems of the laborer are definitely remediable, but have not received the publicity needed to ensure strong action from the government.

AUTOMATION AND THE WORKERS

The development of automated processes in industry is both a source of hope and of fear. The majority of laborers have looked upon it with apprehension, as well they might. Many men of middle age or past have been replaced by automation and have found new jobs nearly impossible to obtain. At the same time automation brings certain types of promise to the world of labor.

Study such features as workmen's compensation, safety regulations, and retirement pay in a job you know at first hand or the occupation you intend to enter.

---

[15]"A Matter of Life and Death," *Newsweek*, pp. 64–66, August 17, 1970.
[16]*Ibid.*

THE ADVANTAGES Hardly anyone in a country geared to industrial progress would assume that automation could be delayed indefinitely. Rapid advances into automation help the United States to maintain a competitive advantage in some areas of foreign trade, although the race for such an advantage is constantly tightening. For the laborer, one of the encouraging developments of automation is the tendency to replace some of the most tedious jobs with those that are more interesting and require higher levels of training. Assembly line jobs are the types most easily replaced. Automation is leading to an economy in which the majority of jobs are in the white-collar or service categories rather than in the mines and mills. Even on the factory floor, the worker in the more automated plant is generally better integrated into the production system and less alienated from management and his fellow workers than in the older type of plant.[17]

AUTOMATION AND THE UNSKILLED The opposite effect of automation is to make the unskilled even less employable than in the past. At a time when the public conscience has been roused to some degree about the problems of poverty and hard-core unemployment in the inner cities, it develops that the unemployed are harder to help than ever before. Even the high school dropout could easily learn an assembly line job, but such jobs are declining. Retraining programs have been instituted, but they can succeed only if jobs are actually available. Only a very small fraction of the unemployed are able to pass the tests for entering the training programs.[18] Another disturbing question is whether the new jobs prepared for will not also become obsolete in a short period of time. Or is it possible that automation is creating jobs in new fields as rapidly as it replaces them in old fields?

EMPLOYMENT The argument that automation creates as many jobs as it replaces would be quite naïve if we assumed that it takes as much manpower to produce the automated devices as the total number of hours they will replace. If that were true, there would be no economic advantage to automating a plant. The more subtle arguments are: (1) automation makes its products available in enormous quantities at reduced prices; consequently, far more products are sold than in the past. Perhaps it takes only half as much manpower to produce the goods as it did before automation, but more than twice as many goods are sold. The result should be an increase in employment; (2) although automation may replace workers in one industry, it adds so greatly to prosperity and the general level of consumption of goods and services that new jobs are generated in other areas of the economy to compensate for the ones lost through automation.

In regards to the first argument, Charles Killingsworth[19] analyzes employ-

[17]Michael Fullan, "Industrial Technology and Worker Integration in the Organization," *American Sociological Review*, vol. 35, pp. 1028–1039, December 1970.
[18]Michael Harrington, "The New Lost Generation: Jobless Youth," *New York Times Magazine*, May 24, 1964.
[19]Charles Killingsworth, "The Automation Story: Machines, Manpower, and Jobs," in Charles Markham (ed.), *Jobs, Men, and Machines*, Frederick A. Praeger, Inc., New York, 1964, pp. 15–47.

Computers, the redistributors of jobs,
give to the trained, take from the
untrained, and count people as
inanimate objects.

ment rate as a consequence of the particular stage of development an industry has reached. For example, Ford introduced movable assembly line techniques during the infancy of the automobile industry while it had an unrealized capacity for expansion. The new process, making possible an expansion of production, resulted in bringing the price of cars down to a level that the majority of people could afford. Now that there is a car for every three people, it is doubtful whether even a revolutionary change in technique could result in a comparable increase in production. In the case of Ford, the production increase was great enough to vastly increase employment, in spite of increased worker efficiency. In a hypothetical modern case, the total sales might increase slightly, but not enough to add to the total demand for labor. This, says Killingsworth, is the essence of why for a number of years Western Europe has progressed rapidly in production and has had full employment. The people of Europe are in the youth of the automotive age, which we passed long ago. Almost exactly the same is true for various kinds of household appliances and television sets. In present-day Europe, new techniques stimulate production enough to increase total employment; in the United States they are unlikely to do so.

A recent study of computer control offers much the same conclusion as Killingsworth. In several industries the introduction of more computers created new jobs and replaced only a few workers, but this seemed to be a temporary situation. It was expected that as process computer applications increased and spread into more industries, "their displacement effect may become even more pronounced."[20]

Leaving the picture of automation at that state, it would be easy to conclude that massive and permanent unemployment is in the offing. Actually, although there was an uncomfortable amount of unemployment at the beginning of the 1970s, it is hard to argue that the problem results entirely from automation. Automation has been under way for many years, but employment has been fairly high most of that time. The unemployment problems have centered more around the business cycle than around the introduction of new techniques. The only possible explanation could be, then, that automation has somehow succeeded in creating jobs in new industries other than the ones it has directly served.

Looking at the overall picture of employment in the United States during the last decade, we can see that jobs have been created in some areas to compensate for the ones being lost elsewhere. While agriculture and mining have declined as areas for hiring, certain services have increased greatly. Education is one of these services; entertainment, recreation, and medical care are others. As the society has felt the increasing need for education, it has supplied the jobs for teachers. As it has become affluent enough to afford more and more entertainment and recreation, it has provided jobs in those fields. The question remains, however, "Will such areas of employment continue into the future in strong enough demand to compensate for any losses taking place in mining, railroads, steel, and automotive industries?" Or

[20]Arthur S. Herman, "Manpower Implications of Computer Control," *Monthly Labor Review*, vol. 93, pp. 3–8, October 1970.

will new jobs, possibly hundreds of millions of hours devoted to improving the environment, take up the slack? Or will the job slack be handled simply by having people work fewer hours?

LEISURE: PROSPECT AND PROBLEMS   Since labor first demanded a ten-hour day there has been concern over what the worker would do with his spare time. Opposition to shortened hours has even taken the form of speculating about whether idle time will lead to drink and degeneration. What usually occurs seems to be more investment of time in home improvement or in driving the family car much greater distances than before. There has been a long decline in the hours of work for the wage earner, and so far it has not resulted in any drastic moral deterioration. In 1962, Local No. 3 of the International Brotherhood of Electrical Workers made news headlines by signing the first twenty-four-hour week contract. There was public reaction against it, but its results have not been catastrophic. The necessary work is accomplished, and there is no sign of increasing family problems as a result of too much leisure.[21]

The twenty-four-hour week is simply a drastic extrapolation from a long-term trend. The work week declined an average of about 0.5 percent per year during the early part of the nineteenth century, reaching a standard of about forty hours in the 1940s and generally remaining fairly stationary since. There is every reason to think it will continue its downward course in the future, especially if economic recessions create a share-the-jobs motive.

THE PSYCHOLOGICAL PROBLEMS OF NONWORK   The real psychological problem is not so much a matter of hours of work as it is having some kind of job to organize time and to give a person a sense of importance. Bayard Rustin sums up the importance of work with a statement that says much about the work ethic with which this chapter is concerned:

> What is a man? A man is his work. If I ask you Who is Beethoven? you will all say, "Composer"; Picasso, a painter; Nat Hentoff, a writer. But if I look at a list of people on relief and ask you, "Who is Mrs. Jones?" [You will tell me] "Nobody!"[22]

Even for some retired persons the same problem often exists. A man who has spent his life thinking of himself as a worker can easily come to think of himself as nobody after he retires. Stuart Chase tells of a group of white- and blue-collar workers in New York on a system of mandatory retirement at age sixty-five. The majority said farewell to New York and headed for the land of their dreams — Florida, California, or Arizona. Within six months most were back. Those with previously developed hobbies and outside interests adjusted fairly well. Several others had mental breakdowns, and one person committed suicide. The man whom Chase designates as the saddest case

[21]Theodore W. Kheel, "How the 24-hour Week Has Worked," in Charles Markham, *op. cit.*, pp. 100–106.
[22]Bayard Rustin, "Education," in Robert Theobald (ed.), *Dialogue on Poverty,* The Bobbs-Merrill Company, Inc., Indianapolis, 1967, p. 59.

of all set his alarm clock for the usual hour and went to the shop every day to watch his old friends work.[23]

The President's Council on Aging confirms the conclusion that many people cannot adjust to retirement and even regard it with shame. Especially among the least educated, hobbies may be regarded with contempt. Often the retired man sits around the house, restless and irritable, and relations between the older married couples begin to deteriorate. Another indication of the American's uneasiness with a life of leisure comes from a questionnaire in which a nationwide sample of workers was asked whether they would continue to work even if they had the good luck to be handed enough money to get along without work. Eighty percent said "Yes."[24] The very same people often defined work as "something you have to do because it's good for you," or "something you don't like." The explanation for wanting to work has to be found in a puritan ethic or in an inability to otherwise find meaning in life. For very few people is industrial work anything but drudgery, but the alternative of uselessness seems to be worse.

For those who have developed other interests and hobbies, the impact of a short work week and early retirement is quite different. Society obviously has the problem of finding recreational activities not only for those with the ability to be creative, but for many others as well. For nearly everyone it also remains vitally necessary that some kind of meaningful employment be found for at least a considerable part of his life. The employment might occasionally have to be created by the government, but it must be something worth doing. Chase uses a quotation from Dostoyevsky about the importance of a meaningful job. Dostoyevsky was no product of the Protestant ethic, but he states the case for meaningful work eloquently. Perhaps the work ethic could be called the ethic of meaning, in which case it belongs to the entire human race. Dostoyevsky wrote:

> If it were desired to crush a man completely, to punish him so severely that even the most hardened murderer would quail, it would only be needed to make his work pointless and absurd.

WORK AND ALIENATION

The idea of the alienation of labor is not a new one. When the hard conditions that are still found among some of the poorest migratory farm laborers were common to nearly all workers, the alienation of labor was equated with poverty. Early nineteenth-century reformists wrote of how the worker was turned against government and church and society generally by long hours of labor, unwholesome conditions, and such abuses as the employment of women and children in factories and mines.

Marx was a little more sophisticated in his analysis of the reasons for the alien-

---

[23]Stuart Chase, *The Most Probable World*, Penguin Books, Inc., Baltimore, 1969, pp. 136–137.
[24]*Ibid.*, p. 140.

ation of labor, but he also attributed it largely to poor conditions and an unequal share in the product of toil. To Marx, the roots of alienation and the factors that made the poor workingman of the industrial period more alienated than the medieval peasant had been was his relationship to the production process. The worker no longer owned the tools of his labor, but worked away from home in a factory owned by others and at the production of goods in which he had no financial stake. He also became part of a long production process in which he was only a minor instrument, so that he had none of the feeling of pride in workmanship that had belonged to the master craftsmen of the earlier guilds.

Whatever the truth of the marxian picture, it described primarily industrial labor and did not anticipate the tremendous growth of a white-collar class or of vast bureaucracies that would be rather similar in both socialist and capitalist states. It was for later writers to turn their attention to new aspects of the technical system, first to white-collar labor, and then to something called the technocratic or the cybernetic state.

MILLS AND THE WHITE-COLLAR WORLD   The late C. Wright Mills was one of the sharpest critics of the conditions that produce and mold the character of the white-collar worker. Throughout modern societies, a majority of people rate white-collar work above industrial labor. A white-collar job is the upward-mobility dream of industrial workers for their children. It has been the American dream of success for millions of immigrants entering the country. Mills nevertheless finds much to criticize in the white-collar class, almost exactly the class of people that politicians are now referring to as "middle America." Mills saw the white-collar worker as part of a class that had gained the whole world but lost its own soul. Centered in a society beset with innumerable social problems, the white-collar worker (Mills includes professionals in this category) loses all social concern in a search for status, a "status panic."[25]

Mills was convinced that the future was not bright for the lower echelons of white-collar workers. Too proud of their status differentiation from that of manual labor, they would not organize. Even more than the common laborers, they could easily be manipulated by what Mills later identified as "the power elite" — the top ranks of government, industry, and Madison Avenue. Since almost everyone now completes high school and becomes eligible for at least the lower ranks of white-collar status, increased effort and strain are required for entering and advancing in the middle class. The white-collar class, or middle America, becomes a battleground of status striving and anxiety. Heart attacks are common among those who have had to fight hardest to work their way up. One recent study found heart attacks three times as common for male white-collar workers from farm backgrounds as for those who remained on the farms.[26] The greater risk seems to be for the upwardly mobile,

[25]C. Wright Mills, *White Collar: The American Middle Classes*, Oxford University Press, New York, 1951.
[26]George Getze, "Successful Men Run Greater Heart Attack Risk," *Los Angeles Times*, July 13, 1970, Part I, pp. 1, 5, quoting Berkeley scientist S. L. Syme.

not for those born of wealthy families. Along with the striving of the white-collar world, Mills finds a very limited concern for social problems and a narrow kind of social-class ethnocentrism. Writing in 1951, he asked questions that were heard more frequently in the years following: Is the white-collar world worth the struggle? Is the end of the struggle a status ambiguity in a world manipulated by a powerful and inexorable technology? Other writers have questioned the morality of certain aspects of the modern world of employment.

FROM MEANINGLESSNESS TO IMMORALITY   In *Growing Up Absurd*, Goodman stresses the number of pointless and meaningless jobs in modern society. In his later book, *Like a Conquered Province*, he goes into the problems of the amorality of many jobs, particularly research projects. Science, in its pure research, claims to be neutral, neither good nor bad. Yet, says Goodman:

> What is striking is that the doctrine of pure science and its moral neutrality always come to the fore when scientists are assigned an official status and become salaried and subsidized, as in the German universities in the nineteenth century or in America today.[27]

The great industrial machine can be geared to purposes that individual scientists or researchers disapprove, but they can always explain that science is neutral. Industry is also neutral. It simply produces what the market demands — harmful drugs, tobacco, dangerous toys for children. The political process also becomes neutral, simply marketing the candidate the best way possible, so that he can feel out public demand and satisfy it or do a good enough public relations job to give the public the illusion of being served.

THE TECHNOLOGICAL SOCIETY   Probably no critic of modern society is more severely pessimistic than Jacques Ellul.[28] In his book, *The Technological Society*, he pictures the course of events in terms somewhat similar to those of Goodman. The essence of the technological society, in Ellul's thinking, is that technique has replaced purpose. The important achievement is efficiency, but efficiency for no particular end. The danger in fascination with efficiency is that it leads one to admire such things as giant engineering projects that desecrate nature, organizations that submerge the individual, and even such marvelous achievements of science as hydrogen bombs. The technological society is essentially immoral. What, then, is its impact on labor?

An illusion is created, says Ellul, that we are moving in the direction of humanism in the world of work. What we are actually doing is studying the physiology of work, the organization of labor, vocational guidance, and techniques for keeping people contented on the job. These, though, are all techniques aimed at serving the cause of efficiency of production, not human happiness. The dream is to create a

[27]Paul Goodman, *Like a Conquered Province*, Vintage Books, Random House, Inc., New York, 1968, p. 302.
[28]Jacques Ellul, *The Technological Society*, Alfred A. Knopf, Inc., New York, 1967.

society in which each man is fitted and measured for an occupation in such a way that he will be as content as the worker in the bee colony, knowing nothing else, dreaming of nothing else. We shall have attained "technological totalitarianism." This is the type of planning we have criticized in the Soviet Union; yet, says Ellul, it is typical of the development of all technological societies and can be anticipated as an increasing trend in the future.[29]

CONFLICTING INTERPRETATIONS Such writers as Mills, Goodman, and Ellul point to dangers under the surface of the social system. It cannot be assumed that the partial winning of the struggle against want and the development of a more thoroughly schooled population means that all is well. On the other hand, none of the critics would expect us to resign ourselves to despair. Is there any way to resist a system that puts each person into his proper, tiny, and fairly isolated little cubicle, where he can spend his life worrying about such irrelevancies as status?

Buckminster Fuller, inventor of the geodesic dome, is a Renaissance-type man with a wide range of interests and ideas. He sees our way out of eventual destruction as a reversal of the present trend toward narrow specialization. He even presents the argument, based on both biological and anthropological studies, that those human tribes and those animal species that have been most vulnerable to extinction are those that have grown most specialized.[30] Applying the same perspective to the modern world, he sees danger in the nationalistic rivalries that keep some types of learning secret and exclusive and the academic specializations that cause even the most capable minds to be narrowly channeled. In his opinion, we must all belong first to the entire world, not the specialist world. Only after relating ourselves to our entire space ship earth should we devote part of our time to work specialties.

Fuller's generalist view is actually very much in line with what many members of the younger generation seem to be seeking—a life in which art, music, and poetry are examined at least as much as business and technology. There is also the wholesome tendency to relate to the entire society and even to the total natural environment, rather than merely to the white-collar world of which Mills complained.

Whether such interests are merely passing fads and we shall eventually channel ourselves into the narrow ways Ellul warned of remains to be seen. What is definitely true on the positive side is that the world of work does not have to be the compelling

---

Survey your community resources for meaningful nonwork activities—
the arts, sports, recreation, entertainment, causes to pursue.
Once again you might want to write suggestions to the city council.

---

[29]*Ibid.*, pp. 349–361.
[30]Buckminster Fuller, *Operating Manual for Space Ship Earth*, Pocket Books, Inc., New York, 1970, pp. 35–36.

The development of leisure time
activities as an alternative to future
empty hours of idleness.

sunrise-to-sunset routine that it was for our ancestors. If the world of work is to become a new form of slavery, it will be unnecessary slavery, of our own making.

EDUCATION FOR THE NEW LIFE   In the previous chapter on education, the complaint was made that school has too much of a rush-to-completion atmosphere. Actually, in spite of this complaint, there are new trends at work in education that could well prepare people for an age in which work is no longer the major part of their lives and the source of their self-concept. For more than a century adult education has been prominent in parts of the world, especially in Denmark. Presently, adult education of all kinds is a very important part of community- and state-college systems. Often the return to school is mainly a diploma quest, but it serves other purposes as well — cultivation of the arts, literature, drama, and the general enjoyment of life. The same sources of social change that have created a utilitarian need for technological education are perhaps now just as surely bringing about a need for education in the creative use of leisure. Ralph M. Goldman of San Francisco State College has made a proposal for Life-Span Educational Insurance, which could conceivably meet both occupational and leisure-time needs.[31] The main selling point for such a policy would be to make retraining immediately available for people whose jobs are replaced by new techniques. It could also be used to pay the educational costs of women who wish to train for jobs after their children are in school. Finally, since all people could take out such an insurance policy, the insurance could be used for leisurely, creative college pursuits for people not seriously in need of its retraining features. Such a proposal would need considerable thought and study, but it at least points to new possibilities for meeting the dual training needs of an industrial system with changing employment patterns and with increasing time for leisure.

SUGGESTED READINGS

Ellul, Jacques: *The Technological Society*, Alfred A. Knopf, Inc., New York, 1967.

> *Ellul's book is concerned with much more than work in the future, but has great bearing on it. He sees the demands of the technological society as overwhelming to the individual, making him a card in a great computer.*

Friedmann, Georges: *The Anatomy of Work*, The Free Press, New York, 1962.

> *A study of the work problems created by the industrial society and the attempts made to deal with them — reducing hours of work, changing relations between labor and management.*

[31] Ralph M. Goldman, "Life-Span Educational Insurance: A Proposal," *Educational Record*, vol. 51, pp. 60–65, Winter 1970.

Goodman, Paul: *People or Personnel* and *Like a Conquered Province*, Vintage Books, Random House, Inc., New York, 1968.

> *The first of these two books (published in one volume) is addressed to the problems of working for the impersonal corporation, the dehumanization and powerlessness of the individual in our most gigantic concerns. The second book, on education, democracy, city planning, and ecology, is equally readable, but only secondarily concerned with work.*

Pavalko, Ronald M.: *Sociology of Occupations and Professions*, F. E. Peacock Publishers, Itasca, III., 1971.

> *A broad introduction to sociological implications of the role of work and occupations in society; presents empirical findings and sociological theory.*

U.S. Department of Labor, *Occupational Outlook Handbook for 1970–1971*, Bureau of Labor Statistics Bulletin No. 1650, Government Printing Office, Washington, D.C.

> *The Labor Department's Occupational Outlook Handbooks, published every two years, are an invaluable source of information for persons trying to guess the future of job security. Although all predictions are risky, the handbooks review the situation and present the best available information on professional, managerial, clerical, sales, service, skilled manual, agricultural, commercial, governmental, and other types of employment.*

U.S. Department of Labor, *Monthly Labor Review*.

> *This frequently overlooked magazine gives all the latest information on wage and price trends, changing retirement age and retirement pay, significant court decisions in labor cases, blue-collar versus white-collar opportunities, female employment, and many other topics of concern to the wage-earning public.*

 **QUESTIONS**

1. What has to be done if the work ethic defeats itself
    by turning out too many goods?

2. What are some of the characteristics of the work world
    that cause uncertainties and reluctance on the part
    of the young?

3. In spite of better wages and unionization, many
    problems remain for blue-collar labor, such as ·. . . .

4. Explain differing views of the ultimate effect of
    automation on employment.

5. What are some of the conflicting interpretations of
    the effects of technological society on meaning and
    purpose in life?

6 *In an older agricultural society the marriage relationship was held together by economic necessity. Economic change and greater female equality have changed the marital relationship into one that is held together almost exclusively by affection. What are the consequences to family stability? Are there peculiarly heavy strains on a marriage relationship that is born in romance and based almost singly on the expectation of happiness and fulfillment? If more marriages dissolve, is the trend a subject for alarm, or is public alarm merely a matter of cultural lag? How realistic are the divorce laws of most states?*

The family bond is a loosening one in respects other than an increased divorce rate. Why are we talking increasingly of a generation gap? In the following pages, an examination of the family will suggest that age-grades are becoming more important than kinship in one's psychological location in society. But are there dysfunctions to separate youth subcultures, middle-America subcultures, and old-age subcultures? What happens to the aged in such a society? Are we drifting into a system of minimal family care for the young and more and more public upbringing of youth? Is there any way to strengthen the psychologically protective features of the family in spite of institutional changes that at present seem to weaken it? Is there any means to prevent further loosening of the kinship bond?

FAMILY: THE LOOSENING BOND

There are great contrasts in family types, and both sociologists and anthropologists have theorized considerably about the connection between family type and societal needs and values. For example, strong lineage systems develop where many of the functions of education, law, and government are carried on by the family or where inheritance is extremely important. Polygynous families have a special value for societies with a high death rate among males (usually caused by war) or in societies that place great importance on male dominance and on the increase of certain lines of descent. Some extremely warlike societies, such as ancient Sparta, found it useful to downgrade the importance of family duties for their young warriors, especially if the warriors belonged to an upper class with servants to care for the household.

The family in modern industrial societies also needs to be structured in ways congenial to societal requirements. The family must give enough freedom to the young so that they can adjust to changing norms, customs, and occupational roles. The family is less bound by tradition and a wide range of duties than many families of the past, but compensates by the idealization of romance and strong affection between mates and between parents and children. The modern middle-class family also has the difficult task of defining the right balance between intergenerational solidarity and growing independence for the younger generation. It senses a need to create personality types with a sense of direction but also capable of change to meet everchanging circumstances. For this reason the typical middle-class family cannot be rigid and authoritarian, with its statuses and relationships tightly structured. However, if the family goes so far to the other extreme as to lack cohesion and is unable to produce a generation of children who feel secure and confident, both the individual and society suffer. At present, more than 500,000 children per year see their parents separate, and the divorce rate is slowly increasing. The reasons given by people who break the bond of marriage are numerous, but underlying the individual reasons are certain basic characteristics of the marital tie in a mobile, industrial society.

SOCIAL CHANGE AND THE MARRIAGE RELATIONSHIP

Certain distinctive characteristics of the family system in the Western World, and in the United States in particular, are the results of economic change, reduced family size, and equalization of status. The economic change of the last century or so has resulted in jobs outside the home for the father, and more recently for the mother. The family no longer earns its living together on a family-type farm as it once did. As a consequence, children do not learn their occupational roles from parents, but are dependent upon the school and other institutions.

The family is smaller than it used to be, especially in the sense that it contains only a married couple and their children, and rarely any outside relatives. Along with the exclusion of relatives from the home there has been a decline in the feelings of responsibility for elderly grandparents. Social security and medicare take care of the aged, and they are less the family's concern than in the past.

The status of family members grows more nearly equal with the passing of time. Only a few grandparents can remember a time when the rule "children should be seen and not heard" was rigid doctrine. Male and female are expected to be companions on a more or less equal footing within the household. Since the children must be reared with a view to independent decision making, their status comes very close to equality with that of the parents.

A few other significant changes have been going on in the family, such as a declining educational role within the home, less of a role in the teaching of religion, and usually a diminishing role in recreation, especially as the children reach the age for driving automobiles and as age specialization in entertainment grows.

GROWING ROLE OF AFFECTION   Students of the family are in fairly close agreement about the types of changes that have come about, but not in the evaluation of the changes. It is true that the family is less concerned with as many functions as it once performed, but is that necessarily bad? Possibly the family of today, with more privacy and with less anxiety about getting a day's work out of all its children is better geared to affectivity and enjoyment than it once was. Philippe Ariès[1] pictures the family of medieval Europe as one with less of an affectionate bond between husband and wife, with far less privacy, and with different attitudes toward children from those of today. Children, although not neglected, were in no way made central to the family as they are now. The special psychological needs of children were not recognized. Portraits showed them as quite undifferentiated in appearance and proportioned exactly as adults. "Most people probably felt that children had neither mental activities nor recognizable bodily shape."

Women likewise were given less of the special consideration of later times. For the upper classes, few in number, there was a cult of chivalry. Centuries later, women of more common birth were also supposed to be accorded chivalrous treatment; but women were seldom considered as people with minds worth developing or capable of carrying on an intelligent conversation. Close emotional relationships between husband and wife were unimportant. Even if they could barely tolerate each other, the family continued, upheld by law, village opinion, relatives, and the church.

In the modern family, by contrast, emotional feelings are particularly intense because of the small number of people sharing a common household, not intruded on by many guests or to any great extent by neighbors or relatives. Under these circumstances preservation of the marital relationship seems especially valuable. Yet it is in this very type of family that the preservation of that relationship presents unusual difficulties.

[1]Philippe Ariès, *Centuries of Childhood*, Alfred A. Knopf, Inc., New York, 1962, p. 39.

The old-style family, bound by status,
propriety, and a marriage vow that says
"as long as ye shall *live*."

The new-style family, with equality and individual fulfillment and bound only by "as long as ye shall *love*."

THE UNSTABLE FAMILY   To speak of the modern, nuclear family, centered only in the parents and their offspring, as an "unstable family" is, admittedly, to use a biased term. It is the term devised by the French sociologist, Le Play, to describe such a family in contrast to the extended or "stable family"—the type of kinship system that linked large numbers of relatives together. Le Play's contention was that the European family of an earlier time had been a large, consanguineal family, rather like the Oriental families of more recent times. Such a family held together and was an ongoing institution, never coming to a close because of the death of any particular member or married couple. The link between generations was stronger than the husband-wife link.

In modern America we think of the ideal marriage as involving the closest link between husband and wife, definitely not to be interfered with by kinsmen. Not all families fit the model, of course. In many old-money families the proper marriage is made with family position in mind. In many other cases, premarital pregnancy of the girl is the reason for marriage, rather than romantic devotion. Some people marry for money or to escape from home, but all such marriages are looked upon as less than ideal. The emphasis on money and position belonged more to LePlay's old-fashioned stable family than to the modern type.

The modern type of family has evolved to meet the requirements of an economic system that places the father's job far from the household and that often needs women too for work outside the home. Partly in response to economic and educational realities, the society has become equalitarian in its sentiments. A society that educates and makes fairly equal demands on both men and women calls for a high degree of equality between husband and wife. In an equalitarian situation, marriage must be based on consent and that consent must be won through love and romance. There are other interests too, of course—children, a home, and possibly many common interests and values—but romantic attachment is vital. Leo Zakuta[2] notes that in this respect there is still a contrast between the European and the American marriage. European marriages are also based on mutual consent and usually follow a romantic courtship, but the idea of singleness of devotion is not played up to quite the same degree. Far more European women, if confronted with the knowledge that their husbands have been having affairs with other women, will take the "boys will be boys" attitude. The American woman, unless she belongs to a particularly liberated segment of modern youth, will feel a sense of hurt, anger, and betrayal.

The problem is that the very characteristic that has made the modern American marriage a particularly intense state of bliss, with full love and gratification for both partners, also makes the marriage more vulnerable to friction than an arranged type of marriage. When the husband had a status far above that of the wife, sometimes relations were very free and easy for him. The greater the difference of status between mates, the greater the freedom of the husband to have a mistress and, concomitantly,

[2]Leo Zakuta, "Equality in North American Marriages," *Social Research*, vol. 30, pp. 157–170, Summer 1963.

the more acceptable was the status of mistress. Even prostitution was tolerated and defended as "ultimately the most efficient guardian of virtue." The idea was that the prostitute not only protected good women from being attacked by evil men, but even protected wives from two frequent demands from their husbands.[3] Now that women are no longer expected to be so inhibited as to not enjoy the pleasures of love, love and romance are much stronger and are almost the total center of marital stability. However, love is such a powerful emotion that, if neglected, it can turn to hate. The husband as authority figure could be respected, or at least accepted, if not loved. The husband as lover may be hated if no longer loved.[4]

The consequences of the equalitarian and romantic marriage are certainly not to be condemned entirely. Certainly no one, including sociologists who analyze the virtues of older systems, wishes to have his marriage arranged by wise parents, and only occasionally are people willing to be paired off by a wise computer. The modern wife is not willing to trade her position of equality or near-equality for the guarantee of a permanent marriage to a domineering man. It is important, though, to see the contrast in sociological perspective and to know that a high divorce rate will not fall under the hammer blows of constant preaching and scolding or of outmoded laws that try to force people to stay together.

The marriage that places high value on equality and companionship, however, is probably more stable in today's society than the one that insists on male dominance and rigid division of labor. The nonequalitarian family might have had stability in an earlier age, but for modern America it is in a state of strain.

THE ANACHRONISTIC FAMILY The family that rejects equality and companionship between the spouses begins to seem out of date, an anachronism. Mirra Komarovsky describes her research in a group of such homes, consisting entirely of white, Anglo-Saxon, blue-collar workers, generally of very limited education. In such a family the male role is an isolated masculine role, not at all concerned with companionship with wife or with other women. "Regular guys don't mess around with women except when they want what a woman's got to give them" said one of the wives. The man was not expected to help around the house, and it was all right for him to be "out with the boys." The situation was uneven, with the woman staying at home with the children. She did not worry about the social adjustment of the children or their psychological problems, but found lots of worries about making them behave and obey.

In pursuing the question of whether such a family is actually happier than the middle-class family with more ambiguous norms, Komarovsky's conclusion is "No." The amount of complaints and general unhappiness seems to be greater. A possible explanation is that in the modern world it is just about necessary for man and wife

[3]Christopher Lasch, "Divorce and the Family in America," *Atlantic Monthly*, vol. 218, pp. 57–61, November 1966.
[4]Zakuta, *op. cit.*

to have the companionate role that is typical of the educated middle class. In the old days such a role was hardly necessary because people stayed in the same neighborhoods, close to their kinsmen and friends. Now they move frequently and neighborhoods are not emotionally close. The consequence seems to be that the wife of the blue-collar worker in Komarovsky's study is isolated from the old-fashioned female gossip of earlier days, but has no role in the mixed company so typical today. The man is often unhappy because his wife is moody. Neither realizes that the source of trouble could be their belief in a God-given, impenetrable wall between the psyches of men and women.[5]

DIVORCE

The right to divorce is recognized in nearly all societies, although Italy did not pass a divorce law until 1970. The grounds for divorce and statistics on divorce vary greatly the world over. There are some tribal societies in which divorce rates are even higher than in the United States, and Egypt and a few other Islamic countries have sometimes had higher divorce rates than ours. Otherwise, the United States has the dubious distinction of being the world leader in divorce. In some tribal societies the reason for high divorce rates bears an accidental resemblance to our own: people marry very young in a kind of trial-marriage situation, not expecting to achieve marital stability until later in life.[6] In parts of the Islamic world the husband still has full authority about divorce, and this custom results in a very high divorce rate.[7]

DIVORCE STATISTICS, USA   The divorce rate has been increasing gradually in the United States along with a more mobile, urban way of life. In 1900 about one marriage in twelve ended in divorce; at present the rate is a little more than one in four. The divorce rate reached its highest point in 1946, at the end of World War II, mainly as a result of many young marriages made on short acquaintance during the war years. In 1967 the divorce rate had climbed to the highest point since 1946 — 11.7 per thousand marriages (2.7 per thousand population). There were, as of 1967, 2.2 million divorced and unremarried women in the United States and an additional 2.9 million separated from their husbands but not divorced. Three out of five homes headed by women included children; 7 million children (about 10 percent) lived in households without fathers. Each year divorces are granted to families having a total of nearly 600,000 children. Of the people over twenty-five years of age at first marriage, only about 15 percent get divorces; of those less than 18 years old, the rate is about 50 percent.[8]

[5]Mirra Komarovsky, "Blue Collar Families," *Columbia University Forum*, no. 7, pp. 29–32, Fall 1964.
[6]M. F. Nimkoff, *Comparative Family Systems,* Houghton Mifflin Company, Boston, 1965, pp. 337, 359.
[7]Even in the Islamic world, the custom is changing, and sometimes there are subtle devices by which a woman can defend herself against the husband's intent to divorce her. See Lawrence Rosen, "I Divorce Thee," *Transaction*, vol. 7, pp. 34–37, June 1970.
[8]Statistics from "The Growing Toll of America's Broken Homes," *U.S. News & World Report*, vol. 65, pp. 92–93, August 5, 1968.

DIVORCE AND SOCIAL CLASS William J. Goode[9] finds that, with rare exceptions, in the industrial countries of the world those people with higher incomes, higher levels of education, and occupations that are given much respect by the community are the least likely to divorce. Highest divorce rates occur at the bottom of the socioeconomic scale, except occasionally when desertion is an easy alternative to divorce and divorces are very difficult to obtain. There are several reasons for the higher divorce rates among the poor. For one thing, the husband's income is likely to be so low that it does not give the wife very much inducement to stay with him; conversely, the man's income is so low that he knows he can probably escape alimony if he is divorced. His job and possessions mean so little to him that he doesn't mind escaping to some other part of the country. For the poor there are often fewer community and kin relationships and pressures to be taken into consideration. Another economic reason is that the higher-income family usually has strong future commitments; divorces will entail heavy economic loss. Finally, there is considerable evidence that marital relationships are more satisfactory between middle- and upper-class members of society than for those in blue-collar jobs or in poverty. The previously cited study by Komarovsky gives a likely explanation for the differences in marital satisfaction. One reservation must be made, however. Although the higher-income families do better than those of low income regarding marital stability, all segments of American society have higher divorce rates now than before 1900.

CHILDREN OF DIVORCE Early studies of children coming from broken homes indicated that the home broken by divorce was the direct cause of high amounts of delinquency. For example, a study made in 1950 found that 60 percent of the troublemakers came from broken homes. A study in Denver in the 1960s found that 75 percent of delinquent Negro youth were from broken homes. Such statistics, however, leave two questions unanswered: (1) would the children be better behaved if their parents remained together even in a quarrelsome, unhappy marriage? (2) Are there factors other than divorce that account for the delinquency? In answer to the first question, most studies agree that a bitter, quarrelsome, intact home is certainly no better an environment for the young than a broken home. In answer to the second question, it must be recalled that divorce and separation rates are highest in the very social-class strata where delinquency rates are highest.

Howard N. Bahr[10] reviews some of the above data on broken homes and concludes that often they are more of a comment on results of poverty and bad living conditions than of family breakup. In his own study, Bahr investigates the relationship between adult homelessness and excessive drinking to early family breakup. Of the alcoholics and vagrants in his study, 30 to 40 percent came from broken homes,

[9]William J. Goode, "Marital Satisfaction and Instability, A Cross-Cultural Analysis of Divorce Rates," *International Social Science Journal*, vol. 14, no. 3, pp. 507–526, Summer 1962.
[10]Howard N. Bahr, "Family Class and Stability as Antecedents of Homelessness and Excessive Drinking," *Journal of Marriage and the Family*, vol. 21, pp. 477–483, August 1969.

but so did the same percentage of nonalcoholics from the same area and social-class background.

Many delinquency studies end in statistics similar to those of Howard Bahr's. Others do show some correlation between broken homes and delinquency, higher for girls than for boys, and for younger than for older delinquents. The difference is not very great, however, and the figures do not answer the question, "What would have happened if an unhappy family had remained intact?"[11]

A study among middle-class college students found less general happiness, less self-confidence, and more difficulty with the opposite sex among students who had come from homes broken by divorce.[12] Since childhood happiness is correlated with later marital success, the unhappy family can easily repeat its pattern in the next generation. Whether or not some studies have exaggerated the effect of broken homes on delinquency rates, there seems to be general agreement that a series of bitter quarrels followed by divorce proceedings has an almost traumatic effect on youth.

DIVORCE LAWS: LEGAL FICTION VERSUS REALITY Divorce laws are slow to change to meet modern realities. One reason is that the majority of states still define marriage in terms of a "legal fiction"—a point of law that has little bearing on reality. The legal fiction is that marriage is a contract set up under civil law and, therefore, its maintenance is a business of the state. Unless one person can be proved to have sinned against another, there are no grounds for breaking the contract; the married couple must remain in holy wedlock, which someone has aptly called "holy deadlock."

Since marriage and divorce regulations are made by state rather than by federal government, the nation has a confusion of divorce laws. All states accept adultery and cruelty as grounds for divorce and often stretch cruelty to mean "mental cruelty," which can mean almost anything from fiendish mistreatment to mere incompatibility. Most states also recognize a variety of other grounds for divorce: desertion, incurable insanity, criminality, "loathsome disease," frigidity and impotence, and many others. In all states but one, however, someone has to be at fault in order for a divorce to be granted. California recently changed its law to make divorce possible simply on

---

> **What constitutes grounds for divorce in your state? Are the divorce laws consistent with modern realities? Try to get a lawyer experienced in divorce cases or a marriage counselor to speak for the class.**

---

[11]Sophia M. Robinson, *Juvenile Delinquency: Its Nature and Control*, Holt, Rinehart and Winston, Inc., New York, 1960, pp. 108–112.

[12]Jack Harrison Pollack, "Are Children of Divorce Different?" in Judson R. Landis, *Current Perspectives on Social Problems*, Wadsworth Publishing Company, Inc., Belmont, Calif., 1966, pp. 190–193.

grounds of mutual consent without anyone having to accept the blame. A result has been an immediate rise in divorces, which may prove only temporary. It is possible that the California divorce rate has risen suddenly as the result of a backlog of people who wanted to divorce but wished to avoid a difficult legal process. The present statistics are, however, almost the ultimate in the perceived trend toward higher divorce rates. In 1970, 114,000 California couples dissolved their marriages, an increase of 39 percent over the previous year. There were 173,000 marriages in 1970—only about one-third more marriages than divorces.[13]

Many of America's divorce laws were passed in the late nineteenth century as a response to women's protest movements. The idea of the laws was to protect women against cruel and tyrannical husbands. Previously, divorces were granted by state legislatures on an appeal that usually came from a man of means and influence. Divorces were virtually impossible for the poor or for women, except occasionally on grounds of adultery or cruelty. Present laws in the majority of states still reflect the idea of protecting the woman from a cruel husband and often result in the husband feeling victimized by the proceedings. They are also strongly criticized for encouraging long court duels, high lawyer's fees, and a struggle that is a bitter experience for the divorcing couple, friends, relatives, and particularly the children.[14]

There are no present indications that the divorce rate will decline in the future. Donald J. Cantor[15] predicts a situation in which first marriages will be regarded almost as trial marriages. The problem will be to do some effective birth control counseling to prevent bringing children into the world until a marriage demonstrates a fair measure of success and stability.

The only types of loosening bonds discussed at length in this chapter have been those of marriage. An off-hand impression of the society makes it look as though the bonds holding generations together are also weakening and that the society is becoming increasingly age graded.

THE AGE-GRADED SOCIETY

Much has been written by anthropologists about age sets in the primitive world, but only a few have commented on the parallel between primitive and modern societies in this respect. In societies that make a strong issue of rites of puberty, those who have gone through the rites together form a bond for life, linking them almost as closely to age mates as to family. Jomo Kenyatta's *Facing Mount Kenya* gives an interesting picture of this strong emotional bond, as remembered by Kenyatta from his youth. In Yoruba society the young initiate into the Egungung fraternity went much further in making his primary link one to the fraternity rather than to family.

[13]"State Divorces Up," *Los Angeles Times*, January 8, 1971, Part I, p. 26.
[14]Christopher Lasch, *op. cit.* See also, Donald J. Cantor, "The Right of Divorce," *Atlantic Monthly*, vol. 218, pp. 67–72, November 1966.
[15]Cantor, *op. cit.*

The initiate was asked, "Are you prepared to go even against your brother? Your father? Your mother?" The answer in each case had to be "Yes."[16] Totalitarian states of modern times have deliberately used youth groups for the same purpose.

At first glance, American society seems to bear no resemblance to the African societies mentioned or to totalitarian states. What, then, could be the reason for a similar development? One trait that all the societies have in common is that the major role-training for life is taken over by agencies outside the family. In some cases, the role-training was largely military. In American society economic change has necessitated role preparation through the schools (the same is the case with other industrial countries, and youth subcultures are very much in evidence). The other trait that all age-graded societies seem to have in common is the necessity of learning universalistic principles.

No antifamily purpose is intended, of course, in the promotion of age sets in American society, but it can be argued that the age-grading system of modern education produces a latent function that is antifamily. It is impossible to understand part of the strain within the modern family relationship without turning to the problem of age grading. S. N. Eisenstadt has made a thorough study of age grading.[17] Most of his book is an anthropological study of age grading and the varieties of the custom in the primitive world. His basic principle is that age grading occurs in societies with universalistic as opposed to familistic values and where major statuses are acquired outside the kinship group. In primitive societies the universalistic values are learned in the process of initiation into the age sets, rather than from the family, and the age sets are a fully institutionalized phenomenon. In modern societies, the very term "age sets" is seldom used, and there is no deliberate attempt to institutionalize such groups, but age sets nevertheless exist and are very important.

As mentioned in Chapter 5, kindergarten has been characterized by Gracey as "academic boot camp." We could just as well call it the first initiation into the age set. More frequently the designation "peer group" is used, but as time passes any particular age group sees itself in terms of a vast aggregate that goes far beyond the peer group of close acquaintances. Even the small child is aware of millions of others like him. In his adolescent years he will be more fully aware of his own generation and will develop a strong identity with it and a loyalty that often flies in the face of family solidarity.

> Make an observational study of a junior high school or grammar school subculture. What changes have come about since you were the same age?

[16]Eugene Victor Walter, *Terror and Resistance*, Oxford University Press, New York, 1969, p. 84.

[17]S. N. Eisenstadt, *From Generation to Generation*, The Free Press, New York, 1956.

There are various reasons why the age set takes on a strong identity and loyalty function. For one thing, as Eisenstadt points out, the child in modern society is learning universalistic norms that are not always part of family norms. The children from families with old-fashioned, puritanical norms will be thrown into contact with a society and generation that is much more permissive. The family with strong racist feelings will probably have its children reared in an atmosphere of increasing racial equality and acceptance. The family that believes strongly in thrift and avoidance of debt will have no choice but to see its children indoctrinated by an age set in which the old Benjamin Franklin ideas are not even a cultural memory.

THE OCCUPATIONAL FUNCTION   The school rather than the family is charged with the responsibility of preparing the young for future occupations. The family in modern industrial society prepares youth for an occupational role only indirectly by sending the young to school. Often the occupation being prepared for is so far from family knowledge that no useful parental advice is possible. Consequently, a gulf opens within the family and leaves the young person looking for advice but unable to find it.

The inability of the family to prepare the young for an occupational role is one of the traits that has caused it to be designated an "inefficient institution." Bright children born in families of low socioeducational status are seldom prepared realistically for the roles for which they are equipped by native ability. Even the age set is of little help in this respect because it is divided along social-class lines, so that those least able to find their way to high status are usually thrown together.

THE RITES OF PUBERTY   In strongly age-graded preliterate societies, there are often extensive and severe rites of puberty or coming-of-age ceremonies, marking the passage from childhood to adulthood. Childhood is left behind, and the new initiate is nearing the age for marriage. Often there will be considerable sexual experimenting before marriage, but eventually a marriage will be arranged. The family usually cooperates in the process by raising money for bride price.

There are no such institutionalized rites of puberty in American society, and there is much more tension about preparation for marriage. Eisenstadt concludes that tensions are most likely to develop between parents and the young in instances of the home's tending to block the road to marital maturity. This is often the case in the American family. Premarital relations are discouraged, with diminishing effectiveness, by the parents. Parents are very much aware of the odds against young marriage, and strongly urge delay. The age set usually counsels differently.

Both the age set and the school take over much of the function of instruction in sex that is the prerogative of the home in many societies. Our schizoid attitudes toward sex make frank discussion between parents and youth difficult. The school does not intentionally encourage early marriage, but there is something about the total informal student subculture that leads to early marriage. In high school or before, a dating pattern develops, sometimes based on infatuation, and sometimes

Modern rites: defiance of convention.

developed as a necessary part of the pursuit of popularity. Popularity is badly needed in a situation where status is more a matter of the age set than of family background. Often the dating goes too far at an early age, and knowledge of the facts of life is acquired in the laboratory of experience under conditions strongly inconsistent with parental ideas of right and wrong.

DATING AND EARLY MARRIAGE   As of 1968 the average age for first marriage in the United States was 20.3 years for women and 22.7 for men, representing a decline in age of about two years for the woman and four years for the man as compared to 1900. There was a considerable difference in socioeconomic class as to the age of marriage, with the lower socioeconomic class usually marrying younger. Regardless of social class, those who started dating before fifteen years of age were inclined to marry younger than the average.[18] The earlier the marriage, the more likely all kinds of marital problems. The only cases in which early dating led to successful marriage were those in which the dating couple went together several years before marriage. According to Mervyn Cadwallader of San Jose State College, 40 percent of

[18]Arthur A. Campbell, "Early Dating and Early Marriage," *Journal of Marriage and the Family*, vol. 30, pp. 236–245, April 1968.

all brides are between the ages of fifteen and eighteen, and half of their marriages end within five years, but a knowledge of such statistics is no deterrent to early marriage.[19]

If our popular literature is even partly correct, sexual frustration can hardly be a reason for early marriage. A desire to start occupational careers earlier is not the answer either. Young couples are usually not economically prepared for marriage and usually are not through school. In spite of all the arguments against early marriage, marriage is not delayed, and part of the reason is at least indirectly connected with the age set.

Time was when the older generation decided the order of maturity. The first step to maturity was economic independence and the second was marriage. Now the first step seems to be marriage. "The Masai becomes an adult when he kills a lion," says Cadwallader, "and an American becomes an adult when he gets married."[20] This statement is hardly a joke. The status of adolescence tends to be long, confusing, and of indefinite termination, except through marriage. A difficult status is terminated by a status that is even more difficult at that stage of life.

AGE SETS AND IDEOLOGIES The intergenerational drift is very pronounced and important in many other respects. New fashions and designs, vocabularies, and vices, such as substituting drugs for alcohol, arise. New ideologies also arise, differing from generation to generation, but never the same as those of the parental generation. There was "flaming youth" in the 1920s, radical youth in the 1930s, delinquent youth in the 1940s, conformist youth in the 1950s, and, again, radical youth in the 1960s and 1970s, and the development of what has been called the "hang-loose ethic." All such epithets exaggerate, of course, but they bear enough truth to illustrate the tendency for particular age cohorts to differentiate themselves from each other and from their elders. Although many college students remain fairly close to the political perspectives of their parents, enough make a radical change to cause ideology to be one of the major factors in the generation gap.

In most places where age grading is part of the institutional policy of a society, it reinforces the religious aspects of life by ritualization. In modern societies, especially in the last decade or two, there has been a strong tendency for youth, especially

---

> **What do you believe to be the stereotypes of middle-aged Americans about college youth? Put your stereotypes in question form and see whether a sample of middle-aged Americans actually holds the assumed attitudes.**

---

[19]Mervyn Cadwallader, "Marriage as a Wretched Institution," *Atlantic Monthly*, vol. 218, pp. 63–64, November 1966.
[20]*Ibid.*, p. 64.

college youth, to reject the old-time religion, sometimes becoming frankly agnostic and sometimes looking for something new. Again the age grading tends to divide the family.

MIDDLE AMERICA   The age set of the parental generation is now referred to by politicians and the mass media as "middle America." Age grading is really not a phenomenon of the middle years, but in our society a stereotype has developed that makes it so. Just as the elders, with the help of the mass media, have stereotyped the young as a generation of purposeless hippies, the young have stereotyped their elders. Middle America is supposed to be conservative, hypocritical, money-grubbing, and definitely past the age for any fun or spontaneity in life. Actually, middle America's enjoyments do seem to be widely separated from the young and not sufficiently concerned with them.

THE STRULDBRUGGS   For the oldest age set there is something equivalent to burial without death. At first there are the activities of elderly groups such as senior citizens' clubs, but the groups are set off into a world of their own. The wealthy can even retire to communities of their own, the most famous of which are the Leisure Worlds in various parts of the country. In these cases the idea of age sets is again strong, just as it was in youth, because the aged are fairly well isolated from the main stream of the culture.

Since people no longer die after enjoying a few years of retirement, and only a few can afford to live in a Leisure World, the majority eventually become a burden on society. They also become pitiful to look upon and must be hidden away from sight. Some of them reach a state of decrepitude that reminds us of the "Struldbruggs" in *Gulliver's Travels*. When Gulliver visited the land of the Luggmaggians, he found that some of their people, the Struldbruggs, did not die at all, but lived for century after century. Gulliver's first comment was that it must be wonderful to have such long life and to be able to learn, to remember, and to advise others. He learned, though, that longer life does not mean longer memory or greater wisdom, but that it only makes people "opinionative, peevish, covetous, morose, vain, talkative, and . . . dead to all natural affection." A further study of the immortals shows that:

> At ninety they lose their teeth and hair; they have at that age no distinction of taste, but eat and drink whatever they can get, without relish or appetite. . . . In talking they forget the common appellations of things, and the names of persons, even of those who are their nearest friends and relatives. For the same reason they can never amuse themselves with reading, because their memory will not serve to carry them from the beginning of a sentence to the end . . . .
>
> They were the most mortifying sight I ever beheld, and the women more horrible than the the men. Besides the usual deformities in extreme old age, they acquired an additional ghastliness in proportion to their number of years, which is not to be described.[21]

[21]Jonathan Swift, *Gulliver's Travels*, The Pocket Library, New York, 1957, pp. 210, 212.

Age and the lonely years of low income,
declining health, and abandonment
by family.

People familiar with homes for care of the aged will find the Gulliver quotation too true to be amusing. Many old people's homes, sometimes euphemistically called rest homes or convalescent homes, are in disgraceful condition. Physician's care is scarce. Drugs are frequently misadministered, or given only to make patients easy to handle. In many cases, food expenditure per person is less than $1 per day. A New York reporter found several New York rest homes "abominable . . . filthy rooms, roaches in glasses, dirt in water pitchers, and indescribable conditions in bathrooms."[22] Throughout the country many such institutions are a scandal, inadequately staffed, exploitative in price, and without the welfare of the patients in mind.

Jules Henry tells of two such institutions, one in which the patients are kept clean and well fed, and the other a place he names "Hell's Vestibule" (from Dante's *Inferno*). Even in the sanitary, "well-run" institution, the feeling of discard and of merely waiting for death is oppressive, and no conversations, entertainment, or hobbies are provided to keep minds from dwelling on the morbid. Such problems are of the type that seldom attract public attention. In Henry's words, "The social conscience cannot be stirred to concern unless some terrible evil . . . rages across the land. Hence the spiritual degradation and hopelessness of its obsolete charges seems none of its affair."[23]

Admittedly, the very aged are a problem, and their numbers steadily increase. In the age-graded society, they are easy to forget. They are not part of the age sets of the able-bodied, and they are not part of an extended family that honors its aged. They are the unwanted; they are the Struldbruggs.

FUTURE POSSIBILITIES

A few commentators on the family have wondered whether it is not time to abandon the family as a defunct institution. Such a question is raised by Barrington Moore,[24] who summarizes the strains in the system quite well, and sees the rising divorce rate as the most significant indication of the poor health of the family. In reading into his essay a little further, however, it becomes clear that what he is talking about is social change, not social burial. Institutions change, sometimes rather suddenly, but they do not "self-destruct" without leaving a trace.

> **Study rest homes in your area; talk to some patients. Do you find that some are almost completely abandoned by their relatives?**

---

[22]David H. Pryor, "Somewhere between Society and the Cemetery: Where We Put the Aged," *New Republic*, vol. 162, pp. 15–18, April 25, 1970.

[23]Jules Henry, *Culture Against Man*, Random House, Inc., New York, 1963, p. 392.

[24]Barrington Moore, Jr., "Thoughts on the Future of the Family," *Political Power and Social Theory*, Harvard University Press, Cambridge, Mass., 1958.

The family, admittedly, is beset with problems. We could add to all the previously mentioned complaints by saying that the family is in some respects a terribly undemocratic institution for an age of equalitarianism, because a powerful family cannot resist exerting its influence in the direction of special favors for its own members. This is one reason why families have often been seen as enemies by totalitarian regimes. This very trait of a family, which can easily turn into a vice, is also its greatest virtue. Irving Goffman makes the extremely significant comment in his book *Assylums* that the family is the greatest possible enemy of total institutions. By total institutions he means jails, prisons, armies, asylums, orphanages, monasteries — any institution that takes total control of the individual. In this sense, an entire state can become a total institution, crushing individual decisions, and even turning son against father and brother against brother. Such a state is antifamily, and the family, battered though it may be, attempts to act as a refuge against such a state.

The family is a prescientific development that gives difficult tasks to the novice, often links incompatible people together, even occasionally gives dull parents bright children, or vice versa. The family provides for the performance of the extremely vital task of early socialization by anyone who happens to be a parent — frequently a disaster of unskilled labor. But anachronistic though the family seems in a scientific age, it is still amazingly popular, as evidenced by the prevalence of early marriage and a 98-percent remarriage rate for the divorced. Flying in the face of our concerns over population explosion, the majority of couples want children, and family planning agencies are almost as busy prescribing remedies to the infertile as they are trying to stem the tide of babies. Whatever its ills, it is better to think of the family as in need of a doctor than in need of an undertaker.

FAMILY TRENDS IN THE WORLD   Nimkoff concludes his book on different family types with an essay on the future of the family.[25] As a world trend, especially in societies changed by industrialization and the need for public education, families are undergoing similar types of change. One change is in the direction of more public upbringing of children through schools and nursery schools, and in some cases through public boarding schools. The public rearing of children is especially pronounced in the Russian boarding schools and in the government communes of China. On a small, voluntary scale, the Israeli kibbutzim represent the same type of development. The age-grading tendency previously discussed is promoted by such institutions.

The second worldwide change that Nimkoff mentions is toward a minimization of function, as is the case with the family of the United States. To a considerable degree, the family loses its secondary functions of economic production and protection, but it maintains its psychological supportive function. It also gains function in the realm of planning, both for children and for the budget.

A third change is the one most central to our discussion — a change in stability pattern. The rising divorce rate in the United States can be expected to be duplicated

[25]Nimkoff, *op. cit.*, pp. 357–369.

elsewhere. However, Nimkoff says that the family is simply reacting to social systems that are in a state of flux. Possibly, despite its marital instability, the family remains more stable than most other social institutions. In times of human storms—war, depression, or revolution—the family, despite its frictions, gives what little protection it can and often provides man with his only reason for survival.

In Nimkoff's opinion, the trend of the family is toward play rather than work as as integrative principle. With more leisure and more recreational activities, he argues, the family can spend more time together. In times of less prosperity, parents were often so busy scratching out a living that they had little time to devote to children. Even the working parents of today often have more leisure time than earlier generations had. In the context of other statements in Nimkoff's book, however, his conclusions about the integrative functions of leisure time sound a little dubious. He mentions, for example, that when the American family had one car, the car served an integrative function. People had to plan their activities together in order to all get a ride. Now there may be several cars in the family, and the possibility of going separate ways for recreation increases. Such an instance can be multiplied by examples from many kinds of specialized recreational activities.

CONFLICTING PROPOSALS   Proposals for helping the family can be based on opposing viewpoints of what is desired. Some would argue that great efforts must be made to preserve the marriage bond. Few would any longer advocate making divorces impossible, but many persons would suggest family counseling before a divorce is considered. Others would not object to attempts at counseling but would take more of a "roll with the tide" attitude. If many young marriages are likely to end, then, they would suggest, why not make divorce easy and free it of stigma as much as possible?[26]

The process of readjustment after divorce is an extremely difficult period at best, entailing a new search for love, new life habits, a restoration of pride and confidence, new social relationships, and often financial problems.[27] Every attempt should be made to prevent adding further problems. At present, although many divorces are arranged without a court scene, they are often bought through bargaining over custody of children, property, alimony, and so forth.

Another proposal for making the marriage relationship more stable is to be more restrictive about marriage. It is possible to imagine a science-fiction situation in which geneticists would examine the applicants for a wedding license to make sure their mating would be in the interests of human perpetuation, and in which psychologists or computers would study their personality profiles to make sure they were compatible. Actually, a certain amount of genetic counseling is already being done, and computers have been used extensively for matching people for a first date. They may someday be a substitute for the old marriage arranger of Asiatic and

[26]Cantor, op. cit.
[27]Willard Waller, The Old Love and the New: Divorce and Readjustment, Liveright Publishing Corporation, New York, 1930, pp. 2–14.

A universal trend: public rearing
of children.

Eastern European tradition. Obviously, though, the computer's judgment would be merely a suggestion, not an order. It is also hard to see how any type of counseling system could be entirely effective, since it would always be possible to leave one's own state or country to get married and since many marriages are a result of pre-marital pregnancy.

THE REARING OF CHILDREN, PUBLIC AND PRIVATE The proposals most frequently discussed for care of children in the future all tend to emphasize nursery school, pre-school training, summer camps, and every conceivable way of taking them away from home and keeping them with the peer group. It is this tendency of parents to want to be free of their children as much as possible that led Moore to ask if there is not some better alternative to the family.

It would be reactionary and unrealistic to propose that child care be returned completely to the home. The question is, though, whether there is not some way of keeping parents and children more emotionally close than is often the case in societies today. Some persons contend that the Israeli kibbutz does precisely this task. For those not familiar with the kibbutz, it is the name for a type of small cooperative community in Israel in which both the mother and father are freed to work in agriculture or to follow military duties by leaving child care entirely to specialists. Parents visit with their children, but only in a fun and enjoyment capacity. The problems of discipline are not theirs. The result seems to be the production of bright, capable, cooperative children who, upon maturity, usually remain in the kibbutzim system.[28]

A kibbutz arrangement would probably be impossible except in the type of small agricultural village in which it is now established. Furthermore, many parents would react strongly against it because of too total a separation of family function from marital partners. However, could some of its objectives be achieved in other societies, especially the free and easy relationship between parents and children? Can child-care centers and more public upbringing be made to harmonize with the objective of close parent-child relations?

Urie Bronfenbrenner discusses a possibility that might resolve the dilemma to some extent.[29] His proposal is that business and government cooperate more with families by providing for child and infant care at or near centers of employment. Communities, he says, should also establish neighborhood family centers, with co-operative efforts at child care and projects in which both young and old could co-operate. The schools, he thinks, could prevent too much separation of ages by finding

[28]Stuart A. Queen et al.: "The Minimum Family of Kibbutz," in *The Family in Various Cultures*, J. B. Lippincott Company, Philadelphia, 1961, pp. 116–136.
[29]Urie Bronfenbrenner, quoted by Marelene Cimons in "Our Children: Love Them or Lose Them," *Los Angeles Times*, December 13, 1970, Sec. F, pp. 1, 21.

projects for children in the adult world and for getting older youth interested in helping children. The present tutorial efforts of many college students are in line with such ideas, and so are recent clean-up-the-environment movements that have involved all age groups.

It is hard to argue with Nimkoff's conclusion that the trend in the world today is toward greater public upbringing of children. To a degree it is inevitable, but means must be found to prevent the total institutionalization of childhood found in some totalitarian regimes, or imagined in Huxley's *Brave New World*.

SUGGESTED READINGS

Atlantic Monthly, vol. 170, November 1966, a special issue on the family.

> *Articles deal with the changing position of women, the brittleness of the marriage bond, and the absurdities of divorce laws.*

Eisenstadt, S. N.: *From Generation to Generation*, The Free Press, New York, 1956.

> *Much of the material in this book is drawn from anthropological studies of societies very foreign to our own, but Eisenstadt shows also how his age-grading theories apply to modern societies, especially to certain totalitarian societies.*

Glasser, Paul H., and Lois N. Glasser: *Families in Crisis*, Harper & Row, Publishers, Incorporated, New York, 1970.

> *A good collection of articles, generally based on empirical research. The general topics covered are family poverty, disorganization, illness, and disability.*

Mace, David, and Vera Mace: *Marriage East and West*, Dolphin Books, Doubleday & Company, Inc., Garden City, N.Y., 1959.

> *Especially fascinating to the student who has never reflected much about a different structuring of marriage. The attitude of the East, placing family permanence, duty, and responsibility far ahead of romance, is so well presented that the book seems almost biased; but it is a good antidote to our narrow definition of family relations.*

Queen, Stuart A., et al.: *The Family in Various Cultures*, J. B. Lippincott Company, Philadelphia, 1952.

> *A fascinating book, well written, it traces the historical roots of the Western family. It also gives interesting comparisons with different traditions — the Hopi family, for example, and the Israeli kibbutz.*

Wiseman, Jacqueline P. (ed.): *People as Partners: Individual and Family Relationships in Today's World*, Canfield Press, San Francisco, A Division of Harper & Row, Publishers, Incorporated, 1971.

A good collection of articles by authorities on family. Parts 5, 6, and 7 are particularly applicable to the previous pages — family partnership, children as junior partners, and marital crises.

QUESTIONS

1. How can a greater cultural emphasis on love, romance, and equality actually make a marriage relationship more vulnerable to breakdown than in the days of arranged marriages?

2. Why is the type of family described by Komarovsky less satisfactory now than in the past (see "the anachronistic family")?

3. In what ways are the divorce laws of most states unrealistic?

4. Why has our society developed such strongly age-graded characteristics?

5. What are the worldwide trends in family as described by Nimkoff?

PART TWO

THE INCONGRUITIES

There are many incongruities that contribute to the worries of our troubled land, such as the paradox of poverty in the midst of plenty, and race and sex discrimination in a society that claims to believe in equality. Another incongruity is that of maintaining fairly rapid population growth at a time when human population is reaching the limits of the earth. The first of these problems has troubled societies since ancient times, and even population growth has been seen as a potential source of danger since the early nineteenth century. What, then, is new about the incongruities?

WHAT IS NEW

In many cases what is new about the problems discussed in the next four chapters is the increasing social awareness of their implications. Racial inequality has been inconsistent with our declared social norms throughout our history, and we find it hard to understand how our ancestors could have been blind to the fact. It is only recently, however, that we have become aware of some of our other incongruities. We thought we had been good to the blacks because they were eventually freed from slavery. We were good enough to allow large numbers of immigrants to come to our shores, including the impoverished, the refugees, and ironically, the draft dodgers from lands of compulsory military service. Only in an age of protest, however, did we begin to realize the full meaning of second-class citizenship for black Americans and a vastly uneven welcome for the immigrants entering our land. The problem of women's rights is similar. We have long believed women achieved equality when the Nineteenth Amendment was passed and have spoken with complacency of an age of female equality. The employment discrimination facts now being publicized have taken much of the nation by surprise.

The problem of poverty is not new, but it is relatively new to have a society that could actually afford not to have poverty. The problem of overpopulation has been perceived by a few people for many years, but by only a few. As recently as the early twentieth century, Theodore Roosevelt was decrying our declining birth rate, fearing "national suicide." Now, with the birth rate much lower, most people are worried about the crowding of the earth.

MEETING THE SOCIAL PROBLEMS CRITERIA

All the problems discussed in the next four chapters involve large numbers of people. All are seen primarily as normative problems, and all are amenable to solution and, as a matter of fact, at least some progress has been made with many of them. The racial problems, however, still present a threat. So little has been done about the racial problems of the ghetto that we could continue to have the bitter, divided society warned of in the *Report of the President's Commission on Civil Disorders*. Persistent poverty is also a threat, for it is costly and alienative, and tends to undermine belief in the viability of our economic system.

As for the problems of male and female, we do not anticipate any literal battle of the sexes, but we do anticipate increasing complaints about the confusion of role requirements of both men and women, and about women's relative deprivation in both the political and occupational spheres. Finally, the potential threat of the population explosion is very great—more so in already crowded parts of the world than here, but potentially dangerous everywhere.

INTERRELATIONSHIPS

The problems of minority groups, female employment, and poverty are intricately related to economic and social change. Poor immigrants from Europe were once able to find jobs in the factories and mines of America. Recent immigrants from the rural South to the urban North, however, have not been able to find work. Increased efficiency and automation have eliminated many jobs for the unskilled and semiskilled. Even when norms change enough to make us realize the need for greater racial equality, our tradition-bound institutions respond slowly—schools, labor unions, industries, and political parties.

The problems of minority groups and poverty are closely related to alienation and deviant behavior. Those whose experiences of life have caused them to feel unwanted and unworthy are not closely bound to the norms of the property-owning middle class. Craftiness is sometimes the price of survival. Outraged feelings can also lead to acts of hostility or a retreat into the world of drugs.

The problems of women's rights are closely connected to economic change as well as to normative change. Women were once employed only in poorly paying sweatshop jobs or in domestic tasks. Even now women's jobs tend to be low paying, but educational equality and opportunities for the skilled and educated have greatly increased the number of women in the occupational world and the number who feel cheated in pay and in opportunities for advancement.

THE INCONGRUITIES PERSPECTIVE

Incongruities always exist in societies to some degree. All societies hold certain social sentiments or values—idealizations of what is believed to be right. Practice seldom lives up to the cultural ideal, and the difference between ideal and practice is referred to as normative strain. There are also cases in which old cultural ideals are outmoded by new events and needs, and normative change becomes necessary.

MANAGING NORMATIVE STRAIN   As noted in the introductory chapter, societies develop means for the management of normative strain. They learn to explain away inconsistencies or to so completely compartmentalize their thinking that they do not even notice them. Men of the Victorian age could glorify and sentimentalize women much more than modern men do, but nevertheless confine them to the kitchen. White men, without the slightest touch of irony, could speak of how they liked black people just as well as anyone else "as long as they know their place." A country boasting of being a land of refuge for the poor was hardly aware of its inconsistency in passing an Oriental Exclusion Act. The poor were to be helped with charity, but only the deserving poor, and those who were unfamiliar with the rules of the middle-class world were not considered deserving.

Education in the social sciences, more travel and acquaintance with other people and customs, an awareness of world opinion, and more experience with the heterogeneity of the city have helped to broaden attitudes. Technical change has had its effect by moving people away from stagnant rural communities. Even these developments, though, might not have produced as much normative strain as is now apparent if our society had not already held sentiments about equality. The inconsistencies between ideal and reality have become abundantly clear and have led to an age of protest.

VALUE CONFLICT   Whereas normative strain refers to an inconsistency between norms and practice, value conflict refers to a real difference of opinion as to what the values should be. Value conflict is often involved in what is called deviant behavior, but it applies to other situations as well. Most Americans believe in democracy, a certain degree of equality of opportunity, the elective process, and other time-honored American ideals and customs. They do not, however, agree in values about poverty. Some think the poor should be given very little for fear they will be happy and content with social parasitism; others believe that poverty is seldom the individual's fault and that welfare payments should be sufficient to prevent degraded status. Similar conflicts occur in the next problem to be considered: population. Most Americans believe in birth control; some do not. Many Americans believe in almost any method to achieve birth control, including abortion. Many others believe this is wrong. Consequently, population issues become involved in value conflict.

Conflicts in values make it impossible to prescribe solutions to which all will agree. There are a few guidelines to take into consideration, though. Are proposals consistent with the needs of a modern industrial society, and will they bring a degree of normative consistency to the culture? Will the solutions leave the society less threatened by internal dissension; will its incongruities be reduced?

7 *Relationships between the majority group and racial and ethnic minorities have long constituted one of our outstanding normative incongruities. The United States takes pride in having been a place of refuge for large numbers of immigrants drifting in from many parts of the world, but why was the welcome so uneven? Why did the descendants of the "old immigration" object so strenuously to the "new immigration"? Why have some of the new immigrants objected to the northward and urban emigration of black Americans?*

What are the various accommodations that have come about between the black and white races in America? Is the next accommodation going to be one of full equality, or will American institutions continue to show racial separation and bias? How much real progress has been made by the black race in job equality, housing equality, and educational equality?

What special problems have been encountered by Hispanic Americans, especially those of Mexican descent? Just what is meant by the word "Chicano," and what are the characteristics of the present Chicano protest movement? Finally, what are the special problems of the American Indians? How are we to understand the ambiguous attitudes of many toward becoming full-fledged members of the white man's society? Do our values call for cultural homogeneity or for pluralism?

THE MYTH OF THE MELTING POT

At the base of the Statue of Liberty is an inscription in honor of the immigration policies of the United States, reading in part:

Give me your tired, your poor,
Your huddled masses yearning to breathe free,
The wretched refuse of your teeming shore,
Send these, the homeless tempest-tost to me,
I lift my lamp beside the golden door!

America has had a right to such an inscription on her Statue of Liberty, for her record of welcoming the stranger has been far more generous than is usual in this ethnocentric world. As with so many idealistic sentiments, though, there have been contradictions between ideal and reality. The "teeming masses" referred to have generally been those of Europe, not of Asia. Preferably, too, they have been those of Northern Europe, not of the South and East, and Protestant rather than Catholic or Jewish. In spite of the preferences made clear in the immigration acts of the 1920s, the gates have actually swung open at times for the latter groups as well as for the former, and many have found America to be their promised land.

A much more serious contradiction to the ideal of a welcoming "lamp beside the golden door" was the exclusion of certain other groups from the implied equalitarian philosophy of the goddess of liberty—the red, the brown, and the black. The red man was already here, but had to be driven away, exterminated, or starved on reservations. The Mexican occupied much of the Southwest, and was brought into the union by conquest. His numbers were swelled over the years by new entrants, but they were truly welcomed only for work that no one else wished to do. The Africans were brought in chains, welcomed only as chattels. For both red and black, a determined effort was made to exterminate all previous culture and, regardless of their external color, to make them culturally white.

Regardless of the fate of the excluded minorities, the people of Europe came by the millions—more than 40 million altogether, escaping hard times and oppression, escaping debtors' jail, escaping wars and conscription, and looking for a future for themselves and their children. America needed people to fill her vast domains, to build her railroads, and to man her factories and mines. However, even with the Europeans some were better received than others; and the people of Asia were eventually excluded. The recent emphasis on the problems of black America, and on the Indians and Chicanos, has superseded an interest in the immigrants from the Old World, but an examination of the immigrant record is still important. The record will tell us much about why the ideal of the great American melting pot applies to some but not to others. So, before turning to the more distressing problems of the racial minorities, it will be good to review the story of the Anglo-Saxons and the "white ethnics," for the mingling of ethnic streams was often turbulent, even when they flowed mainly from the same European source.

JOINING THE NEW SOCIETY

Joining the new society was not always easy even for the European, and especially not for the poor. The ocean passage was long and often accompanied by sicknesses that killed the aged and the weak. Many of the poor came over as indentured servants and had to work for years to pay off their passage. Sometimes their children likewise became indentured servants and had to work for masters until they reached their majority. After the indenture was paid, they were not always prosperous, and many had second thoughts about having left Europe. Generally however, the time came when financial improvement was possible for most of the early immigrants. They came largely from Northwestern Europe, resembled the dominant racial type already here, and were overwhelmingly Protestant. In the census of 1820, the United States numbered 9½ million Americans, one-fifth of whom were Negroes; most of the remainder were of Northern European descent. Indians were not counted.

There were a few early protests against the immigration of Quakers, Unitarians, and Catholics, and after the 1820s there were protests against the Germans and Italians who were migrating into the country. It was not until later in the century, however, that feelings against foreigners began to rise to fever pitch. As the pace of immigration increased, people became less willing to welcome "the wretched refuse of your teeming shore."[1]

American racists in the late nineteenth century listened to such writers as Madison Grant, author of *The Passing of the Great White Race*. From overseas, John Stuart Chamberlain of England and Gobineau of France were writing of the dangers of the "bastardization" of races by intermixtures. Their use of the word "race" was different from the meaning given the word today. To them, Mediterranean and Eastern European people were of different "race" from those of the West. It is also discouraging to know that learned authorities, including sociologists, anthropologists, and psychologists, were inclined to give credence to the racist view. A senate immigration commission of 1911 drew on the writing of the learned authorities in concluding:

> The new immigration as a class is far less intelligent than the old, approximately one-third of all those over 14 years of age when admitted being illiterate.[2]

Obviously, lack of education was being equated with lack of intelligence for the white ethnic groups. President Wilson did not agree with such an assumption and opposed restriction of immigration on a literacy basis.

THE OFFENSES OF THE NEW IMMIGRANTS Often the offenses of the new immigrants were merely those mentioned in an old Irish national song, ". . . And denouncing us for being what we are." What the new immigrants were was something a little different

---

[1]Peter I. Rose, *The Subject is Race*, Oxford University Press, London, 1968, pp. 21–25.
[2]*Ibid.*, p. 24.

An outcry arose against the so-called
New Immigrants from southern and
eastern Europe and Asia: they were
guilty of being different.

from the American tradition. Many were Catholics, a few were Jews; some were Greek, Russian, or Romanian Orthodox. Their customs and appearance seemed strange, and it was assumed that they could never become really Americanized. They were accused of coming just to save money so they could live prosperously back home. In fact, some did not intend to stay permanently. Many young immigrants from Greece and other parts of Eastern Europe came to earn dowry money so that their sisters could get married; only then could they marry with a clear conscience. Most eventually decided to stay and wrote home for brides to be sent to them. Some lived very frugally and had a hard time in the New World, but most Eastern Europeans were inured to poverty, knew how to live more cheaply than native Americans, and managed to flourish in the New World.

Seen from the point of view of the racist, the real offense of foreigners was simply "being what they are." From labor's viewpoint, their offense was often a willingness to work for low wages. Manufacturers and builders of railroads seemed like paragons of racial liberalism, urging more immigrants to come over. Laborers protested immigration, seeing immigrants merely as competitors for jobs. To this day a perceived economic threat can rouse hostilities against the outgroup, and there is a slight parallel between the urban migration of black Americans today and the transoceanic migration of Europeans in the past.

MELTING TEMPERATURES   W. Lloyd Warner and Leo Srole[3] have analyzed the rates of assimilation of various ethnic groups into American society and described the sharp contrasts in rate of "melting" in the great melting pot. To no one's surprise, those who were white, Protestant, and English-speaking faced the least difficulty in assimilation. Those who were white and Protestant, but non-English-speaking (Dutch, Germans, and Scandinavians) came in a close second. Behind them were those who spoke English but were Catholic, mainly Irish. Then came Czechs and Poles and various others who physically resembled the Western Europeans, but were neither English-speaking nor Protestant. After them were Southern Europeans and near Easterners, also non-Protestant, and darker in complexion. In the long run, it seemed that physical appearance was more important than cultural difference in the rate of absorption into American society. Afro-Americans, having been deprived of all their African cultural inheritance, were culturally part of America since the seventeenth century, and yet their real assimilation was still in the indefinite future.

It might be argued that the Chinese and Japanese, although of different appearance, have been well received at times; but animosity against them can be aroused easily. The antiforeign protests of labor in the late nineteenth century were aimed more at the Chinese than at any other minority, and they were the first people to be excluded from migration to the United States.

[3]W. Lloyd Warner and Leo Srole, *The Social Systems of American Ethnic Groups*, Yale University Press, New Haven, Conn., 1945, pp. 283–296.

THE INSCRUTABLE OCCIDENTAL   There is a whole body of Western literature filled with clichés about the mysterious, inscrutable Oriental. Surely the Occident must have been even more inscrutable to the Chinese who began to arrive in California during the Gold Rush. They had been told of opportunity and were welcomed to work in mines and on railroads. It soon developed, though, that they were highly competitive in both labor and business, and this fact changed the good, diligent men of the Far East into the "yellow menace." They were excluded from the country, and those who were already here were not allowed to bring their wives. In 1890 there were more than 100,000 Chinese men but only 3,868 Chinese women in California, and white America wondered why there was prostitution in Chinatown! The Chinese were not allowed to own land or to farm, nor were they allowed to enter any businesses except laundries and restaurants.[4]

The Japanese also came to California, and their arrival too was protested. They were partially excluded in 1907 and completely excluded in the 1920s. When World War II came, the Japanese had the honor of replacing the Chinese as the Oriental peril, even those who were United States citizens. For the safety of the West, they were incarcerated in relocation centers, sustaining hardship and heavy financial loss, while their sons fought for America in Europe. Oddly enough, in Hawaii, where Japanese were much more numerous than in California, they were left free. Inscrutable, indeed, is the Occidental!

THE UNEVEN RECORD

Even for those people who entered America years ago in answer to the call of opportunity, the record of success has been very uneven. One reason is connected with the reception given them, although the less preferred position has not been an absolute barrier to upward mobility. A fair percentage of Catholics succeeded quite well, even in the days when anti-Catholic prejudice was strong, and many Jews, Eastern Orthodox, and Buddhists have also succeeded in American life. An analysis of why some groups succeeded better than others may cast light on the current problems of the racial minorities whose opportunities seem so severely limited.

THE CRITERIA OF SUCCESS   Obviously, one criterion of success was being of the "right" type—culturally, socially, and religiously. Another important aid to success was possessing the right kind of skill for working in the new land. The type of skill required differed from time to time, and what was helpful in one period was not necessarily helpful in another. For example, the hardy European peasants were well equipped for facing the clearing and developing of land before the closing of the frontier. Many others, common laborers, found their strong backs greatly needed for building

[4]Charles Hillinger, "Why Chinese in U.S. Had to Be Laundrymen," *Los Angeles Times*, February 20, 1971, pp. 1, 24.

railroads, working the mines, and developing the resources of the country. Both farm experience and physical strength decreased in importance as the economy of America became less purely extractive and more urban-technical. In a later period of migration, soon after World War II, the people most strongly desired were scientists, engineers, rocket experts, and doctors. Manufacturers by that time could easily agree with union laborers in seeing no need to bring unskilled migrants into the system. Often today, the unskilled migrant entering the city is a black man, looking for the type of job that is disappearing.

There were definitely other criteria for success, which were closely connected with the values of the people arriving in the new land. Many of the early arrivals from Northwestern Europe represented the basic, hard-striving ethic that Max Weber describes in *The Protestant Ethic and the Spirit of Capitalism* (and which we shall say more about in Chapter 10). There were certain traits about the early Protestants that made them compulsive in their struggle to get ahead rapidly, but many non-Protestant people had similar values. A study by Bernard Rosen,[5] which compares several immigrant groups, finds the Jews and Greeks doing particularly well in achieving middle-class status, and finds also that they stress the values of success striving and independence training in the rearing of their children. Included in Rosen's study is the idea that a slight handicap acts almost as a goad to greater effort; an overwhelming handicap in prospects for the future leads to discouragement. The Jewish admonition to children was to "Remember you must do a little better than others in order to get the job, because you are a Jew." The much stronger hiring prejudice against the black has, in the past at least, been more of a discouragement than a goad to increased effort.

Other immigrants tilled the same American soil but reaped little harvest. Many early arrivals, even from the preferred British Isles, settled in marginal agricultural regions where a handful of their descendants continue to live in poverty. Many miners from Europe entered American coal mines, devoting their lives to an unwholesome task that has declined in manpower requirements. Generally speaking, the Europeans found America to be a land of opportunity. The opportunity for the later arrivals — the white ethnics — was not quite so great, however, as it had been for the original settlers.

> **By conducting a few interviews, see what you can find out about differences in success orientation of different minority groups. How demanding are they of their children in school work? What would they consider an adequate life goal?**

---

[5]Bernard Rosen, "Race, Ethnicity, and the Achievement Syndrome," *American Sociological Review*, vol. 24, pp. 47–60, August 1959.

_1968_

TOTAL POPULATION	200,000,000	
minus	50,000,000	Roman Catholics
minus	22,000,000	Negroes
minus	6,000,000	Jews
minus	4,000,000	Eastern Orthodox
minus	1,000,000	Oriental and Polynesian
minus	550,000	American Indians
minus	650,000	Others
equals	116,000,000	WASPs

THE WASPS Fears are sometimes expressed that the white ethnics (Italians and Greeks, Poles and Czechs, Jews, Armenians, and others) are increasing their economic stake in America and are about to "take over"; but the evidence indicates that the WASPs (White Anglo-Saxon Protestants) are still doing extremely well. The WASPs still are a majority of the population, although not so large a majority as in former times. The figures[6] for 1968 were approximately as presented in the above table.

Economically, the advantage of the WASPs is more impressive than their numerical majority. Of the directorships of the fifty largest corporations, 88 percent are held by WASPs. Of the ten largest commercial banks, WASPs hold 83 percent of the directorships; Roman Catholics come in second in directorships, and Jews third. Even the Bank of America, founded by Amadeo Giannini, and with many Italian holders, is said to be "infiltrated" by WASPs. The WASPs hold 80 percent of the directorships of the five largest insurance companies in America. Minority proprietors are common in clothing stores, entertainment, construction, and even in research laboratories, but the big, basic production industries are still largely WASP. Occasionally one encounters an anti-Jewish fanatic convinced that the Jews control most major industry. Actually, they make up only about 7 percent of big-business executives, although they constitute 3 percent of the population and 8 percent of college graduates.

For the WASP descendants it would be comforting to believe that the reason for the difference in economic power is a matter of basic ability. The prevailing opinion of the nineteenth century was that such superior ability was the obvious explanation. Recent investigators such as Mills (*The Power Elite*), Gabriel Kolko (*Wealth and Power in America*), G. William Domhoff (*Who Rules America?*) and Ferdinand Lundberg (*The Rich and the Super-rich*) present no such explanation. They perceive a class of inherited wealth descended from people who inhabited this land when the foundations of industrial empires were laid. More so than the equally able members of ethnic minority groups, their ancestors were "in on the ground floor." Mills presents evidence that the ascent from rags to riches has been growing more and more unlikely for nearly a century. Of the early arrivals who were allowed into the competition, the majority were white Anglo-Saxon Protestants. The other early arrivals—Negroes and the indigenous Indians—were not allowed into the game.

[6]Fletcher Knebel, "The Wasps: 1968," *Look*, pp. 69–72, 75, July 23, 1968.

THE FIRST BACKLASH The word "backlash" has come into common use since the days of strong racial protest movements, but it could easily have been applied at an earlier time to the opposition of the old-type Americans to the new immigration of the late nineteenth and early twentieth centuries. Antiforeign sentiment became so strong that restrictive laws were passed in the 1920s to stem the tide of immigrants. There had already been acts to exclude the Chinese and nearly all the Japanese, but the Immigration Act of 1924 was much more thoroughgoing. The aim was to keep the ethnic composition of the population the same as it had been in the past. Using surnames as an index to the lands of origin of the people already in the country, a quota system was adopted to limit the new immigrants on a national origins basis. By the new law, approximately half the people allowed to enter the United States each year were allocated to the British Isles and about one-quarter to Germany and the Netherlands. Eastern and Southern Europe had to be content with very small quotas, and Orientals were completely excluded. Although occasional modifications of the law were made in order to admit hardship cases after World War II and after the Hungarian uprising of 1956, the quota system remained the basic law until its revisions in 1965 and 1968.

The Immigration Act of 1924 had clearly negated the old American value of equality in favor of preferential treatment for Nordic and Protestant areas. The law reflected not so much a reversal of American opinion as a set of circumstances that allowed political control to be gained by the narrow, provincial elements of American society.[7] It was during a decade of backlash against United States involvement in world affairs, of uneasiness over the increasing urbanization of society, of fear of subversive influences creeping in from Russia, and of a new type of puritanism that insisted on preventing people from drinking. It was the decade of the Scopes Trial, aimed at defeating evolution in the name of fundamentalism. It was a decade of revival of the Ku Klux Klan in a form at least as much antiforeign and anti-Catholic as it was anti-Negro. Apparently reactions against the inevitable onrush of world events can, under some circumstances, call forth authoritarian sentiments that have long lain dormant.

THE ETHNICS AND THE NEW BACKLASH Ironically, a new kind of backlash is said to exist among the very ethnic minorities who were once the victims of a backlash that

---

Make an opinion survey of racial attitudes. Do you find age and social-class differences? Do you find antiblack prejudice among white ethnic groups? Are the white ethnics of your study actually any worse than the WASPs for prejudice?

---

[7]Seymour Martin Lipset, *The First New Nation*, Doubleday & Company, Inc., Garden City, N.Y., 1967, pp. 289–301.

led to discriminatory immigration laws. In their case there is uneasiness about the entry of the black racial minority into the competitive labor market. Such anxiety is heightened by the presence of fairly frequent racial riots. At such a time it is sobering to recall that the Irish, Poles, and other minorities have had their episodes of violence. In 1870 and 1871 the Irish turned New York City into a battleground between the Orangists and the Catholics,[8] and the Molly Maguires employed terrorism in their labor demands of the 1860s and 1870s. When feelings run high, discrimination occurs, and hopes for progress are thwarted, any group can riot.

Another idea that bothers white ethnics (and some WASPs) almost as much as the threat to jobs is a feeling about traditional success striving. Many whites see themselves as having started poor, but nevertheless having worked their way up in a competitive labor market without special legislation or special aid. Why, they ask, can't the black minority of the poor urban ghettos do the same? To answer that question requires a glance at black history and at the present condition of our labor requirements.

RELUCTANT JOINERS: BLACK AMERICA

More than any other racial minority, the Negro points out the mythological element in the great melting pot story. To a very great degree the same can be said for two other minorities, the Mexicans and Indians. All three are distinct from the minorities we have previously discussed. Throughout most of American history the Indians have not been admitted into the dominant society, the Mexicans have lived only on its fringes, and the blacks have lived only in a symbiotic relationship to it, working for it but not belonging to it. All three groups must be examined before leaving the myth of the melting pot, but the case of the black Americans must be examined first, partly because of their vast numbers and partly because they alone endured centuries of slavery.

THE STAGES OF ACCOMMODATION Accommodation, in its sociological meaning, is any arrangement for reducing conflict between groups that are potential enemies. A slave-to-master relationship is one kind of accommodation, the most unequal kind possible, in which the potential conflict is settled by giving all the force and all the rights to one side. The story of slavery in America is sufficiently well known to need little repetition, except to point out that it was an unusually severe type of slavery. In many slave systems encountered in the world slave status is not absolute; even the slave is given certain rights, such as the right to marry, and sometimes even the right for his children to be born free. In the earliest days of American experience, there were actually such limitations on slavery, and the slave condition was not expected to be eternal. As slavery became increasingly profitable, however, it

---

[8]Thomas N. Brown, *Irish-American Nationalism, 1870–1900*, J. B. Lippincott Company, Philadelphia, 1966, p. 80.

The second stage of accommodation:
debased status.

became increasingly permanent and absolute. The field hand in particular had no rights whatever—no right to family life, to eventual freedom, or to learn to read and write; and various publications gave good advice on how to keep him firmly under control. The beginnings of social-class differentiation within the slave system arose with household domestics and craftsmen, who had a better chance at life than the field hands. Their descendants, along with those of freed slaves, were to be the forerunners of what black sociologist E. Franklin Frazier called the black bourgeoisie.

With the end of the Civil War and the beginning of freedom, it looked as though an entirely new type of accommodation was coming about, one of both freedom and equality. In the early years of freedom, the black man could vote, ride the trains, and enter any part of town he wished. In fact, there was a period of twenty years when it seemed that interracial feelings were improving and equality was near.[9] Then in rapid succession the Jim Crow laws were passed, to help divide poor whites from poor blacks and prevent an overturn of the old upper class of the South. In many states the black man had to ride in separate train compartments, keep off the sidewalk, stay out of public parks, avoid white restaurants and theaters, stay out of white quarters of town after dark, avoid glancing at white women, and learn to say, "Yes sir, you're right, boss," regardless of how humiliating the circumstances. He could not be a man, but must be called "boy" all his life.

Nevertheless, the chains had been partly broken. A few blacks were able to get an education. Men left the South and found de facto rather than de jure segregation and situations that were more bewildering than ever, but not quite so hopeless. Events occurred that began to upset the accommodation. Two world wars took place, and black troops saw other parts of the world and other conditions. Especially in World War II, many knew a temporary taste of prosperity and hope for the future, and all heard lectures on the evils of racism overseas, in spite of the fact that they were fighting in a segregated, racist army. The irony of their situation became more and more apparent and galling. "There comes a time when people get tired," Martin Luther King said; "We are tired of being segregated and humiliated, tired of being kicked about by the brutal feet of oppression."[10] The Montgomery Bus Strike had started, and it signaled the beginning of a revolt which has not yet died.

Since 1952, leadership and methods have changed. From Dr. King's completely nonviolent methods there was a change to occasional violence. A nonviolent method is particularly infuriating to some of the opposition. Nonviolence, as Mahatma Gandhi once observed, depends on an opposition with a sense of humanity, and not all the white opposition had a sense of humanity. Several of the oustanding pacifist leaders were assassinated, and an escalation of passions took place.

Eventually the American public became accustomed to riots in the cities, to Eldridge Cleaver and H. Rap Brown, to Malcolm X and the separatist Black Muslims,

[9]C. Vann Woodward, *The Strange Case of Jim Crow*, Oxford University Press, New York, 1966.
[10]Quoted in Louis Lomax, *The Negro Revolt*, Signet Books, New American Library, Inc., New York, 1962, pp. 101–102.

and to the violent Black Panthers. There was talk about a white backlash — something that was measurable to a degree, but hardly enough to swing elections in most parts of the country. There came also the cry of Black Power, and the very words were electrifying to many black Americans, even though the expression was never clearly defined.

THE SEARCH FOR IDENTITY   One reason the cry of Black Power had considerable force for rallying support was that it gave a sense of importance to people who had long suffered ego destruction. The works of such black writers as Richard Wright, James Baldwin, and Ralph Ellison are full of references to the problems of identity. One can seek a feeling of identity in various ways. He can look to his own achievements and to those of people in his group. He can look to the past and identify with his ancestors and the land of his origins, or he can turn inward, developing his intellectual and contemplative powers. But in none of these ways could the black American find his sense of identity. Accomplishments were seldom possible, and his history was erased or distorted. He could not look backward to Africa, for all his roots had been torn out in the days of slavery, and old lineages, clans, and tribes were as foreign to him as they were to the white world that surrounded him. Spiritual contemplation was not admired in American society. Power was respected, however. One has a sense of identity if he can make his presence felt. For the black man with the strongest sense of the mark of oppression, a new identity came through violent protest.

THE NEXT ACCOMMODATION   In the years of protest much was won. The poll tax was brushed aside by court decision, and so was most of the Jim Crow legislation, and black enrollment in colleges began to rise. New civil rights organizations supplemented the old ones, and what had once been largely black bourgeoisie organizations now became mass movements of the poor and lower class. White leadership of civil rights organizations, which had generally been well meaning but too patronizing, was replaced by black leadership in all cases. A new identity, a new drive, and new purposes were found.

In spite of progress, dangers remained. The country began to argue increasingly about whether busing should be used to integrate the schools or whether children should always be sent to schools in their own neighborhoods. The observant realized that the whole argument evaded a much more embarrassing question: why were all the neighborhoods segregated? Was not the society basically hypocritical as long as such segregation not only existed but continued to grow? How could educational, economic, and occupational integration come about while the blacks continued to be segregated in the ghetto?

The institutionalized segregation of neighborhoods is very costly to society. The present course is leading to what the President's Commission on Violence characterized as "two societies, separate and unequal." What the commission should

Percent of persons leaving school as high school graduates, 1960–1968

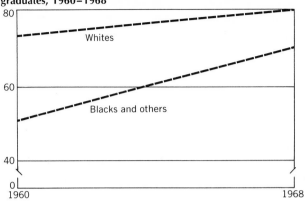

Unemployment rates by race for persons dropping out or graduating from high school

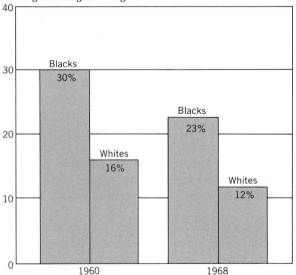

have added is that we have always had two societies, separate and unequal. The first inequality was slavery; the second was (and to a degree still is) Jim Crowism; the third accommodation is that of the ghetto and its attendant deprivations, and of essentially racist institutions. The real fear for the black man in modern American society is that the third accommodation will have the degree of permanence that the first and second have had. One of the dangers is the argument that says, "Look, you've got a Civil Rights Act, the right to go to school, and the right to vote. What more do you want?"

THE INSTITUTIONS OF RACISM   Some of the worst atrocities of racism have declined; there is a growing white consensus that blacks are not, after all, inherently inferior and subhuman. A majority at least speak the sentiments of racial equality, especially a majority of the young, and most of those who are somewhat racist do not consciously realize they are. Nevertheless, ingrained habit and institutionalization continue to be racist. Economically, as we have seen, the real power is in the hands of whites, generally of Anglo-Saxon descent, but it is not only in the main economic power centers that the black man has no foothold. He lives in run-down ghettos that are owned mainly by whites, and he usually buys at stores with white proprietors. In proportion to their share of the population, black Americans own only one-tenth as many businesses as do whites, and what they own are mainly very small concerns. The reason does not seem to be bad management; the Small Business Administration has been very successful in collecting on loans to black proprietors.[11] For the most part such businesses are located in poor areas, patronized only by the poor, and must buy wholesale from major producers—all white—and generally must pay very high interest rates on loans. Furthermore, most starts in small businesses have occurred at a time when most small proprietors, black or white, have a hard time continuing to exist.

For the consumer the same kind of economic disadvantage is present and is well documented in David Caplovitz's *The Poor Pay More.* Prices are higher, interest rates are much higher, and the goods are more apt to be shoddy. An FTC study found that an item selling wholesale for $100 would sell in a high quality store for $165, but in a store in a low-income area for $250.[12]

Employment practices continue to discriminate against blacks. In a study of large corporations in fifteen Northern cities it was found that blacks held 20 percent of the unskilled jobs, but only 2 percent of the skilled jobs and 1 percent of pro-

---

Have you been discriminated against because of race, color, or creed?
Write to Equal Employment Opportunity Commission, Department of
Labor, Washington, D.C., if it is a job covered by federal law.
Otherwise take your case to a minority group organization such as
NAACP.

---

[11]Louis L. Knowles and Kenneth Prewitt (eds.), *Institutional Racism in America*, Prentice-Hall, Inc., Englewood Cliffs, N.J., 1969, pp. 16–17.
[12]*Ibid.*, p. 25.

fessional positions. The same study found that 40 percent of black students attended schools that were at least forty years old, whereas only 15 percent of whites attended schools of equal age.[13] The ward politician in the black community finds it hard to do anything for his area because he must buck strong white economic interests. The previous figure, based on data from the U.S. Census Bureau, compares the amount of black versus white people graduating from high school and the unemployment rates of various races if they do not complete high school. More and more blacks are graduating from high school, but the unemployment rate between blacks and whites remains the same—twice as many black dropouts as whites remain unemployed. The police watch the boys of the ghetto area more closely, frisk them more frequently, and break up their gatherings more than in other parts of town.

Not only are the schools, on the average, of poorer quality, but the black child finds himself left out of the reading books, and especially out of the history books. A study in California found some schools still using history books that failed to mention a single Negro after the time of the Civil War. This is the type of neglect that has led to black student demands for courses in black history. They are incensed that more than 20 million Americans should be treated as though they have no historical existence.

The officer corps of the armed forces remains overwhelmingly white, especially in the Navy and Marines. Blacks make up 12 percent of the Marine Corps, but just over 1 percent of its officers. In the Navy, they fare about the same; in the Air Force slightly better. The Army is the branch of the service that comes closest to having black officers in the same proportion as black enlisted men, but even there the officers number only about one-third as many (11.2 percent enlisted men to 3.2 percent officers).[14]

Something needs to be said, too, about the political institution, where the legal right to vote does not always mean what it seems to mean. Gerrymandering is accomplished in many areas to dilute the voting power of the blacks. This has been done in the Los Angeles area to keep down the electoral effectiveness of the Mexican-Americans as well.[15] In Southern states there is occasionally still a fear of possible violence, but more frequently blacks are kept from the polls by fear of economic reprisals. Wherever it is completely clear that their jobs depend upon staying on good terms with white racists, the percentage of voters is quite low. Yet another problem is that the national political party organizations tend to be exclusive clubs. The delegates with the decision-making power are all white.

In spite of this fact, considerable political progress has been made. 1970 saw a 22-percent increase from the previous year in the number of black officeholders in the United States, and a fourfold increase compared to 1966. Even with this

[13]David Boesel et al., "White Institutions and Black Rage," *Transaction*, vol. 6, pp. 24–30, March 1969.
[14]Ray Cromley, "Military: Too Little, Too Late," *Bakersfield Californian*, p. 23, February 18, 1971.
[15]Knowles and Prewitt, *op. cit.*, pp. 52–53.

dramatic increase, blacks still held only 1 percent of the public offices in America in 1970, although they make up 11 percent of the population.[16]

No institution remains more rigidly segregated than the church. Proper sentiments are often expressed, ministers meet in integrated ministerial associations, church conventions pass resolutions in support of an integrated society, but on Sunday morning, black is black and white is white.

THE CONTRAST   The discussion of the institutions of racism fairly well answers the question, "Why haven't the black Americans succeeded as well as the white ethnics, and why do they still complain?" It is only in recent years that the black has even come close to educational equality and the opportunity to enter the competition of American life. He has entered the competitive market for jobs at a time when high skills are required, but he is at a disadvantage in attaining those skills. He carries a burden of generations of educational and cultural neglect, and of discrimination that has embittered him and vitiated his creative energies. His subcultural background has provided him with neither the knowledge, the habits, nor the strongly competitive attitudes in monetary matters that are needed for success in the capitalistic world. Against these barriers he has done remarkably well, but he must still struggle in education, in politics, in community action, and in propaganda in his own behalf or be stopped at what has been described as the third level of accommodation—a step above Jim Crow, but a long step below equality.

RELUCTANT JOINERS: THE BROWN AND THE RED

The black man was brought to America in chains and slavery. The Indians were equally reluctant to join our society, having been brought in largely by conquest and treaty violation. The Mexicans are of several types historically, differing from those who were already in the Southwest before acquisition of the territories from Mexico to those who have entered the country of their own volition. For them the reluctance is not so much over the joining of the society as over being totally engulfed in it. They would like to retain an identity of their own. Just as the blacks call their man who is too deeply involved with the whites an "Uncle Tom," so do the Mexicans sometimes use the word "Tio Tomás," or "Tio Taco," and the Indians sometimes refer to an "Uncle Tom-ahawk." Sometimes the Indian who is too thoroughly assimilated into the white society is called an "apple"—red on the outside but white on the inside. The meaning of all such terms of derision is quite clear: there are differences of opinion as to how far assimilation should go. Does one want to leave all that is African, all that is Mexican, or all that is American Indian and become a total *asimilado*?

[16]"Blacks Show 22 Percent Rise in Officeholders," *Los Angeles Times*, May 3, 1971, Part 1A, p. 6.

La huelga **(the strike) of California grapeworkers brings a new sense of Chicano solidarity and power. A protest march to Sacramento.**

WHO ARE THE CHICANOS? Choosing the right terminology for the American of African descent is difficult, but for the American of Mexican descent it is nearly impossible. Such terms as "Spanish-American," "Spanish-speaking," "Mexican-American," "Hispanic," and "Spanish-surnamed," have all been used and would be a little more inclusive than the term "Chicano"; but they are not liked by the young militants. To some members of the younger generation the older names seem to imply that a polite euphemism must be found for "Mexican," as though the word itself denotes some type of inferiority.[17] Many Americans of Mexican descent refuse to abandon Mexican in favor of Hispanic and even prefer the newer word "Chicano." The word "Chicano" omits many people of Hispanic culture—Puerto Ricans, Cubans, and other Latin Americans. It is not acceptable to the descendants of many old Spanish families of the Southwest or to many middle-class business and professional people of Mexican descent; but it is the preferred term for a significant group and is coming into wide use. As one Chicano student states the case:

> It used to be that it was a put-down for a Mexican-American to be called a Chicano, but today the new breed Mexican-American has learned to identify with the adjective in much the same way the Afro-American has learned to identify with Black. It's their thing, and because it's their thing they are proud of it.[18]

[17]Ruben Salazar, "Who is a Chicano?" *Los Angeles Times*, February 2, 1970, Sec. 2, p. 1.
[18]Angel Campos, Letter in *The Renegade*, Bakersfield College, Bakersfield, Calif., March 5, 1971.

Those who call themselves Chicano identify more with the poor than with the middle class. Their parents have brought some of the values of the Mexican peasant—a strong sense of family, and a sense of manhood that comes from the type of work which makes men hard and muscular, but wears them out early. In many cases they are farm laborers, especially those most recently arrived from Mexico, and a life in the fields starts in childhood. For those living in the cities, segregation is prominent and increasing, unemployment rates are high, and school dropout rates are equally high. The average educational level for the younger generation is tenth grade, although it is somewhat higher in New Mexico and California and lower in Texas.

EDUCATIONAL PROBLEMS In older generations, when race was taken for granted as an explanation for all cultural differences, little thought was given to the fact that the Chicano child did not generally do well in school. At times his deficiency in English has been a convenient excuse for segregation, and such segregation has served mainly to perpetuate a set of values that could fit him for nothing but lower-class existence. To this day, he is still stereotyped as a candidate for the stable lower class, or at best lower-middle class, and is counseled into programs that terminate with a high school diploma but are not intended for college preparation.

The explanation for a rather poor record in school, which was once blunt racism, has now changed to bilingualism. George I. Sanchez points out the partial falsity of such an explanation.[19] Many ethnic groups have done well in school in spite of bilingualism. If a foreign language is learned at the right time it can even increase a person's perception of language and linguistic principles and broaden his thought patterns. If, however, the child's mother tongue is looked upon with scorn, not understood by his teachers, forbidden, and treated as though it is purely an instrument for expressing evil thoughts, bilingualism presents serious problems. It is also well known that a person can best learn the art of reading if he first learns to read in his native language rather than in his acquired language. For the Chicano, the learning process is reversed, just as it is for American Indians.

Sanchez further says, however, that even though the language problem is important, even more important problems are often ignored. In Texas, where the socioeconomic condition of the Chicano is particularly depressed, the Mexican child needs far more attention to enculturation into American ways. A good school for such children should keep classroom size to a minimum and employ teachers who understand Spanish and are familiar with the Chicano subculture. They should understand the kinship loyalties that tend to hold him close to his own culture and should encourage him to think of improving conditions for his people, not just for himself. Too often the individualized Yankee norm is taught: try to rise above the level of your family and friends. To people of one ethnic background this might seem admirable; to others it is the mark of an ingrate, if not a traitor.

[19] George I. Sanchez, "History, Culture, and Education," in Julian Samora (ed.), *La Raza, Forgotten Americans*, University of Notre Dame Press, Notre Dame, Ind., 1966, pp. 1–24.

Above all, a school system should not leave the Chicano out of its books and its accounts of history and it should not vilify his ancestors for having tried to defend their territory against Yankee imperialism. It also should not judge him and start him on the path to a "failure syndrome" by assigning him an IQ score based on tests in a language he understands poorly.

CONFLICTING CULTURAL BACKGROUNDS Organizations of a political activist type have been formed by the Chicanos, although there have been some strongly retarding problems. One problem is that the people are not all of a kind. Some are strongly Americanized; at the opposite pole are those newly arrived from Mexico and speaking little or no English. There are also old rural communities, dating back to Mexican rule in the West, where leadership has been of a traditional patronlike type, and where the family is so strong as to virtually preclude other types of organization. One Texan community study says, for example:

> The strength with which a person is bound to his family so overshadows all other bonds in importance that it contributes to the atomistic nature of the neighborhood. Socially, if not spacially, each household stands alone.[20]

Some Mexican leaders are offended by studies done by Anglo-American social scientists; these studies tend to picture Mexicans as of one particular cultural and psychological type or as uniformly tradition-bound people. Octavio Romano and Rudolfo Gonzales both stress the multiple origins of *La Raza* and the cultural range from tradition to modern sophistication. There was, for example, a great exodus of Mexican intellectuals following the Mexican Revolution of 1911; the exodus brought in a type very different from the peasant who has been studied so much by anthropologists. An interesting contrast in interpretation is offered by two translations of a fairly common Chicano saying. The American anthropologist William Madsen[21] explains the term *cada cabeza es un mundo* (literally, "each head is a world,") to imply the Chicano's sensitive nature, his resistance to probing questions, and his right to his own opinion. Octavio Romano[22] interprets the saying quite differently. He relates it to the great multiplicity of the Chicano culture, but not to any distinctive psychological patterns. The people came from all parts of Mexico and from all classes, the exploited and the exploiters, the educated and the illiterate, Michoacans, Chihuahuans, and Aztecans, the Hispanicized and the pure Indian; each has his own mind. He cites the expression in connection with the movement to get all together as part of *La Raza*—no longer *cada cabeza un mundo*. Parenthetically, it should be

[20]Arthur J. Rubel, *Across the Tracks: Mexican-Americans in a Texas City*, University of Texas Press, Austin, p. 25.
[21]William Madsen, *The Mexican-Americans of South Texas*, Holt, Rinehart and Winston, Inc., New York, 1964, pp. 20–21.
[22]Octavio Romano, "The Historical and Intellectual Presence of Mexican Americans," *El Grito*, vol. 2, p. 37, Winter 1969.

added that many Chicanos have never heard the expression, a good illustration of wide cultural differences.

THE COMPLAINTS SUMMARIZED Some of the most common complaints have already been mentioned: treating Spanish as an inferior language, judging children on the basis of unfair IQ tests, and segregating them educationally on that basis. All that has been said about the institutions of racism for blacks applies to a degree to the Chicanos. There is de facto segregation of the Chicanos into their own barrios; there is no treatment of Chicano culture or history; there are complaints of unfair treatment by police and courts; like the black, the Chicano tends to be the last hired and the first fired; his children go to the oldest schools in the district; and his sons die in disproportionate numbers in the war in Asia. He also feels himself to be left in an ambiguous position between citizen and foreigner.

This last complaint needs a little elaboration, for it is true that the more militant Chicanos want a certain degree of cultural self-determinism, but not as foreigners. Their feeling is that the goddess of liberty can accept "your tired, your poor" despite considerable cultural differences. Defining how far cultural differences can extend in a nation of nations is a problem for all Americans; finding the right fit between pride in *La Raza* and in United States citizenship is a problem for the Chicano. He wishes to be judged as a man, not as an ethnic category, but at the same time he does not want to be completely cut adrift from his mother culture.

Chicano organizations are becoming much more active now than formerly in trying to achieve economic advancement for their people, while retaining an interest in their culture. The college entrance rate for Chicanos is on the increase, although still inadequate. The University of California at Los Angeles had only 300 Mexican-American students as of 1970, but even this number represented an increase from the mere 79 of 1967. The number (less than one-tenth of 1 percent in a state where people of Spanish surnames number nearly 10 percent of the population) is pitifully small, but it still represents progress. The Los Angeles situation is typical. Throughout the Southwestern states there is a rising demand for more access to college and jobs and, it seems, the beginning of a new identity and a new spirit and militancy.[23]

THE RED DILEMMA We have long been told that the "vanishing American" is no longer vanishing, but many Indians feel that they are vanishing in a spiritual sense. Even in a physical sense the plight of the Indian is extremely bad. In both educational achievement and in income he ranks far below either the black or the Chicano. The average income of the Navajo reservation family is just under half the government's official poverty level.

There has not been the close identity between Mexicans and Indians in the United States that is sometimes found in Mexico. South of the border, those leaders

[23]Editors of *Newsweek*, "Tio Taco is Dead," *Newsweek*, pp. 22–25, June 29, 1970.

who were most Indian are often the most idolized—Juarez, Zapata, and even Pancho Villa. In the United States there is hardly a barrio that doesn't have someone nicknamed "El Indio." There is a resentment of the way Indians are depicted in American movies, but it is only recently that there have been attempts to make this a common cause.[24] Although many Anglo-Americans feel a strong sense of sympathy for the Indian, no Indian leader has ever been elevated to the rank of national hero in the United States.

WARPED HISTORY The story of the American Indian is an often told tale, but it has been told with little attention to detail. Most Americans know that the Indian was somehow cheated out of his land, that he was moved westward, that he was defeated and broken in spirit. We know the fight was an uneven one, with heavier force of manpower, weapons, and technology on one side than on the other, but we like to think it was otherwise fair combat, and often our histories lead us to think it was. Histories are more likely to be written by winners than by losers and to give an implied blessing to superior power. "History, in its written version," says the Mexican writer Miguel Méndez, "is a vulgar prostitute who disdains those people who do not adore gold and power."[25] Hence, many details have been omitted. The Negro has been forgotten, the Mexican has been vilified, and the Indian has been recorded as a strange combination of romantic, villain, and madman. There have, it is true, been historians who have told the story truthfully, but the garbled folk history that comes through our children's texts and motion pictures fits the characterization Méndez assigns it. Nothing is told of giving the Indians blankets contaminated with smallpox germs and of the indiscriminate killing of women and children as late as 1890.

In the tragic episode known as the Trail of Tears, in which five civilized tribes were exiled to what is now Oklahoma, 4,000 Indians died from exhaustion and cold on the way. Yet President van Buren told the nation on December 3, 1838, "The measures [for Indian removal] have had the happiest effects . . . . The Cherokees have migrated without any apparent reluctance." To this day aged Cherokees, Creeks, and Choktaws tell their grandchildren what their grandparents told them—that history is a lie.[26] The president did not bother to tell the country, either, that Chief Osceola was seized while approaching under a flag of truce and died of mistreatment.

White children learn the history of Kit Carson, the wilderness scout, the hero, the knight of the West. Aged Navajos tell their grandchildren how he encouraged the Utes to plunder their land and steal their women and their horses, and how his troops destroyed their wheat and corn and their animals until they were starved into surrender and captivity. Then there was the Long Walk to Fort Sumner, 300 miles away, where preparations for detention were so poor that many died, and the funds

[24]Romano, op. cit., pp. 37–39.

[25]Miguel Méndez, "Tragedias del Noroeste," El Grito, vol. 2, Winter 1969. "La historia en su version escrita es una puta vulgar. Desdena a los pueblos que no otorgan la lisonja del oro y del poder."

[26]John Collier, Indians of the Americas, Mentor Books, New American Library, Inc., New York, 1957, p. 125.

appropriated for their care were swindled. After four years in captivity they were sent home to a land in ruins, where they spent more years in malnutrition and misery.[27]

Soon, however, the government showed its protective hand and supplied sheep and seed. A treaty was drawn up making the Navajos (the same as nearly all other Indians) wards of the state. If they would obey and let the government think for them, plan for them, show them how absurd their religion and their customs were, and send their children off to school to learn to develop contempt for their parents, then all would be well. There is no better way to create a dependency syndrome; many Navajos are now on welfare, as are many tribes. At first the Indians hid all their best children and sent only the lame, the unintelligent, and the misfits to school; but eventually more and more children were rounded up by the authorities and sent to school. A society that told all immigrants they could practice their own religion set about determinedly to stamp out the Navajo religion. When the religious education succeeded, and a young Navajo "followed the Jesus trail," he would find himself rejected by his own people, but still regarded as a "dirty Indian" by the whites.

It must be admitted that the Navajos had been raiders and a nuisance to the surrounding Pueblos and the whites. The Pueblo Indians had never made any trouble, and were not even supposed to be considered wards of the state, according to Supreme Court rulings in 1910. Yet every possible type of deception was used by white raiders to try to seize the Pueblo lands. Bills were introduced before Congress in the 1920s to take away Pueblo rights and to make their priests subject to arrest for subversion. The harmless Pueblos were denounced as a "red menace" — possibly because of their rather communal way of life. Fundamentalist churches were aligned against them on grounds that they were godless heathens, and false stories were spread to the effect that their ceremonies were somehow pornographic and evil. The Pueblos, for the first time in more than 200 years, all united, hired lawyers, and started the first modern counterattack. They had been swindled of 16 million acres of their land, and when they started suit for their rights, all the governing body of the Taos tribe were imprisoned for "religious crimes" — a strange type of crime to reconcile with the First Amendment to the Constitution. Finally Representative Frear of Wisconsin sought to investigate their "animalistic rites," and found they had been lied about. He and Senator King of Utah and Senator "Fighting Bob" LaFollette of Wisconsin championed the Indians and a unique victory was won. In 1933 their lands and religious liberty were restored.[28]

THE LEGACY OF HISTORY These historical episodes may seem a digression, but they have an important purpose. It is necessary to know the legacy of bitterness that has been left, or the white man can never understand the phenomenon of "blanket Indians" — Indians who are given all the blessings of being dragged away from home to a white man's school, but eventually return home to their old people and their old

[27]Ruth M. Underhill, *The Navajos*, University of Oklahoma Press, Norman, 1956, chaps. 8 and 9.
[28]Collier, *op. cit.*, pp. 143–154.

Led by young Mohawk Richard Oakes, Indians showed revived spirit by temporary seizure of Alcatraz Island for use as an Indian culture center.

ways. It is necessary to know a little history to know why the Indian has not jumped eagerly at the white man's ways, why 40,000 Navajos have never learned English, and why they look with hostility at the tourists who drive through their reservation and stare at them as though they are animals in a zoo. It helps to explain why they have resisted the white man's ways, even though their economic future would seem to require such a solution.

This does not mean that all people who have worked with the Indians have been either stupid or villainous. Many have meant well, and there are Indians who have seen the benefit of becoming urbanized and have been glad for what education has been supplied. The majority, however, even when necessity drives them to Chicago, or Los Angeles, or Oakland, are lonely persons, torn from their people and their gods, but far from being assimilated. They seek the company of their own kind, and they seek a new identity that is neither that of their autochthonous origin nor of modern urban America.

THE NEW MOOD   White America has been a little shocked at such episodes as the seizure of Alcatraz. A people long considered to be either dead or changed into whites is again making its presence known. Stan Steiner was the first to write a book on

Red Power.[29] Like all power terms, it sounds a little threatening, but the essence of Red Power is the idea of allowing the Indian to control his own destiny, to bring to a long delayed halt his status as a ward of the state. The young warriors returning after World War II expected a new status in American life. They had been praised for their service to their country. Then they had returned to find themselves "not the last hired and the first fired, but never hired at all."[30] They found the old complaints about the Indian who had tried to become white, but found no place. They witnessed a case or two of Indian soldiers being refused burial in white cemeteries. They found that even the Indians with high academic potential were likely to drop out of college, not for intellectual, but for emotional reasons. They believe that the Indian has a compelling need for an independent identity, one that will fit him for the modern world but not swallow him into the white society.

At one location in the land of the Navajos—Rough Rock, near the center of the reservation—is a school completely run by the Indians. There are other persons present, but they too speak Navajo and have a feeling for the traditional ways of the tribe. There the children can learn in a manner that acquaints them with the needs of the white man's world, but does not alienate them from their essential Indian identity. There they can learn to read and write both English and Navajo. There they can practice Christianity if they wish, but they need not be told that the sacred views of their ancestors are madness or evil. They can gaze in reverence at the sacred San Francisco Peaks; they can learn the legends of First Man and First Woman, and of Changing Woman—the inner being of the earth, who gives life and renews life. They can learn the healing ceremonies of the Beauty Way and the Enemy Way, and what it is like to live in harmony with the holy people and all the wondrous spirits their ancestors have known.[31] They can belong to the land that is sacred to them and have some type of psychological moorings, regardless of how far the search for jobs may take them. They can eventually find a place in the modern world, but in their own way and at their own pace.

The Census Bureau reports an interesting sidelight to the new feeling of Indian pride. The reported Indian population increased from 523,000 in 1960 to 792,000 in 1970, a jump of more than 50 percent. Census Bureau officials speculate that many people are now reporting the Indian identity they once tried to hide.

THE PROSPECTS

Over a period of years the distinctions between the Anglo-Americans and the white ethnics have become less important. Legal discriminations against Chinese and Japanese have been removed, and hard feelings have declined. Antisemitism is also on the decline, although it still exists among extremists of both the right and left wing. Un-

[29]Stan Steiner *The New Indians*, Dell Publishing, Inc., New York, 1968.
[30]*Ibid.*, p. 24.
[31]The Long Walk," National Education Television documentary, 1969.

less international events or some other crisis causes an unpredictable shift in public opinion, we can probably look forward to a continuing decline in prejudice against most of the groups included under the term "new immigrants."

The distinction between the majority group and the three minorities just discussed, however, continues. Although public opinion polls show a marked decline in prejudiced beliefs, the actual pattern of segregated neighborhoods, churches, clubs, recreation halls, and schools makes the society look much more racist than stated opinions would indicate. The three major minorities, although they have their differences, have a number of problems in common.

COMMON GROUND   Mexicans, Negroes, and Indians all find difficulties in the attempt to follow the upward-mobility pattern of both the old immigrants and the new. They see a need for intense effort in education, and they are calling for an education that not only prepares them for economic life, but gives their people dignity and pride. They are all entering an economy that has a decreasing need for the untrained and that, because of its pace of change, makes the catching-up process in technical and scientific fields more and more difficult. They all have a backlog of bitterness that only time, social justice, and new opportunities can heal. They are all tempted to confrontation, sometimes of a violent sort, if they find no other way of making their grievances known.

Collectively, however, the three minorities are a potent political force. The future depends upon their learning to use their political and legal powers more fully in order to overcome the craftiness and wiles of some whites and the complacency of others. The future depends also on the majority group's willingness to understand the plight of the minorities and not block their progress by neglect, indifference, or parsimoniousness about supplying education and the other necessary opportunities.

SUGGESTED READINGS

Knowles, Louis L., and Kenneth Prewitt (eds.): *Institutional Racism in America*, Prentice-Hall, Inc., Englewood Cliffs, N.J., 1969.

Knowles and Prewitt show us that even though public attitudes have changed, the consequences of ingrained institutional policy keep our society strongly racist in such areas as education, justice, politics, health care, housing, and employment.

> **If you live in a big, multiracial city, work with minority-group children through a Head Start or school tutorial program.**

Pettigrew, Thomas F.: *Racially Separate or Together*, McGraw-Hill Book Company, New York, 1971.

> *One of several books by Pettigrew, a social psychologist of great knowledge and experience and strong moral conviction about the need for a united society. Covers housing, police relations, education, attitudes, and possibilities for political action.*

Samora, Julian (ed.): *La Raza: Forgotten Americans*, University of Notre Dame Press, Notre Dame, Ind., 1966.

> *Many books are now appearing on the problems of the Mexican-Americans. This is one of the best, especially on educational problems and employment. It strips away considerable mythology about the complacent Mexican. (Not available in paperback.)*

Steiner, Stan: *The New Indians*, Dell Publishing Co., Inc., New York, 1968.

> *A loosely structured account of travels, meetings, and conversations with Indians in many parts of the United States. Steiner allows the Indians to explain their attitudes in their own terms. The book gives a feeling of the emergence of a new awareness and self-concept.*

Young, Whitney M., Jr.: *Beyond Racism*, McGraw-Hill Book Company, New York, 1971.

> *An eloquent plea for an open society by the late president of the Urban League. Presents a program of action for government and individuals to ensure democracy, justice, and equality.*

Magazines: people unacquainted with the publications of other racial groups should examine a few issues of *Ebony*, and also of one of the Chicano magazines, of which *El Grito* (Berkeley, California) is a very good example.

 **QUESTIONS**

1. Why were the immigrants to America given an uneven welcome?

2. Compare the causes of the backlash of the WASPs against the white ethnics with that of the ethnics against the blacks.

3. Describe the type of racial "accommodation" known as Jim Crowism.

4. Explain and give examples of "institutions of racism."

5. What are some of the special problems faced by the Chicanos?

6. Why have many American Indians been slow to integrate into the general culture of the United States?

FOX.S.M.
304 W 39st

8 *The incongruities between ideal and practice noted in Chapter 7 are applicable also to a discussion of male and female. Why had we assumed that once the Nineteenth Amendment was passed, women should have no further complaints regarding equality of opportunity? What are the actual grounds for women's complaints about employment, promotion, and social acceptance as equals? What are the demands of most of the leaders of the women's liberation movement? Does social change, through its influence on employment opportunities, have a bearing on the case of female equality? Since most social roles are reciprocal, can we expect greater rights for women to have a negative effect on the position of men? Will the role expectations of men become more difficult, or will men be relieved of certain role burdens they would be glad to discard? Are there any demands of the women's movement that could be helpful for both sexes? What will happen to the traditional roles of women? Will the women's liberation movement add considerably to the pressures that are even now resulting in more public rearing of children?*

We shall note that by no means all women show a great interest in the demands of women's liberation. Nevertheless, the movement is very strong and vocal. New adjustments are being made, and even more will have to be made in the future if we wish to remove the incongruities existing between our professed belief in human equality and the actual case of male monopoly of the most important leadership roles in society.

MALE AND FEMALE

As the values of society change in the direction of greater equality, it seems only natural that the increasing equality should apply to women as well as to men. The preponderance of societies, of course, have rated man as superior to woman and have given higher status to the work done by men than to work done by women. The unequal status assigned to work roles was noted by Ralph Linton in his definitive essay on status and role. In one society women make the pottery and in another men are the potters; in the former society the potter's trade is a lowly one, in the latter, a high art. In modern society there has been an equivalent point of view, holding that women excel in many types of routine, tedious tasks, but the more creative tasks are performed best by men. Philip Goldberg gave a test to women students in which they judged the quality of written articles bearing the pseudonyms John T. McKay and Joan T. McKay. Although the articles were all written by the same person, even the women students rated the articles they believed. to have been written by John as superior to those by Joan.[1] Apparently even women have been sold the idea that men are more creative.

The attitudes of inequality used to be more marked. Ancient societies generally had little use for female liberation. Even the creative period of the French Enlightenment found Condorcet almost alone in pronouncing women the intellectual equals of men. As recently as 1873, Dr. Edward H. Clarke wrote that a boy could study for as much as six hours per day without injury, but if a girl spent that long studying her "brain or special apparatus will suffer . . . leading to grievous maladies which torture a woman's earthly existence, called leuccherea, amenorrhea, dysmenorrhea, chronic and acute ovaritis, prolapsus uteri, hysteria, neuralgia, and the like."[2] Not only was study and thought too much of a strain for a woman, but her delicate nature imposed other limitations. Apparently her "brain and special apparatus" could easily suffer from too much sexual activity or from any employment outside the home. Of course, there were a few bad women who seemed able to entertain any number of evil men and even to break the employment rules.

Attitudes have changed, of course, but there is a Women's Liberation Movement today that contends attitudes have not changed very much. There are other groups that question unshakable tradition regarding male and female, including the Free Sex Movement, the Gay Liberation Movement, and Zero Population Growth. All have one point in common: they tend to challenge the traditional idea that male and female differences should serve solely for species perpetuation and a division of labor primarily structured to serve that ancient cause.

THE INCONGRUOUS ROLES OF WOMEN

In the early days of the Women's Rights Movement it was supposed that the right to vote would be the key to full equality. High political office would be within the grasp

---

[1]Cited by Jo Freeman, "Growing Up Girlish," *Transaction*, vol. 8, p. 37, December 1970.
[2]Quoted by Marijean Suelzle, "Women in Labor," *Transaction*, vol. 8, p. 56, December 1970.

Baby boom — a liberation road block.

that respectable women should have the right to enjoy sex as much as men. Victorian ladies simply yielded to their husbands' "animal nature," supposedly with great reluctance. Now women are also allowed to have an animal nature, and every sex manual emphasizes the point. The greater emphasis on woman's role as a partner in love, however, had a tendency to reemphasize basic physical differences. In some ways woman had gained, but perhaps in some ways she had lost in her battle for entry into the status of equality.

ENTER DR. FREUD The awareness of freudian psychology had a profound effect on the relations of male and female. We are not concerned here with whether or not the great Vienna psychiatrist was correct in all his interpretations of dreams; what is important is that he was heeded. Freud was able to convince much of the Western world that it was suffering from a puritanical hang-up that was causing frigidity, 213 impotence, and neurosis. The forbidden subject of sex came to the fore, and it threw a roadblock in the way of liberated women. Why did women want to be doctors, lawyers, engineers? In freudian writings was the implication that they desired such careers because they were sexually frustrated, not normal, not able to bask in the glory of sexual attractiveness. In a freudian phrase detested by the feminists, they were suffering "penis envy."[7] Friedan makes a strong point of the effect of Freud. Women turned too frequently from reading liberation journals to reading sex manuals.

An equally important reason for the decline of the earlier feminist movement was a change in breeding habits. Some militant feminists interpreted the change as a deliberate attempt to sell out the cause of womanhood; others more plausibly interpreted it as a reaction against the dislocations of war. Whatever the reasons, the 1940s and 1950s showed a renewed interest in the home. The normal woman, the one not rendered neurotic by suppressed desires, should be interested mainly in the blessings of husband, home, and children. The old German phrase *Kinder, Kirche, und Küche* (children, church, and kitchen) was almost applicable. Those who remember the end of World War II will recall the enormous prevalence of pregnant women and baby carriages. Woman, in spite of her relative sexual freedom, was still linked strongly to her traditional role. Its demands had increased in various ways, but basically it was still a home role. In the 1920s the college coed was looking for liberation and a career; in the 1950s she was looking for a husband.

THE IMPOSSIBLE ROLE   What had actually happened was a type of liberation that in some ways increased frustration. Now it was granted that woman should be educated, but not for a life career. She should be educated in order to help her husband earn a living, if necessary, and to keep up with her husband intellectually and make a good companion for him. At the same time, her household role had diminished but little. There were more labor-saving devices, but there was also more labor. Baby care had become more demanding, including considerable reading about child care, more fussing with formulas, psychological needs, greater attention to diet and vitamins, and more permissive training. At the same time she was not permitted, as her grandmother had been, to put on weight and recognize age. She was expected to be fascinatingly beautiful and shapely. There is an old Chinese saying that a man's needs are three: a wife to keep house and bear children, a concubine for sexual pleasure, and a friend with whom to communicate his philosophy and dreams.[8] The American wife must be all three.

THE DESCENT OF MAN

At the same time that woman worries over whether she has really ascended in status, man has little doubt that he has descended. He has descended from a status that

---

[7]Betty Friedan, *The Feminine Mystique*, Dell Publishing Co., Inc., New York, 1962, chap. 5.
[8]David Mace and Vera Mace, *Marriage East and West*, Dolphin Books, Doubleday & Company, Inc., Garden City, N.Y., 1959, p. 224.

was unquestionably one of superiority. In the upper classes, his status was that of manager of affairs, guardian of the estate, a major link in an important lineage. In the lower classes, male status often implied merely physical dominance rather than the intellectual direction of affairs, but with a strong feeling for division of labor and manliness and a total avoidance of housework.

ECONOMIC ADVANCE: STATUS LOSS   Over the years the major change has come about in the middle class, but middle-class norms include an increasing proportion of Americans. The man is educated and has achieved an advance in economic position. He is aware, nevertheless, of another type of status loss — a loss in male dominance. If society had a consistently equalitarian definition of sex roles, there would be no great problem for the man, but such is not the case. The male is still expected to be decisive and assertive, to accept military service if need be, to be as brave as his forebears, to prefer rough, competitive, and adventurous sports; but at home he is dethroned.

Even in more traditional societies the woman has often been defined as the ruler in certain domestic areas, with not too much interference in the manner of running the house and caring for the children. But outside, in the fields or with the cattle, the man ruled and taught his sons to rule in later years. Now there is no outside. The family is confined to the house for its range of collective activity, and to a great extent that is the woman's domain. In older societies, and to a decreasing extent now in lower-class circles, the man could escape to the tavern. Now the women invade taverns and clubs and are battering down the last remaining walls of masculine refuge. Courts have ruled in their favor about bars, restaurants, race tracks, and every conceivable occupation.

There are conflicting views of the consequences of this change. Many men seem to show little concern about the declining differences in the assignment of occupational roles to male and female. On the other hand, the view expressed by psychiatrist Dr. Hendrick Ruitenbeek[9] is that man is psychologically castrated. Ruitenbeek sees impending disaster for man. The consequence of lowering male status in the home is increasing anxiety for him, especially in the United States, where the man's role was previously a very active one. The concept of the man was of the conqueror of the West, the clearer of land, the builder of railroads. His was active work in an extractive economy. The passive role, the quiet home role, was clearly identified only with the woman. It is possibly for this reason, says Ruitenbeek, that the American man has been more downgraded within the home than his European counterpart, who has had longer experience in coping with a confining situation. Whatever the case, the American man is less dominant than the European.

SEXUALITY AND STATUS   The double standard that permitted philandering on the part of man but not the woman gave man an enviable status. Within his own bedroom,

[9]Hendrick Ruitenbeek, *The Male Myth*, Dell Publishing Co., Inc., New York, 1967.

The military-masculine stereotype and
the cult of masculinity: is it passing
into oblivion?

Declining role differentiation in the
paternal image: can such a change aid
both male and female?

also, it was the man who was to be pleased. His knowledge of woman's greater demands upon him, says Ruitenbeek, leads to uncertainties and self-doubts. Not only in the physical sex role, but in the personality that has long been assumed to accompany maleness, there is a change that is damaging to the male ego. The way of woman has been stereotyped as the way of manipulation, persuasion, and even minor deceit and craftiness. The way of the man has been that of direct statement, forcefully supported by his role, if nothing else. The salesmanlike society of today demands the manipulative personality for both male and female, an idea expressed some years ago in David Riesman's analysis of the "other-directed" personality. Increasingly the male is becoming other-directed, both in his physical sex role and in his social and occupational roles.

THE NONROLE OF FATHER It is increasingly difficult for a boy to grow up into a male role in modern society, mainly because the father is barely able to provide the proper model. The boy's parents are "apparently more neurotic and less competent to fill their own difficult role . . . hence the young male is affected by indifference or hostility to a mother seen as dominating and to a father perceived as inadequate."[10] The situation is not true of every family, but often the father, who complains of the woman's dominance, is not very interested in the role of father and is happy to shift care of the family to the wife. He may pretend to dominate, but the children see him manipulated and controlled by the mother. Such fathers often turn compulsively to their work, seeking identity there more than at home; but often their jobs are not psychologically rewarding enough to give the sense of strength that the older farmer, cattleman, or ironmonger enjoyed.

The father of an earlier time was more likely to cast a strong image—not necessarily a lovable one. If he were greatly admired and loved by his son, he could be emulated. If he became an object of hate, he could be rebelled against; and the son, through his very act of rebellion, gained his sense of manhood. Now, Ruitenbeek's argument goes, the father is a nonperson, neither a model to be followed nor a power to be overcome. Occasionally "palship" emerges as a weak shadow of what was once the father role, but this too is inadequate. The young man must turn to his peer group for identity and support.

Ruitenbeek's work, intended as a defense of the male, sometimes sounds almost like a polemic against him. A major point he makes, and one of the stronger points in his work, is concerned with a deeper identity crisis. Neither male nor female is to be blamed particularly, but the occupational structure and the social relationships and kinship structures of modern societies have changed so drastically as to make alienation a part of the experience of both men and women.

Just as a member of the Women's Liberation Movement can complain that women are appreciated only in the sex roles brought to mind by the offensive expres-

[10]*Ibid.*, p. 82.

sion "baby doll," the man can see himself reduced to "lover boy," "hubby," and "daddyo." In one sense the problem of male and female seems beyond resolution. If man's status was once at the top, then it can go no way but down. Does this mean that the Women's Liberation Movement is a threat that will cause man to descend further, or are there possibilities for a mutual adjustment? Considerable space has been given to the nature of the women's complaints, but do all women complain? What are the proposed solutions? Can an increase in freedom in one area of life lead also to an increase in freedom in other areas of life?

THE DEMANDS

For believers in traditional roles it may be comforting to know that large numbers of American women hold beliefs almost as ancient as the Chinese principles of Yang and Yin. Yang, the male principle, is active; Yin, the female principle, must be passive or the harmony of the universe is upset. A recent Gallup poll found that the wives of workingmen generally saw their Yin role as quite satisfactory. The role might be too passive, but only 30 percent thought men have an easier time than women; 46 percent thought women have an easier time than men. The remainder had no opinion.[11]

Among the college women, however, there was more discontent with woman's lot. Whereas the national sample showed 65 percent saying that women get as good a break as men in this society, only 50 percent of college women agreed. It is obviously the 50 percent in disagreement who are the most vocal on the matter of male-female relations. The Women's Liberation Movement probably does not express the convictions of the majority of women, but what makes it important is that so many of its champions are among the most capable and active members of society. They are the cutting edge of the blade, as were their female counterparts in the first Women's Rights Convention of 1848. As mentioned previously, the movement for women's rights has been less productive than might have been expected, but now it is being pursued with a renewed zeal and at a time when equalitarian norms of various kinds have been proclaimed more loudly than ever before.

THREE SPECIFIC DEMANDS In an earlier age the primary demand of women was for voting rights, and the secondary one was the right to jobs. Today the demand for equal

---

Attitude survey. By a simple questionnaire, see if you can find differences between generations and social classes in what are considered proper male and female roles. (For example, should men be nurses? Would you vote for a woman for President?)

---

[11]"Life is a Toil," *Transaction*, vol. 8, p. 10, December 1970.

rights to jobs and equal rights to pay and promotion has moved into first place. Women's groups do not all agree about their demands, but nearly always they include jobs and certain other rights that will increase a woman's employability, for example, the right to child-care centers, and the right to abortions if babies are unwanted or are due at unacceptable times. A recent scholarly book on the history of women's movements in America attributes their failure primarily to the basic female problems of child bearing and infant care.[12] If women are to succeed in careers, they must find means of regulating these basic demands. The possibility is greater now than in the past. Family planning is almost universally accepted, but child-care centers leave much to be desired.

Several European countries, especially Sweden and Denmark and the Soviet Union, have concentrated much more on child-care centers than has the United States. Since Russia has long had a manpower shortage (there are 18 million more women than men, largely because of World Wars I and II), the U.S.S.R. has to rely upon women's labor and has provided day-care centers and boarding schools. The Scandinavian countries are much more comparable with the United States, and in those countries equal employment opportunities have been aided by low birth rates and readily available infant and child care. Recently the American government has recognized the need for child-care centers, but mainly to make it possible for women to hold jobs that will get them off welfare. The demand of the women's rightists is for child-care centers for all working mothers, even those receiving good pay and married to men with good jobs. They see child care as a right needed to guarantee equality.

Perhaps progress will become fairly rapid in child-care centers. The 1970 White House Conference on Children heard a series of demands for infant- and child-care centers and for schooling at an earlier age than at present. So far, however, child-care facilities have remained inadequate in number and poor in quality, hardly keeping pace with the worldwide trend noted in Chapter 6. There are about 5 million children of preschool age with working mothers, but the highest estimate of day-care facilities available is 640,000, most of which will not take children under three years old.[13] Research in New York led to the conclusion that many people take care of children because they are too sick physically or emotionally to handle other types of jobs. The majority of child-care centers are run by people who seem fairly pleasant, and the researchers found no cases of real abuse; the major problem was that the centers were run by people interested in business rather than in children. The facilities were physicially adequate, but the atmosphere was usually one of unrelieved boredom. It takes trained and imaginative people to keep children busily occupied and happy and to see that they have the types of learning experiences that prepare them for school and for life. The majority of working mothers cannot feel assured

[12]O'Neill, *op. cit.*

[13]Joseph Featherstone, "Kentucky Fried Children," *New Republic*, pp. 11–16, September 12, 1970.

Needed: care centers for children of
working mothers.

Labor force participation rates of married women by presence and age of children, March 1960 to March 1969

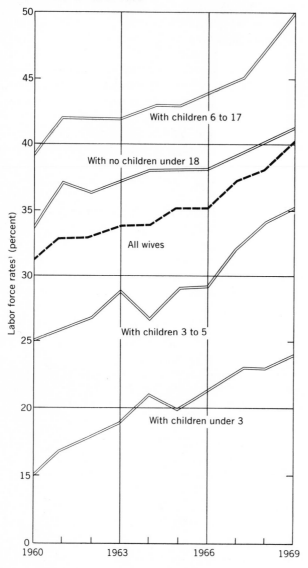

Labor force rates¹ (percent)

With children 6 to 17

With no children under 18

All wives

With children 3 to 5

With children under 3

50

45

40

35

30

25

20

15

0

1960   1963   1966   1969

¹Labor force as percent of population

that their children's needs are being met in these respects.[14] In the meantime, figures from the Department of Labor show the increased need (see page 222).

Another important demand of the Women's Liberation Movement is for the right of abortion. The present trend in the United States is toward liberalization of abortion laws, but there are many states in which legal abortions are virtually impossible to obtain. Only New York and Hawaii have fully permissive laws on the matter. The California law has been liberalized to a degree but depends upon certification that a woman's physical or mental health would be damaged by having the baby.

The legalization of abortion becomes involved in value conflicts. The strongest statement in favor of fully legalized abortion is that a woman should have the full right to determine what happens to her own body. The opposite view is that a fetus has equal status with developed human beings and must be considered just as much a living individual. Daniel Callahan[15] has written about the results of opposite philosophies regarding abortion in various parts of the world. All countries with either moderately or highly restrictive laws, he found, show high rates of illegal abortion and higher rates of maternal deaths than do countries that make abortion easy. On the other hand, countries that make abortion easy have a harder time with contraceptive programs, especially among the poor. Callahan, a moralist, cannot be happy with easy abortion, but feels that restrictive laws are worse. He would recommend at least formal counseling on the matter, and following abortion, counseling on contraception. Few feminists would take issue with such a recommendation.

The total right of the woman to decide on an abortion, of course, runs counter to a man's rights in the matter. In an article titled "Adam's Rib, or the Woman Within," Una Stannard[16] shows how strongly men are involved in the desire for children. She even demonstrates that many cases of "womb envy" are apparent in the anthropological world. Nevertheless, the woman can always argue that a child not desired by its own mother is brought into the world with a very poor start in life.

THE METAPHYSICS OF WOMEN'S DEMANDS Going beyond the immediate and practical demands for equal opportunity are others that get into the field of emotions, self-image, and conceptualizations of reality. Kate Millett,[17] for example, generalizes

---

Does your school have a special program in women's studies? Such classes are becoming increasingly common. Take up the matter with your dean of instruction or equivalent administrator.

---

[14]*Ibid.*
[15]Daniel Callahan, *Abortion, Law, Choice, and Morality*, The Macmillan Company, New York, 1970.
[16]Una Stannard, "Adam's Rib, or the Woman Within," *Transaction*, vol. 8, pp. 24–32, December 1970.
[17]Kate Millett, *Sexual Politics: A Manifesto for Revolution*, Doubleday & Company Inc., Garden City N.Y., 1970.

beyond mere occupations to the description of a society that has been insensitive to woman's basic humanity and has systematically subdued her politically, by which she means in all power-structured relationships. Males are still given a "birthright priority" to rule females, and the right is perpetuated by fables about the natural abilities and temperament of woman.

Suelzle,[18] a little less vehement than Millett, also gives a number of the generalized complaints about inferior status (as do most women leaders). She lists several myths about females that are antagonizing to the militant women of today. The idea that few women really want a career she considers a myth. Women are, in fact, taught that they should not want a career, and they are treated as though they should not desire one. Women are taught always to underestimate themselves—a reason why they start out well in school but often lag in the college years. Suelzle also presents some statistical evidence for attacking the myth that women are absent from the job more than men. A Women's Bureau study found them doing slightly better than men. She also spikes the statement that most women are working only for pin money and that women control a majority of the wealth of the country.

In summary, there are many complaints. The most persistent are the complaints about employment and the lack of facilities for child care. Most of the others are concerned with a feminine image that is probably becoming passé. Do the women's demands, then, amount to such a repudiation of the male that society is somehow threatened?

COEXISTENCE

One consolation about a battle of the sexes is that the two must ultimately arrive at some form of accommodation. The major demands repeated most frequently by women would not be impossible for men to accept. The emotional tone of the Women's Liberation Movement is at times antagonizing to men, but movements are seldom led by the calm and complacent. Equality of employment and pay seem reasonable, and it can be argued that bringing women's pay to the same level as men's prevents the possibility of replacing male workers with cheaper labor. Similarly, the provision of better care centers for children is hardly a male versus female issue. If the care centers are to be subsidized by the government, they are a political and monetary issue, but an issue along which people divide on partisan more than sex lines. The issue of abortion presents more normative difficulties, but again, opinion differences are probably more a matter of religion and ideology than of sex. When it comes to the last types of demands, the ones that insist upon equal status for women and for discarding all the old stereotypes, it is a little harder to see the complete reconciliation of the sexes. It will be good to recall Ruitenbeek's conclusion that both suffer from types of alienation under conditions of modern society.

[18]Suelzle, *op. cit.*, pp. 52–60.

If we use the word "anomie" rather than alienation to describe the situation of modern sex roles, we shall be looking at such roles in more clearly sociological terms. Anomie is a situation that exists when roles are rapidly changing, or when they call for contradictory demands or are not properly internalized. In this sense the roles of both male and female have become anomic. Although women complain of having been assigned too many conflicting roles in the modern family, men can complain about a large degree of role loss. Men are often bewildered to find themselves attacked for their inhuman domination over women at a time when they often consider the situation to be almost the reverse. This is one of the many perplexing problems of modern American society. At present there is more family breakup than in the past, which superficially seems to argue that relationships between the sexes are less harmonious than they once were. It is likely, though, that those marriages that do persist and that are based on equality, are happier than many of earlier times. It is possible that we stand on the threshold of improved relationships between the sexes, if new status adjustments are made and internalized.

MUTUAL LIBERATION Mary Calderone, director of the Sex Information and Education Council of the United States, reminds us that we are living in an age of increasing sensitivity to human relationships. Different groups and races are more aware of each other than in the past and more capable of viewing each other as human. Possibly the stereotyped roles of male and female are more persistent even than those of race and ethnic group, but we do know that different societies stereotype the sexes differently. In Arapesh society both male and female are kind and gentle. In Mundugamore society both are fierce and warlike, according to Margaret Mead's *Sex and Temperament in Three Primitive Societies*. Social systems seem to be able to modify whatever temperament is associated with one sex or the other. Certainly in the Western world the female has changed greatly from the faint and delicate creature of Victorian literature. Certainly, too, the American man has changed from the various stereotypes of several generations ago: the six-shooting Westerner, the ignorant backwoodsman, or the hearty farmer or blacksmith.

Calderone contends that man is just as much a victim of stereotypes and myths as is woman — "stereotyped grooves of earning, governing, and fighting and . . . compulsively fixed patterns for masculinity in dressing, professions, recreation, and life style."[19] She cites a case in which men had to listen to half an hour or more of women's comments on what they would like. The final conclusion was that the men admitted having been asked to express sentiments that were part of their inner lives but that they had not dared express because of social conventions. Men, she concludes, could stand to be released from some of their self-imposed demands of impassivity and stoicism; and all learning of social processes should relate primarily to being human rather than to being of a particular sex, color, or race. Calderone can, of course, be

[19]Mary Calderone, "It's Really the Men Who Need Liberating," *Life*, vol. 69, p. 24, September 4, 1970.

accused of mere sermonizing, but she states a position in line with modern trends when she suggests that the "iron man" view of masculinity is declining.

THE ECONOMICS OF SEX DISCRIMINATION In the earlier days of women's rights, an antifeminist argument frequently used was that women would take jobs away from men who have to support families. The argument was very similar to the argument against the importation of cheap foreign labor. In both cases there was a threat of the undermining of pay standards and union benefits.

As of 1969 nearly 10 million women were employed at clerical work in the United States, as opposed to only about 3½ million men. Clerical work is notoriously under-unionized, as is much of the work done by women in the United States. Nationally, 85 percent of women workers are in nonunion jobs. At present they receive some protection from various state laws calling for maximum hours of work, maximum amounts of materials to be lifted, sanitary conditions, and overtime. However, there are attacks against such laws, spearheaded by a number of employer groups, but also often receiving the approval of some of the women's rightists themselves.[20] The National Organization for Women (NOW), in its enthusiasm for equality seems willing to forego protective laws for women. Joan Jordan suggests that the stand should be one of keeping all protections at present on the statute books, but extending them in similar degrees to men. For example, restrictions on how heavy a load can be lifted could be retained, with less severe restrictions, but restrictions nevertheless, for men. Instead, the present movement seems to be away from protective legislation. Since 1964 twelve states have either amended or repealed hour laws for women.

The net result of these changes is to make women more employable for those seeking to exploit cheap labor. A study made in 1950 found that manufacturing companies saved a total of 5.4 billion dollars by paying women less than they would have had to pay men.[21] Exactly the same situation can be continued and intensified if present undermining of protective laws continues.

If there is any area in which the vested interests of male and female are alike, regardless of how much they might bicker, it is in the area of employment. Nothing can be worse for men than to be fired so that their jobs can be filled more cheaply by women. Nothing is worse for the conditions of labor in general than having a large percentage of workers willing to forego the benefits of union regulations or state laws for their protection. To achieve equal rights, the women need to battle at least as much in the area of unionization as in the political field. Their lawyers must also look into the possibility of additional clauses to a women's rights amendment to make sure that no present rights are undermined in the name of equality. Men and women could be mutually supportive in many of the employment areas that still need more safety and health regulations.

[20]Joan Jordan, "Working Women and the Equal Rights Amendment," *Transaction*, vol. 8, pp. 16–22, December 1970.

[21]*Ibid.*, p. 16

It is probably in the upper-level jobs that full equality for women would demand more moving over on the part of men. It is at university levels of skill and education that the largest amount of complaint is voiced. It is also among men of such levels of education that a reasonable attitude toward equality would seem most easily realizable. As we have seen, this is not the case at present, judging from actual employment. Women are grossly cheated in the number of professorships awarded, in the number of openings in medical schools, and in administrative jobs. It seems possible that working-class men and women may relate to each other better on plain bread-and-butter issues than do the educated men and women of the middle class.

EMPLOYMENT OPPORTUNITIES   As stated, women failed to hold their own in the professions in the 1960s. While total professional employment rose 4.4 percent, women's employment in the professions rose only 1 percent. Of all professional women, 36 percent were teaching in elementary and secondary schools by 1969, and this field was being oversubscribed. A great difficulty with female employment was that half of all women workers were concentrated in only twenty-one occupations; a fourth were in only five occupations: secretary-stenographer, household worker, bookkeeper, elementary school teacher, or waitress.[22] Rapid growth of opportunities for women seems likely in employment as physicians, architects, and draftsmen. Women are grossly underrepresented in science and engineering, but these, at least at the moment, are not expanding fields of employment. In medicine it is distressing for women leaders to note that of the twenty-nine countries reporting to the Tenth Congress of the Medical Women's International Association, in only three did women comprise a smaller percent of physicians than in the United States—South Vietnam, Madagascar, and Spain.[23]

REFUSING THE ROLES

There are various indications of a reduced difference between the sexes, not only in superior-inferior relationships, but even in hair style and manners of speech and dress. It would seem rather natural in a society that no longer has a wild West, and

---

Have you been discriminated against in housing or employment on the basis of sex? Write to Equal Opportunity Office, Department of Housing and Urban Development, or Health, Education and Welfare Department, Washington, D.C.

---

[22] Janice Neipert Hedges, "Women at Work," *Monthly Labor Review*, pp. 19–29, June 1970.
[23] *Ibid.*, p. 24.

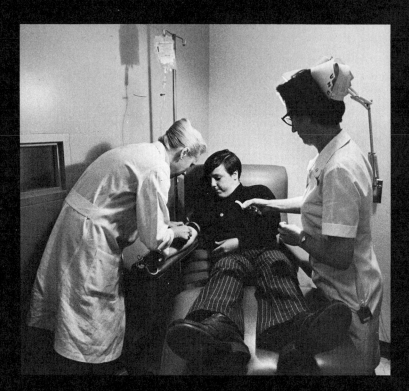

The woman doctor, unusually rare in
America, is discouraged by prejudice,
false stereotypes, and restrictive
medical school practices.

where increasing numbers of jobs can be held by either sex, that sexual dimorphism would decline. Some have dubbed the dress customs of certain elements of the younger generation as "unisex" and have worried about whether a man is a man and a woman is a woman any more. Almost at the same time the elders are worrying about premarital relations between the young, abortion, and the increased rate of venereal disease. The actual change is simply one of rejecting certain stereotyped expectations for male and female, but probably not a change in the attraction of one sex for the other. The most radical changes are limited to a minority. The majority of young people expect to marry and to eventually rear a family. There are fewer people committed to a single life now than in the past, unless a very recent change is developing.

THE REPRODUCTION ROLE   There are interesting contradictions about the attitudes of the public in regards to population control. The realization that birth rates should be kept down to approximately the level of zero population growth has been rather generally accepted. At the same time, the average desire for children expressed by married couples is for more than three children, too many for no population increase and certainly too many for the women desiring a virtually uninterrupted career. To be consistent with the desire for low birth rate, it would seem that the time has come to honor people who wish to remain single and/or childless, but such is not the case. A women's rightist complains that single, women-hating men are merely regarded as eccentric, but that man-hating women are "automatically labeled some kind of pervert."[24] As a matter of fact, male and female are both given a negative appraisal unless they marry—one of the present pressures toward young marriage.

Presently there is no evidence of a growing resistance to marriage, only to staying married to the same partner. There is also little evidence of a desire for childlessness in marriage. In terms of the brittleness of early marriages, most marriage counselors would suggest delaying children, but few young couples do. Dr. Alan Guttmacher, president of the Planned Parenthood World Federation, claims to see evidence that many of the educated middle class are losing their prejudice against the childless couple.[25] He points out, with perfect logic, that for the couple primarily interested in careers and/or impatient with children, the childless idea makes perfect sense, and it also makes sense for the women's rightist. Sensible or not, the childless idea still runs counter to the general public statement. A series of polls, mainly by Dr. Gallup, shows that year after year the "desirable" family size is about 3.3 children, and that the limit is set mainly on the basis of how many children a couple can afford.[26] Whatever else may prove a source of worry in the Women's Lib Movement, no one need fear that reproduction is drawing to a close!

[24]Julie Smith, "What They Want: A Survey of the Campus Lib Movement," *California Monthly*, p. 40, June–July, 1970.
[25]"Make Love, Not Babies," *Newsweek*, p. 111, June 15, 1970.
[26]Ruth B. Dixon, "Hallelujah the Pill?" *Transaction*, vol. 8, pp. 48–49, December 1970.

THE SEX LIBERATION MOVEMENT   In spite of the continued emphasis on the family duties of procreation, there are various types of sex liberation movements in society. An age of greater freedom of expression and equality and decline in respect for conventions is almost sure to be accompanied by open criticisms of the old moral standards. The Sexual Freedom League goes much further than most people would countenance, with nude parties, wife swapping, and the general attitude that everything is right as long as it is not conventional.[27] Some policies advocated by the Sexual Freedom League are in line with the thinking of the modern age: abolition of laws that invade the privacy of the bedroom, legalized abortion, abolition of most kinds of antipornography laws, more humane treatment of homosexuals and lesbians, allowance for transsexual operations, and less falsity about standards. The 1957 Wolfenden Report to the British Parliament advocated abolishing laws against homosexual practices between consenting adults. Although it was not adopted, it has led to far more discussion of the problem than in the past and an increasing tendency toward kindly treatment of the problem in a number of plays and films, more in Europe than in the United States.

The pornography laws have been entirely eliminated in Denmark, and on a de facto basis are nearly nonexistent in many American cities. In 1970 the President's Commission on Obscenity and Pornography presented its report to President Nixon. The report advocated abolition of laws against the reading or viewing of pornographic materials by adults. Three members objected to the report, and much was made of the fact. What received almost no newspaper attention was that two members (Larson and Wolfgang) believed the recommendations were still too restrictive. Whatever the case, the President, Vice President, and Senate turned down the report's recommendations. The commission had done its duty of gathering facts, but facts do not necessarily influence political leadership. The constant reassurance of the commission that there was no connection (or possibly a negative connection) between sex crimes and pornography seemed to impress no one.[28] Commissions often experience the same fate as sociologists!

SIMILARITIES IN PROTEST MOVEMENTS   In an age of protest over inequalities, it seems likely that a women's liberation movement will continue in one form or another, as will many movements aimed at greater equality. So far the women's protest movement has convinced many people that the sex equality once believed to have been attained with the Nineteenth Amendment has fallen far short of its goal. Now, with less compulsion about reproduction, with limited family size, with considerable public rearing of children, and with many years of life left after the children are grown,

[27]Jack Lind, "The Sexual Freedom League," in Walt Anderson, *The Age of Protest*, Goodyear Publishing Company, Pacific Palisades, Calif., 1969, pp. 181–197.
[28]Clive Barnes (ed.), *The Report of the Commission on Obscenity and Pornography*, Bantam Books, Inc., New York, 1970.

women are much less restricted by their traditional biological roles. The possibilities for greater liberation are at hand.

The women's protest movement is very closely linked to, and was probably partly inspired by, the protests of racial and ethnic minorities discussed in the previous chapter. In both cases there has been a wide gap between ideal and reality, and in both cases the society has been only vaguely aware of the incongruities and has even prided itself on having handled the situation well. Complaints about employment have been prominent in both types of movements, but the issues have gone deeper than mere economics. Even more important has been the desire for a new self-concept of full equality and a denunciation of anything vaguely resembling second-class citizenship. Protests will probably continue as long as the normative incongruities continue.

SUGGESTED READINGS

Barnes, Clive (ed.): *The Report of the Commission on Obscenity and Pornography*, Bantam Books, Inc., New York, 1970.

The work of the commission suffered an even worse political fate than most such commissions, but many of its findings are very interesting. See especially Sections 1, 2, and 3 on findings, recommendations, and the impact of erotica.

Friedan, Betty: *The Feminine Mystique*, Dell Publishing Company, Inc., New York, 1962.

The first volley in the present feminist movement. Analyzes the problems of inequality and their causes; refutes large numbers of myths and stereotypes about femininity, working mothers, and educational and occupational opportunities.

Morgan, Robin: *Sisterhood is Powerful*, Random House, Inc., 1970.

An anthology of writings from the women's liberation movement.

Packard, Vance: *The Sexual Wilderness: The Contemporary Upheaval in Male-Female Relationships*, Pocket Books, Inc., New York, 1970.

Vance Packard has a flare for sensational titles and is not a sociologist by training, but he documents his studies well. His book deals with changing sex norms and male-female roles, as well as with the problems of marriage and speculations about the future. As with all of Packard's books, it is very readable.

Ruitenbeek, Hendrick: *The Male Myth*, Dell Publishing Co., Inc., New York, 1967.

This book, probably intended as an answer to Betty Friedan, shows a real perception of the problems of both sexes, but is particularly concerned with what the author sees as the demasculinization of men.

Transaction, vol. 8, December 1970.

Entire edition is devoted to the Women's Rights Movement. Excellent articles on occupations, feminine and masculine self-image, need for child care, and need for greater political activity.

QUESTIONS

1. Explain how some of the attitudes resulting from Freud's writings and the "baby boom" slowed down the attempt at female equality.

2. Compare the role problems of women and men in contemporary society.

3. What are three specific demands of many members of the Women's Liberation Movement, and what are their more generalized demands (referred to as "the metaphysics" of women's demands)?

4. What are the facts about the increase in total employment of women? How does this contrast with the quality of jobs they hold and their pay and promotions?

5. What changes in attitude and what policies in employment could possibly bring benefit to both men and women?

6. How prevalent is the tendency to reject traditional feminine roles of marriage and family?

9 *Nowhere is the disparity between possibility and accomplishment more worrisome to well-meaning reformers, to critical taxpayers and to the poor themselves than in the area of poverty and dependency. Progress has been made, but the big question is "Why has progress against poverty been so limited?" Why does poverty appear so everlasting? Why have we not done at least as well in developing a rational, uniform approach to poverty as many Western European countries have done? What are the characteristics of the poor — age and sex distribution, regional distribution, and racial and ethnic distribution? Poverty includes many besides the unemployed. What are some of the occupations that pay so poorly as to leave their workers in poverty? In particular, what are the conditions of seasonal labor in agriculture? Is "Poverty U.S.A." merely relative, or do we have actual malnutrition, ill health, and early death resulting from poverty?*

We shall look at all these questions and also at various programs that have been tried or are being advocated for improving welfare and/or ending dependency. Can education and retraining do most of the job of ending dependency, or must we look more deeply into characteristics of the economy? What will have to be accomplished to prevent the poor from being "the everlasting poor"?

THE EVERLASTING POOR

In an age of abundance and in a particularly wealthy society, it is easy to think of poverty as a purely relative matter—the lack of funds for a new car or fashionable clothes or the inability to keep up with the neighbors or to reach that ill-defined plateau called "the American standard of living." It is easy to rest in the assurance that Americans are well off compared with the poor of bygone times and distant places. There is a certain amount of truth to such a viewpoint, of course. The impoverished are a smaller percent of the total population than they were decades ago.

The poor have not disappeared, however, nor is there any prospect that they are about to do so. The poor are very much with us—often unobserved, it is true—but nevertheless in our midst. They suffer not just from relative deprivation; they suffer from absolute deprivation, from a lack of medical care, from a lack of housing and privacy and good food. They suffer from an inability to aid their children to find a place in the mainstream of life and from deprivation of a sense of self-worth and dignity. Even more than the numerous and hungry poor of the past, they are the "poor in spirit," pushed into the backwashes of life, more than ever before stigmatized as the inept, the retarded, the subhuman. Many are of the everlasting poor because they have no way to help themselves and no future; such is the case with many of the aged and sick, the blind, and those crippled in body and mind. Many more of the poor are children, and unless society does better in the future than in the past, they will perpetuate the poverty of their parents; they too will be the everlasting poor.

Not only does poverty exist in America, but it exists on a scale not commonly found in the other prosperous countries. The phenomenon is puzzling to much of the world, for even the most caustic foreign critics of America generally give us credit for being a people with a heart, with a fair measure of generosity and charity in our character. Why is it that a people well known for their generous efforts to rescue Europe from poverty after two world wars, a people with a sense of mission, a people who have sent generous amounts of aid to relieve historical crises in China, India, Latin America, and Biafra are unable to cope with poverty at home? What kind of lenses make it possible to see suffering more clearly in foreign lands than at home—in slums, ghettos, reservations, and such rural backwashes as Appalachia?

THE INCORRIGIBLE AND THE DAMNED

Certainly part of the reason for the different appraisal of poverty abroad and at home is a matter of awareness. Sudden tragedies such as floods, hurricanes, and wars receive vast amounts of publicity and sympathy. The undramatic, monotonous accounts of domestic poverty do not attract the same attention. However, the difference in dramatic quality and publicity is but a minor part of the problem of focusing public attention on poverty. Much of the problem has to do with values that are held more strongly by the American public than by much of the rest of the world.

THE ACHIEVEMENT ETHIC The achievement ethic runs strong in American literature and viewpoint. In essence, it is the attitude that Max Weber characterized as the Protestant ethic. Originally the Protestant ethic was based on a religious belief in the value of hard work and thrift, and the resulting prosperity was viewed as a sign of the Lord's blessing. Those who failed to achieve success were, according to Weber's interpretation of early Protestantism, obviously the incorrigible and the damned, not partaking of the grace of God. Such a philosophy is not believed in literally today, but it has a long carryover effect. The modern equivalent can probably be stated as the conviction that those who have not succeeded, with very few exceptions, are highly deserving of their poverty. To help such people may be commendable, but is by no means morally necessary.

The achievement ethic was well summarized at the turn of the century by the stalwart conservative sociologist William Graham Sumner:

> In general, however, it may be said that those whom philanthropists and humanitarians call the weak are the ones through whom the productive and conservative forces of society are wasted. They constantly neutralize and destroy the finest efforts of the wise and industrious, and are a dead-weight on the society in all its struggles to realize any better things. Whether the people who mean no harm, but are weak in the essential powers necessary to the performance of one's duties in life, or those who are malicious and vicious, do the more mischief, is the question not easy to answer.[1]

Not all Americans agreed with Sumner's viewpoint. A social reformer of the same period, Robert Hunter, wrote an impassioned book about the conditions of the poor. A quotation of his on child labor is enough to demonstrate why some people grew up weak:

> For ten or eleven hours a day these children of ten and eleven years stoop over the chute and pick out the slate and other impurities from the coal as it moves past. The air is black with coal dust, and the roar of the crushers, screens, and rushing mill-race of coal is deafening. Sometimes one of the children falls into the machinery and is terribly mangled, or slips into the chute and is smothered to death. Many children are killed in this way. Many others, after a time, contract coal-miner's asthma and consumption, which gradually undermines their health. . . . There are in the United States about twenty-four thousand children employed in and about the mines and quarries.[2]

In the long years since Sumner and Hunter wrote, there has been a softening of the tone of the Sumner philosophy, and there has been a softening of the conditions of child labor described by Hunter, but both philosophy and conditions have their counterparts today.

---

[1] William Graham Sumner. *What Social Classes Owe to Each Other*, Harper & Row, Publishers, Incorporated, New York, 1900, pp. 19–20.
[2] Robert Hunter, *Poverty*, The Macmillan Company, New York, 1904, pp. 237–238.

The costs of neglect: dilapidated housing, high infant mortality, tuberculosis, and the incurable damage of childhood malnutrition.

THE PHILOSOPHY OF "BENIGN NEGLECT" Robert L. Heilbroner[3] notes the striking contrast between the United States and many of the other highly industrialized nations of the Western world. In no other prosperous country that he has visited has he found anything like the squalid living conditions of parts of American cities, nor so much neglect of the conditions that exist. Apparently the reason for the bad showing of the United States is not that the Scandinavian countries, the Netherlands, Switzerland and others have no poverty potential to deal with; the reason is that they devote more effort to coping with the problems. Welfare expenditure in the United States is 6.5 percent of the gross national product (GNP). For the nations of the European Economic Community (France, Belgium, Luxembourg, West Germany, Italy, and the Netherlands) the average expenditure is 14 percent of the GNP; for the Scandinavian countries it is about 13 percent; for Canada, 9.9 percent.

Our neglect of poverty shows in many areas. Since 1950 we have fallen from fifth to eighteenth place among the world's nations in the prevention of infant mortality. Our relative position in life expectancy has declined, and our tuberculosis

[3]Robert L. Heilbroner, "Benign Neglect in the United States," *Transaction*, vol. 7, pp. 15–22, October 1970.

rates are higher than in Western Europe. We also have diseases of malnutrition, "including kwashiorkor — long considered a disease specific to underdeveloped areas."[4] We have not actually moved backward in most criteria of health and longevity, but we have failed to make as rapid progress as much of the technically advanced world has done.

Juvenile arrest and commitment rates are much higher here than in other countries of comparable income. Juvenile crime can by no means be attributed exclusively to poverty, but actual juvenile incarceration is largely a hazard of poverty. Whereas the President's Crime Commission in 1967 reported that 90 percent of American youth had broken laws that could call for commitment by a juvenile court, 95 percent of the juveniles sent to institutions came from families in "less than comfortable" circumstances. There is another interesting contrast in the area of crime, bearing on our policy of neglect. In Denmark the prison psychologist has an average case load of 20 to 30; in the United States his average load is 179.

EXPLAINING NEGLECT Heilbroner explains next the relative neglect of welfare and juvenile rehabilitation in the United States. He explores two major possibilities, but partially rejects the first one. It is sometimes assumed that the problem in the United States is that of a more heterogeneous population. Yet Canada and Switzerland both have the problems of ethnically heterogeneous populations but have not neglected the problem of poverty to the extent we have. Heilbroner at this point, perhaps, makes too little of the problem of racial prejudice in the United States, but he is certainly correct in pointing out that neglect exists regardless of race. Some of the all-white communities of Appalachia are among our most neglected poverty areas.

His final conclusion is similar to the one mentioned as the Protestant ethic or the achievement ethic. Heilbroner, however, proceeds to explain why this particular ethic has remained much stronger in the United States than in many other countries once thoroughly imbued with the same point of view. His conclusion is that we have suffered from too much success. The rags to riches myth has had a degree of plausibility in the past, and we have failed to note that the plausibility has declined in an age of economic giantism, bureaucracy, and restructuring of the employment situation.

There is yet another twist to the American norms regarding poverty. With our emphasis on democracy and belief in the possibility of nearly universal middle-class

---

> **Attitude survey. Is poverty mainly the fault of the poor themselves, or is it usually beyond their control? Ask this question of young and old groups, Democrats and Republicans, Catholics and Protestants, church members and nonchurch members, blacks and whites. Note differences in attitudes.**

---

[4]*Ibid.*, p. 16.

attainment, we have had little of the same noblesse oblige attitude that has generally prevailed in societies of recognized inequality. It has not seemed a part of the role of government to dispense charity to those in need. The equality ethic has, in fact, been so strong that it has been hard to believe that any but the wicked or the lazy can possibly remain in need. It is for this reason that many Americans characterize the welfare effort much as Sumner would have done—an attempt to reward the lazy, the weak, and the indifferent. In fact, many are unaware that the overwhelming majority of welfare aid goes to the aged, to needy children, and to the disabled. They do not realize that in nearly all states needy children cannot receive welfare aid if they have an able-bodied father at home, even if there is a high rate of unemployment in his area and he is unable to find work.

WELFARE AND WORK INCENTIVE   It is also possible for a society to have a vested interest in poverty. Such a condition exists when wages and working conditions are so bad that only poverty will drive people into accepting jobs. Vested interest in poverty is a diminishing reason for its existence in industrial societies, but, as we shall see, there are a few places where it is still evident.

Frances Piven and Richard Cloward[5] show how in the past the amount of relief given the poor was regulated by two principles: giving enough money to prevent riots and disorder, but little enough so the poor would be forced to take any jobs available, regardless of how low the wages or how bad the conditions of labor. This type of thinking still prevails to some degree because care of the poor is costly. We still have a tendency to weigh the cost of helping the poor against the indirect costs of suffering, crime, and alienation that result from too much neglect.

THE EQUIVALENT CONDITIONS   When Hunter wrote *Poverty* nearly seventy years ago, he was writing a bitter denunciation of a total system. Poverty was more abject, and it included a much larger part of the population than it does today. In one respect, however, poverty is the same: its worst victims are the young, and they are the ones who will perpetuate its pattern in later years. For example, compare the above quotation from Hunter's *Poverty* (1904) with the following quotation from Senator Mondale (1970):

> Nearly a million of them (the impoverished children) live in families which subsist primarily on migrant or seasonal farm work . . . the child is physically unable to attend school regularly. He begins working at a very early age. He not only suffers from malnutrition, but moves in a never-ending cycle of bending, lifting, and carrying. By the time he is 10 or 11 he has stopped going to school. He is often married at 14 or 15. Soon his health deteriorates. His back shows the damaging effects of constant stoop labor. . . .[6]

[5]Frances A. Piven and Richard A. Cloward, "The Relief of Welfare," *Transaction*, vol. 8, pp. 31–39, May 1971.
[6]Walter F. Mondale, "Think of These Children," *New Republic*, vol. 163, p. 15, December 26, 1970. Reprinted by Permission of THE NEW REPUBLIC, ©1970, Harrison-Blaine of New Jersey, Inc.

THE DIMENSIONS OF POVERTY

Poverty concentrates more in some parts of the country than in others, and more in periods of economic decline than in periods of prosperity, but there is still a stubborn omnipresence about it. John Kenneth Galbraith[7] was the first to use the descriptions "case poverty" and "insular poverty" to describe the situation of today. Case poverty is in all communities and is usually related to characteristics of the person in poverty—physical disablement, sickness, mental deficiency, alcoholism, or old age. Insular poverty refers to the islands of poverty existing in exhausted coal-mining regions of West Virginia, worn-out agricultural areas of the rural South, and Appalachian hamlets that have never known the affluence of the twentieth century. There are also islands of poverty in the ghettos of our large cities, in the Mexican communi-

[7]John Kenneth Galbraith, *The Affluent Society*, Houghton Mifflin Company, Boston, 1958.

Percent of persons in poverty, 1968

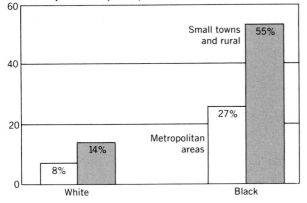

Percent of families below poverty level, 1968

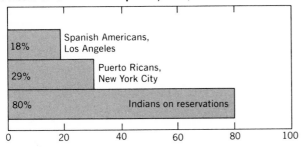

ties of the Southwest, and on the Indian reservations. The word "insular" must not be construed to imply few in number or vanishing.

WHO ARE THE POOR   As of 1968 the Census Bureau listed 25,389,000 people below the poverty line; two-thirds of these were white and one-third were nonwhite. The nonwhites are vastly overrepresented in the poverty statistics in proportion to their numbers, but poverty belongs to every race. The Census Bureau's definition of poverty is given in terms of monetary income, ranging from below $1,702 per year for a single person to a ceiling of $5,722 for a family of seven or more.

The poor comprise more than 5 million families, nearly 2 million of which are headed by women. Of the poor families, 2.3 million live on the rapidly dwindling small farms; more than 23 million are nonfarm families. In the South, 20 percent of all families live in poverty; elsewhere only 9 percent are below the official poverty line.[8] Although much attention in recent years has been focused on urban blighted areas, a larger percentage of rural than of urban people are poor, and high poverty rates exist among Spanish-speaking Americans and Indians on reservations (see figures based on data from the U.S. Census Bureau, page 241). Much of the poverty of the South is among nonwhites, but nearly 2 million poor white families also live in the South—42 percent of all the poor whites in the United States. The other major concentration of poverty is in the inner cores of the cities, where jobs are scarce and ill paying, and transportation to get people to areas of employment is virtually nonexistent. In terms of age, the two largest categories of poverty are the very young and the very old. More than 6.4 million aged people and 10.7 million children live in poverty.

The composition of the poor, then, explains part of the reason for the persistence of poverty. The present poor tend to vastly overrepresent the aged, children, and families with female heads. Many of the adult male heads of poverty families are in ill health, crippled, or lacking in the needed skills for employment. Many work but do not earn enough to keep their families above the poverty line.

Of all the categories mentioned, the children are the most likely to attract the sympathy of the public. Two Christmas news items from Los Angeles illustrate this point. A wealthy restaurant owner decided to give a Christmas dinner for 100 children, but only 50 arrived. All the available children had been rounded up; the orphanages were drained for Christmas. A Los Angeles lady, frustrated in her efforts to be lady bountiful, complained that helping some other day just wouldn't be the same. The reporter commented rather caustically that to help a poor orphan in August would be as out of season as summer eggnogs or Christmas trees.[9] Off-season charity is no fun! Apparently the good city of the angels also saw little joy in helping the

[8]The President's Commission on Income Maintenance Programs, *Poverty Amid Plenty: The American Paradox*, U.S. Government Printing Office, Washington, D.C., November 1969, p. 29.
[9]Mike Royko, "Where Did All the Needy Go?," *Los Angeles Times*, December 22, 1970, pp. 2, 22.

**One of the 6.4 million poverty-stricken
aged Americans.**

elderly. While the children were being feasted, the radio announcers had to put out frantic, last-minute appeals for food baskets for the aged.

The children, at least in some areas, seem to be assured of a good meal at Christmas time. What about the rest of the year? Apparently the normative problem is not so much a lack of human kindness as it is unawareness in the vast, impersonal society. Only special occasions bring the poor to mind.

THE CHILDREN OF THE POOR The majority of the poor children of America, those who live in the urban slums and ghettos, must face some of the worst conditions and institutions the nation has to offer. Infant mortality for the poor is about four times as high as the national average. In the twenty largest city school systems, children are, on the average, a year or more behind the national achievement norms. The schools become "dropout factories." Hospitals are crowded, with long waiting lines. Venereal disease is epidemic. Welfare is at its most inhumane and degrading.[10] There is much less safety from violence, robbery, or rape in the urban slums than elsewhere, and much of the theft is of the meager possessions of the poor, to be hocked for the price of dope. Drugs are everywhere, and the pressures toward drug use are greater than in any other part of society.

Many poor children of America are Indians. Seven thousand Navajo children under nine years old are in boarding schools run by the federal government; several have frozen to death trying to escape to get back home during the cold winter. Alaskan Indians are sent as far away as Oregon or Oklahoma to federal boarding schools. Most Indian children sent to Bureau of Indian Affairs schools have no knowledge of English, and their chances are only one in twenty of having a teacher who knows anything of their language. Their culture is ignored.[11]

A million or more Chicano children are sent to school without a knowledge of English and no effort is made to compensate for their language difficulties. In one school in southern Texas, Chicano children are made to kneel and beg forgiveness if they are caught speaking Spanish. Neither in educational skills nor in attitudes are they being taught how to pull out of the poverty of their parents. The culture of America remains not only foreign, but hostile as well.

The greatest concentration of poor whites is in Appalachia, where family size is also much larger than the average. More than 900,000 of the children of Appala-

---

> Visit and see if you can cooperate with agencies, public or private, dealing with poverty — welfare offices, Office of Economic Opportunity, Salvation Army, and various Catholic and Protestant charitable organizations.

---

[10]Mondale, *op. cit.*, pp. 16–17.

[11]*Ibid.*

chia are poor; only 6 percent receive welfare assistance. If the father is at home, no welfare assistance is given. The system encourages fathers to desert for the sake of their families.[12] In most of Appalachia, however, there is a father and there is a home. For the child of the ghetto the father is frequently missing. For many poor children, the home is missing.

CHILDREN OF MIGRATORY LABOR During the last few years newspaper comments on migratory labor have been mainly about Cesar Chavez and the determined attempt to organize farm laborers, especially in California. Elsewhere, farm labor makes no news because it is the same virtual peonage it has always been. In 1960 the late Edward R. Murrow presented a televised program called "Harvest of Shame," showing the conditions of migratory labor in America. Ten years later, in August 1970, NBC televised a program titled "Migrant." The commentator was different, and scenes of the prosperous parts of Florida were different, but otherwise, as NBC pointed out, the two programs were virtually interchangeable. The migrant laborers pictured in the Southeastern United States were 55 percent black, 35 percent Mexican, 10 percent Anglo-American, and 100 percent wretched. On a national scale the migratory laborers' families account for nearly 1 million of the children of poverty. They go to school from four to seven months per year, but never to the same school throughout that period. The teachers find them "uneducable." The other children make fun of them. "They think I am a bum," said one of the children interviewed; "Well, I guess I am!"

Such is the self-image imposed. Dr. Robert Coles, a psychiatrist who has spent years among the migrants, says that the children eventually become "dazed, listless, numb to everything but immediate survival," with special psychiatric problems of "extreme confusion, disorientation, depression, and even suicide." They also have specific physical diseases, often resulting from the pesticides to which they are constantly exposed. For those who stereotype the poor as shiftless or lazy, Coles says:

> No group of people I have ever worked with—in the South, in Appalachia, and in our Northern ghettos—tries harder to work, indeed travels all over a country working, working from sunrise to sunset, seven days a week when the crops are there to be harvested.[13]

Not only do adults work, but children work. Child labor laws are evaded, and childhood ceases at the age of nine or ten. It is no exaggeration to call the conditions those of peonage, for various devices are used to keep the laborers constantly in debt. "Many of these families are owned for all practical purposes," says Coles, "by

[12]*Ibid.*, p. 16.
[13]Robert Coles, M.D., Research Psychiatrist, Harvard University, in testimony before the Senate Subcommittee on Labor and Public Welfare, *Migrant and Seasonal Farmworker Powerlessness*, Part 2, U.S. Government Printing Office, Washington, D.C., pp. 334–335.

crew leaders who transport them around the country, sometimes with guns at their sides."[14]

Coles is especially concerned with the psychological effects of the depressed, rootless life on the children. "I do not believe the human body and the human mind were made to sustain the stresses the migrants face," he says, "worse stresses than I have ever seen anywhere in the world, and utterly unrecognized by most of us."[15]

His evidence of psychological damage to children is extremely convincing and damnatory. The child is born not in a hospital, but by the side of the road, or in the field, or in a one-room shack without running water or electricity. No doctor is at hand. To go to any authorities—hospital, sheriff, or welfare agency—is "just like asking for trouble." The people take care of themselves, and have correspondingly high death rates.

As the children grow up they have only negative experiences of school and of the great society outside. Psychiatrists are interested in the self-portrayals of children and the subtle stories they tell. One of the children, an eight-year-old girl, when asked to draw something, couldn't think of anything to draw except her birth certificate. Why? That was the one special thing she owned, her one source of identity. She had no house. The children do not normally draw houses, as other children do. One girl drew only Yo-Yos, because they were just like her, she said, always bouncing around but with nowhere to land. The people in the children's pictures are faceless. The outstanding feature in one boy's picture is a high, forbidding fence. Questioned, the boy told of a conversation with his parents in which he said he would like to go to other places than just the fields:

> But mother said we had better be careful; we can't keep asking to go here and there. We should close our eyes and imagine there is a big fence on each side of the road and we can't get off even if we wanted to because of the fence. That is why I put the fence in, to keep the car from getting into trouble with the police.[16]

There is probably no better symbol than the little migratory boy's high fence to sum up the effects of a childhood of degrading poverty. The child is fenced into the limited world of his subculture and fenced out of the world of opportunity and hope.

Coles asks why such conditions continue in a country whose wealth and whose values should have made them obsolete decades ago. To a degree, Heilbroner's essay on "benign neglect" answers the question: we have tended to exclude some groups in the heterogeneous society, and even more important, we have blamed the poor for their poverty. There is, however, in the case of migratory farm labor yet another reason: the poverty of some subsidizes the affluence of others. Farms are highly competitive, and the depression of wages gives a competitor an advantage over his rival.

[14]*Ibid.*, p. 353.
[15]*Ibid.*, p. 335.
[16]*Ibid.*, p. 342.

Migratory farm labor and nomadic children, homeless and unschooled, destined to repeat the cycle if neglect of rural poverty continues.

The market is competitive too, and affluent Americans keep down the prices of their vegetables by tolerating the conditions that produce what Murrow so aptly called America's "harvest of shame."

HUNGER

In 1967 a committee of doctors sent to Mississippi by the Senate subcommittee on poverty was shocked to find that they were not looking at mild cases of malnutrition, but at starvation. They saw children suffering from damage to bodily tissues, with eye and ear diseases, skin diseases, physical weakness and fatigue—all associated with a lack of food.[17] There was considerable publicity about the matter in Mississippi and about similar conditions discovered in the Carolinas and Texas. The government, which had been distributing surplus food through the Agriculture Department to counties willing to pay part of the cost, turned to a food-stamp program. Food stamps are supposed to supplement the family diet and thus prevent hunger. The recipient pays a certain amount and gets enough stamps to buy considerably more; the amount paid depends upon his income. If, however, he has no income, or medical and other expenses have wiped out his income before he gets around to buying his food stamps, he is out of luck. Furthermore, many counties do not actually make the food stamps available. In Mississippi eight counties switched from commodity distribution to food stamps, and one year later 32,000 fewer people were receiving food aid. The same situation applies on a smaller scale throughout the country. Although 6 million people were being given food aid in 1967, a larger number had been receiving aid six years before.[18] The situation continues.

In 1970 Dr. Arnold Schaefer of the Department of Health, Education and Welfare reported findings in line with the previously cited ones from Mississippi. His studies were conducted among poverty groups in Texas and Louisiana. He found high rates of anemia, vitamin deficiency, and protein deficiency, especially among those of lowest income. He also found that large numbers of people were not able to pay enough money to get the food stamps that have been thought of as a cure-all for malnutrition.[19] At about the same time, two young army officers, Capt. Terrence P. Goggin and Capt. Clifford Hendrix, were sent to conduct an investigation for the President's Urban Affairs Council. Their report concurs with many others. Only 16 percent of the poor were receiving food stamps in the counties they studied. They blamed failure largely on racial prejudice, political blackmail, and inept or underfinanced local governments. They also have accused official Washington of suppressing their report.[20]

[17]Elizabeth B. Drew, "Going Hungry in America: Government's Failure," *The Atlantic Monthly*, vol. 222, pp. 53–61, December, 1968.

[18]*Ibid.*

[19]Dr. Arnold E. Schaefer, in *Nutrition and Human Needs*, Hearings before the Select Committee on Nutrition and Human Needs of the United States Senate, U.S. Government Printing Office, Washington, D.C., 1970, pp. 764–779.

[20]Robert Rawitch, "Food Stamp Survey," *Los Angeles Times*, September 9, 1970, Part II, p. 4.

A CHEAP SOURCE OF PROTEIN People in poverty look for bargains, and often the search is self-defeating. The well-to-do can explain that it is foolish to buy shoddy goods, even when the price is low, but when there is virtually no money there is no alternative. Malnutrition is often the obvious result of food shortage, as we have seen. It may also be the result of very inferior food or food that is potentially dangerous.

Two officials of the Lexington Rendering Company of Lexington, Nebraska, testified before the Senate Committee on Nutrition. The senators were surprised that their testimony concerned pet food rather than human food. The men testifying were incensed that their state allowed careless handling of meat for animal food and permitted the use of dead and putrefying animals, some of which had died of botulism, salmonellosis, anthrax, or rabies. But what bearing has this on the problem of human nutrition and food bargains for the poor? The testimony reads:

> A portion of this nation's canned pet food is consumed by humans. The economically disadvantaged, particularly those in the South and Southwest — I speak here of the Negro, Indian, and Mexican population — receive little benefit from the small print on the labels of cans which say, "Not for human consumption." Our moral and medical responsibility to this nation's 30 million poor demands further protection, especially in view of the current "humanization" approach by the pet food industry in promotional campaigns.[21]

By the "humanization" approach, the spokesmen referred to advertisements making it sound as though the pet food is just as good as any other food in the store. They presented many examples of advertisements to this effect. They also complained that the loathsome meat used for pet food is stored so close to meat processed for humans that some of it could easily end in the wrong category.

PHYSICAL AND MENTAL EFFECTS A number of efforts have been made to prove a relationship between physical inferiority and such problems as criminality and dependency. A famous old study by Lombroso is often mentioned in psychology and sociology classes, mainly as an example of faulty research work. Lombroso made a study of inmates of prisons and found a surprising number of physical defects, which he interpreted as genetic in nature. Many years later, E. A. Hooton made a similar study in the United States and found similar results. Neither study is now believed

---

Do the poor really pay more? Do a study of your own community, comparing quality and prices of groceries in the poorest parts of town with middle-class areas. Also check on appliance stores, especially on rates of interest and other special charges.

---

[21]David E. Gauger and Clifford L. Johnson, in *Nutrition and Human Needs, op. cit.*, Part 13A, p. 3913.

to have proved what was expected, namely, a genetic factor in criminality. What had been demonstrated is quite apparent: more poor people than rich people are sent to prison, and the poor are more likely to have been malnourished. The poor do not have their teeth straightened, or eyes and ears inspected and corrected, or careful attention to well-balanced meals and vitamins. Most of the poor cannot afford private medical care, and often public facilities are too far away or too crowded. Some fragments of testimony from the President's Commission on Poverty illustrate this point:

It took me nine months to get a man in the nursing home. He fell and broke his hip and injured his foot. He was ninety-two years old. When we finally got an opening he had died because the foot had already become infected, gangreous [sic], and it was too late.

I can't get a dentist appointment for my two children. "We don't take welfare patients" — and these are people that the Welfare recommended. . . .

I went in [to the County Hospital] and told the head nurse about it [his son was hit by a car], she said, "Well, we can't take him." Of course he was in pain. His leg was just smashed all to pieces where the bumper hit him.

The only place we can refer for charity hospitalization is in University Medical Center in Little Rock [150 miles away]. But even then, they are so crowded that the doctors always have to make prior appointments and make sure space is available.[22]

Small wonder the poor often seem physically inferior! What about the mental effects of malnutrition and lack of medical care? More study must be done, but present indications are that malnutrition takes a heavy toll. Brain growth in the fetus can be retarded by poor nutrition of the expectant mother. Protein deficiencies can also retard brain growth in early childhood. We need to know much more than we do about ways to keep poverty from being self-perpetuating, but there is no doubt that the first step is to feed the children.

Studies among black children in impoverished areas of the South found 54 percent and 80 percent of the two school populations tested suffering from intestinal worms. The roundworms consume much of the skimpy food supply of such children. A 1968 study also found cases of scurvy, pellagra, rickets, kwashiorkor, and marasmus. Kwashiorkor is a result of protein deficiency; marasmus is a result of caloric deficiency—less politely called starvation. Schaefer showed a senate committee the result—a film of an emaciated baby with "staring eyes and match-stick arms." The film was not of Biafra, but of Mississippi.[23]

Several prominent senators have been startled at the findings of their committees on poverty and are determined to improve our methods for the relief of poverty and malnutrition. What legislative progress has been made in the past? Why is previous legislation inadequate? What kinds of new proposals are under study?

[22]The President's Commission on Income Maintenance Programs, *op. cit.*, p. 18.
[23]Robert A. Liston, *The American Poor: A Report on Poverty in the United States*, Dell Publishing Co., Inc., New York, 1970, pp. 122–126.

PROGRAMS AND PROMISES

Consistent with the achievement ethic, past programs have been geared to exclude the undeserving. Even in the New Deal period of the 1930s, when it was abundantly clear that hard-working people had been laid off by the millions through no fault of their own, attempts were still made to prevent giving a direct handout. Makeshift jobs were provided under WPA (Work Projects Administration), the CCC (Civilian Conservation Corps), and various other agencies. Some work projects were severely criticized, but they at least made it possible for people to remain at work, and some made remarkable improvements in the type of environmental and conservation work advocated today. Such projects may again become means of coping with unemployment.

SOCIAL SECURITY The major New Deal accomplishment for coping with poverty was the Social Security Act. The old age and survivor's features provided benefits for the aged and for widows and children. Later the program was extended to aid disabled workers and to provide health insurance for the aged (medicare). One trouble with the Old Age, Survivors, and Disabled (OASDI) benefits is that they are proportionate to a person's earnings. The poorer a worker is at retirement, the less retirement pay he receives. The retirement pay is low enough so that many of the aged on social security fall below the poverty line. Another problem is that the aged find it very difficult to supplement their social security incomes. Until they have passed the age of 72, there is a limit to how much they can earn without having their earnings deducted from social security benefits. The present limit is $1680 per year. This places the aged in a position where they cannot necessarily collect all the retirement pay they are entitled to, and flies in the face of one of the otherwise enlightened features of the act—the principle that payments are rights earned by the worker's own tax contribution to the system, not merely charity. There is no equivalent to a pauper's oath.

State unemployment insurance laws (supplemented by the federal government) add benefits to those laid off from their jobs, but such benefits are uneven and short-ranged, with a maximum of twenty six weeks in most states. During recession periods the length of time of payments is insufficient. Twice in the 1960s Congress extended the period of payments at federal cost. The amount of payment depends on wages, but ranges widely from a low of $34 per week in Mississippi to $72 in Hawaii.[24] As of 1968 almost one-third of the labor force was exempted from unemployment insurance. Some (state and government employees in most cases) had other insurance policies. Others, especially migratory agricultural workers and domestic workers, had low pay, no private insurance, and no state unemployment insurance. To those of comfortable incomes and just below, insurance is provided. To the poorest it is denied.

AFDC Because social security leaves many gaps in aid to the poor, other programs have been developed. The largest in cost is Aid to Families with Dependent Children

[24]The President's Commission on Income Maintenance Programs, *op. cit.*, p. 109.

(AFDC). Although an indispensable aid, AFDC has many shortcomings. Consistent with the ethic of "no work, no pay" most states do not provide benefits to children whose fathers are able-bodied. Actually, if the head of a family of four or more works full time at the federal minimum wage of $1.60 per hour, his family will still fall below the poverty line. No provisions are made to supplement his income. If the father is able-bodied but cannot find work, his children are ineligible for aid in twenty five states and actually receive such aid in very few cases. As of 1970 only 100,000 families with men present were receiving aid for dependent children. The present policy makes it seem that children should be punished if there is the slightest hint that their fathers are indolent. It also makes it seem better for fathers to desert than to stay at home when they are unable to find jobs.

The definition of able-bodied is often extremely strict. In Wolfe County, Kentucky, 5,000 of the 6,500 inhabitants were below the poverty line in 1968, but few received welfare. Johnson, a typical case, suffered from silicosis, which results from years of coal mining and which causes shortness of breath and a feeling of smothering. However, his family could not receive welfare because Johnson was not regarded as "permanently and totally disabled." In his case, at least, food stamps were provided. The Johnson family was permitted to buy $82 worth of food stamps for only $3. Sometimes not even $3 was available, but it was paid by the Office of Economic Opportunity (OEO).[25]

The welfare system also assumes that "unemployment and receipt of assistance are mutually exclusive. This view is untenable in a world in which employable persons may have potential earnings below subsistence standards."[26] It is this policy that gives rise to a peculiar social injustice by which an unemployed family head can make more money than one who is employed full time.

Another difficulty with existing systems is that AFDC payments are very low in most states. In 1969 the average payment per dependent child in the United States was $43 per child, but the national average failed to describe many states. In Mississippi the average recipient got $10 per child per month; in Massachusetts, $65 per month.[27] For a child to live on 33¢ per day (the Mississippi requirement) would call for a spartan discipline reminiscent of the orphanage in Dickens' *Oliver Twist*.

THE OFFICE OF ECONOMIC OPPORTUNITY The Johnson Administration launched what it called a "war on poverty," the major feature of which was the creation of the Office of Economic Opportunity. The effort was not the type of war that called for drastic institutional changes, but it did launch a number of experimental programs that have been helpful. More than 1,000 Community Action Agencies were created in various cities, with such aims as establishing industries, building rental houses, establishing cooperative buying organizations, providing child care, exchanging information on

[25]Liston, *op. cit.*, pp. 78–79.
[26]The President's Commission on Income Maintenance Programs, *op. cit.*, p. 5.
[27]*Ibid.*, pp. 6–7.

employment, and repairing houses. The philosophy of the program called for participation by the citizens of the poverty areas themselves.

Another widely acclaimed policy of OEO was the establishment of Head Start programs aimed at giving children of depressed poverty areas a better start in school. Studies of its results indicated only partial success in spite of general agreement that a real effort was made. While he was Secretary of Health, Education and Welfare, Robert Finch concluded that an even earlier time of help was needed; the development of mentality can be damaged at an extremely early age.[28] He could have well added that good mental development starts with proper nutrition of the mother while she is carrying the child.

One of the most promising services of OEO has been provision of legal assistance in many states. Lawyers serving the poor have done much to help them from being denied their rightful earnings, being overcharged by merchants, victimized by garnishment proceedings, or denied the right to organize. Although bitterly opposed by Governor Reagan, the California Rural Legal Assistance Program (CRLA) has been particularly successful in handling many cases for the poor. The victimization of people who have no schooling, no influence, and no knowledge of how to obtain their rights is often accomplished with virtually no resistance. Dr. Hector Garcia tells of an interview with a law-enforcement officer who worked 30 years among Mexican-American migratory workers:

> I said, "In this 30 years or so of your law officer's work, have you ever got a search warrant, have you ever gone to the justice of the peace or the judge and gotten a search warrant? And the answer was "No."
> And this is fantastic, that this ranger would have worked 30 years and arrested thousands of people and never been able to get a search warrant—or arrest warrant![29]

The importance of legal assistance can hardly be overemphasized. A number of enclaves of poverty have taken their first steps toward a feeling of human dignity and mastery over their fate when they have learned that access to justice is possible.

The OEO has also concentrated on training plans, especially for people who have had very little education and lack any of the skills needed for employment. A large number of people have been aided by the program, but it has been criticized on grounds of its great expense in terms of the number of people aided.

THE FAMILY ASSISTANCE PROGRAM All the aids and programs discussed omit many people and result in uneven benefits throughout the United States. Hardship and hunger and child labor still continue. There is a tendency for the very poorest areas to be helped least, and there is no effective floor for family income.

[28]Liston, *op. cit.*, pp. 155–156.
[29]Hearings before the Senate Subcommittee on Labor and Public Welfare, *op. cit.*, Part 4B, p. 1528.

The President's Commission on Income Maintenance Programs advocates a program of income supplement to be federally administered and to provide for the same minimum income level in all states. The original committee recommendations were for a floor of $2,400 per year per four-member family, which is slightly below the poverty line. The actual administration proposal to Congress cut the ceiling to $1,600 per year for a family of four—substantially below the poverty line.

A secondary feature of the proposal would be to supplement existing income on a graduated scale. If, for example, a family of four received no income whatever, the government would provide $2,400 by the original commission proposal. By the same proposal, if a family earned $1,800, the government would supplement its income by $1,400, making it seem worthwhile to work in order to earn more than the bare minimum. Supplements would be possible up to a maximum income of $5,000 per year.[30] These figures are only indicative of the philosophy of the program and will be sure to change in accordance with the mood of Congress and administration and conditions of inflation or deflation.

The intent of the system is to provide enough incentive so that family heads will continue to work, except mothers with young children who might consider it best for their families to stay home. Only about 30 percent of present-day welfare mothers would be better off staying at work, so low are their average earnings.[31] The principle would be instituted that families are entitled to assistance even if headed by an adult male. The adult male would be required to register for work, but his family would not be penalized if no job could be found. In the words of the commission:

> It is time to design public policy to deal with the two basic facts of American poverty: the poor lack money, and most of them cannot increase their incomes themselves.[32]

OPPOSITION TO FAMILY ASSISTANCE PROGRAM At present there is strong opposition to the Family Assistance Program. Conservatives oppose the idea on the grounds that it would add many recipients to public welfare costs, probably increase the total cost of combating poverty, and philosophically, it would go too far in the direction of admitting that a plain handout is the most rational way to handle the poverty pro-

---

There is considerable pressure for welfare reform and many proposals for consideration. Study these; express your opinion to your congressman and senators.

---

[30]The President's Commission on Income Maintenance Programs, *op. cit.*, p. 58.
[31]F. Helmut Weymar, "The Poor Should Be Paid Bonuses," in Robert Theobold (ed.), *Social Problems for America in the Seventies*, Doubleday & Company, Inc., Garden City, N.Y., 1969, pp. 55–71.
[32]The President's Commission on Income Maintenance Programs, *op. cit.*, p. 6.

gram. The AFL-CIO is also opposed to the program unless it carries minimum-wage provisions. Organized labor does not want to see a system that will require recipients of benefits to agree to work as soon as a job is available, regardless of the wages paid. A number of liberal members of Congress oppose the plan because the income floor is well below the poverty level. Present legislation would demand continued payment under AFDC, in spite of the Family Assistance Program.

OTHER ATTACKS ON POVERTY

In the discussion of population, it was pointed out that considerable headway against poverty could be made simply by discouraging the poor from having large families. Present population statistics indicate that some headway is being made, but it is still true that the poor have more babies than the well-to-do. Only recently have public agencies in most states made family planning and birth control devices available to the poor. Although the population approach to poverty is useful, it must not be seen as a panacea. Even families with a small number of children are not able to break out of the pattern of poverty if the family is surrounded by unemployment, dilapidated housing, high delinquency and drug-abuse rates, poor schools, and a general atmosphere of hopelessness. Above all, there must be employment opportunities. Education is needed too, but, like population control, it is not a complete answer in itself.

THE EDUCATION PANACEA The United States has placed a great emphasis on education as the answer to all problems. For many people it has been the road to upward mobility, but is has two major limitations. First, some people do not do well in school, because of lack of native capacity or lack of the necessary stimulating home background. Whatever the reason, many children become involved in a vicious circle of failure leading to discouragement, which in turn leads to further failure. Much more effort must be put into education before it can solve this problem. Secondly, education alone does not create jobs. There must be opportunity, or the road out of poverty becomes impossible.

Bayard Rustin[33] sees correctly the limitations to the education solution when he contrasts the poor of today with the large numbers of immigrant poor that entered America in the nineteenth century. The latter found opportunities, not because they were educated—they were not—but because there were opportunities open. There was land to settle, and there were jobs for men with muscle, jobs for "a strong back and a weak mind," according to the old expresssion. We have long since grown accustomed to saying there are no longer jobs for the physically strong but uneducated, but we are also going to have to face the fact that there are not always jobs for the educated, either. This is the dilemma of education and retraining. In times of job

---

[33]Bayard Rustin, "Education?" in Robert Theobald (ed.), *Dialogue on Poverty*, The Bobbs-Merrill Company, Inc., Indianapolis, 1967, pp. 53–60.

Man pitted against man in the predawn rush for the dwindling supply of jobs for those with obsolete skills.

shortages, the newly trained man can find a job only by taking the job from someone else. The situation creates a crisis that can pit man against man and race against race. To state the matter cruelly, in times of high unemployment, every man with a job has a vested interest in keeping his competitor unemployed. Education will not solve the problem; the only solution lies in more jobs.

CREATING JOBS Creating jobs is particularly difficult in these days of rapidly developing automation, and yet there are countries with a fair degree of automation and with labor shortages—Germany especially. When the economic system is operating in high gear, with full production, job opportunities seem to present themselves. In the United States, the long period of unemployment of the Great Depression ended with wartime prosperity. War, of course, must not be the solution. If we can have prosperity only through death, we will do well to forego prosperity. But surely there are other possibilities. The solution we seek must not be the false prosperity of war, or the illusion that all is well because nearly everyone is getting enough of a handout to keep himself alive. As Michael Harrington has said, the only proper solution must "bring these millions of poor to the point where they can make their contribution to the United States.[34]

Even the most sanguine proposals about bringing the poor into the general society must recognize that some direct giving of aid will be necessary. There will always be widows with dependent children, the physically ill, the aged, and others incapable of productive activity, but there are proposals for reducing the poverty level far below its present 25 million.

ECONOMIC GROWTH AND EMPLOYMENT Leon Keyserling,[35] one-time head of the President's Committee of Economic Advisors and one of the authors of the Full Employment Act, has long advocated means of keeping the economy in high gear. This, he contends, is the only way of really combating poverty. If employment rates are high, then retraining simply has the effect of changing the personnel of the unemployed. Recent social legislation has been worthwhile in that it is aimed at giving black as well as white Americans access to what jobs exist, but it has not done much to actually create jobs.

Keyserling and Rustin both suggest that we spend much more government money to increase our rate of economic growth. Their argument is that if there is a balance between the amount of economic goods produced and consumed and the amount of money poured into the economy, we shall have little inflation. The much more wasteful spending of wartime probably adds greater inflationary pressure, but

[34]Michael Harrington, *The Other America*, Penguin Books, Inc., Baltimore, 1963, pp. 178–179.
[35]Leon Keyserling, "The Problem of Problems: Economic Growth," In Robert Theobald (ed.), *Social Problems for America in the Seventies*, Doubleday & Company, Inc., Garden City, N.Y., 1968, pp. 1–24. See also Leon Keyserling, "Programs: Present and Future," in Robert Theobald (ed.), *Dialogue on Poverty*, The Bobbs-Merrill Company, Indianapolis, 1967, pp. 91–104.

Keyserling reminds us that during World War II we maintained a fantastic rate of production, along with full employment and the uneconomic waste of war, but we did not have very rapid inflation. He is convinced that we can solve most of our poverty problem by the investment of many billions of dollars (even through deficit spending if necessary) on housing, hospitals, rest homes, parks and playgrounds, cleaning of rivers, lakes, and forests, general beautification of the land and cities, and improvement of the quality of life. In some respects Keyserling's viewpoints are about as consistent with the traditional achievement ethic as any program can be: all idle manpower and equipment is seen as inexcusable waste as long as there are jobs to be done. In other respects, his approach is not congenial to more conservative American views. Conservative economists would fear that his approach is too inflationary. It is also hard to see how the program could work without making the federal government an even larger employer than it is today.

Keyserling's ideas are by no means unprecedented. During the days of the New Deal, a far more burdensome problem of poverty was partly solved by work projects. Under the WPA, 5,000 public buildings were constructed and 85,000 repaired; 46,000 bridges and viaducts were built or improved; and more than 15,000 parks and playgrounds were built. Some people would call for such types of projects every time unemployment becomes high, whether or not we go into the extensive deficit spending advocated by Keyserling.[36]

CAPITAL FOR THE POOR The idea of trying to help the poor, especially the ghetto poor, to open businesses of their own has had a certain amount of political appeal, but it has not been carried very far. Louis L. Kelso and Patricia Hetter suggest a much greater concentration on this area. Their contention is that undesirable jobs and government handouts, although a means of keeping body and soul together, do nothing toward making full participation in society. The millions who came to America for the opportunities it could offer were looking for more than jobs. They wanted to own part of America; they wanted the secret of how one becomes affluent.

Kelso and Hetter say, in effect, that there will be a hard core of poverty as long as there is a "hard core of affluence," that is, as long as all the capital goods are owned by outsiders. The situation of which they speak is most typical of the black ghetto, but it exists in all slums, both urban and rural. Kelso and Hetter advocate low interest (or even no interest) loans to make possible the creation of business among the poor, black and white. Only this could give them the optimistic sense of participation so badly needed.

There are several proposals, then, that go beyond the mere welfare approach to poverty. Many of OEO's projects—community projects and legal assistance programs—aim at self-help and pride. The idea of employing all those who need jobs

---

[36]Garth L. Mangum, "Guaranteeing Employment Opportunities," in Robert Theobald (ed.), *Social Policies for America in the Seventies, op. cit.*, pp. 25–54.

in the great task of contributing to the future of America is another approach that combines access to indispensable money with a measure of pride in accomplishment. The idea of Kelso and Hetter, in a more conservative, proprietary way, attempts the same hopeful approach.

PROBLEMS RELATED TO POVERTY By now we have noted that poverty is related to many aspects of the social system. It is inextricably linked to the types of industrial change that have brought automation and shifting job requirements and that have dried up the demand for rural labor. It is closely connected to education and the need for retraining programs. Although the majority of poor people are white, the proportion of poverty is greater for blacks, Chicanos, and Indians, so the study of poverty is partly a study of racial and ethnic problems. Above all, poverty flouts the moral norms of the country, especially at a time of real potential for universal abundance. Even the proposed solutions to poverty are linked to the normative order and the work ethic, with many leaders expressing a desire to provide work rather than having to resort completely to the present welfare system.

As the title of this chapter suggests, the problems of the poor are much more persistent than optimistic America had ever supposed they would be. These problems need constant attack on many fronts. If we merely scold the poor for being incorrigible, or deny that poverty exists, or assume that all poverty will be buried inevitably under a mountain of American productivity, the problems will remain. If the present mood of searching for new solutions continues, perhaps the time will come when we will no longer have to say "the everlasting poor."

SUGGESTED READINGS

Kain, John F. (ed.): *Race and Poverty: The Economics of Discrimination*, Prentice-Hall, Inc., Englewood Cliffs, N.J., 1969.

Discusses the close connection between being black and being poor. The last few selections are on policy alternatives and represent such varied views as those of the Kerner Commission, the late Robert F. Kennedy, and President Nixon.

Liston, Robert A.: *The American Poor: A Report on Poverty in the United States*, Dell Publishing Co., Inc., New York, 1970.

A short, hard-hitting book on poverty and hunger, defects in the welfare system, and various attempted improvements and recommendations.

Seligman, Ben B. (ed.): *Aspects of Poverty*, Thomas Y. Crowell Company, New York, 1968.

An excellent collection of excerpts from works by Herman P. Miller, Kenneth B. Clark, Jules Henry, and several others. Includes the ghetto, human obsolescence, schools, housing, race, and poverty, and an antipoverty strategy.

Theobald, Robert (ed.): *Dialogue on Poverty*, The Bobbs-Merrill Company, Indianapolis, 1967.

A series of dialogues on poverty and education, poverty and religion, poverty and inadequate economic growth, and programs for the alleviation of poverty.

The President's Commission on Income Maintenance Programs, *Poverty Amid Plenty: The American Paradox*, U.S. Government Printing Office, Washington, D.C., November 1969.

Not all will agree with the proposed solutions presented, but there can be little argument with the facts disclosed by the commission—and they are grim facts—or with the need for a reexamination of our present system.

 **QUESTIONS**

1. Why has the United States neglected poverty more than many other well-to-do countries have done?

2. Who are the poor in terms of age, region, rural-urban distribution, occupation, and race and ethnic group?

3. What conditions of migratory agricultural labor in parts of the U.S. tend to create a perpetual culture of poverty?

4. What are the physical and mental effects of malnutrition?

5. What are the inadequacies and inequities in the present program of welfare?

6. Why would some economists say that education and motivation will not necessarily solve the problems of poverty?

10 The problem of overpopulation has received so much publicity that it is hardly necessary to point out the incongruity between the needs of the times and the older ethic of maximal reproduction. Many questions remain, however. Just how severe is the problem of overpopulation in the underdeveloped world? Do underdeveloped countries have possibilities for mitigating the problem by the same rapid increase in productivity and decline in birth rate that has taken place in Europe? If overcrowding goes on indefinitely, will it have serious psychological, as well as physical, effects on the human race? Are we possibly undermining the quality of future populations by chromosome-damaging drugs, chemicals, and pollutants?

Nearly all these questions are alarming. Some could be answered, partly, by pointing out that the United States is not really densely populated compared to much of the rest of the world. Why, then, is overpopulation a worry to us? Another thought that might prevent too much alarmism is that trends do not always continue indefinitely. Are there any new ideas and values in the most crowded regions of the world that might reverse the high-birth-rate value? If so, will such changes occur in time to prevent disaster? Finally, are there any policies that might be pursued on an international scale to head off the population disaster that so many experts see looming over the horizon?

BE FRUITFUL, MULTIPLY

According to the accounts of the ancient Aztecs, the earth has been destroyed four times, but each time man has reappeared and reproduced. Certain Brazilian Indian tribes claim the earth has been destroyed seven times. Many stories of the Near East relate only one disaster of such proportions—the Great Flood, told in the Babylonian story of Gilgamesh and the Hebrew story of Noah. In all the destruction stories the narrators have assured us that at least one male and female survived, and that they multiplied rapidly. The Biblical story is by far the best known in the Western World, and its results are unique among Bible stories. In all other cases God gave man commandment after commandment—not only the famous ten, but the hundreds of minor rules and regulations of Leviticus and Deuteronomy. Man immediately went forth and broke all the rules and regulations but one. One rule he obeyed with vigor, enthusiasm, and glee—"Be fruitful, and multiply, and replenish the earth."

Not only was man happy to obey that commandment, he was compulsive about it. In many societies men without offspring have married wife after wife to try again for issue. Sometimes they have set up rules whereby other people's children ceremonially can become their own. There are even cases of "ghost marriages" in which a devoted widow marries to the memory of her deceased husband so as to bear him children posthumously. Everywhere the desire for offspring has been evident. For aristocracies, there has been an ambition to continue the dynasty; for the humble there has been a desire to somehow avoid the oblivion of genetic death. In most cases there has been the desire for children to love, to teach, and to put to work. Children have also helped to rekindle the fires of memory of youth in parents and grandparents, and to prevent the disaster of an old age of loneliness and misery.

Once man replenished the earth, he proceeded to replenish it again and again. All the reasons for desiring children continued, even though the earth suddenly began to shrink. The earth, which once was as vast as eternity, was seen in new perspective. It became a tiny island isolated in the infinity of space, capable of being crowded, overcrowded, eroded, mined, and destroyed. This, too, man set out to accomplish.

THE OUTDATED NORM

The reproduction norm is obviously outdated, but it is not easily laid to rest. There are countries where a considerable majority of people have only from one to three children per family and where population is, consequently, stabilizing, but much of the world continues to be excessively fruitful. The United States in the 1970s shows a birth rate that has declined considerably below that of the "baby boom" years of the 1940s and 1950s, but the population is still increasing rather rapidly. Before discussing the demographic problems of the United States specifically, however, it will be good to look at certain population characteristics of the entire world. A historical study of world population will lead to an awareness of certain general

Once the vast, empty earth called for human habitation; now nature is desecrated by the swarming multitudes that invade her once silent places.

principles about the reproduction habits of people, and to an intimation of whether the current population explosion is only temporary, or whether it may continue far into the future.

DEMOGRAPHIC TRANSITION A demographic transition, or population change, has occurred in the last three centuries, changing the earth from a rather sparsely populated planet to a crowded planet. Such changes have taken place before, but only on a minor scale. The biologist Edward S. Deevey contends that the world has actually known three different human population explosions. The first population explosion took place in the dim beginnings of humanity when our ancestors first learned to use stone tools and make themselves better competitors for survival than most other animals. In a mere million years the population increased from only 1,000 or so to about 5 million inhabitants. The human race was growing at an unsteady pace, averaging perhaps 0.5 percent per century.

The second population explosion began about ten thousand years ago, when man began to learn how to cultivate crops and live from the agricultural produce of the land, rather than purely from hunting, gathering, and fishing. Food became more plentiful and dependable, and the world's population increased more rapidly, doubling itself in from one to two thousand years.

The third great population explosion came with the industrial-scientific age. It seemed fairly gradual at first, with the population doubling in a little over a century back in the 1600s and 1700s, but presently it is changing much more rapidly. In 1960 the world's population seemed to be doubling about every fifty years.[1] Since then people have really knuckled down to the task and are doubling the world's population in about thirty-three years.

The most common use of the concept of demographic transition is to describe the third transitional period mentioned by Deevey. It seems important to mention the first two, however, because otherwise a question might arise as to whether population explosions have been merely temporary phenomena followed by reversals in growth rates. The answer seems to be an emphatic "No," even though there have been temporary downturns caused by war, famine, or plague. There was, of course, nothing disturbing about the first two population explosions, but the third one has most of the world's demographers deeply worried.

DEMOGRAPHIC TRANSITION IN THE WESTERN WORLD In Europe and many other areas of European settlement, such as the United States and Canada, population in the last two or three centuries has increased more rapidly than in the rest of the world. From 1600 until 1950, people of British descent increased from 3 million to 150 million, a fiftyfold increase, while the world as a whole increased about sixfold. Between 1750 and 1950 the United States broke all records by increasing from 2 million to 166 million. During the same period Europe (excluding Russia) increased in population from 125 million to 392 million, and Russia from 42 to 180 million. While most European countries were increasing population at least three or four times, China, India, and Pakistan little more than doubled their populations. In recent decades the population increase pattern has changed, with China, India, and Pakistan all expected to more than double their populations from 1950 to 2000, while Europe will increase her inhabitants by only one-fourth.[2]

The reason the population increase has slowed down in Western Europe is primarily a shift in values. Kingsley Davis believes that whenever and wherever urbanization, industrialization, education, and rising living standards take place, new values begin to replace those that are rooted primarily in family and kinship. The change is not merely a matter of availability of contraceptive devices, which are often available but not used in underdeveloped countries, but an attitude change. When standards of living and education reach a particular level, people become interested in their own careers and in the amenities of life that are finally within their reach. They do not want to jeopardize their prosperity and opportunities by too large a family.[3]

[1]Edward S. Deevey, Jr., "The Human Population," *Scientific American*, vol. 208, pp. 194–198, September 1960.
[2]E. A. Wrigley, *Population and History*, McGraw-Hill Book Company, New York, 1969, pp. 205–207.
[3]Kingsley Davis, "Population," in Garrett Hardin (ed.), *Science, Conflict, and Society*, W. H. Freeman & Company, San Francisco, 1969, pp. 101–110.

In contrast to the reduced birth rates of the industrialized countries, what is referred to here as "the outdated norm" continues in many parts of the world. There are numerous reasons besides the overall sentiment that family alone gives life meaning and value. Family also ensures a supply of children to help with the farm work and to take care of parents in their old age. Not only must there be children, but there must be many children. Until the most recent generation, large numbers of children have died young, so at least five or six children have been thought necessary to guarantee the survival of the family. The large-family norm continues even after the reasons supporting it begin to diminish under the impact of inoculations and medical care. Often religious norms insist on high reproduction rates, and sometimes large numbers of children are necessary to demonstrate a man's masculinity.

Sentiments, too, are important. Even for many ambitious, career-oriented modernists there are moments when family and children provide the greatest psychological security in life. There is an old African folktale that is rich with wisdom about man's emotions regarding children. God created a man and a woman and gave them a happy world in which to live. They asked him if they could live there forever or whether they must someday die. He explained to them that there were two kinds of death and that they would have to choose between them. "You can die as the moon dies, or as the banana tree dies. The moon dies, but returns again the same. The banana tree dies and does not return, but it sends up the shoots that are its children." The man and woman pondered the question, and then decided to choose the death of the banana tree so that they could have children. Since then children have been more important than life itself.

We know from comparative sociology and anthropology that the urge to have children is not uniform for all people, but it is very close to being a species universal. To deny people the right to parenthood is considered cruel. In only a few societies have even slaves been denied that right. The real question, though, is one of numbers. Can people of the underdeveloped portion of the world be persuaded to face old age with only one or two children, or will they continue to desire large families? In many parts of the world even a stable population is disastrously high. Even now China is reaching the 800 million mark and will probably pass the billion mark well before the end of the century.

BIRTH RATE AND DEATH RATE Crude birth rate and death rate are both given in terms of numbers per thousand population. The birth rate of the United States during the baby boom after World War II reached about 25 per thousand population, but dropped to just over 17 by 1970. Some of the world's underdeveloped countries have birth rates of between 40 and 50 per thousand, and death rates of only 15. Such vital statistics show a rate of natural increase that has been rare in the world's history.

If Deevey's estimates are correct, Old Stone-Age man increased his population at about 0.05 percent per year. By 1750 the world's population was growing nearly ten times as fast, 0.4 percent per year. By 1900 the annual growth rate was 0.8

Stages of population growth

Occupational distribution of employed workers 18 years old and over
with selected amounts of formal education, March 1970

percent, and by 1965 it was 1.8 percent. The United Nations projections expect a slight decline to about 1.25 percent by the year 2000. The population history of the world can be presented graphically as above.

Although birth rate eventually begins to decline, it is still far ahead of death rate, and the third population explosion goes on. There is a tragic irony in the situation: the medical advances that have lengthened human life now threaten to make that life extremely cheap.

The problem is overwhelmingly one of lowered death rate, but there are even places where birth rate has increased as death rate declines. These are all in the less industrialized parts of the world. There are various reasons, one of which is that the improved medical care has prevented stillborn babies and maternal deaths at childbirth. Better medical care has also meant that far more girls live to reach the reproductive years of life and that there are fewer widows in the world. Another change has been the general abandonment of the practice of infanticide — the killing of unwanted babies. Yet another change in the direction of greater population has been the abandonment of old taboos about sex avoidance for lactating women. When women nursed their babies for two or three years and observed rules of sex avoidance during that time, the birth rate slowed down. (The custom was generally observed only in polygamous societies in which men could continue mating relations with their other wives.) Eventually, it is hoped, the underdeveloped world will reduce

---

Try tracing your own family tree several generations back. How many children were born? How many survived to maturity? Compare with the present generation.

its birth rate, but the immediate result of modernization is often an increase in birth rate, as well as a rapid decline in death rate.[4]

The result of changes in birth rate and death rate is that while the industrially developed parts of the world increased by 11 percent during the decade from 1960 to 1970, the underdeveloped regions increased by 24 percent.[5] Such figures explain why population, a problem everywhere, has reached the state of crisis in the underdeveloped world. The crisis involves malnutrition and poverty, approaching starvation, and perhaps various kinds of pathologies.

BEYOND THE MALTHUSIAN NIGHTMARE

One hundred seventy years ago Thomas Malthus wrote an essay on population that has been a subject of discussion ever since. The malthusian idea can be stated very briefly: population tends to increase more rapidly than food supply. Consequently, if a population is not checked by some kinds of controls, there will eventually be pressure against the limits of food supply, and resultant starvation. Malthus even reduced his idea to the mathematical principle that population increases at geometric progression (1, 2, 4, 8, 16, 32) and food supply at arithmetic progression (1, 2, 3, 4, 5, 6). Such a formulation is highly dubious, and even if it correctly describes a general tendency, has many exceptions. The population of the United States increased very rapidly throughout most of our history, but the food supply increased even more rapidly. A more likely implication of Malthus' ideas is the principle of diminishing returns, although the term "diminishing returns" was never used by him. The law of diminishing returns holds that a time comes when increased effort and investment put into the land (or any type of production) pays less and less in dividends, until the point is reached when the payoff is not sufficient to attract further effort. Even stated this way, the idea of exhaustion of food supply is sometimes debated. In recent years there has been a "green revolution" in many underdeveloped areas of the world. New varieties of wheat, rice, and other grains have increased the yield of lands so much that anticipated famines have been averted — or maybe only postponed. If the idea of diminishing returns is applicable, the time will come when additional increments in work, fertilizer, better strains of seed, and all other artifices known will not be sufficient to avert famine. The only possibility in the long run will be to restrict population increase.

Malthus suggested gloomily that there are other natural controls on population besides famine: war, disease, and vice. None sounds like a very attractive alternative, not even vice. His suggestion was that people could become so debauched by vice

[4]Dudley Kirk, "World Population: Hope Ahead," in *Stanford Today*, pp. 10–11, Winter 1968. For a more thorough description of primitive controls on birth rates, see Burton Benedict, "Population Regulations in Primitive Societies," in Anthony Allison (ed.), *Population Control*, Penguin Books, Inc., Baltimore, 1970, pp. 165–179.

[5]M. A. El-Badry, "Population Projections for the World, Developed and Developing Regions," *Annals of the American Academy of Political and Social Science*, vol. 369, p. 11, January 1967.

as to undermine their strength, health, and reproductive vigor. A few periods in history suggest such a possibility—the roaring orgies of the degenerative period of Roman history, for example. Francis L. K. Hsu suggests that such was often the fate of some families of old China. After they made their way to wealth and position, they began to decline through inactivity or vice or some type of social pathology.

If we substitute the term "social pathology" for Malthus' word "vice," we may be looking at a result of population crowding that also acts as a brake on population increase, although not one to be recommended. Several animal studies suggest that crowding has natural limits, but some also suggest a horror that goes beyond the nightmare of Malthus. Deevey's essay, "The Hare and the Haruspex: A Cautionary Tale,"[6] tells, for example, of the mysterious death of overcrowded snowshoe hares in Minnesota. "Life quickly leaves them, and they die from the slightest injury." The reason is not famine or war or predators or even disease. The reason is atrophy of the liver caused by conditions of stress due to overcrowding. A haruspex was an ancient Roman soothsayer who believed he could divine the future by reading the entrails of animals. Deevey suggests that we might be reading the future of the human species in a similar way. He mentions many other cases of illness caused by overcrowding and other stress, but one is particularly striking. A report from the Philadelphia zoo blames "social pressures" for a tenfold increase in deaths from arteriosclerosis among the animal population.[7]

Probably the best-known experiment on the crowding of animal populations is the one done by John B. Calhoun.[8] Calhoun conducted a number of experiments with rats, allowing them to breed to a population of very great density in his laboratory. As the population density increased, the rats would no longer eat alone, but seemed always to crave company. At the same time they seemed not to really *like* company. Some became detached and somnolent; others became quarrelsome. Some became "pan-sexual," attempting relations not only with estrous females, but with unwilling females and also homosexual relations with males. The female rats no longer built adequate nests for their young, and many did not take care of them, but simply let them die. Male rats in some cases became cannibals, eating baby rats. By methods that could easily be subsumed under Malthus' category of vice, the population stabilized, but at a tremendously high level. Often in the final stages of crowding no sex object was sufficient to cause arousal, and the male rats showed no interest in mating.[9]

In another work, Calhoun presents some of his surmises concerning human populations. In setting up his rat colonies, Calhoun had always started with two to four breeding pairs. A friend, not knowing the procedure, started with sixteen breed-

[6]Edward S. Deevey, "The Hare and the Haruspex: A Cautionary Tale," in Eric Josephson and Mary Josephson, *Man Alone*, Dell Publishing Co., Inc., New York, 1962, p. 577.

[7]*Ibid.*, p. 584.

[8]John B. Calhoun, "Population Density and Social Pathology," *Scientific American*, vol. 206, pp. 139–146, February 1962.

[9]John B. Calhoun, "Population," in Allison (ed.), *op. cit.*, pp. 110–124.

Crowding the subway, as in a scene from *The Human Zoo*, with muggings, rapes, and the types of behavior noted in experiments with crowded rats.

ing pairs. It was observed that in the latter case the rats reached a much greater level of crowding before showing pathological behavior. Calhoun's conclusion is that they had been sufficiently crowded from the beginning so that they did not stake out a territory of their own to defend. Their conceptualization of space differed from that of normal rats. Calhoun conjectures that the same trait may apply to humans. Is it possible, then, that as far as psychological tolerance is concerned, we could reach a standing-room-only situation? Not quite, Dr. Calhoun assures us. There is a limit to our reconceptualizing space, and probably the maximum psychologically safe population for the world would be about 7.5 billion. That is a number we should reach early in the twenty-first century.

Desmond Morris, noted for his frank and brutal interpretations of human nature, wrote a book titled *The Human Zoo*. The title is drawn from a comparison between the pathological behavior of animals held captive in a zoo and what Morris considers the pathological human behavior caused by crowded, urban living. We live in a zoo, a place of unnatural crowding and stress. All species, Morris contends, have developed mechanisms for limiting their numbers, whether by increased aggressiveness

271

and fights over territory or the reduced reproductive capacity noted in the rat study. He even speculates that in unconscious ways mankind has tended to set brakes on his population growth by such practices as infanticide, human sacrifice, mutilation, head-hunting, cannibalism, and various sex taboos. In later societies:

> new sexual philosophies emerged that had the effect of reducing group fecundity; neuroses and psychoses proliferated, interfering with successful breeding; certain sexual practices increased, such as contraception, masturbation, homosexuality, fetishism and bestiality, which provided sexual consummation without the chance of fertilization. Slavery, imprisonment, castration, and voluntary celibacy also played their part.[10]

Whatever the explanation of the customs described by Morris, they have not succeeded in holding the world's population in check, as a daily increase of 150,000 people assures us. Not even combat, which urban civilizations changed from skirmishes to devastating wars, has been able to hold population in check. Despite pathologies, the human being remains far less restrained in his breeding habits than most of the crowded animals in the zoo. Is he in danger of decline in quality as his numbers increase in quantity?

POPULATION QUALITY

The problem of population quality poses two important questions: are we producing populations of favorable genetic stock, and can we provide an opportunity for good physical and mental health for the huge numbers now being born? The first question is highly controversial and open to every possible bias, but since it is frequently asked, it should be examined.

POPULATION QUALITY: GENOTYPE The observable physical traits of people constitute their phenotype. The phenotype can be modified in various ways. Hair can be curled or dyed, crooked teeth and noses can be straightened, girdles and bras can make remarkable modifications, and in a few extraordinary cases even sex can be changed through surgery. Behind all the superficial changes, however, is a genotype—the genetic structure that is inheritable and not easily given to tampering. Genetic changes do occur, however, usually through mutation—a modification of the genes that is nearly always unfavorable. Genetic change also occurs when the numbers of people having particular genetic traits, whether they are such unseen traits as blood types or such obvious traits as dwarfism, are increased.

What makes genetics controversial are the questions of what types of people are reproducing in largest numbers and what effect they will have on the future of the human race. Evolution, according to darwinian theory, tends to encourage reproduction among the "fit" and to eliminate the "unfit." The big question is "Who is

[10]Desmond Morris, *The Human Zoo*, McGraw-Hill Book Company, New York, 1969, pp. 150–151.

fit?" The layman who has not thought too deeply about the problem is inclined to judge fitness by physical strength, intelligence, moral goodness, or good looks. None of these criteria has much bearing on darwinian fitness. Fitness in the evolutionary sense can be defined only by a type of circular reasoning—those who survive long enough to bear offspring are fit simply because they have survived and reproduced; by the same reasoning, those who die too young to have reproduced are unfit. Hence, in one environment those people most resistant to endemic malaria are fit, be they tall, short, fat, thin, wise, dull, ugly, or beautiful. It is possible that such a pandemic as the black death changed the genetic composition of the human race to some extent, with the survivors being the descendants of those most fit in terms of resistance to disease. Tuberculosis may have had the same effect on many Indian tribes in more recent history.[11]

It would be reassuring to believe that intelligence is always connected with survival. In a general way it probably has been throughout the course of human evolution. Certainly it has been man's ability to create cultures that has made him the dominant species of the earth, and such cultures would have been impossible without mental development. The question at the present stage of cultural development, however, is whether the cultures of today are so protective as to eliminate beneficial natural selection, either for intelligence or physical strength, or for resistance to disease.

This question is subject to bias in interpretation. Every convinced racist thinks the other race is inferior. Social-class snobs tend to think of lower classes as genetically inferior. Hitler's program of so-called eugenics was sometimes corrupted into a practice of sterilization of the political nonconformist. Any attempt to define such categories of people as inferior is extremely dangerous nonsense.

A frequently occurring question is one of differential birth rates, with lower classes generally having more children than middle and upper classes. In most school populations it will be noted that there is a negative correlation between family size and the scores made on intelligence tests. If the low scores really do indicate low intelligence, and if the low intelligence is a truly genetic trait, then we would expect to see a gradual decline in intelligence with each passing generation. So far the evidence does not bear this out. What few old tests have been given to school children of the present generation indicate that they are doing at least as well, on the average, as the parental generation. A number of surveys were conducted by the Scottish Council for Research in Education to determine whether differential breeding habits were causing an intelligence decline among Scottish school children. The tests actually showed a generational increase in IQ scores. Whether the explanation is better nutrition, better educational methods, or simply being "test wise," the scores tend to foil the prophets of doom.[12]

---

[11]Theodosius Dobzhansky, *Mankind Evolving*, Yale University Press, New Haven, Conn., 1962, pp. 302–305.
[12]*Ibid.*, pp. 315–316.

Dysgenic effects of war: killing the strong.

There are not enough studies of the type conducted in Scotland for us to be sure of the answer to the problems of low achievement in particular families. It seems likely that for many such families the explanation can be failure in such areas as home training, education, motivation, self-image, and hope for the future. There is a second type of educational retardate whose IQ scores average considerably below those of the families merely deprived of equal opportunity. In some cases extreme mental retardation is caused by such genetic defects as gargoylism, mongolism, phenylketonuria, and amaurotic idiocy. In other cases defectiveness results from nongenetic problems such as congenital syphilis, encephalitis, rubella in the mother, Rh incompatibility, and cerebral trauma.[13]

In a less protective condition of human society people in the above categories would tend to be eliminated by natural selection. It is probably true that advanced cultures help the human race to carry a larger number of unfavorable genes than it once did. There are mitigating circumstances however. Many unfavorable genes are only occasional mutations (hemophilia, mongolism, and phenylketonuria, for example) and occur in families that are generally healthy and normal. There is no question that we need to know much more about genetic problems than we do, and long-term dysgenic trends are a definite possibility, but at present our major aim should be avoiding any man-made genetic defects.

INCREASING NATURE'S ERRORS If unfortunate mutations and differential selection are seen as errors of nature, it must be admitted that man can again improve on nature at erring. Natural mutations are frequent and almost invariably harmful, and now man is adding to the burden of mutant genes that the human race must carry. Atomic fallout is a major source of mutation, although authorities disagree as to how severe it is at present. Linus Pauling contends that we have already caused the births of hundreds of thousands of defective babies because of atomic fallout. Edward Teller considers the amount "tolerable," but no one denies that it increases the rate of mutation to some extent. Even overexposure to X rays can increase mutations. As mentioned in Chapters 3 and 4, there are other known or suspected sources of genetic damage: many types of drugs, both legal and illegal, various chemicals and food additives, and possibly contaminants entering water supplies.

We also do a bad job of dysgenic selection—that is, eliminating many of the physically and mentally strong from the human breeding grounds. Warfare at some earlier time in human development may have tended to eliminate the weak. Now it is much more likely to eliminate the strong. In a grim joke played against the processes of natural selection, the strong and well become the unfit—often selected to die in warfare and leave no descendants. Those with physical or mental defects are lucky; they are the fit.

[13]Edward Zigler, "Familial Mental Retardation: A Continuing Dilemma, *Science*, vol. 155, pp. 292–298, January 20, 1967.

Dobzhansky suggests that we may be also including another type of person among the unfit. Those who are particularly sensitive and intelligent may be more likely than the average person to succumb to heart attacks and other killing conditions in an age of tension and nervous strain. Certainly man needs to give more thought to the quality of his genetic product.

POPULATION QUALITY: PHENOTYPE The other major question about population quality is whether we will be able to bring the people of the world up to the potentials with which they are naturally endowed. During the twentieth century, social scientists have generally studied environmental influences on the human material at hand—the phenotype—almost to the exclusion of biological heredity. It is good that this has been the field of emphasis, because it is the area most amenable to improvement.

One population problem that makes it difficult to bring all people up to their potential is the extremely large number of children in the world. In the United States the average age is under twenty five. In some of the underdeveloped countries of the world, more than half the people are fifteen years of age or younger. Our very high birth rate of the 1940s and 1950s has been a serious problem for us; the much higher birth rate for many underdeveloped countries has been a disaster. Even well-meaning governments, struggling hard to improve the conditions of their people, find it impossible to provide minimal education for such hordes of children. The same age-distribution problem makes health care and rising production standards difficult, and probably will create a serious job shortage in the future.

The other way in which population problems make it difficult to provide opportunities for people is a matter of differential birth rate. As noted, the poor have more children than the well-to-do and are often unable to give them the opportunity, the motivation, or even the hope for success. Reduced birth rate on the part of the poor is a necessity, but focusing on birth rate should not obscure the sight of society's duty to those who are already here. With good social policies, many of the disadvantages of poverty can be greatly reduced in the wealthy countries of the West. For the impoverished countries of the world the problem is at present hopeless.

POPULATION U.S.A.

The crowding of the earth is part of the problem of the United States. We inhabit the same planet as the lands of greatest population explosion, and we are making our

---

Attitude survey: ask a sample of college students how many children they would like to have. Compare with a group of noncollege people of approximately the same age.

276

own contribution to the crowding of the earth. We must give help when famines occur. We can lose in the search for friendly relations in the world if insoluble poverty drives more underdeveloped lands into communism or into some other form of totalitarianism. If overcrowding becomes either a reason or an excuse for war, we can easily become entrapped in such conflicts. The United States is, obviously, involved with the rest of mankind, but what about the productive land at home? Are we also in danger of overcrowding and overtaxing our land?

POPULATION TRENDS IN THE UNITED STATES   A first impression of the population trends in the United States is strangely at variance with the picture painted by the population alarmists. From the time of the landing of the Pilgrims until about 1900, the growth rate of the United States was rapid enough to have frightened the world, but no one was concerned. In fact, Theodore Roosevelt spoke in alarm about our declining birth rate and worried about "national suicide" through the production of too few babies. In his day the birth rate was more than 30 per thousand. It had been a sensational 50 or more in colonial America.

Another interesting way of thinking about birth rate in the United States is to refer back to the period of the baby boom. What actually happened during the post-World War II baby boom was that married couples, on the average, had about one more child than they had had during the all-time low reproduction period of the Great Depression. This slight increase in fertility occurred mainly among the middle class. Although it was true as always that the poor had more children than the rich, there was a slight downturn in the size of poverty-stricken families relative to the middle class.

By the late 1960s the baby boom was over. For two decades the Census Bureau had been revising its future estimates upward; now it is revising them downward.[14] The highest estimates were for 361 million by the year 2000; current estimates are for 283 million.

On a comparative basis our people are not particularly crowded; there are just over 55 per square mile, compared to approximately 200 per square mile in China, 400 in India, about 600 in West Germany, more than 950 in the Netherlands, 1,100 in Java and 2,000 in East Pakistan. What gives us the sensation of crowding is that we all choose to live in the same places. Many rural counties give the impression of having been stricken by the plague, so shrunken are their populations. Meanwhile, the vast industrial, suburban complexes of the East and the Pacific Coast spread as aggressively as the leaping roots of a mangrove forest. Like the crowded mice in one of Calhoun's experiments, we seem to have a compulsion to snuggle up to each other in vast aggregates. The obvious reason is that industrial areas provide more jobs than do scenic areas, but the crowding alarms us and makes us think that our population explosion is the worst in the world.

[14]Ben Wattenberg, "The Nonsense Explosion," *The New Republic*, vol. 162, p. 10, April 1970.

THE REAL PROBLEM In spite of these reassurances about the United States population, problems remain. The rate of increase diminishes, but the population total still grows. Even the downwardly revised estimate of the Census Bureau predicts an addition of 80 million people to our population in the last three decades of the present century. Although the large family of poverty is less common than it once was, it still exists. About 42 percent of American families with five children or more are found among the poor, whereas only 10 percent of families with one or two children are poor.[15] In spite of the prevalence of contraception and abortion, large numbers of unwanted babies are brought into the world, some to be neglected or battered children. It is estimated that 40 percent of the unwanted children are born to the poor.[16] Little genetic counseling is done, and dysgenic traits continue in the population.

The major reason why the American birth rate is a problem is that the average American will use resources at a rate unmatched in any other part of the world. In his lifetime he will wear out from ten to twenty automobiles (assuming that he is a moderate, cautious driver) and burn up nearly 100,000 gallons of gasoline in his automobiles alone. He will probably also require such hobby items as snowmobiles, dune buggies, speedboats, motorcycles, and airplanes, all pouring out their contaminants and eating their quota of the world's limited resources. It is this tendency for the affluent American to use up the earth that causes such environmentalists as Ehrlich and Commoner to say that the birth rates of the poor are only minor problems compared to the fairly high birth rates of the affluent. Their point of view about the environment is fully understandable, but in other respects high birth rates among the poor are the larger problem, helping as they do to perpetuate poverty.

THE EXTENSION OF FAMILY PLANNING If the declining birth rate of the educated, urban population can be duplicated by all segments of the American public, the United States will be able to reach population stability. A few population experts—Donald Bogue and Dudley Kirk, for example—expect this to happen. There is evidence that most of the poor are no longer committed to large-family values, but by accident have more children than they desire. In a 1960 Growth of American Families study, lower-income families were found to want slightly smaller families than higher-income couples. The stated desire for the above $10,000-income family was for 3.3

Is there a Planned Parenthood Association in your community? Invite a
speaker from the organization. Find out what is being done on the local level.

---

[15]Paul R. Ehrlich and Anne H. Ehrlich, *Population, Resources, Environment*, W. H. Freeman and Company, San Francisco, 1970, p. 246.
[16]*Ibid.*, p. 246.

The real problem in America, not just
numbers of people, but the squandering
of products and resultant waste and debris.

children. Families with incomes of $3,000 and below wanted an average of 3.1 children. Nonwhites stated a wish for fewer children than whites—an average of 2.7.[17] There is presently a considerable gap between stated desire and actual fertility, but even the stated desire would result in continued population growth.

In spite of the availability of pills and intrauterine devices, unwanted pregnancies occur, and they occur twice as frequently among the poor and near poor as among other segments of the population. Only New York, Hawaii, and California have laws that are fairly permissive about abortion, but it is estimated that about one-fifth of pregnant women throughout the United States seek abortions. For the well-to-do, safe abortions are possible, even if they involve moving to another state or country. Among the poor, a sizable number of pregnant women go to quacks or attempt self-induced abortions, sometimes mutilating themselves in the process. An estimated 800 to 5,000 women die each year as a result of illegal or "home made" abortions.[18] Dr. Warren Hern of the OEO proposes national planning services for families of the poor.[19] Surveys generally show an increasing public acceptance of the idea of more permissive abortion laws that would prevent the births of hundreds of thousands of unwanted children. Ehrlich[20] makes a four-step proposal for the United States, addressed to the entire population, not just to the poor:

1. A Federal Population Commission whose major task would be birth control propaganda.

2. Replacement of all income-tax deductions for children with a graduated scale of tax increases, depending on the number of children.

3. Mandatory instruction in birth control in all public schools.

4. A biomedical research program to encourage population regulation and environmental sciences, rather than the present emphasis on death control.

    Ehrlich admits his program has little chance of adoption. The second point,

---

How realistic are the laws of your state regarding birth control information and availability of pills and devices, especially for minors? Can poor women get the pill free at clinics? If not, make your views known to supervisors, welfare agencies, and state legislators.

---

[17]Frederick F. Jaffe, "Family Planning and Poverty," *Journal of Marriage and the Family*, vol. 26, pp. 467–470, November 1964.
[18]Warren M. Hern, "Family Planning and the Poor," *The New Republic*, vol. 163, pp. 17–18, November 14, 1970.
[19]*Ibid.*, p. 19.
[20]Paul R. Ehrlich, "World Population: A Battle Lost?" *Stanford Today*, series I, no. 22, pp. 5–6, January 1968.

in particular, could be opposed as a way of penalizing babies for having such bad judgment as to be born. The problem of population limitation is undeniably urgent, but so is the problem of providing life opportunities for the children already here. The one objective should not be pursued at the expense of the other.

AVOIDING EXHAUSTION OF THE EARTH

Sometimes demographers take a grim delight in calculating how many people there will be in the world at a particular date if present trends continue, or how fast the rate of increase is at present. One film on population (*Standing Room Only*) states that every time your heart beats, three babies are born. On the cover page of Ehrlich's *The Population Bomb* is the statement:

> While you are reading these words four people will have died of starvation. Most of them children.[21]

In the same book, Ehrlich gives the estimate that if the world's population could increase at the present rate for 900 years, there would be enough people to fill a continuous 2,000-story building covering the entire earth.

No one really expects such a fantasy to come true, but will enough of it come true to make life unlivable or to damage the earth's ecology beyond recovery? Commoner thinks that the critical mark could be as low as the 6 or 8 billion mark, which we are almost sure to attain between the years 2000 and 2050. "Any attempt to raise more food than will support 6 to 8 billion people will probably strain the ecological system very severely. That is about as high as we can go."[22] Not all authorities would be quite so pessimistic in their predictions as Commoner, but none would give us more than another century or two at present rates.

The next question, then, is how to stop the world's runaway population growth. It can, of course, be stopped by the malthusian formula of war, famine, and pestilence; but the world has been through enough of the horrors of war to wish for more. We have recently seen both war and famine in Biafra, with spindly legged children with distended stomachs and glazed eyes staring blankly at approaching death. The scene is familiar to human history; Biafra actually involved far fewer people than earlier famines in India, Russia, and North China. In recent years it has usually been possible to avert famine by supplying food from regions of surplus, but there may come a day when the "have" countries can no longer produce the surplus needed to save the "have not" lands of the earth. The products of the earth may be exhausted without feeding its billions of mouths.

[21]Paul R. Ehrlich, *The Population Bomb*, Ballantine Books, Inc., New York, 1968.
[22]Rudy Abramson, quoting Barry Commoner, "Biologist Says World Faces Survival Crisis," *Los Angeles Times*, December 30, 1969, Part I, p. 1.

DEESCALATION? Until now the world's population has been growing at an everincreasing pace. As mentioned, though, the United Nations projections call for a tapering off of growth rate by the end of the century, but by that time there will already be well over 6 billion people in the world. The question is whether the decline in birth rate will be too little and too late.

Donald Bogue is one of the very few population experts to believe the population problem may be solved before widespread famine starts (there is, of course, the slow famine of malnutrition at present). Bogue says "It is quite reasonable to assume that the world population crisis is a phenomenon of the 20th century, and will be largely if not entirely a matter of history when humanity moves into the 21st century."[23] As grounds for his optimism he cites the growing interest in birth control throughout much of the world, even including Catholic countries where church policies have been assumed to be an insurmountable barrier to birth control. He also mentions aroused political leadership and better research into methods of control. He takes comfort from a possible reversal of the trend toward greater death control. It looks as though the rapidly declining death rate of much of the world may be tapering off, if for no other reason than that neonatal and childhood death rates have already been reduced close to the vanishing point, and there is no way to extend the old-age end of the life cycle much further.

Dudley Kirk also takes an encouraging view of the population situation, because "the world is moving from 'viewing with alarm' to action."[24] Kirk tells us that the situation of the last decade or two has been unusual not only in phenomenal progress in death control, but as we have seen, in actual increases in birth rate in some of the modernizing countries. Since 1960 a growing awareness of population pressures is beginning to reverse the increased birth rate. Only a few underdeveloped lands were launched on a birth control program before 1960: Taiwan, Singapore, and Puerto Rico. Since then they have been joined by the Ryukyus, Korea, Hongkong, and Malaysia. In Latin America, Argentina and Uruguay have brought about great declines in birth rates, and Chile is headed in the same direction. Communist countries of Eastern Europe have cut birth rates, in spite of Communist ideology. Argentina, Uruguay, and Puerto Rico have cut birth rates in spite of the official Vatican position. It seems that no official ideology can stand against various types of cultural factors that lead to a decision to limit family size. Even China has joined with such other population giants as India and Pakistan in establishing family planning programs. The official propaganda has long contended that a Communist state can feed any number of people. Nevertheless, the Chinese are encouraged to delay marriage and family so as to have more years to devote exclusively to service to the Communist state. Thus China tacitly admits what she has tried to deny—not even a Communist state can do the impossible. The fertility of the soil is far more limited than that of the human species.

[23]Donald J. Bogue, "The End of the Population Explosion," *The Public Interest*, no. 7, p. 11, Spring 1967.
[24]Dudley Kirk, "World Population: Hope Ahead," *op. cit.*, p. 8, Winter 1968.

CONTINUED WORRIES In spite of all the words of cheer from Bogue and Kirk, at present the world's population is increasing more rapidly than ever before, and the earth already has more people than it can possibly support on anything that Americans would consider even a minimum acceptable standard of living. One-third of the world's people are chronically hungry. The only countries to approach population stability are those with high levels of industrialization, urbanization, and education, including the United States, most of Europe, and Japan. Let it be repeated that these countries merely *approach* stability but have not actually achieved it. Such countries have been joined to some degree by Korea, Taiwan, and a few others. But, despite considerable effort on the part of governments, the great population giants of India and China, together containing nearly half the world's people, are still growing at a rate that will double their populations within thirty-five years or less. Parts of Latin America are gaining population even more rapidly. Much stronger action is needed. Ehrlich, again, has some suggestions for action on the part of the United States:

1. Refuse to send food to any country unable to demonstrate that it is doing everything in its power to lower its birth rate.

2. Refuse to help countries that are already beyond hope because of the imbalance between food supply and population.

3. Give all possible help in birth control knowledge and pills to any country willing to use the knowledge.

4. Help any country that applies for such aid with knowledge of how to increase farm yield.

5. Accept the fact that it is just as easy to use our knowledge, our wealth, our technology, and even our sacred tax money for the aid of mankind as for fighting wars.[25]

Suggestion 1 sounds harsh, and suggestion 2 sounds downright cruel. As usual, Ehrlich states his case in a dramatic manner to emphasize the gravity of the crisis, but it is hard to argue with his basic viewpoint: there is no question that more drastic steps are needed in the future than in the past if disaster is to be avoided. Man must increase the fruitfulness of the earth and decrease his own, or the nightmare of Malthus will become reality.

SUGGESTED READINGS

Allison, Anthony: *Population Control*, Penguin Books, Inc., Baltimore, 1970.

A collection of articles including animal population studies, growth of the world's human population, control attempts in several countries, and the food-supply problem. There is also a very interesting article on birth control in primitive societies.

[25]Ehrlich, "World Population: A Battle Lost?" *op. cit.*, p. 7.

Ehrlich, Paul R.: *The Population Bomb*, Ballantine Books, Inc., New York, 1968.

> *A frequently quoted book with a dramatic presentation of the problem of overpopulation and proposed solutions. The last parts are addressed to the individual with suggestions for action groups, such as Zero Population Growth.*

Morris, Desmond: *The Human Zoo*, McGraw-Hill Book Company, New York, 1969.

> *This spicy and entertaining portrayal of the human race, now crowded and living in unnatural quarters, has its serious side. We must find small-community life, says the author, and we must not out-breed the planet's limits.*

The Annals of the American Academy of Political and Social Science, vol. 369, January 1967.

> *The entire issue, subtitled "World Population," is devoted to population trends and problems.*

Thomlinson, Ralph: *Demographic Problems*, Dickenson Publishing Company, Inc., Belmont, Calif., 1967.

> *"A sociological analysis of selected population problems, trends, and controversies," as the author says in his preface. Concise and well presented.*

Wrigley, E. A.: *Population and History*, McGraw-Hill Book Company, New York, 1969.

> *With many illustrations and charts the author shows the great fluctuations in population of the past and the rapid upward trend of today. Compares industrial and nonindustrial parts of the world.*

QUESTIONS

1. Explain why demographic transition was not a great problem for Europe, but is much more serious for the emerging nations of the underdeveloped world.

2. If humans are similar to experimental animals, what pathological traits might result from overcrowding?

3. What policies and accidents of today could cause genetic problems for the future of the human race?

4. In what respects is the United States much less of a population problem than much of the world, and in what respect is the United States a very serious problem?

5. What is the evidence *pro* and *con* on whether the population growth of the world will slow down soon enough to avoid major disaster?

PART THREE

ROLE FAILURE AND DEVIANT BEHAVIOR

As noted in the Introduction, societies can be described as networks of statuses and roles. Each member holds a number of statuses or positions relative to others, such as husband, wife, employer, employee, doctor, lawyer, and many others. Each position is accompanied by a type of expected behavior, or role. Some people are unable to fulfill their roles because of sickness, mental illness, or other disablement. Such people need to be cared for, and the problem of their care is becoming increasingly a public, social issue. Heavy users of drugs and alcohol also suffer role impairment and become a serious problem to society. The various types of crime to be discussed in Chapter 13 are cases of deviant behavior and could also be thought of in role terms — substituting illegal roles for socially prescribed roles. Many kinds of role failure and deviance are present in all societies at all times. What is new about them in American society that causes them to be part of the difficulties of the troubled land?

WHAT IS NEW

The first development that is new and troubling is in the field of care of the ill and mentally ill. Medical knowledge has advanced tremendously, but so has the cost of medical care, and the United States has no comprehensive plan for taking care of the medical needs of its people. Medical science has made exciting advances in ability to save lives, and by extending lives into advanced age, has added to its tasks. Many modern nations have made ample provisions for increasing medical demands, but we have not. In the case of mental illness, too, knowledge has advanced, but public attitudes lag. The mentally ill are still stigmatized, and so are large numbers of people with other types of stigmata.

Narcotics addiction was mainly a problem of the slums of certain major cities for most of the period from 1914 until about 1960. Now it spreads throughout society, especially among the young. In the meantime, the use of a less dangerous product —

marijuana—has become widespread and has created a great value conflict over law and law enforcement.

In the field of crime, all indications are that the rate is increasing, and evidence will be presented to show that the underworld is better organized now than in the past. At the same time, the machinery of justice is bogged down by a greater burden of cases than it is equipped to handle.

MEETING THE SOCIAL PROBLEMS CRITERIA

The physically and mentally ill cannot meet role obligations, and the lawbreakers who defy many of society's demands are very numerous. The former do not constitute the same type of normative problem we have generally taken into consideration, but there is normative failure on the part of society in not meeting the cost of their care to a greater degree than it does and in not providing enough physicians. The problems of sickness and crime cannot be eradicated, but they are certainly amenable to improvement. As the situation stands now, failures of adequate health care are causing the United States to lose its position of world leadership in health and longevity, and many people are suffering needlessly. Crime is increasingly threatening as a problem, for there are indications that organized crime is penetrating ever deeper into the fields of legitimate business and government.

INTERRELATIONSHIPS

Social change has made it possible to live a life of relative idleness, without clearly defined norms. The strongly competitive ethic of earlier days does not seem so relevant as it once did, and a retreat from the struggle becomes more common. Unfortunately, such an attitude seems to be one of the causes of a search for new "kicks," usually only through liquor and marijuana, but increasingly through extremely dangerous drugs.

Social change has also made the world a much more anonymous place than it once was, and the restraints of neighborhood and community are greatly reduced. The consequence is that society must depend more exclusively upon formal police power to enforce its laws and less upon primary-group controls and possible social ostracism. Like all other problems, deviant behavior is closely related to other aspects of society.

PERSPECTIVES OF ROLE FAILURE AND DEVIANCE

Deviance is related to social change, to value conflict, and to anomie. Anomie, as the word is used by Robert Merton, refers to norms that conflict with each other and leave the individual in a normative dilemma. Merton's theory of deviant behavior, referred to briefly in the Introduction, contends that societies prescribe proper goals for individual striving and proper means for achieving those goals. In American society the proper goal is generally material success. However, people do not have equal access to success goals, partly because of varying social backgrounds, abilities, financial starts in life, and encounters with discrimination. Consequently, some people resort to illegal means to attain the success goals admired by the society. Others give up and become "retreatists"—a term Merton originally used for tramps and vagrants, but which seems highly applicable to cases of drug addiction as well. Merton has one other deviant category in his theory—rebellion. By rebellion he originally referred to political rebels such as Communists and Fascists, but his term is also very applicable to mere "rebels without a cause"—including many destructive and belligerent juvenile gangs.

The person who is ill or the person who is mentally ill is also in an anomic position. There is no way of fulfilling role obligations, and life is thrown into confusion. Anomie is also a problem for the physically disabled, who are sometimes expected to fill normal roles and sometimes expected to play the role of dependent. What norms to follow in different situations, whether to give up the search for independence or to continue to try, what unintended insults must be met and how—all these are problems that make the lives of many handicapped people confused and anomic.

Certain types of role failure are inevitable for the sexual deviant—the homosexual or the lesbian—and the situation is another one of anomie. There is usually an internal conflict of guilt feelings over an inability to follow social norms and defiance against the norms of the "straight" world.

Another perspective on deviance is to look upon it as a type of learned behavior. It is the point of view of sociology and of the social sciences in general that human nature is causative, subject to rules of cause and effect, and that nearly all kinds of crime can be accounted for in environmental terms. For this reason the ideas of Edwin Sutherland are given considerable prominence. Sutherland shows how different types of crime are learned under different circumstances; he says that they can best be explained as learnings, not as the results of particular personality types, races, or ethnic groups. Impoverished urban areas are associated with burglary, petty theft, fighting, and drug use. Business organizations, on the other hand, often make possible the learning of an entirely different type of crime, which Sutherland calls "white-collar crime." Examples of white-collar crime are tax violations, record disguising, unfair measures, and false advertising. It can be seen very readily that such types of crime are learned, and they are learned under completely different circumstances from those of burglary and petty theft.

The idea of crime as learned behavior brings us to a final perspective on deviant behavior: it would seem that the worst way to deal with crime would be to put all criminals into confinement together where each can learn from the other. Yet this is what we do, and it constitutes one of the great dilemmas of punishment and one of the reasons why the problems of law enforcement and justice are included along with role failure and deviance.

11 The "afflicted and the possessed" include varying types of people, but all are people who are suffering in some manner. In all cases, they are unable to fully perform the roles society expects, or, in the case of the stigmatized, they can fulfill such roles only with unusual effort or heavy psychic costs.

We are accustomed to complaints about how the mentally ill are poorly understood and provided for, but now we are also asking about the physically ill. Why do we not provide more facilities for the sick? Why is adequate medical care so difficult to obtain, and why are costs out of reach for the common man? Is it really true that the poor can always receive help in county hospitals?

Are there still prejudices against the mentally ill? What is the meaning of the prescientific word "possessed?" Is it still believed in? What are the role characteristics of mental illness that cause it to be ignored in some countries and among some segments of the population? What other types of conditions can cause a person to be stigmatized? Why is the stigma of sexual deviance stronger than that caused by other types of role impairment? Why has the word "possessed" been applied to the sex deviant?

What proposals are being made for meeting the health needs of the nation? What attitudinal changes are still needed for the "afflicted and the possessed?"

THE AFFLICTED AND THE POSSESSED

An affliction is a condition of torment, whether the problem is one of disease, degenerative condition, or accidental disablement. Also afflicted are those who are seen as abnormal and are therefore stigmatized—the dwarf, the pathologically obese, the mentally defective, the ugly and disfigured, and the sexually maladjusted. For most people, the only affliction of a type to be considered here is occasional sickness, but even such an affliction can be disorganizing socially and financially. A kindly society should be expected to make all possible arrangements for the relief of any type of affliction and should seek an understanding of the possessed.

To speak of the possessed is to use an ancient and unscientific terminology for certain types of affliction. In ancient times those whom our courts might now call "of unsound mind" were believed to be possessed of evil spirits. Possession is referred to frequently in the Bible; for example, in the fifth chapter of Mark, Jesus commands the unclean spirits to leave a possessed man and to enter instead a herd of swine. There are reasons for using the ancient term "possession" in spite of our now living in a scientific age. One reason is that a belief in possession has lingered for hundreds of years, and societies have acted as though mistreatment of the victim would be a means of exorcizing the unclean spirit. Our word "bedlam" comes from the nickname of a London insane asylum where patients were kept on display like animals in a zoo and where passersby, to drive out the possession, were allowed to tease them until they "raised bedlam." Care of patients has improved in recent years, but there is still a stigma against the mental patient, still the feeling that he is possessed, and often the feeling does not go away even after he is pronounced well and released from psychiatric care.

In discussing the afflicted and possessed, we shall examine first the most common type of affliction, physical illness, and how well our society provides for its care. Next we shall look at the problems of those who are now usually designated as mentally ill and finally to certain other types of people who are treated as though they had an "unclean spirit," whether or not they are regarded as ill.

WHEN ILLNESS STRIKES

For the average person, illness strikes occasionally; for some it is persistent. Whatever the case, occasional or chronic, the chances of recovery are improved if there is an assurance of good medical care and of good medical care unaccompanied by financial ruin. Such cannot be guaranteed. There is no question that over a long period of years the medical profession of the United States has improved its knowledge vastly, developed wonder drugs and wonder machines for taking care of even the most unusual complaints, and that the profession is advancing rapidly in further research. The American Medical Association has assured the public that there is no better medical care anywhere than in the United States. Such a statement is true, but only with the qualification "if you can afford it."

MEDICAL COSTS   The stock answer to the complaint that only a few can afford the price of good health is that the aged are now covered by medicare and that about 75 percent of younger Americans are covered by some type of medical insurance policy. Two problems remain, however. First, what happens to the quarter of the population not covered by any type of health insurance? Secondly, are the policies adequate to meet the needs of medical disaster?

In answer to the first question, recall the discussion of poverty in the United States. Many rural poor live in areas that are remote from medical service. The city poor go to large public hospitals that are overcrowded and bureaucratically run. In New York, the health commissioner estimated that in a recent year 13,000 poor people died because adequate medical care was not available to them. Often the middle class considers itself worse off than the poor in some respects because the poor are eligible for free public care, whereas those with higher income are not. Admittedly, there are usually some opportunities for medical care for the poor, but "the public facilities that do exist perpetuate a grotesque circle of personal humiliation and medical lunacy."[1] There is often a long, bureaucratic runaround, a referral to one clinic after another, hours of waiting, and derogatory comments. The institution begins to think the poor are unconcerned and fail to even try to take care of themselves. Perhaps some of the poor, more than the educated middle class, are inclined to ignore the need for medical aid, but much of the trouble is with the circumstances under which they must go begging for medical care, the distance to go, and the time of waiting. In Chicago, the medical headquarters of America and the center of the AMA, there are eighty hospitals and medical schools. Yet the west-side ghetto, with 300,000 people, has only one hospital. More than 1,000 patients per day must go to Cook County Hospital. Disease rates there are three or four times the national average. The hospital staff does its best, but cannot cope with the situation.[2]

For the middle class, feeling protected by medical insurance policies, there are equally serious problems. Doctors, who still feel a sense of obligation to provide medical services to the poor, continue to play Robin Hood by overcharging those able to pay. It is fairly common practice to increase the rate for an operation if it is known that the patient has medical insurance. Insurance companies set guidelines on the amount to be paid for particular services, and the majority of doctors try not to exceed the suggested limits; but some *do* exceed the limits considerably. Tunley mentions a surgeon who raised his fee from $150 to $300 for an operation because the patient had an insurance policy that paid $150.[3]

However, doctor's fees are only part of the rising costs of operations. Daniel Schorr[4] gives the following as the cost of a typical operation in 1970:

[1]Elinor Langer, "The Shame of American Medicine," in Jerome H. Skolnick and Elliott Curie, *Crisis in American Institutions*, Little, Brown and Company, Boston, 1970, p. 337.
[2]Daniel Schorr, *Don't Get Sick in America*, Aurora Publishing Company, Nashville, Tenn., 1970, pp. 44–45.
[3]Roul Tunley, *The American Health Scandal*, Harper & Row, Publishers, Incorporated, New York, 1966, p. 86.
[4]Schorr, *op. cit.*, p. 64.

Long waits, dreary facilities, crowds, and perfunctory treatment in hospitals for the poor, and reduced chances for restoring health.

Hospital	$ 641.35
Surgeon	300.00
Anesthetist	76.50
	$1,017.85

A record of another operation, involving eye surgery and several weeks in the hospital, totaled $15,270.[5] By 1971 the average cost of hospitalization had increased to $70 per day for the United States as a whole and to $100 per day in New York City. There are many reasons besides the fee policies, but the important point for consideration now is that most insurance policies will not bear the entire cost, and the closer they come to bearing the costs, the higher the rates have to be. At present, medical costs are rising 15 percent per year.[6]

[5]Fred J. Cook, *Plot against the Patient*, Prentice-Hall, Inc., Englewood Cliffs, N.J., 1967, p. 60.
[6]T. R. B., "Here We Come, Otto," *The New Republic*, vol. 164, p. 8, February 27, 1971.

INSURANCE ESCALATION There are certain built-in difficulties with the types of health insurance policies held in the United States. One problem is that they are generally intended as disaster insurance, not insurance against minor illness. Although there is much to be said for such policies, they often fail the family with small children. Many times medical costs mount up for small children because of a series of sicknesses, not because of a single major disaster. Usually only surgery or chronic complaints are paid for.

Another problem with present policies is that there is a tendency for them to keep escalating insurance costs. If the insurance policy reads "for hospitalization of at least two days duration," then there is a fair chance that the patient will be hospitalized for at least two days, even though he might have been just as well off at home. The intent of the doctor in such a case is to be considerate of the patient, but a result of such policies is that the insurance companies must pay larger claims and hence increase their rates.

Even for patients benefiting from medicare, premiums have escalated. In 1966 the patient had to pay the first $40 of medical costs; now he must pay the first $52. Coverage under medicare is far from complete; the government estimates that it pays about 45 percent of the health bill for old people.[7] There have also been many complaints of doctors overcharging medicare patients and "converting socialized medicine into predatory capitalism."[8] Such a charge is by no means true of all doctors, however. The fact that some make considerable incomes from medicare is sometimes a clue to how many services were once rendered for a nominal charge. No one bothers with nominal charges, though, when insurance will pay the bill!

THE QUALITY OF CARE Medicine has been able to eliminate the threat of most childhood diseases, to nearly eliminate tuberculosis and pneumonia as killers, and to stop the spread of most infections. The American Medical Association, over a period of more than a century, has eliminated most, but not all, the medical quacks and insisted on standards of competence in medical practice. The AMA in the period from 1900 to 1920 was the leading organization to advocate a system of national medical insurance. During the following forty-five years it reversed itself completely and

---

Attitude survey: survey public opinion in your community regarding the quality and cost of medical services. Use such questions as (1) have you ever postponed seeking medical help because of the costs? (2) Is your medical insurance adequate?

---

[7]Schorr, *op. cit.*, p. 105.
[8]Editorial, *Christian Century*, vol. 87, p. 228, February 26, 1970.

fought a last-ditch action against any such insurance, thus alienating a fairly large segment of the public.

In spite of all the efforts at good, honest medical practice, there remains much to be desired. Some doctors still manage to operate on a basis of old-fashioned quackery. The diet-pill specialist is a good example. Susanna McBee,[9] working for *Life*, visited ten diet doctors in various parts of the country. A few had been in trouble with the medical profession, but most seemed to be tolerated reasonably well. Although the writer was not overweight, they all took her case and charged their fees, congratulating her on stopping her problem in its early stages. Few prescribed either diet or exercise, but all prescribed pills. From the ten doctors she gathered 1,479 pills on her first visit, including amphetamines, barbiturates, sex hormones, diuretics, thyroid, and digitalis. None are drugs to be used except by a person with real need as established by careful medical examination. All are potentially dangerous. Sometimes the rewards of the unscrupulous physicians exceed those of their more conscientious colleagues.

Just as distressing as the continued presence of medical quacks is the fact that many unnecessary operations are performed. Langer tells of a common joke among medical students: "What are the symptoms calling for a hysterectomy?"—"Two children, a Blue Cross card, and a uterus."[10] A Columbia University study of medical care of a group of Teamsters and their families concluded that one-fifth of the hospital admissions were unnecessary, and one-fifth of the operations were poorly performed.[11] In another case, reported by Dr. Paul A. Lembcke of the University of California, during a particular audit period of a hospital, when the entire staff of gynecologists was on salary, they performed 26 hysterectomies. In the same hospital at a later period, when the doctors were on a fee-for-service basis, they performed 130 hysterectomies.[12] Tunley concluded that Bernard Shaw stated the real source of the problem years ago when he said

> That any sane nation . . . should give a surgeon a pecuniary interest in cutting off your leg is enough to make one despair of political humanity. But that is precisely what we do. And the more appalling the mutilation, the more the mutilator is paid.[13]

The implication is not that doctors are peculiarly greedy; in fact, their concern for medical ethics may make them a little more conscientious in some respects than the majority of the population. Nevertheless, the doctor has a vested interest in persuading himself that an operation is warranted.

A more important reason for the inadequacy of our medical care is that we do not have enough doctors. The proportion of doctors to the total population has been

---

[9]Susanna McBee, "Diet Pills," *Life*, vol. 64, pp. 23–28, January 26, 1968.
[10]Langer, *op. cit.*, p. 338.
[11]*Ibid.*
[12]Tunley, *op. cit.*, p. 128.
[13]*Ibid.*

declining for fifty years. We need about fifty thousand more doctors than we have, but at the rate we are going we will slip even further behind existing needs in the future. Even now we have fewer doctors per population than Canada, Germany, Sweden, England, or almost any country of Western Europe,[14] and in none of those countries are people financially ruined by medical costs. Not only do we have too few doctors, but there are also too few nurses. The United States has 700,000 practicing nurses and needs about 850,000. At the same time, we have 285,000 trained nurses who do not practice, largely because of the low status and insufficient pay given nurses.[15]

The United States is the only major Western country that does not produce doctors and nurses for export. The usual pattern is that the "developed" countries of the world produce a medical excess that is sent to the "underdeveloped" countries. By this criterion, the United States is one of the "underdeveloped" countries, importing 20 percent of its doctors from abroad.[16] The brain drain of European countries to the United States may be drawing to a close in aeronautics and many fields of science and engineering, but not yet in medicine. We are grossly deficient in the number of medical schools, which guarantees a continued deficiency in doctors.

HOSPITALS: THE TRIPLE AFFLICTION

One goes to the hospital only when afflicted with sickness. In the past the affliction had to be extremely severe, even critical, before a person was sent to the hospital. Now, as we have seen, he might be sent because the hospital is the only route for collecting on his medical policy. In the more serious cases, though, the hospital is a place of great concern and anxiety. The reasons for hospitalization are such that one should expect to be reassured by every possible psychological device. Such is definitely not the case. If the first affliction is that of the sickness itself, the second affliction is caused by the nature of the hospital, and the third by the financial worry of meeting the bills.

> Medical facilities survey: find the number of doctors in your community (information probably available through local AMA) and the number of hospitals and hospital beds. Also survey conditions of crowding in the county hospital.

[14]*Ibid.*, pp. 115–213.
[15]Leonard Gross, "Introducing the Supernurses," *McCall's*, vol. 98, pp. 128, 219, March 1971.
[16]Tunley, *op. cit.*, p. 92.

THE PSYCHOLOGICAL AFFLICTION In one of Margaret Mead's[17] numerous books on primitive societies, she speaks of the problems of hospital care for primitive tribes. Much of their worry is over superstitions that do not concern us, but even more worrisome to them is the psychological problem of being placed in a building run by foreigners. They cannot be surrounded by their own kin, or by people who seem to care. Although Mead is speaking of primitives, her description sounds strangely familiar to the modern, sophisticated, twentieth-century American. The hospital tends to be a large, cold, forbidding place. It has about it an unmistakable odor of antiseptics and urine. Its cold white walls and cold white nurses and various instruments on display are unnerving. More important, the place achieves a degree of impersonality rare even in the bureaucratic world of today, with patients referred to not by name but by room and bed number or possibly as "the appendix in 107A." There are all kinds of papers to make out, proddings and probings and needles, early-morning wakings, and also long periods of relative inattention. The emphasis is heavily on science, but neglectful of human relations.[18]

Sometimes hospitals are so short on personnel that they cannot give the necessary attention to patients. Edward M. Brecher[19] tells the pathetic story of how he and his son had to take turns sneaking into the hospital late at night to make sure that his wife, a cancer patient being fed intravenously, was being properly cared for. There was grave danger, they were told, if the bottle of liquid being fed her should run dry; yet it would have happened without their intervention.

In the old days the family physician was in charge of the patient at the hospital; now he has only a casual arrangement with the hospital. Sometimes the internist fills the role of friend and confidant, and in other cases, as we shall see, the psychiatrist fills this role. For many patients, however, there is the feeling that no one is really in charge except an impersonal bureaucracy. The hospital often closely resembles the "total institution" described by Erving Goffman (see Chapter 14). Some of the characteristics of the total institution are: robbing the individual of status, dignity, and personal identity, and placing him in a situation where all types of decisions are made about him without his knowledge or consultation. The needed relief from anxiety is not accomplished under such circumstances.

HOSPITAL COSTS: THE REASONS The third affliction, financial worry, seldom vanishes when a patient becomes hospitalized. For many people, insurance helps greatly, but it seldom meets the total cost of hospitalization. Congressional hearings in 1969 led to the conclusion that insurance, on the average, pays 74 percent of hospital

[17]Margaret Mead, *Cultural Patterns and Technical Change*, Mentor Books, New American Library, Inc., New York, 1955, pp. 205–208.
[18]Luke M. Smith, "The System—Barriers to Quality Nursing," in Jeanette R. Folta and Edith S. Deck (eds.), *A Sociological Framework for Patient Care*, John Wiley & Sons, Inc., New York, 1966, pp. 134–142. See also Richard M. Titmuss, "The Hospital and Its Patients," in Folta and Deck (eds.), *op. cit.*, pp. 236–238.
[19]Edward M. Brecher, "With a Life at Stake," *McCall's*, vol. 95, pp. 96–97, 132, 134–135, October 1967.

Amazing equipment and skill, but pro-
hibitive costs in spite of underpaid
nurses and assistants.

costs, 38 percent of doctor bills, and almost nothing toward drugs and private nursing care.[20] One of the reasons for limited payment is that medical costs rise so rapidly. Another reason — the tendency to hospitalize more people — has already been mentioned. Another problem, of course, is inflation, which has driven up all costs. Along with inflation there has been a demand for higher pay for hospital workers — an employee group that has been grossly underpaid in the past. The hospitals are also better equipped today, and the new types of equipment are extremely expensive. Another expensive policy, but one that is quite justifiable, is trying to provide more beds in case of emergency. Costs seem to rise in proportion to facilities available, whether or not they are in use.

There is still another reason for price increases that is much harder to justify: hospitals tend to be run wastefully. "Although hospitals are the third largest industry in the United States, employing about 1.7 million persons (about as many as steel and autos combined), their methods would bankrupt any other business.[21] Materials are wasted. Sometimes various departments duplicate purchases of equipment that is used little by any of them. There is seldom any getting together (as in many businesses) for purchasing purposes, in order to take advantage of reduced prices for large orders. Although there is increased specialization in the medical field, many hospitals compete with each other in generalization, each providing all possible services, even when they are close together. In Westchester County, New York, for example, four hospitals each wanted to buy a cobalt unit, which costs $100,000, for cancer therapy. In this case a planning council prevented waste by duplication, since the hospitals were within fifteen minutes of each other and could easily share the seldom-used equipment. Usually such economies are not achieved.

Whatever the reasons, some of which are unavoidable, the cost of hospital care has increased so greatly that present insurance policies are no longer adequate. New solutions to the hospital problem are needed.

PROPOSALS The crises in American medical care for the aged was severe enough to cause the passage of a social security-based medical insurance, which is at least a minimal disaster insurance. The proposal, led by the late President Kennedy, was passed during the Johnson administration, in spite of the determined opposition of the AMA. There have been complaints of unfair practices arising from medicare, but the strong opposition to it from the AMA died down almost immediately, and an attitude of living with the inevitable was adopted. Threatened strikes did not develop.

Since the passage of medical insurance for the aged, shortcomings of the program have become obvious, but the principle of government-backed health insurance was examined and found not to be the disaster its opponents had predicted.

[20]Schorr, *op. cit.*, p. 91.
[21]Tunley, *op. cit.*, p. 130.

There are also other types of suggestions for improvements in medical care. One suggestion is to hire nurses with higher degrees of training; they could take over part of the doctors' functions.[22] There are suggestions for improvement in home-care facilities, with the possibility of providing adequate nursing care at costs much lower than the costs of hospital care. Certainly there is room for greater efficiency on the part of hospitals and for new clauses in insurance policies that will stop the tendency of rushing more people than necessary to the hospital.

All such changes, however, would still leave the United States with a medical-care system that is in many ways years behind the other progressive countries. In 1882, Otto von Bismarck of Germany instituted the first program of universal medical insurance in the world. Since then, many governments have adopted similar schemes, and none have abandoned such policies once they were adopted. The German system is decentralized and rather complex, but it seems to guarantee good medical care without heavy costs to the ill. The British system has been greatly vilified in the United States, but it is sufficiently well liked in Britain to have passed off the stage as a political issue; neither Conservative nor Laborite wishes to tamper with the system in any major way. The national medical policies of the Scandinavian countries and the Netherlands are similarly accepted and viewed with pride.[23]

In the United States a change of thinking seems to be coming about. Senator Edward Kennedy is proposing a national health insurance program to cover the entire American population and the Nixon administration is also making such a proposal. There is a wide difference between the two proposals, as is to be expected. President Nixon proposes leaving insurance in the hands of private corporations, with employers and employees contributing to the cost, as now. For the poor (below incomes of $3,000 for a family of four) the government would pay the cost. The insurance would have some limitations. The first $100 or $200 of hospital costs would be borne by the patient, but the insurance would take care of the high costs of major disasters. The present counterproposal of Kennedy and Representative Martha Griffiths would come closer to being a nationalized public health service like the European model. The AMA has its own proposals, not too different from those of the administration. None of the plans at present deals very firmly with the problem of regulation of

---

Study the new proposals (at present there is a proposal by the Nixon Administration and one by Senator Kennedy) for more complete health insurance. Study alternative proposals and let your congressman know your opinion.

---

[22]Gross, *op. cit.*, p. 75.
[23]Schorr, *op. cit.*, pp. 148–161.

medical practice or of preventing undue increases in fees. Such policies would undoubtedly bring down the wrath of the AMA, but they will probably be among the issues of controversy in the future.[24]

Another problem that is dealt with little, if at all, by the present health proposals is that of psychiatric care. It is noteworthy too that most insurance policies do not cover psychiatric costs, although between one-fourth and one-half of all hospital beds are occupied by the mentally ill. Even in our attitudes toward insurance, we could be accused of looking upon the mentally ill more as possessed than as sick.

THE POSSESSED

"Physical illness can play queer tricks with our thoughts and our behavior," says Dr. Richard Titmuss, "but this does not mean we are neurotics. In being querulous and ungrateful, demanding and apathetic in turn, we are in fact behaving as ill people."[25] In this description, Titmuss is clearly showing that the physically sick person can display some of the same annoying symptoms as the neurotic or psychotic, but there are marked differences. The differences are of such a nature, in fact, that at least one noted psychiatrist, Thomas S. Szasz,[26] objects to the very use of the term "mental illness." Illness is one thing; mental malfunctioning is quite another, as he sees it. The mental case does not behave as a patient is expected to behave. Using Talcott Parsons' definition of how the patient should function in his role, we can see that the physically ill patient meets role expectations, but the so-called mentally ill person does not. The patient's role, says Parsons, involves four major aspects:[27]

1. Exemption from normal role responsibilities

2. The recognition that the sick person cannot "pull himself together" and function again just on the basis of will

3. The desire to get well

4. The obligation to seek technically competent help

With few exceptions the physically ill patient accepts these aspects of his role, and his family also accepts them. If he fails to abide by such expectations he is not being a good patient. When long institutionalization destroys the desire to get well, then the patient has lost his status as one to be sympathized with. To quite a degree the same is true if he is ill but refuses to accept competent help.

[24]John Osborne, "To Your Health," *The New Republic*, vol. 164, pp. 12–14, March 6, 1971.
[25]Titmuss, *op. cit.*, p. 236.
[26]Thomas S. Szasz, *The Myth of Mental Illness*, Harper & Row, Publishers, Incorporated, New York, 1961.
[27]Talcott Parsons, *The Social System*, The Free Press of Glencoe, New York, 1964, pp. 436–443.

The obligations of the patient role are not usually fulfilled in what is designated as mental illness. The subject is often viewed as one who ought to continue his responsibilities but will not; he should be able to pull himself together, but does not. He acts as though he is not himself; he acts like a man possessed. In a more modern comparison, we might say it is as though something had shorted out a number of circuits. The result is often a personality that makes the victim a much less sympathetic type than the physically ill, and often an object of scorn.

HYSTERIA OR MALINGERING In his criticism of the term "mental illness," Szasz concentrates rather heavily on the type of mental illness referred to as "hysteria." The person suffering from hysteria has the symptoms of illness—pain, indigestion, or even paralysis—but without any physical causes. There are, of course, also people called malingerers, who simply pretend to be ill in order to escape obligations, and sometimes there is an argument as to what is the true state of the patient claiming to be ill. Szasz shows that under such circumstances the psychiatrist tends to be the man who speaks up for the mentally ill person, showing that he is truly afflicted. In modern times, with many people covered by some type of medical insurance, the insurance company tends to take the side against the patient, not wanting to meet its obligations unless a physical symptom can be found.

In the Soviet Union very little attention is paid to psychiatry, and Szasz suggests that the reason is rather similar to that used by the representative of the insurance company. The Russian government tries to keep a person at work. Only if he can prove a clear and definable physical reason for his illness can he be out sick. A psychiatrist does not have the power to play the role of "lawyer" for his patient, trying to prove that he is actually afflicted. In Western countries, the psychiatrist does play such a role, and in some respects takes on the position of the old-fashioned family doctor.

Despite nis objection to the expression mentally ill, Szasz shows that the concept of mental illness has actually done considerable good. The very term may serve to keep some psychologically disturbed people under competent care. It is also much better than seeing all such persons as malingerers or possessed of a devil. Nevertheless, Szasz argues convincingly that thinking of psychological problems as cases of mental illness produces an unfortunate result—the tendency to treat such cases as sickness, with idiosyncratic causes, but not as mental malfunctions that might have social causes.

SOCIAL CLASS AND MENTAL ILLNESS It is generally known that tuberculosis is more likely to occur among the poor than among the rich, but once it occurs it is properly treated as the same disease. When it comes to what is called mental illness, the conclusion is not necessarily the same, even though the term mental illness makes it seem the same. A well-known study by August B. Hollingshead and Frederick C. Redlich[28] verified what would generally be expected about social-class differences in the likelihood of consulting a psychiatrist. Members of lower classes generally perceive personality problems as cases of "John's getting ornery, cantankerous, abusive, and mean lately," but they are not likely to define the problem as one of mental illness. Others have observed that among lower-class people psychiatric disorders bear far more stigma than they do among the educated. A frequent complaint among prisoners in the California prison system is against the insistence on making them admit there is something wrong with them, that they are "ill." The prisoner can stand to be told that he is bad, but he bristles at other implications. "The shrinks try to make you think you're a kook." This viewpoint is important for various reasons. In the Hollingshead and Redlich study, the lowest class accounted for 18 percent of the people sampled but for 38 percent of the mental patients. Lower-class mental patients also had a tendency to develop more severe conditions and to be hospitalized much longer.

A natural question that arises is whether the conditions are more severe simply because they are ignored in the early phase, because they receive poorer attention, or because the conditions of life among the poor lead to more severe mental problems. Probably all three factors have some relevance, but there are indications that the last one is most important. A very thorough study of midtown Manhattan by Srole and others[29] confirms the Hollingshead-Redlich figures about mental illness and social class. Those with moderate psychological problems were fairly evenly distributed across social-class categories. For the highest-income categories about one-sixth were designated as "impaired"; for the lowest socioeconomic group, one-third. In further refinements of their figures, the researchers found that downward mobility has a strong effect on mental impairment, both as cause and as effect.

Harry Turney-High[30] presents good evidence of an anthropological nature to show the relationship between life conditions and psychological problems of various kinds. The adjustment of whole tribes of so-called "Digger" Indians to the American way of life could be characterized as malingering, but it is only the rejection of a culture and its status system that could explain such an adjustment for an entire people. Black Americans have higher blood pressure, on the average, than white Americans, but such is not the case with their racial relatives in Africa. Hypertension is part of the way of life imposed upon black Americans. The upward strivers in the dominant American society, especially those who strive hard but achieve little, are subject to psychosomatic disorders. In the case of downward mobility, there are strong suggestions that alcoholism may be as frequently an effect as a cause.[31] In general,

[28]August B. Hollingshead and Frederick C. Redlich, *Social Class and Mental Illness*, John Wiley & Sons, Inc., New York, 1958, pp. 171–175.
[29]Leo Srole et al., *Mental Health in the Metropolis*, McGraw-Hill Book Company, New York, 1962.
[30]Harry Holbert Turney-High, *Man and System: Foundations for the Study of Human Relations*, Appleton Century Crofts, New York, 1968, pp. 557–579.
[31]*Ibid.*

differential stresses of life result in differential rates and types of psychiatric problems on a social-class, ethnic, and racial basis. The mental illness of the poor is a different phenomenon from that of the wealthy. As with so many of the problems of the poor, more understanding of the differential strains of life is needed, with more attempts at prevention of mental problems.

INSTITUTIONAL CARE   One-quarter to one-half of all hospital beds are occupied by people designated as mentally ill, but the majority are released within a few months, except the extremely old with chronic brain syndromes or those with major psychoses entailing delusions and other serious derangements of thought processes.[32] Better medication than was available in the past helps to bring many patients to a sufficiently stable condition to make outpatient care possible. Many states have increased facilities for care outside of hospitals, but the health clinics are nearly always short on public funds. Long waiting periods are required for appointments, and large numbers of people are left untreated until their mental problems lead to disaster.

State mental hospitals have long been regarded with horror. Like public mental health clinics, they are usually understaffed and underfunded. Because they have the problem of caring for quite a few dangerous patients, some of them are prison-like. In spite of these problems, physical conditions in most mental hospitals have improved in the last thirty or forty years. Nevertheless, they need far more public attention. In all cases where custodial care is important, it is very possible for it to become the major function of an institution, as it is with prisons, and for the aim of cure to be largely neglected.

Mental institutions have undergone a complete cycle in America in the course of a century. In the 1840s the philosophy was to treat the patients with the utmost consideration, hoping that kind treatment and the naturally restorative powers of the human body would return them to health.[33] Later in the century, with increasing crowds of patients and mounting costs, and especially with an attitude of contempt for some of the people of foreign origin who became hospitalized, there was a change in policies. For many years exposés of mental institutions showed up cases of malnutrition, filth, and neglect, excessive severity, and little attention to any possible

---

> **Individual help: many hospitals call for volunteer aids, something very helpful and also good training. Another helpful and educational project is to visit the aged in so-called convalescent homes.**

---

[32]John A. Clausen, "Mental Disorders," in Robert K. Merton and Robert K. Nisbet, *Contemporary Social Problems*, Harcourt Brace Jovanovich, Inc., New York, 1966, pp. 30–39.
[33]Ailon Shiloh, "Sanctuary of Prison — Responses to Life in a Mental Hospital," *Transaction*, vol. 6, pp. 28–35, December 1968.

In the best hospitals, resocializing replaces tranquilizing in the rehabilitation of mental patients. In contrast, many public institutions offer only custodial care.

improvement. The main aim was control, and this was often brought about through humiliation and degradation of status, and even by the creation of an atmosphere of terror.

A recent study of a Veterans' Administration hospital in Illinois[34] showed a very great change in some respects, but a persistence of a tendency to develop an institutionalized personality. Most patients were happy with the good food, television, clean, comfortable beds, and generally good standards of care. They were inclined to interpret shock therapy as some kind of punishment, however, and to have no awareness of the meaning of therapy. About 40 percent of the patients were "institutionalized"; they did not want to leave; they had found a home. The institutionalized patients were a little uneasy about the man making the survey and wanted to

[34]*Ibid.*

be reassured that he wasn't involved in some kind of scheme for making them go away. Although they complained that the institution was a place of loneliness and that sometimes they might be punished by isolation, they did not want to leave. They were mentally detached from the world, hardly able to conceptualize family or friends on the outside.

The criticism that the researcher (Shiloh) makes is that despite merciful treatment in other respects, not enough is done to prepare patients for normal life. Neither the institutionalized nor the noninstitutionalized patients had any concept of what they might do to help themselves when released or where they would look for outpatient services. Not only in veterans' hospitals, but wherever large masses of patients are held, it becomes impossible for the hospitals to utilize the knowledge medical science has developed for rehabilitation of mental patients.

Shiloh's conclusion could be generalized: any program of therapy that makes the patient dependent on the therapist or the institution for too long can result in chronic illness. Even welfare dependency can become a chronic illness, or a type of "addiction."

Occasionally we are horrified by a case reminding us of the inhuman treatment of the mentally ill; we thought such treatment had disappeared long ago. In the spring of 1971, five inmates of an Ohio hospital for the criminally insane were freed. None had ever been convicted of anything; they were simply being held for observation. They had been held for twenty-two to forty years. Dr. T. J. Reshetylo, who finally released them, commented that the institution was very short of doctors and had received no replies from the courts about the cases. Dr. Reshetylo comments that there are over 100 other patients in the same category whom he hopes to release in the near future.[35]

AFFLICTION AND STIGMA

The previous pages considered physical and mental illness as the main types of affliction. Often a distinction is made between the two on the grounds that physical illness carries no implication of stigma, but mental illness does. Although the observation about a societal tendency to stigmatize mental illness can hardly be denied, there are many exceptions to the statement that physical illness is not stigmatized. Some physical illnesses certainly are not; they even attract immediate sympathy. When poliomyelitis was still a major crippler, pictures of little crippled children went right to the heart of the American public and large donations were made. On the other hand, if one were to appeal for funds to help people who have been physically impaired by the long-range effects of syphilis, his campaign would probably collapse. It has been difficult to raise funds for clinics to help people who are in physical and mental trouble with drugs. It can be objected that the latter affliction was "brought

---

[35]"Forgotten by the Courts, Five Finally Freed," *Los Angeles Times*, April 24, 1971, Part I, p. 6.

on themselves," but such is not always the case with afflictions that bring stigmatization. What of ugly cases of facial disfigurement, of missing ears or noses, or of severe mental retardation? We tend to sympathize with the blind, joke about the deaf, and shun the deformed.

THE UGLIEST MAN IN CANADA A depressing illustration of the tendency for society to completely exclude certain stigmatized individuals was reported in the summer of 1970. The incident occurred in Canada, but its setting could have been anywhere. More than anything else, it points out the tendency to exclude certain of the afflicted and stigmatized to avoid thinking about them. Certain people who, in the normative definition of social problems, should be those of greatest concern, are usually excluded from the social-problem category because they are few in number and incapable of any major protest. "Lumpy Willie" is a good example.

Recently, the ugliest man in Canada died. He had been spending the last year or two of his life working as a night watchman to pay off some debts. He liked to go out only at night so people wouldn't see him and stare at him. He even washed and shaved in the dark so he wouldn't see his own reflection in the mirror. He was called Lumpy Willie because he had hundreds of knobs and lumps all over his body and face, caused by a rare condition called Von Recklinghausen's neurofibromatosis. No one would give him a job; restaurants and bars refused to serve him. Children had shunned and teased him when he was a child; he had never had a date, rarely a friend. Unable to work, he stole and used credit cards fraudulently for a living and spent most of the second half of his thirty-nine-year life in prison. He drank by himself in a cheap hotel, and once while drinking he attempted suicide.

Then a good doctor, Theo Wilkie, took mercy on him and worked long hours at surgery, removing many of the lumps from his face until he was nearly normal in appearance. He was over being "so ugly that I am hated by people who don't even know me." He worked, paid off his fines, made good on his fraudulent checks, and very soon thereafter, on August 11, 1971, Alex Samuel Chapelski (Lumpy Willie) died.[36]

MANAGING STIGMA The stigmatized often band together for mutual support. There are organizations of dwarfs, the obese, alcoholics, wives of prisoners, the hard of hearing, the blind, and the crippled. Misery loves company and often finds company. Not many are as alone as was Lumpy Willie.

There is another side to the banding together of the stigmatized, however. Often they are segregated and have no choice. The "normals" fear to associate with them too much for fear of taking on something of the stigma.[37] This is particularly true at certain ages of childhood. Even the goodhearted child hardly dares champion the one

[36]"'Ugliest Man'—He Paid Debts Before He Died," *Los Angeles Times*, August 21, 1970, Part I, pp. 1, 18.
[37]Erving Goffman, *Stigma: Notes on the Management of a Spoiled Identity,* Prentice-Hall, Inc., Englewood Cliffs, N.J., 1963, p. 30.

who is stigmatized, whether the stigma is that of having a father in jail, of belonging to the wrong race or religion, or merely looking odd. Often the institutions of society work to set the stigmatized apart. Who else should the aged and infirm visit except the aged and infirm? So institutionalized arrangements are made. The blind must know the blind, lead the blind, and identify with the blind. A newly blind girl comments on her attempt to readjust to familiar places and routines, but tells how she was firmly led, instead, into the valley of the blind:

> I was to spend the rest of my life making mops with other blind people, eating with other blind people, dancing with other blind people. I became nauseated with fear, as the picture grew in my mind. Never had I come upon such destructive segregation![38]

Goffman's book *Stigma: Notes on the Management of a Spoiled Identity* analyzes the ways in which people try to manage the problem of damaged identity that results from stigma. There are attempts to interrelate, to promote kinder terminology for their affliction ("hard-of-hearing," please, not "deaf"), to publish small newspapers, to learn how to ward off intended or accidental insults, how to manipulate prestige symbols in order to compensate for stigma, how to "pass" as though there were no stigma, when to hide and when to reveal the scars of identity, and when to be on guard and when it is possible to be one's self. Always there is a psychological strain, minor for some kinds of stigma, devastating for others. Many people bear at least a slight stigma, for as Goffman says the only completely unstigmatized person in America is "a young, married, white, urban, Northern, heterosexual, Protestant father of college education, fully employed, of good complexion, weight, and height, and with a recent record in sports."[39]

Goffman, as always, gives a sensitive, probing picture of a problem of individual management of a difficult situation. Outside intervention is difficult because the problem is understood only by people with that particular stigma. Often there is also a sense of fear in intervening. The doctor who devotes his time to working with drug abusers, the minister who befriends the homosexuals, the leader in a drive against venereal disease—all such people can take on a little of the stigma of those they befriend. Therefore, these and many other kinds of stigma are generally ignored—the ex-convict, the mental case, the attempted suicide.

THE CASE OF SUICIDE The person who has attempted suicide is badly stigmatized, and various explanations are guessed at: some type of insanity, drugs, or a disgraceful secret. Actually, the usual case of suicide or attempted suicide involves an individual who seems quite normal. The suicide rate among the young has risen very sharply in recent years in the Los Angeles area (from 12.2 per 100,000 in 1960 to 28.4 per 100,000 in 1969) and is one of the leading causes of death among people of

[38]*Ibid.*, p. 37.
[39]*Ibid.*, p. 128.

college age. The Los Angeles Center for Suicide Prevention finds that the public generally believes the suicide rate to be highest among drug users and radical college students. Actually, the rate is about the same among drug users and nonusers and considerably lower among college students than among the noncollege group. Many persons who attempted suicide have complained of heavy pressures from parents or of feelings of hopelessness about society, but the most common symptom is a great feeling of loneliness. "My guess is that we have more conditions that lead to that [loneliness] today," says Michael Peck, director of the Center—"a lack of responsiveness among people and institutions."[40]

EVEN THE BRAVE: THE VETERANS' HOSPITALS   When a man fights for his country and is wounded in action, every effort is made to rush him to a military hospital, where his chances of survival despite wounds are the best they have ever been. He comes home, perhaps with his legs amputated, but deserving the status of hero; he has been called upon to serve, and he has served.

Years go by. Some amputees are never completely rehabilitated, or perhaps they are unable to find jobs. Being less than whole, living restricted lives, and envying those who remained civilians does nothing for dispositions. The brave young hero changes into an old cripple, ill tempered and ill kept, and possibly has to spend most of his time in a veterans' hospital. Since the cost of hospitalization is very great, and there are always thousands of demands on the federal budget, the hospitals are only half-financed. The heroic words of old, that one can "bear his afflictions proudly," cease to apply. "Heroized" becomes "stigmatized."

The Senate Subcommittee on Veterans' Affairs conducted an investigation into veterans' hospitals from November 1969 to April 1970. What they found does not reflect against the hospital personnel. Attempts were being made to handle the increasing load of patients as well as possible, but the situation was growing difficult. There seemed to be just as great a tendency to forget veterans in hospitals as there is to forget all people who get hidden away in institutions. "It's like you've been put in jail or been punished for something," Marine Marke Dumpert, an amputee, said in an interview in the Bronx VA Hospital.[41] That hospital is one of the oldest ones still used, and the picture of it in *Life* is not reassuring. Not only is it old, dirty, and crowded, but there are far too few personnel to staff the hospital adequately. An amputee, almost unable to move, woke one night to find a rat crawling across his hand. There were also complaints of inadequate equipment for training and rehabilitating the types of paralytic injuries resulting so often from the booby traps used in the Vietnam War.

It must be admitted that the *Life* article has been criticized for being excessive in its condemnations; but the cautious, conservative *U.S. News & World Report* re-

[40]"The Youthful Suicides," *Newsweek*, vol. 77, pp. 70–71, February 15, 1971.
[41]From "Assignment to Neglect," by Charles Childs, *Life*, May 22, 1970, © 1970 Time Inc.

ported a few months later along rather similar lines. No particular hospital was taken to task, nor was the Veterans' Administration blamed, but the conclusion was that inadequate preparation was being made for the increasing numbers of wounded veterans. There has been no expansion of beds or doctors or nurses (although some growth in the number of interns), since 1965. In 1966 a payroll cut was necessitated by economy moves from the government. It has been hard to hire adequate personnel.

Senator Alan Cranston has been particularly sharp in his criticism of the treatment of our wounded.[42] The implication of the present analysis is that over a period of years the status of the wounded soldier tends to change from that of hero to that of forgotten or even stigmatized. In the opinion of Dumpert, the only thing wrong with this analysis is that it doesn't seem to take a number of years:

> I feel that the way we Vietnam veterans are being treated is abnormal. I regret having to say this, but now I have nothing but disgust for my country. I used to hate the guys who ran off to Canada to avoid the draft. Now I don't hate them. I don't like them, but I respect them for what they did. If I had known what I know now, I would never have enlisted. I don't mean just my injury, but the insensitivity and lack of care. They would have had to drag me into the service kicking. It makes me wonder about Vietnam—about whether the people I saw die, and people like me who are half dead, fought for nothing.[43]

STRANGE AFFLICTION: SEXUAL MALADJUSTMENT

The problems of the sexually unusual are as old as history. Condemnations of various sex acts are dealt with in the Hebraic laws, laws against onanism, homosexuality, and bestiality. Strange practices were known to the Greeks and Romans and are discussed in the Kama Sutra of India. The word "lesbian" (female homosexual) is derived from the Island of Lesbos of ancient Greece, where Greek poetesses declared their love for one another.

Unusual sexual attractions have been accepted with little criticism in some societies, but in our immediate historical tradition, sex interest in one man by another or one woman by another has been seen as an affliction or as deliberate wickedness. It has even been explained as some form of possession—a man with a man's body but a woman's mind; the morphology of one sex, but the psyche of the opposite. Such a description is more poetic than scientific, but it describes well how some homosexuals have felt about their affliction. Some have spoken defiantly of their right to love, whether the world sees it as normal or not. Others have hidden the problem, appalled at themselves. Pëtr Ilich Tchaikovsky and his brother Anatol spoke of their affliction only in whispers as "it," "the curse." Pëtr Ilich loved the widow Nadejda Filaretovna von Meck, who made no demands on him, but came to loathe his wife, who expected normal relations.[44]

---

[42]"Growing Concern over Veterans' Hospitals," *U.S. News & World Report*, vol. 69, pp. 63–64, August 31, 1970.
[43]Childs, *op. cit.*, p. 28.
[44]Catherine D. Bowen and Barbara von Meck, *Beloved Friend*, Garden City Publishing Company, Inc., New York, 1941, chaps. 7–9.

The lives of millions of other people have been cursed by deviation from the range of normal sexual desire. The prevalence of such a problem historically is to be stressed because many uninformed people believe homosexuality to be something that has occurred on a large scale only very recently and only in what they regard as effete societies. Actually, homosexuality occurs in all societies and in nearly all mammalian species. In many societies it has been regarded as perfectly acceptable for males to have both homosexual and heterosexual relations. On the other hand, some religions have been extremely condemnatory of many kinds of sexual practices. The condemnatory attitude has been especially prominent in Zoroastrianism, Judaism, and Christianity.[45]

There is a lack of statistical material on homosexuality and lesbianism from the past, but there is enough literature about the subject to convince us that the problems have been very common through the ages. It will be interesting, however, to speculate on whether its incidence is increasing and also to look into the matter of cause. There are a few cases in which the cause is clearly physical, and they are the only cases in which an explanation seems fairly clear and easy.

TRANS-SEXUALITY

> When the doctor told me I was a hermaphrodite, it seemed like all the pieces of the puzzle of my life began falling into place. All my life I went along thinking I was a queer. I adjusted to that.[46]

The person quoted, and referred to as R. M., was an extremely rare case of hermaphroditism. In the majority of such cases the external sex organ is male, but there is also one ovary and a uterus. The trans-sexual in this case wished to be a female and was operated on to make the change. Such operations are an unusual occurrence but increasing in number. The male to female operation is much easier than the opposite, but even the opposite transition is sometimes performed.

In a case of lesbianism, a woman, T. J.,[47] states:

> I always had a crush on some girl. . . . I thought of myself as one of nature's terrible mistakes, rather than as a boy or a girl. . . . I always like to think of myself as neuter.

T. J. had her breasts removed, then started taking the male sex hormone testosterone so her beard would grow and her voice deepen. Eventually she expects to have full surgery. Hers is not quite as certain a case of true hermaphroditism as R. M.'s, but

[45]Wainwright Churchill, *Homosexual Behavior among Males: A Cross-Cultural and Cross-Species Investigation*, Hawthorn Books, Inc., New York, 1967, pp. 70–85.
[46]A case quoted by Harry Nelson, "Surgery Ends Sex Identity Riddle," *Los Angeles Times*, October 25, 1970, Part C, pp. 1, 4–5. Copyright, 1970, Los Angeles Times. Reprinted by permission.
[47]*Ibid.*

314

it seems to have a physical as well as a psychological cause—a greater than normal amount of male hormone, even before she deliberately started taking testosterone.

THE PSYCHOLOGICAL CAUSES   In the vast majority of cases, homosexuality, male or female, seems to have more of a psychological than a physiological cause, although all explanations remain in doubt. Contrary to earlier opinion, there is no homosexual personality type. Some are effeminate, but most are not. Similarly, with lesbians, some are masculine, but most are not. The psychological roots of homosexuality are complex. In the case of T. J., her father left home, and her mother treated her as the man of the house right from the first; thus, psychological factors might have been added to a physiological predisposition. In some cases male homosexuality develops in a family in which the father has done little to create a responsible image for the son, and where there has been antagonism between father and mother. In such a case, especially if there are no girls present, the boy might be taken as his mother's friend and ally against the father and begin to identify with the mother in a way unfortunate for his later sexual adjustment. The trouble with such an explanation is that it seems to be demonstrable only part of the time. Much of the causation of homosexuality is unclear. It is definitely not all of one type.

At least a few authorities think that in any family lacking a father, the chance of producing a homosexual child is increased. Dr. Robert P. Odenwald[48] agrees with this viewpoint and also contends that a society where sexual differentiations in dress, manners, developed temperament, and job preference begin to disappear, there will be a marked increase in homosexuality. If such an explanation is correct, then we would expect the amount of homosexuality in American society to be on the increase. Odenwald also expects an increase in lesbianism among women for the same reason of insufficient role differentiation. His ideas must be considered speculative, however. Other authorities would disagree, believing that male or female dominance or insufficient role differentiation is irrelevant.[49]

A NEW PHYSICAL THEORY   At an earlier period of speculation about sexual problems, there was a fairly common belief that homosexuality had a physical base. The discovery of hormones and knowledge of endocrinology seemed to be the key to a "cure." With very rare exceptions, however, hormone treatment has been a failure.

Recently, though, the researcher Dr. Margolese reports a new approach to a possible organic base for homosexuality. Research in the amount of testosterone present in the individual has not resulted in a clue to sex deviancy, but there are two chemical components of testosterone whose proportions differ. For the man of exclusively heterosexual interest, the amount of one of the components (androsterone) is greater than the amount of the other (etiocholanolone); for exclusively homosexual

[48]Robert P. Odenwald, *The Disappearing Sexes,* Random House, Inc., New York, 1965, chap. 8.
[49]Churchill, *op. cit.,* pp. 100–120.

males, the reverse is invariably the case, according to Margolese. Converse results have been found in women. It is also speculated that the bisexual may be a person without a real dominance of either androsterone or etiocholanolone.

Margolese was challenged by a psychiatrist to identify a group of homosexuals and heterosexuals by studying the presence of the two chemical hormone components in their urine. To the psychiatrist's amazement, Margolese correctly identified each subject.[50] Even Margolese is cautious about his conclusions, however, merely speaking of such chemical substances as "correlations," not causes. The subject at present is highly controversial, but more research work is being pursued at UCLA.

THE PROBLEM OF STATISTICS The first statistics on homosexuality that have any reliability are those of Alfred E. Kinsey.[51] He found four percent of his male subjects and from 1 to 3 percent of his females to be true homosexuals, that is, exclusively homosexual in interest. What was much more surprising was the discovery that 13 percent of the females and 37 percent of the males had had at least one homosexual experience. It is this latter statistic that makes widely varying estimates of homosexuality all seem somewhat plausible. Jess Stearn's[52] book *The Sixth Man* implies that one man in six is homosexual. This estimate would harmonize with Kinsey's data only if we assume that about half of his 37 percent may be bisexual, generally having normal relations, but at one time or another having had homosexual affairs. Somehow Stearn's figure sounds much too high in terms of other estimates. William J. Helmer[53] estimates that there are about 100,000 homosexuals in New York City— roughly 5 percent of the city's male population over sixteen. A recent study by *Psychology Today* almost completely duplicates Kinsey's findings of more than twenty years ago, with precisely 37 percent having had at least one homosexual experience,[54] which would indicate no marked increase in homosexuality.

Certainly discussion and awareness of homosexuality are increasing, but that may be the only difference. It also seems possible that if public attitudes become more permissive, there might be a slight increase in the amount of overt homosexuality, with a few of the 37 percent mentioned by Kinsey remaining homosexual rather than eventually developing heterosexual interests. Such a conclusion, however, is merely speculative.

MYTHS AND HALF-TRUTHS ABOUT HOMOSEXUALITY The very use of the word "gay" for many homosexuals is a little deceiving. At parties among their own kind, both male and female homosexuals may seem to be gay in the dictionary meaning of the word —

[50]"Homosexual Chemistry," *Newsweek,* vol. 77, pp. 54–55, April 26, 1971.
[51]Alfred E. Kinsey, *Sexual Behavior in the Human Male*, W. B. Saunders Company, Philadelphia, 1948, p. 651. Also, *Sexual Behavior in the Human Female*, W. B. Saunders Company, Philadelphia, 1953, p. 488.
[52]Jess Stearn, *The Sixth Man*, Doubleday & Company, Inc., Garden City, N.Y., 1961.
[53]William J. Helmer, "New York's Middle Class Homosexuals," *Harper's Magazine*, vol. 226, pp. 85–92, March 1963.
[54]Robert Athanasiov et al., "Sex," *Psychology Today*, vol. 4, pp. 39–52, July 1970.

lighthearted and happy. Much of their lives, however, is lived in the straight world, where they must be on guard. Furthermore, there is tragedy about the whole world of the homosexual, for his life must necessarily be incomplete. Old age is especially pathetic. One of the last chapter's of Stearn's book is entitled "Old and Gay," and it pictures a life sinking into loneliness and dejection. Liaisons between partners tend to be short lived. A marriage of man to woman, although somewhat brittle in modern society, at least has societal sanction and familial support. The liaison of man to man or woman to woman is viewed as odd by the tolerant and as evil by the intolerant. The gay is, generally speaking, anything but gay.

A common fear regarding increasing tolerance of homosexuality is of whether exposure to it will "infect" the young. Literature about this subject *seems* to indicate that this is true only for boys who have begun to think of themselves in homosexual terms. An indication that most people do not become permanently homosexual, in spite of exposure to such relationships, comes from a study of prisons.[55] Although much homosexuality takes place in prisons, and young men especially are victimized, after release the men who were heterosexual before imprisonment seem to resume heterosexual interests. It must be admitted, though, that conclusions of prisoner studies might not be applicable to the general population.

Another fairly common assumption is that the homosexual, being perverse in sexual affairs, must be thoroughly bad in other respects. Oddly enough, André Gide, himself a homosexual, often pictured the homosexual characters in his novels as rather perverse and evil. Possibly he was expressing his guilt feelings about his own abnormality. What seems more likely is that the traits of emotional instability, deceptiveness, and heavy drinking have been developed by the homosexual mainly because of his stigmatized position and fear of discovery. Freud himself felt that there was no reason why the homosexual could not be an acceptable, normal personality in most respects.[56]

CHANGING ATTITUDES Ever since the Wolfenden Commission Report in England a decade ago recommended to Parliament that homosexual relations between consenting adults should be legalized, there has been a gradual relaxation in laws and law enforcement regarding sex. Several states regard homosexuality as a sickness and treat it as such. Many cities simply ignore it. A Gay Liberation Movement has become almost militant in its demands for an end of harassment. Most "gays" are genuinely unhappy about their condition but simply do not wish to be hounded about it. One such person states "If I had been given a choice (but people are not), I would prefer to have been straight."[57] If we wish more people to be straight, it might be

[55]William J. Drummond, "State Tries to Offset Prison Homosexuality," *Los Angeles Times*, February 7, 1971, Section H, pp. 1–3.
[56]Helmer, *op. cit.*
[57]Merle Miller, "Homosexual's Story: No More Quiet Desperation," *Los Angeles Times*, January 31, 1971, Section F, p. 2.

wise to make present homosexuals less defensive, so that more could be known about the affliction. Knowledge may not lead to cure, but certainly ignorance will not. Possibly the time will come when most of the affliction can be removed by improvement in child care, psychiatry, or even the use of hormones and chemistry. In the meantime, nothing is to be accomplished by adding to an affliction.

SUGGESTED READINGS

Churchill, Wainright: *Homosexual Chemistry among Males: A Cross-Cultural and Cross-Species Investigation*, Hawthorn Books, Inc., New York, 1967.

> This is the most thorough and careful recent work on the subject. Presents many surprising facts and tentative explanations in an objective manner. Not available in paperback.

Goffman, Irving: *Stigma: Notes on the Management of a Spoiled Identity*, Prentice-Hall, Englewood Cliffs, N.J., 1963.

> Goffman writes with great sensitivity and feeling and also analyzes problems in the context of social-psychological theory. An analysis of how one manages to cope with the stigma resulting from physical defectiveness, blindness, deafness, or outcaste status.

Health Policy Advisory Committee, *The American Health Empire*, Random House, Inc., New York, 1968.

> "A comprehensive analysis of . . . the American medical system." The report charges that the present system squanders money, ignores the needs of patients, and will require more than national health insurance to cure it.

Schorr, Daniel: *Don't Get Sick in America*, Aurora Publishing Company, Nashville, Tenn., 1970.

> Closely parallels a TV documentary on health care problems in America. Documents inadequacy of health insurance, lack of clinics, shortage of doctors and medical schools. Shows how the United States, a leader in medical research, lags behind in the problem of means to pay for medical treatment.

Silverstein, Harry (ed.): *The Social Control of Mental Illness,* Thomas Y. Crowell Company, New York, 1968.

> A collection of excerpts from some of the best works in the field—social class and mental illness, mental health in the metropolis, the psychiatric hospital, the myth of mental illness, and the divided self.

Szasz, Thomas S.: *The Myth of Mental Illness*, Harper & Row, Publishers, Incorporated, New York, 1961.

> A novel point of view about mental illness is presented. Although the present designation "mental illness" is meant to be a kindly definition of troubles, it lumps too many phenomena together and fails to explain age and social-class differences in type of affliction.

 QUESTIONS

1. What are the special problems of the middle class and the poor in trying to get proper health care?

2. Explain what is meant by "psychological affliction" and "financial affliction" relative to the hospital.

3. Why does Szasz criticize the whole concept of "mental illness?"

4. What are various types of stigmata and what methods are used to try to get along in spite of them?

5. How can even the heroized turn into the stigmatized?

6. How prevalent is male and female homosexuality and what are alternative explanations for it?

12 *The search for euphoria through the use of dangerous drugs is definitely classified as deviant behavior. But there are some agents of euphoria whose use is permitted, and societies differ in the types of drugs they prohibit and the degree of penalty imposed for violation of the norms. Under what conditions can such a very common drug as alcohol be used fairly safely, and under what conditions does it produce alcoholism? Why is heavy use of any type of drug seen as a societal threat? Why do governments not simply take the attitude that one's retreat into alcoholism or addiction is his own problem? How is the common good involved?*

How has the drug problem changed over the years in America in legality, amount of use, and type of user? What situations seem to produce the highest incidence of illegal drug use? Are the various illegal drugs now in use properly classified as to their degree of danger? Is the present prohibition of marijuana almost the same thing as the prohibition of alcohol in the days of the Eighteenth Amendment? What are the pros and cons of legalizing marijuana? There is very great diversity of opinion on the issue of marijuana, but practically none on the harder drugs. Why, then, are we losing the battle against heroin? What actions are being taken now, and what new philosophies and proposals are coming about?

THE SEARCH FOR EUPHORIA

A state of euphoria is a feeling of unusual well being or elation that transports the individual to a realm of temporary freedom from the cares of everyday life. Evidence indicates that euphoric experience is sought much more in fast-moving, modern society than it was in previous generations. Sometimes the euphoria is mild—a mere relaxation, heightened conviviality, or a pleasant dream. Sometimes the euphoria seems as beautiful as the passions of love or the mystic experience of religious ecstasy, but sometimes it descends to an ugly state bordering on paranoia.

Certain societies have developed ceremonies to induce strange states of consciousness in their followers or have accomplished the flight from the everyday world of reality through the use of alcohol or drugs. The ceremonies have had the function of rousing fighting blood, of releasing shamanistic powers by which the medicine man can cure disease, or of inducing spiritual visions in young men being initiated into manhood. In nearly all cases, however, the use of the agents of euphoria has been limited by social custom and ritual. Even tribes that have seen strange states of consciousness as sources of power have also seen them as sources of danger.

RITUAL CONTROL

Alcohol and drugs have been used for ritual purposes by both primitive and advanced societies. Wine has long had a social and even a semireligious function, not only in the rites of Dionysus but even in the ritual observances of many Christians and Jews. Cannabis, from which marijuana is derived, was once considered a sacred plant, with magical and medicinal powers. Hallucinatory mushrooms of Mexico and northern South America have had sacred ritual uses for many Indian tribes.[1] Some American Indian tribes required a vision quest of their young men as part of the transition to manhood. For many the vision quest was accomplished by long periods of deprivation and even the sacrifice of a finger by the blow of a tomahawk. The South American Jívaro accomplished the vision quest by using drugs so strong that they caused convulsions and terrifying hallucinations; the drugs were used to contact the spirit world, not merely for pleasure.

PEYOTE AND THE NATIVE AMERICAN CHURCH Peyote has been used by certain American Indian tribes for centuries. The use was very limited, however, and did not spread rapidly from tribe to tribe until the decline of old tribal ways. In the late nineteenth century the Ghost Dance developed as an expressive movement for rekindling Indian loyalty to their own culture, and later the peyote-using Native American Church served the same purpose. The rationalization for peyote use was that God

---

[1]John M. Allegro of the University of Manchester, England, equates the classical Nectar of the Gods and Indian *soma* with the psychedelic mushroom. He also contends there was a connection between early Christianity and certain mystery cults, which found both mystery and ecstasy in the sacred mushroom, John M. Allegro, *The Sacred Mushroom and the Cross*, Doubleday & Company, Inc., Garden City, N.Y., 1970.

had given peyote to the Indians to compensate for their heavy losses at the hands of the white man.

Paul Radin[2] relates a tale told by an Indian who joined the peyote cult. He was a Winnebago of youth, vigor, and good looks, but not happy even though he had access to all the women he desired. He was told by some relatives who had joined the cult that a life devoted to the pursuit of women was wrong. He must learn, they said, to possess only one woman and give up his tobacco and medicine pouch and listen only to Earthmaker (God), whom he would learn about at the peyote ceremonies. Eventually he consented to listen to the strange god, as a man confused between two cultures will sometimes do. He went to the ceremonies, took the peyote, had strange feelings and visions (along with nausea), until at last:

> As I prayed I was aware of something above me and there he was; Earthmaker to whom I was praying; he it was. That which is called the soul, that is it, that is what one calls Earthmaker. Now this is what I felt and saw. The one called Earthmaker is a spirit, and that is what I felt and saw. All of us sitting there, we had all together one spirit and soul. That is what I learned.

From that day on, the young Winnebago settled down to married life and attended the Native American Church services once a week. Peyote, being less potent than the mescaline derived from it and being ritually controlled and difficult to take, did not become mentally disorganizing to any serious degree. It was easily adapted to a culture that had long emphasized a vision quest.

ALCOHOL AND GROUP CONTROLS   Alcohol was also readily adaptable to the cultures of the Great Plains tribes who had enjoyed exciting ceremonies and vision quests, but its use extended beyond ceremonial occasions and became destructive. Certain tribes had opposite value orientations. Ruth Benedict tells us that the Zuñi Indians, whose values called for quiet cooperation and a calm, imperturbable disposition, rejected alcohol as a disturber of traditions and values. The contrast between two types of Indian societies is a small-scale replica of much of the world in its attitude toward the use of mind-altering drinks and drugs. Some permit considerable use of such substances; some limit them strictly to ceremonial occasions; others prohibit them.

Studies in the United States on the subject of alcoholism show some of the results of group controls. Among Orthodox Jews, who permit the use of wine in ceremonies, alcoholism is extremely low. Alcohol, apparently, is strongly associated with religious ritual and only with religious ritual. Jewish people who defy the norms probably find some other means. Among Mormons, who decry any use of alcohol, the rate

---

[2]Paul Radin, *The Autobiography of a Winnebago Indian*, University of California Publications in American Anthropology and Ethnology, no. 16, University of California Press, Berkeley, 1920, pp. 48–64. Reprinted in Philip K. Boch, *Culture Shock*, Alfred A. Knopf, Inc., New York, 1970, pp. 316–326.

The ritual use of wine, as in the Consecration, defines and limits its value to occasions of group integration.

of drinking is very low. However, for those few Mormons who do drink, the possibilities of drinking to excess are considerable. Alcohol for these people is apparently a means of defying authority, and when that is its use it seems to be more dangerous than when used on ritual and social occasions. In some respects the prevailing norms of America come somewhere between those of the orthodox Jews and the Mormons. Liquor is not good enough to be used as a part of religious ceremony. It is seen as bad enough to be frowned upon but not really proscribed. This is probably one of several reasons why the rate of alcoholism in the United States is higher than in most countries.[3]

CONDITIONS OF FAILURE OF GROUP CONTROLS When the group that defines norms about alcohol is unsure of itself, the possibility of alcoholism rises. It would be reassuring to conclude that there would be no alcohol problems for a society that trains its people in the "proper" use of alcohol. This is probably an oversimplification of

[3]Seldon Bacon, "Social Settings Conducive to Alcoholism: A Sociological Approach to a Medical Problem," *Journal of the American Medical Association*, vol. 165, pp. 171–181, May 1957.

the case. In Italy it is reported that a pattern of family drinking of wine seems to produce very few problem drinkers. In France, the same pattern—even more permissive—seems to result in a high rate of alcoholism. One reason for the difficulty is that in parts of rural France wine is related to manhood and virility and good health.[4] Apparently alcohol has dangers even in a society that does not create an urge to use it as a symbol of protest or liberation.

In a society with little primary-group control or strong traditional ties and with very little meaningful ritual, old patterns of behavior are vulnerable to rapid change. Modern America also has the problem of normative confusion, value conflict, discontentment and protest—all the unsettling conditions discussed so far as part of The Troubled Land. Many people try vigorously to work at the problems that beset their society; others follow their own pursuits in a manner as close to old cultural patterns as possible. Many others, however, find normative confusion an excuse for a certain amount of normative rejection. In a society with a fairly well-defined habit of using alcohol to show independent status (and the older generation has certainly done this), it is not surprising that a new symbol of independent status—marijuana—should be taken up rather readily. Unfortunately, for many the drug experience does not stop with marijuana.

THE LAND OF THE LOTUS EATERS

In Homeric legend, Ulysses, on his way home from Troy, had to take his ships and crew through many perils, including the Land of the Lotus Eaters. In that peaceful and dreamy land the people lived on the blossoms of the lotus tree, which had a blissful narcotic effect and kept them in a state of perpetual sleep or near sleep. The lotus eaters gave some of their honey-sweet blossoms to two of Ulysses' crewmen. The allure was too strong for their willpower, and they wished to stay and dream their lives away. To stout Ulysses, determined to return to his kingdom and his wife and son, the lotus blossom was a trap to be avoided. He had his lotus-eating crewmen seized and put back on the ship.

Ulysses can be thought of as a symbol of one approach to life, and the lotus eaters as the opposite. To Ulysses the problems of life had to be faced; to the lotus eaters they were to be escaped from or forgotten. For this reason nearly all governments, especially those trying to lead a dynamic society, discourage the use of drugs and the excessive use of alcohol. Most Western countries have steadily opposed marijuana; India outlaws both alcohol and marijuana, although the latter is used considerably. There are gross inconsistencies as to how various countries think of drug problems, but they all see the lotus blossom as unacceptable. The lotus blossom comparison is overdrawn in the sense that not all sensations sought are those of blissful dreams, but they always have at least an element of escape about them.

[4]Barbara Galliton Anderson, "How French Children Learn to Drink," *Transaction*, vol. 5, pp. 20–22, June 1968.

THE FUNCTIONS OF DRUGS   As has already been suggested by cross-cultural examples, the functions of drugs and alcohol are various. To the Native American Church the function is largely magicoreligious. For less exotic cultures, wine also often has a religious ceremonial function. Bernard Barber[5] names other functions of drugs besides the ones already listed, but several are very similar to the present use of the concept of euphoria.

Some types of drugs are believed by their users to have an esthetic function. The peyote cult discovered new ceremonial dances and new music under the influence of peyote. Rock musicians are famous for their flirtation with such drugs as LSD and marijuana. Coleridge and DeQuincy both smoked opium, but complained that although it stretched the imagination it made the completion of ideas extremely difficult.

Certain types of drugs have been considered aphrodisiacs, but if they have worked for the purpose of sexual arousal, it has probably been for the same reason that placebos (pills without substance given to hypochondriacs) seem to work. People who believe in magic can make themselves think it works. The other reason some drugs might work as aphrodisiacs is that they lower inhibitions.

The admittedly useful purpose for many kinds of drugs is medicinal, a fact that gives the word "drug" two different meanings. This discussion is concerned with medical drugs only in cases where their improper use may produce some of the same health hazards as illegal drugs—possible chromosome damage or prenatal damage, or a tendency toward addiction. The other relationship between the two meanings of drugs is that some of the present illegal products were originally considered therapeutic, for example, marijuana, alcohol, opium, and LSD.

Berbar uses the term "ego disrupting" to describe another function of drugs. Their effects take one away from the usual routines, "out of the rut." Alcohol is used often for this purpose. The idea expressed by certain popular musicians, "step outside your mind," gives an exaggerated version of the same function.

Psychological support is a similar function, but it can be extended beyond the "ego disrupting" function to include tranquilizers and energizers. Under this heading could also be included the drugs used for calming the hyperactive child.

There are a few cases in which drugs have been used for political reasons. During World War II the Japanese encouraged the use of opium in China. There is shrewd reasoning behind the policy of making lotus eaters of one's enemy. There is even a suspicion in American society that some lower-class boys' gangs are not pursued too energetically if they are on drugs. The drug crowd is often more quiet than the energetic gang engaged in interneighborhood fights. The peyote cult was not deliberately started by white Americans, but it served the purpose of quieting whatever aspirations for resistance still existed in Indian America.

Recently another factor could be added as contributing to the use of drugs, the idea of defying conventional norms. LSD and marijuana have served this purpose

[5]Bernard Barber, *Drugs and Society*, The Russell Sage Foundation, New York, 1967.

The ego-disrupting function of drugs,
a dangerous road to ecstasy, followed
by oblivion and despair.

especially well, and to a degree, alcohol had the same function for youth in the days of Prohibition.

All these are rather obvious functions of drugs and/or alcohol. There are other functions, or other ways of looking upon the same functions: for relaxation, kicks, excitement, or for drowning sorrows. All these are included under the idea of euphoria.

THE SEMANTICS OF DRUG USE Before asking whether America is a land of lotus eaters, it is time to clear up some confusion in definitions. Alcohol and drugs have not been categorically separated because it has seemed unnecessary to draw too much of a distinction between them. Dr. Joel Fort, consultant to the World Health Organization, gives an analysis that helps to clarify definitions and to justify the grouping of agents of euphoria used in this chapter.[6] He shows that the semantics of drug use has a strong effect on popular ideas about their acceptability. For example, the advocates of LSD have wanted to call it "mind expanding," implying it does something useful; its opponents refer to it as hallucinogenic or even "psychotomimetic" — imitating states of psychosis. The idea of classifying alcohol with drugs is offensive to many people who use alcohol but think they would never use anything that could be called a drug. The word "drug" has the fault of being an omnibus term including all the functions mentioned above and probably many more.

Fort suggests that the words "mind-altering drugs" should apply to a whole range of agents, including sedatives, stimulants, tranquilizers, LSD, narcotics, marijuana, alcohol, and, to a degree, even nicotine and caffein. More frequently, though, in the public mind classification is made on the basis of "good" and "bad," or legal and illegal. Both such pairs of terms imply value judgments that not all societies agree with. During the days of the Eighteenth Amendment alcohol was illegal and bad; now it is legal and almost elevated to the plane of goodness, in spite of the serious alcoholism problem in the United States. In countries of Moslem influence and also in India, on the other hand, alcohol is both illegal and bad. Marijuana use is generally illegal, too, but in some countries it is not condemned as strongly as alcohol.

The semantics of drug use should lead to some basis for comparing drugs in terms of types of effects. In medical terminology there are such descriptions and they are fairly precise. "Tolerance," "dependence," "addiction," and "drug abuse" are all part of the necessary vocabulary. Tolerance implies increasing use of a drug in order to produce the same degree of "highness."[7] "Addiction," or physical dependence, includes tolerance, but it also includes withdrawal pains and sickness when use of the drug is terminated. There is also psychological dependence that occurs when a drug is necessary to "make life worthwhile" or to overcome feelings of weak-

[6]Joel Fort, M.D., "The Semantics and Logic of the Drug Scene," in *Drug Awareness: Key Documents on LSD, Marijuana and the Drug Culture*, Richard E. Horman and Allan M. Fox (eds.), Avon Books Division, The Hearst Corporation, New York, 1970, pp. 87–98.
[7]*Ibid.*, pp. 88–90.

ness, timidity, or depression, or to bolster the self-image. Drug abuse can be defined as "excessive use of a drug or substance to the point that it interferes with the individual's social or vocational adjustment or his health."[8] "Narcotic" is generally used to apply to dangerous and illegal drugs, although in medical use it refers to pain-relieving drugs, including opium and its derivatives (morphine and heroin) and certain synthetics with a similar effect. Dangerous drugs, in federal and most state laws, also include barbiturates and amphetamines, although both have a legal medicinal use.

DRUG MYTHOLOGY Despite definitions, there is a certain mythology about drugs, for example, the idea that marijuana produces unpredictable results and that the results of alcohol are perfectly predictable. Any drug produces differing effects in different individuals and in the same individual under different circumstances. Even tranquilizers prescribed by a doctor seem to calm most patients but not some; they are even known to have excitatory effects occasionally, aggravating rather than relieving the patient's state. This is not to suggest that all drugs are equally harmful; the point is that dichotomizing drugs into goods and bads is an oversimplification. In their degree of danger, drugs fall along a continuum, but not even the continuum is consistent from individual to individual or from occasion to occasion.

As we have seen, there is some validity to classifying large numbers of agents of euphoria together. Their various functions for a tension-ridden society have made much of modern America a land of the lotus eaters. The severity of the problem, however, depends upon the types of drugs used and the degree to which they are used. Both the types of drugs used and the extent of usage have become disturbing to traditional values and to the physical and mental effectiveness of a large segment of the population.

THE DIMENSIONS OF THE PROBLEM

The daily press rarely fails to mention cases of arrest for narcotics or to headline new discoveries in the problems of drug abuse. We are informed that drug abuse in

---

Attitude survey: many studies of the use of drugs on campus have been made, but they seldom ask why. It would be interesting, although a little difficult, to probe this question. The easiest way would be an alternative choice question. What has influenced you—friends? resentments? a feeling of meaninglessness in life? mere curiosity? and other choices suggested by the class.

---

[8]*Ibid.*, p. 90.

the Armed Forces is reaching the proportions of a national scandal, that the age of drug use for the young is regressing downward from college to high school to junior high school, and that the problem may be simultaneously moving up the age scale to include a few of the middle aged. Most frequently the drug referred to is marijuana, but sometimes the reference is to strongly addictive drugs, especially heroin. There have been drug scares in our nation's history before. When a social worker tells of heavy drug use in a blighted area or of the alcoholics on skid row, he is telling a familiar story. Many current reports about narcotics are less familiar or were less familiar until recently. Several kinds of changes have come about in the use of alcohol and drugs during our nation's history.

A BRIEF HISTORY In spite of the statement that the search for euphoria seems contrary to American values, alcohol and drugs have long been around. Our ancestors in colonial America included large numbers of heavy drinkers. The West was a brawling region where whisky was consumed in large quantities. There seem to have been more abstainers in earlier days than now, but those who drank were even heavier drinkers. Our ancestors thought ill of the Indians but not of their tobacco, which they chewed, snuffed, and smoked to their hearts' content (at one time both Turkey and Persia punished tobacco smoking by the death penalty)![9]

There were cases of the use of opiates in the early nineteenth century, and morphine became common during the Civil War. Many soldiers who had had morphine administered to them as a pain-killer built up a tolerance for the drug and became addicted to it so badly that morphine addiction was sometimes called the soldiers' disease. Morphine was also used in many patent medicines and soothing syrups for babies. Late in the century opium smoking became a fad in the underworld, but the use of opium and its derivatives was coming under increasing criticism from the medical profession.[10]

Opposition to narcotics led to the passing of the Harrison Act in 1914. The Harrison Act, along with court interpretations and amendments, made most drug use illegal and largely a phenomenon of the underworld. A few years later the Eighteenth Amendment was passed, outlawing the use of alcohol and placing the United States on a road to purity unusual among the nations of the world. The failure to enforce the Eighteenth Amendment, and the enormous problem of bootlegging that it created, eventually led to its repeal. During the days of Prohibition, many people of the respectable world never gave up the desire for a drink or the temptation to patronize the criminal world to get it. In contrast, the narcotics world sank further below the level of respectable society, and marijuana was classed as evil along with

[9]Stanley F. Yolles, Director of the National Institute of Mental Health, "The Problem—an Overview," *Narcotics Addiction and Drug Abuse*, U.S. Government Printing Office, Washington, D.C., 1969, p. 46. Hearings before the Special Subcommittee on Alcoholism and Narcotics of the Committee on Labor and Public Welfare, United States Senate.

[10]John A. Clausen, "Drug Addiction," in Robert K. Merton and Robert A. Nisbet, *Contemporary Social Problems*, Harcourt Brace Jovanovich, Inc., New York, 1966, pp. 199–202.

heroin. Apparently many of the old users of morphine managed to break the habit, and later they began to die off. Narcotics were confined increasingly to a subculture of the outcast and despised, except for a slight increase among juveniles after World War II. For many years the number of hard-narcotics addicts stabilized at about 60,000, but in the 1960s the number began to increase. The more dramatic increase in drug use, however, was in the new psychedelic drugs and in marijuana. Much less obvious was a steady increase in the use of drugs with medical utility, but drugs that could easily be abused. Amphetamines, often prescribed for weight reduction but capable of building extreme psychological dependence, are produced at a rate of 8 billion pills per year, according to some estimates.[11]

In the United States today more than 20 million people use sleeping pills, more than 10 million use amphetamines, and about 50 million use tranquilizers.[12] Of the users of amphetamines and barbiturates, about 400,000 are excessive users. An estimated 20 to 40 percent of college students have at least experimented with marijuana and about 5 percent with LSD.[13] Although practically all statistics are estimates, they are in fairly close agreement as to the extent of the drug problem. New York City reports that 8 percent of all persons sent to penal institutions from 1956 to 1965 had an admitted drug history (mainly heroin). By 1969, the comparable figure was 40 percent.[14] In connection with these statistics it should be added that counter to an old stereotype of the "drug fiend," offenses against the person among drug users are fewer than for nondrug users.

Jack Anderson, in his syndicated column of August 15, 1970, charged that drugs are readily available at Walter Reed Army Hospital. He quoted a decorated combat soldier, who is also a pusher, who said he made $6,300 in the last nine months selling marijuana, mescaline, LSD, and demerol. Harry Nelson reports similar cases in California State Hospitals.[15] The Pentagon has not been very open about publishing statistics on drug use in the Armed Forces but has had to admit its large scale existence. In an investigation before Senator Dodd, all officers interviewed admitted growth of the problem "at an alarming rate" for both marijuana and hard narcotics. Witness reports about marijuana use were highly inconsistent, however, ranging from 30 to 90 percent.[16] Even the lower figure shows an involvement that until recently would have been regarded as impossible. By the spring of 1971 the newspapers were reporting 40,000 to 50,000 users of heroin in the Armed Forces overseas. At the same time, the head of the Bureau of Narcotics admits we have not been able to reduce the amount of heroin available in the United States.

[11] "Slowdown for Pep Pills," *Newsweek*, p. 77, August 17, 1970.
[12] Kenneth L. Jones et al., *Drugs, Alcohol, and Tobacco*, Canfield Press, San Francisco, 1970, p. 16.
[13] Senator Ralph Yarborough, in *Narcotics Addiction and Drug Abuse, op. cit.*, p. 46.
[14] *Crime in a Free Society: Selections from the Presidential Commission on Law Enforcement and the Administration of Justice*, Robert W. Winslow (ed.), Dickenson Publishing Company, Belmont, Calif., 1968, p. 234.
[15] Harry Nelson, "Dope Smuggled Inside," *Los Angeles Times*, August 12, 1970, Part II, p. 1.
[16] Warren Rogers, "Drug Abuse in Services Rises Alarmingly," *Los Angeles Times*, September 21, 1970, Part I, pp. 1, 22.

A major problem finally admitted by the
military, sometimes taking more lives
than combat, and requiring long and
uncertain rehabilitation.

Accounts are beginning to appear about drug use in the respectable white-collar world. Major corporations found it necessary to send representatives to a conference in New York on the problem of drug abuse by employees. The Attorney General estimates that one out of forty workers is on drugs, mostly marijuana, but occasionally heroin. One corporation even pays disability money to get employees to undergo treatment.[17] Estimates of the total costs of drug abuse vary greatly. Yolles gives the figure as 2 to 3 billion dollars per year. A recent *Newsweek*[18] article states that in 1969 California alone prosecuted 60,000 narcotics cases at a cost of 100 million dollars.

THE PREVALENCE OF ALCOHOLISM   With the national concern for drug abuse, it is easy to forget the older problem of alcoholism. People are seldom physically destroyed with such dramatic suddenness by alcohol as by some types of narcotics, but it is still true that more people suffer from alcoholism than from the results of other drugs. In 1964, just over 22 percent of the first admissions of male patients to mental hospitals were alcoholics. In 1965, of all arrests in the United States, nearly one-third (1,535,000) were for public drunkenness. Problem drinking occurs in 10 to 25 percent of families on welfare. In 46 percent of fatal traffic accidents, at least one of the drivers had very high blood alcohol concentrations.[19] About five million people are considered problem drinkers. The consumption of alcohol is increasing rapidly, as shown in the following graph based on data from the U.S. Census Bureau and the Internal Revenue Service.

EXPLANATIONS OF DRUG USE   Until ten or fifteen years ago it was common to explain drug use as the consequence of the development of an "inadequate personality,"[20] stemming from a deprived or poorly structured home background. Such an explanation probably has validity in characterizing the type of person who goes from LSD and marijuana to heroin, but it seems very inadequate for the total phenomenon of drug abuse. Today people of deprived backgrounds are still engaged in drug use, but they have been joined by many others. By far the largest element to have joined

---

If such an organization is available and will permit visiting, visit a chapter of Alcoholics Anonymous or Narcotics Anonymous. They make an informative study in the importance of group support.

---

[17]"The Rising Problem of Drugs on the Job," *Time*, pp. 70–71, June 29, 1970.
[18]"Marijuana: Is It Time for a Change in Our Laws?" *Newsweek*, pp. 20–29, September 7, 1970.
[19]Thomas F. A. Plant, *Alcohol Problems: A Report to the Nation*, The Cooperative Commission on the Study of Alcoholism, New York, 1966, pp. 17–20.
[20]D. P. Ausubel, *Drug Addiction*, Random House, Inc., New York, 1958, p. 44.

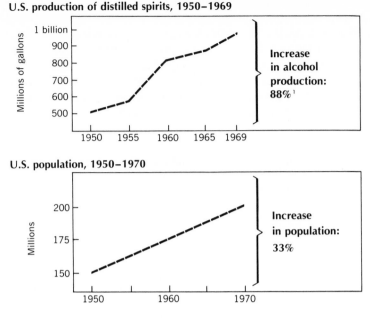

U.S. production of distilled spirits, 1950–1969

Millions of gallons

1 billion
900
800
700
600
500

1950   1955   1960   1965 1969

Increase
in alcohol
production:
88%[1]

U.S. population, 1950–1970

Millions

200

175

150

1950   1960   1970

Increase
in population:
33%

[1]Does not include beer or imported spirits figures

the drug users are young people, often college students from middle-class back-grounds. The drugs also are different. At first there was a great flirtation with LSD, but its use has declined, and the milder hallucinogen marijuana has become the overwhelming favorite. The reason for drug use on campus is different to some degree from the reason for its use in the urban slum. For the middle-class users, the search is for conviviality, belonging, and excitement; for the deprived classes it has often become a search for at least temporary oblivion.

There are differences, then, in the type of people, the type of drugs, and even the type of euphoria. Are there any elements in common? For many of the new drug users the answer seems to be "Yes." For both the urban poor and the "turned-on" student generation, there are all the characteristics of the counterculture. Old values are rejected; there is a feeling of resentment about the striving society. The gap be-tween social value and social reality is seen starkly by the younger generation and greatly elaborated upon. For many, the feelings of resentment against the dominant society are comparable with the resentments felt by minority groups in ghettos.

There are other similarities. Long periods of inaction and boredom make a good background for drug experimentation. For the ghetto the case needs no elaboration. For college students, the comparison is not clear at first, but for some the course work is a long grind. Goals are not clearly in sight. To the elders, youth seems like a period of constant activity and excitement, but the young nevertheless experience long empty hours and uncertainties. The quest for exciting new experience is natural to youth. In older times the parental generation always feared drinking parties; now many parents hope that is the worst that will happen. In previous analyses we have linked drinking and drugs. In one type of motivation the two drift apart for the younger generation. To drink is traditional and "old generation." To use marijuana is the subcultural requirement. This does not mean that the younger generation has never tasted liquor. As a matter of fact, alcohol use still far exceeds marijuana use for any group in the United States, and far more people eventually die of the effects of alcohol than of drugs. But alcohol no longer serves an important psychological function for members of the youth counterculture.

It must be added that as the use of marijuana spreads it is taken up increasingly by other people whose values are not countercultural in the same sense. Servicemen form a distinctive subculture of their own but with only the slightest implications of counterculture. Conditions that the ghetto dweller, serviceman, and student all experience to some degree are separation from strong community opinion in opposition to drug use, and often from the usual routines of integrated family life. In some cases there is a lack of direction and purpose. In the old days servicemen often took strongly to drink; now they have added another ingredient to the potion that temporarily relieves the boredom and anomie of a disorganized life. In veterans' hospitals, drugs apparently have appeal for the same reasons.

A word should be added about a pseudoreligious trait connected with the use of psychedelic drugs. Some young drug users have been off on a vision quest as surely as the Great Plains Indians pursued such a quest. In an age when old orthodoxies are no longer followed by many of the young, but there is still a feeling of religious need, a spirit quest can lead down various paths, one of which is to the perilous land of the lotus eaters.

It cannot be denied, either, that drugs have been promoted, and not just by the stereotyped pushers. The drug industry has convinced the world that there is a specific remedy for every ill; just take the right pill and it will go away. The result is a philosophy of escaping problems rather than facing them. There is also a merchandising tendency to play up the drug culture as long as it will help to increase sales, and many people push the art and fashions of a drug scene that they otherwise hold in contempt.

THE DANGERS

On philosophical grounds one might condemn any habit that turns into a pattern of escapism, even as innocuous a habit as watching TV all day. The type of escapism referred to here as "the search for euphoria" has further dangers. It includes the ingestion of substances that change inner feelings about life without making any real improvements in life. When one returns from the flight from reality, the old problems are still there. This problem belongs to some degree to all drugs, including alcohol, but the severity of the problem differs widely from drug to drug. A description of all the dangerous drugs is impossible in a single chapter, but the relative dangers of a few of the most commonly used should be discussed.

Barbiturates (called "sleeping pills," "goof-balls," or "reds") are sedative type drugs, somewhat similar to alcohol. At first they produce relaxation and good humor; heavier use can produce gloom or quarrelsomeness. The barbiturates are much more dangerous than alcohol because large dosages can be taken without producing nausea, so they are not quickly purged from the body. Barbiturates in combination with alcohol can cause death. Barbiturates are addictive; withdrawal for heavy users can cause convulsions. Contrary to public opinion, withdrawal from barbiturates is at least as dangerous as withdrawal from heroin.[21]

Amphetamines are nonaddictive stimulants, but they are dangerous for other reasons. They have been prescribed in some cases for weight reduction, but their use for that purpose is highly questionable. Amphetamines are commonly called "bennies" (benzedrine), "pep pills," and "speed." Speed (methedrine) is the most dangerous and can induce temporary paranoid symptoms. The amphetamines stimulate the nervous system, depress appetite, and prevent sleep for long periods of time. Truck drivers sometimes use them to stay awake on the road, and students sometimes use them when cramming for examinations. Excessive use can cause all the results of prolonged sleeplessness: mood changes, mental depression, suspiciousness, hallucinations, and even psychosis.[22] Dr. David Smith of the Haight-Ashbury Clinic in San Francisco states that there is no more connection between marijuana and heroin than there is between alcohol and heroin—but the correlation is with speed, the most dangerous amphetamine. A majority of the heroin addicts known to him used speed before turning to heroin.[23]

The powerful hallucinogen LSD is declining in use, but it is still fairly common. The drug is not physically addictive and has been used by various cultists looking for mind-expansion and pseudomystic-religious experiences. Usually the LSD trip produces excitement and wondrous hallucinations; sometimes it produces agonizing panic and temporary psychosis. There have been several dangerous results reported, such as fleeing in fright and falling out of a window.[24] Since such events are rare, they did not seem to dissuade many early LSD experimenters. In the opinion of Yolles, the decline in use came about as a result of reports of chromosomal damage, possible leukemia, and possible damage to the unborn. More research is needed before the full potential effects are known. Yolles is careful not to overstate his case, but he gives strong warning against the drug, especially for expectant mothers.[25]

[21] Jones et al., *op. cit.,* p. 25.
[22] *Ibid.,* pp. 32–33.
[23] Berenice Chipman Fritts, "Young Doctor David Smith," *The Bakersfield Californian*, October 11, 1970, p. 19.
[24] Richard B. Allan, "LSD: The False Illusion," in Horman and Fox (eds.), *op. cit.,* pp. 259–269.
[25] Stanley F. Yolles, "Recent Research on LSD, Marijuana, and Other Dangerous Drugs," in Horman and Fox (eds.), *op. cit.,* pp. 67–86.

Peyote, also a hallucinogen, is still permitted for the Apaches and certain other Indians in religious ceremonies. Since it nearly always causes vomiting, it is not used much by drug experimenters. Mescaline, developed from peyote, is used a little more, but it is very much stronger and more dangerous. A motiveless murder of a family of five in northern California has been attributed to mescaline-induced psychosis.[26]

The drug generally regarded as the most addictive is heroin, derived from opium. Since it is an extremely powerful drug, it is usually cut drastically for the illegal market. Sometimes it is not cut sufficiently and a user gets a much more powerful shot than he is accustomed to—one reason for many deaths from overdoses. The heroin addict typically loses ability to complete tasks or hold jobs and becomes enslaved by the drug. Family ties, recreation, nutrition, and sex interest all suffer, as well as work efficiency. In England, where addicts are treated at clinics, many are able to function to some degree in spite of their addiction. In the United States, where the user is an outlaw, the alienation from work and the rest of normal life is much greater. In the past, few real recoveries from heroin addiction have been recorded. At present methadone is being used as a substitute for heroin and is showing considerable promise. Although its use can be characterized as simply switching from one drug to another, people using methadone are able to function quite normally in society.[27]

MARIJUANA   Marijuana has been left to the last because in some ways it belongs in a different category. Expert opinion is more divided on the effects of marijuana than on most of the other drugs described here. "It is estimated that nationwide it has been tried by 20 to 40 percent of college and high school students and that its use is spreading to junior high schools and grade schools."[28] It seems to be readily available in spite of all that law enforcement authorities can do.

The majority of those who try marijuana are merely experimenters, but about 35 percent continue to use it to some degree. About 10 percent become chronic users. For the mere experimenter or very occasional user, the results are in some ways comparable with alcohol: conviviality, relaxation, release of inhibitions, unsteadiness, drowsiness, impaired judgment. The chronic user may develop the habit of withdrawal from problems and from reality and also may suffer from chronic bronchitis. More study is underway by the National Institute of Mental Health to assess the long-range results of chronic use of marijuana. Meantime, Yolles[29] summarizes one of the areas of concern:

> One needs to be particularly concerned about the potential effect of a reality distorting agent on the future psychological development of the adolescent user. We know that

[26]Jerry Gillam, "Murder Suspect: A Transformation Caused by Drugs," *Los Angeles Times*, October 25, 1970, Part I, pp. 1, 22.
[27]John Walsh, "Methadone and Heroin Addiction: Rehabilitation without a Cure," *Science*, vol. 168, p. 168, May 8, 1970.
[28]Yolles, in *Narcotics Addiction and Drug Abuse, op. cit.*, p. 94.
[29]*Ibid.*, p. 95.

adolescence is a time of great psychological turmoil. Patterns of coping with reality developed during the teenage period are significant in determining adult behavior. Persistent use of an agent which serves to ward off reality during this critical developmental period is likely to compromise seriously the future ability of the individual to make an adequate adjustment to a complex society.

At almost the same time that Yolles expresses deep concern about marijuana, another federal report from the National Commission on the Causes and Prevention of Violence states:[30]

There is no reliable scientific evidence of harmful effects, nor is there evidence of marijuana's being a stepping-stone to hard narcotics. Through our harsh criminal statutes on marijuana use, and in light of evidence that alcohol abuse accounts for far more destruction than any known psychoactive substance today, the report concluded, we have caused large numbers of our youth to lose respect for our laws generally.

In April 1971, considerable publicity was given to a marijuana study reported by the American Medical Association.[31] Two psychiatrists reported thirty-eight cases of marijuana users who had come to them for psychological help. Several, including those most disturbed, had had no previous symptoms of mental troubles. Nevertheless, eight subjects showed definitely psychotic symptoms after fairly heavy use of marijuana. One, for example, developed delusions of grandeur, believing himself to be the secret head of the Mafia. Another—a seventeen-year-old boy—called himself a new messiah.

Others showed no symptoms of a psychotic type, but nearly all suffered loss of ambition, loss of goal orientation, and two or three became a little incoherent— "spaced," in the current slang phrase. Many smokers will admit marijuana leaves them temporarily lazy but deny that the symptoms last. The psychiatrists' study has been criticized as a piece of empirical research because it gives no figures on how frequently types of mental impairment develop and no comparative data about marijuana users who have not suffered such symptoms. The study seems to imply, however, that marijuana, like alcohol, can become a severe problem for at least some people.

THE SEARCH FOR SOLUTIONS

Currently there are several practices for attempting to solve the drug abuse problems. The first is repression by legal devices. For many years it has been wise for political candidates to promise to crack down hard on narcotics. At times the feeling

[30] Ronald J. Ostrow, "Violence Panel Staff Report Asks Legalization of Marijuana," *Los Angeles Times*, September 8, 1970, Part I, pp. 1, 22. Copyright, 1970, *Los Angeles Times*. Quoted by permission.
[31] Harold Kolansky, M.D., and William T. Moore, M.D., "Marijuana and Mental Disturbance," *Journal of the American Medical Association*, vol. 216, pp. 486–492, April 19, 1971.

has been almost equally strong against both the users and pushers of narcotics. As more and more middle-class youth from influential homes have become involved in drug use, the clamor has been louder against the pusher and a little more moderate against the users.

THE DILEMMAS OF PUNISHMENT One trouble with clamping down on narcotics peddlers but not users is that, except for the upper echelons of the narcotics racket, peddler and user are often one and the same. If one member of a marijuana crowd knows where to find a supplier, he often gets a supply and sells part of it to his friends. This makes him a pusher, as defined by law. Five boys and one girl in Boise, Idaho, ranging in age from sixteen to eighteen years, were each sentenced to five years in prison for supplying drugs to other teenagers in town, although they did not meet the stereotype of the evil underworld character sought by punitive laws.[32] Most had the misfortune of coming from families of poor reputation. They lacked good legal representation and went before a judge who felt it necessary to make an example of someone. The community felt even more strongly than the judge about the supposed good effects of long and severe punishment. One irony in the case, however, is that the judge himself is doubtful about any reformative effects of prison. Equally disconcerting to Boise is the fact that many of its youth doubt that the sentence had any deterrent effect in the long run and that the case has attracted so much public sympathy from other parts of the country for the youthful convicts. A majority of similar cases get probation in other states or at worst, short sentences to juvenile institutions—not five years in prison. Punishments tend to be grossly uneven.

Another point that must be made very clearly about the punitive approach to drug control is that, although it has been the basic approach of the United States since 1914, it can certainly not be characterized as a success. Dr. John Kramer, psychiatrist and pharmacologist at the University of California at Irvine, in testifying before Senator Hughes' committee on narcotics, said "We in the United States have been on the wrong track for 40 to 50 years" in our punitive approach. He continued to suggest that if even 10 or 20 percent of the amount of money spent on apprehension, trial and punishment of addicts had been spent on research, "there is no doubt in my mind that our drug abuse problems would this day have been handled not only more humanely, but more effectively, and, in the long run, more

---

If you need help, consult your local telephone directory for NARCOTICS INFORMATION, or HOTLINE, or DRUGS: PREVENTIVE EDUCATION. If there are no helpful local listings, write to Synanon, 1910 Ocean Front, Santa Monica, California.

---

[32]Loudon Wainwright, "A Town Deals Sternly with Its Own," *Life*, vol. 69, pp. 40–47, November 6, 1970.

sparingly of both money and human life."[33] Although the most recent narcotics bill signed into law by the President provides for more clinics, its approach is still basically punitive. It also continues to list the amphetamines, including the very dangerous speed, under the relatively harmless drugs, and marijuana along with the most dangerous.[34]

Another word must be said about the difficulty with a punitive approach to addiction treatment—the place of punishment has all the problems of any other prison. John Brooks,[35] a former addict, and founder of an organization that tries to cure addiction, states that he was in five different prisons, and that in all every type of drug was available. His statement continues:

> In prison, everybody is clannish. All the drug addicts, all they talk about is shooting dope. A man may be physically clean while he is in prison for a while, but psychologically he is still being processed through the drug medium, so that when he comes out . . . psychologically, he is still on drugs.

THE SICKNESS APPROACH A second possible approach to drug problems is to treat them as a sickness. Such has been the case for years with the treatment of severe alcoholism, but even with alcoholism the policy has not been consistent. James P. Spradley tells of the endless cycle of arrests, nights in the drunk tank, "drying out," repeated drunkenness, rearrest, and escape to other cities that is a part of the meaningless round of life of the skid row drunkard.[36] Some alcoholics do not respond to treatment or to such an organization as Alcoholics Anonymous, but whether they can be helped or not, it seems that no purpose is served by constant harassment. Those who advocate a medical approach to drug addiction believe that the same is true even for the advanced heroin addict. Permanent cure is unlikely, but with outpatient care and the use of methadone, he can still live a useful life.

The federal government has long had two centers for the care of addicts and is now increasing facilities. More important for the young drug offender are some of the many community projects, supported by private donations, such as the Haight-Ashbury Clinic in San Francisco, NARCO in Atlantic City, CONCERN in Winchester, Massachusetts, and Marathon House in Attleboro, Massachusetts. Such centers make it possible for young offenders (in their philosophy the term should be "young patients") to receive care, encouragement from others who understand them, and help in returning to the world outside the drug subculture.

Synanon,[37] in Santa Monica, California, is by far the best known self-help clinic. It now houses about two thousand members and has several thousand participants

[33]Dr. John Kramer, in *Narcotics Addiction and Drug Abuse, op. cit.,* pp. 147, 152.
[34]John Brooks, in *Narcotics Addiction and Drug Abuse, op. cit.,* p. 255.
[35]*Narcotic and Drug Abuse Hearings, op. cit.,* p. 255.
[36]James P. Spradley, *You Owe Yourself a Drunk: An Ethnology of Urban Nomads,* Little, Brown and Company, Boston, 1970.
[37]Lewis Yablonsky, "The New Youth Rebellion," *Narcotics Addiction and Drug Abuse, op. cit.,* p. 105.

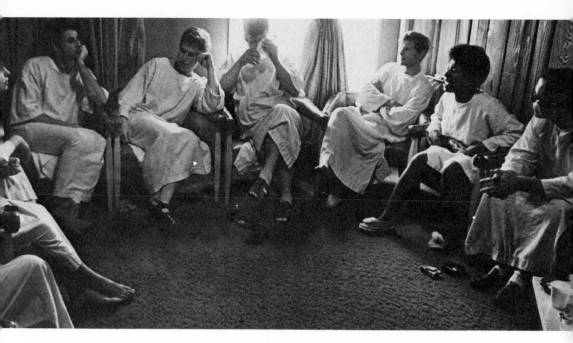

Synanon, the leader in the self-help approach to the drug problem, offers group solidarity, mutual concern, and the arts of creative expression.

who live outside. The self-help program of rehabilitation includes group-interaction and educational sessions, and business, financial, and self-support training. Founded in 1958 by Charles Dederich, Synanon has overcome vehement community opposition and is now accepted as the model for other self-help organizations.

LEGALIZATION OF MARIJUANA? The most serious proposals for the legalization of any of the outlawed drugs regard marijuana. Although recent polls have shown that a majority of Americans are in favor of some relaxation of the marijuana laws, less than a majority agree to full legalization. Nevertheless, the possibility of full legalization is at least being discussed by the national press. *Newsweek* summed up the arguments pro and con recently.[38] Proponents of legalization of marijuana say:

1. Although marijuana probably does some harm, the punishment goes far beyond the crime. Alcohol is probably at least as harmful to the health as marijuana.

[38]"Marijuana: Is It Time for a Change in Our Laws?" *Newsweek,* pp. 20–23, September 7, 1970.

2. The tasks of enforcement are so great as to nearly immobilize some courts for almost anything else. The monetary cost of enforcement is estimated at 100 million dollars for California alone in 1969.

3. The present policy increases the antagonism of the younger generation toward the law.

4. The present situation widens the gap between generations, causing constant parental worry about the law, a felt need for parental snooping and lecturing. Since parents know little about marijuana, but feel compelled to give warnings, they often create a credibility gap.

5. The marijuana traffic is a major source of support for the underworld. Legalization would dry up this source of funds just as legalization of alcohol did after the repeal of Prohibition.

All such arguments have counterarguments. Opponents of legalization reply:

1. Marijuana is a stepping stone to harder drugs because it acquaints people with the drug subculture and the sources of supply.

2. Marijuana may not be addictive, but it leads to psychological dependency.

3. Marijuana users, if their use becomes heavy and chronic, become apathetic and lacking in ambition.

4. Marijuana may have long-term dangers that we do not know of as yet.

5. We cannot give in on every law just because it is hard to enforce or just because it antagonizes part of our population.

Whatever the arguments about the legalization of marijuana, it is clear that we are making no headway in control at present. At the same time, full legalization might give an implication of condoning the use of the drug or even of admitting there are no problems or potential dangers in its use. A possible compromise might be legalization, but with strict government control of its sale so that no profit could be made from marijuana and so that there would be no compulsion to advertise it. In fact, it might even be good to make any advertisement illegal. To treat both the older and younger generations alike in their vices, there would be merit to also stopping

---

Discuss and debate the issue of whether the use of marijuana should be legalized, and if so, at what age level.

the advertisement of alcoholic drinks, sleeping pills, or any drugs that might prove harmful.

EDUCATION   The latest bill on narcotics to be passed by Congress calls for greater effort in education about drug abuse. Most states and communities are also interested in the educational approach. There is some hope that an educational approach can be helpful, provided it is scrupulously honest. An estimated 10 million Americans have stopped using tobacco in recent years, but only after the evidence against tobacco became clear and unequivocal. Before that time even referring to cigarettes as "coffin nails" did little or nothing to discourage smoking. The case is similar with drugs. The evidence against many types of drugs is unequivocal, but educators must be careful of their facts. As Yablonsky says, if students are instructed that "pot will surely lead to heroin," they will be very skeptical.[39] They are almost sure to know people who smoke pot but who would not turn to heroin. Even Yolles estimates that only about 1 percent of marijuana users ever turn to heroin.

BEYOND EDUCATION   Educational efforts can be helpful, but something more is needed. In the earlier type of drug use that was almost entirely a phenomenon of the slums, what was needed was a life of hope and purpose. The concerned reformer could have said that if we cure poverty, discrimination, and despair, we shall have cured the disease of drug addiction. The problem seemed to have been that of bringing into the main current of society those who had been excluded.

Again following Yablonsky's analysis, the new drug problem, that is, the drug problem for middle-class youth, is in some ways precisely the opposite. Many young people of the new period of youth rebellion "claim to use drugs to help unlearn the values, attitudes, and life styles generally accepted by most middle-class people."[40] This is the most disturbing aspect of the entire new drug scene, and the one that is not easily given to cure through laws, medical treatment, or even education. Some consolation is to be found in the fact that the alienation of youth is partly a matter of time and degree. For some, the use of drugs declines with maturity, and for the great majority the only drug used is marijuana. However, there are enough young people who go on to the use of other drugs, and there is enough human wreckage along the drug trail to make drug abuse a source of tremendous anxiety for the parental generation.

The same conclusion made regarding other problems of youth must be repeated here. Clinics, new medicines, and self-help communities are only palliatives for a disease. The solutions lie in making youth a more purposeful experience, with real work to do and real involvement in society. Those most motivated by other types of quests — be they socially idealistic or frankly self-centered — do not require the oblivion of bottle, needle, or pill. The tragic products of inadequate homes, rich or poor,

[39]Yablonsky, *loc. cit.,* p. 105.
[40]*Ibid.,* p. 99.

are the ones most vulnerable. There is no sure remedy, but the preachment to the older generation of those who have worked in such areas as the Haight-Ashbury district should be heeded: keep open the door between generation and generation and between culture and counterculture.

SUGGESTED READINGS

Geller, Allen, and Maxwell Boas: *The Drug Beat*, McGraw-Hill Book Company, New York, 1971.

Advertised as a complete survey of the history, distribution, uses, and abuses of marijuana, LSD, and the amphetamines, the book does a thorough job on all three. Authoritative and interestingly presented.

Horman, Richard E., and Allan M. Fox (eds.): *Drug Awareness: Key Documents on LSD, Marijuana and the Drug Culture,* Avon Book Division, The Hearst Corporation, New York, 1970.

Although the book consists mainly of official documents, many are very readable. The writers have the merit of being cautious about conclusions so that when warnings are sounded they are more likely to be heeded.

O'Donnell, John A., and John C. Bell (eds.): *Narcotic Addiction*, Harper & Row, Publishers, Incorporated, New York, 1966.

A very sound treatment of the subject, divided into a history of addiction, causes and effects of addiction, and the treatment of the addict. Statistics will have to be supplemented with periodical accounts of the last year or so; otherwise excellent.

Spradley, James R.: *You Owe Yourself a Drunk: An Ethnology of Urban Nomads*, Little, Brown and Company, Boston, 1970.

Although the title sounds a little farcical, the story is a pathetic one of homelessness, irresistible drinking habits, long and futile periods in jail, fleeing from city to city and from life itself. The author sees our treatment of the derelict drunkard as both fruitless and cruel.

Trice, Harrison M.: *Alcoholism in America*, McGraw-Hill Book Company, New York, 1966.

Professor Trice's book is built around the theme of our normative contradictions in drinking—the demand to drink, along with the even stronger demand to control drinking behavior, and the condemnation of those who cannot. Also makes a comparison between alcoholism and opiate addiction.

QUESTIONS

1. What are the cultural conditions under which alcohol and certain types of drugs are most likely to be used only in moderation?

2. The story of Ulysses and the Land of the Lotus Eaters is used to symbolize the attitude of most societies toward the use of most euphoric drugs. Why do societies consider it their business to regulate such drugs?

3. Contrast the drug problem of modern America with the problem as it existed before the Harrison Act of 1914 and with the problem of the 1930s and 1940s.

4. What situations seem to cause an increase in the incidence of drug use?

5. What are the arguments pro and con on the legalization of marijuana?

6. Discuss several current proposals for what to do about the drug problem.

13 *What are the facts in the problem of crime rate? Do we really have more criminals, or do we simply report more of their crimes? What difference does it make whether a lawbreaker is young or old, rich or poor? What are the explanations of crime? Is crime a consequence of certain types of people or of certain kinds of circumstances? What are the variations in type and rate of crime for different social classes, and what is the reason for such variations? Is there really an organized underworld, or are reports of a Mafia mere sensationalism? Finally, how do we fight crime? Does policy fit with theory of crime? If not, what improvements can be made?*

In the following pages we shall examine crime statistics on a rural-urban basis, age basis, and rich-and-poor basis. White-collar crime will be differentiated from other types of crime, both in type of offender and in difficulty of prosecution. We shall refer to several recent studies that include the organization now called Cosa Nostra and see what inroads it is making into legitimate American business. Finally, we shall look at new suggestions for fighting crime, especially the organized crime that has so far seemed to defy our efforts at control.

THE LAWBREAKERS:
YOUNG AND OLD, RICH AND POOR

The problems of making laws, justifying laws, and dealing with the violators of laws become increasingly difficult in modern societies. We do not have the primary group controls that were possible for simpler society in which people all knew each other and in which the threat of ostracism or ridicule was a major force in the maintenance of social control. Neither do we have the sacred attitudes that laws are somehow the manifestation of divine will and that the evasion of earthly justice will only make an offender more vulnerable to the fires of divine wrath. In the secular society all laws are seen as merely a far-from-perfect manifestation of the will of the people and their legislators and just as fallible as all the other handiwork of man. The laws, the means of detection of crime, the courts of justice, and the means of punishment are all subjects for argument and debate. At the same time, the heterogeneity of society increases, adding normative strain and confusion; urban concentrations grow; the continuing disparity between poverty and riches becomes more repugnant to the values of the social system, and a gulf widens between the norms of older and younger generations. All such developments are to some degree "criminogenic."

Against the consequence of the forces leading to higher rates of crime, society summons its defenses, often treating symptoms rather than causes. Jails and prisons overflow. Police forces, courts, and the whole machinery of justice expand, but not as rapidly as their burden of work. Detection becomes increasingly scientific. Seldom has a society devoted more time and effort to the apprehension and processing of criminals than the United States does today. More and more lawbreakers are caught, but the amount of crime continues to increase. Apparently, for many elements of the underworld the means of evasion have become just as scientific as the means of detection. By the corruption of government, by the purchase of friends in high places, and by the manipulation of the law and its enforcement system, the lawbreakers and their henchmen continue to thrive. The public is aroused over juvenile offenders and drug abuse, and the FBI concentrates on political crime and various forms of violence. All such problems become important political issues. Meanwhile, organized crime goes on its way, occasionally losing a battle, but never losing the war.

THE PREVALENCE OF LAWBREAKING

The FBI reports that there was a 148-percent increase in the crime rate during the 1960s while the population increased by only 13 percent. As we shall see, FBI reports are far from perfect measures of crime and might have a tendency to exaggerate the amount of increase, but there is little doubt that many kinds of crime have increased greatly, especially crimes against property. Although the public has thought of the 1960s as a period of very great violence, having witnessed many riots and demonstrations, the decade did not produce as much increase in crimes of violence as it did in various categories of theft. Homicide rates actually declined slightly for the entire period of 1945 to 1965 but showed an increase in the late 1960s.[1] The United States has had a history of violence, including labor unrest, outbursts against foreigners, violence of the police and against the police, race riots, draft riots (during the Civil War, New York was taken over for three days by the rioters), and lynchings—4,500 cases between 1882 and 1930.[2] The public has been alarmed over crime waves before, and it would be a distortion of fact to picture the present course of events as uninterrupted deterioration into violence and disorder. However, well-informed government commissioners and other investigators fear that the power of organized crime is reaching new heights, equaled, if at all, only in the Prohibition era.

One factor that can have a strong effect on the crime rate is the law itself. The Eighteenth Amendment had the effect of increasing the crime rate by defining all distributors of alcoholic beverages as lawbreakers. At present one of the problems of America is enforcing gambling, marijuana, and narcotics laws. Since drug abuse was the topic of the preceding chapter, problems regarding drugs will be repeated here only insofar as they have a bearing on other types of crime—theft to support addiction or the organization of the underworld. For the purpose of the present chapter we are mainly interested in the overall statistics on crime and how they relate to different segments of the population: the young, the poor, the minorities, the white-collar world, the "syndicate," and the government itself.

THE CRUDE STATISTICS   The FBI Uniform Crime Reports for 1969 indicated more than 14,000 cases of murder, 36,000 cases of rape, and 306,000 cases of aggravated assault. In the major categories of crimes against property, the figures were:

Robbery   298,000
Burglary   1,950,000
Larceny   1,513,000 ($50 and over)
Auto theft   872,000

All categories represented increases from the previous year.

Anonymous surveys indicate that the majority of people have committed at least an act or two defined as felonies, not mere misdemeanors. Try some anonymous polling in class or on campus. (Better stick to the campus; students are more likely than their elders to answer honestly.)

---

[1]*Crime in a Free Society: Selections from the President's Commission on Law Enforcement and the Administration of Justice*, Robert W. Winslow (ed.), Dickenson Publishing Company, Belmont, Calif., 1968, pp. 44–46.
[2]*Ibid.*

The FBI figures include large numbers of other offenses as well, although the figures on many others are less complete. For example, there were nearly 200,000 cases of narcotics violations, 1,270,000 cases of drunkenness, and 45,000 offenses against family and children. In the white-collar crime category, which must not be omitted, there were 5,500 cases of embezzlement, 30,000 cases of forgery and counterfeiting, and more than 40,000 cases of buying stolen property. In a time of worry over violence, it is interesting to note that there were 81,000 arrests for weapons violations.[3]

CRITICISM OF STATISTICS   Often the FBI Uniform Crime Reports are published in the daily press as though they were the perfect answer to all questions about crime rate. Actually, they have many problems, in spite of the fact that they have been improving somewhat over the years. By no means are all crimes known to the police. The most frequent reason for not reporting crimes to the police is a lack of confidence in law enforcement; consequently an increase in crimes "known to the police" could possibly indicate greater confidence in the ability of police forces to do something about crimes. Another difficulty with the Uniform Crime Reports is that not all cities report. Some sections of the country are more thorough in their crime reporting than others. For example, in one recent year only 45 percent of the known crimes in Mississippi cities were reported in the Uniform Crime Lists.[4]

Another problem is that police forces have been known to disguise statistics in order to look good. Since statistics in the past were much less reliable even than present figures, comparisons of the present with the past are risky. Nearly all these problems add up to making crime statistics rise even more rapidly than crime. However, a good reason for believing the crime rate actually is increasing is that many cities with records of good reporting have shown steady increases. Also, the characteristics of increasing urban growth, mobility, and normative conflict make an increase in crime rates seem plausible.

CRIME: RURAL AND URBAN   Since ours is a highly urbanized population, it is important to know whether or not the traditional prejudice against the city as a center of crime is valid. As a matter of fact, the rates of most types of crime are highest in the big cities, especially the central cities. Twenty-six such central cities, containing 18 percent of the nation's population, accounted for more than half the indexed crimes against the person and 30 percent of the crimes against property. Murder rates vary from 2 to 4 per 100,000 in rural and suburban areas to 10 per 100,000 in cities of 500,000 or more. Larceny varies from a low of 176 cases per 100,000 in rural areas to 359 in suburbs and 734 in cities of more than 1 million.[5]

[3]Statistics from *1971 World Almanac*, Newspaper Enterprise Association, New York, 1971, p. 78.
[4]Leonard Savitz, *Dilemmas in Criminology*, McGraw-Hill Book Company, New York, 1967, p. 33.
[5]Winslow, *op. cit.*, pp. 54–55.

CRIME: AGE AND SEX The general public is particularly concerned about juvenile delinquency, fearing that delinquency is a prelude to adult crime. Certainly there is reason for concern about problems of narcotics, vandalism, and delinquency rates in general, not only among the disadvantaged, but among middle-class youth as well. Several investigations, however, indicate that the type of crime committed by middle-class youth is likely to be outgrown with the passing of time. An investigation by Ronald J. Chilton,[6] for example, indicates a strong economic factor in the type of delinquency most likely to become persistent. The middle-class offenses were more typically matters of drinking parties, sex affairs, and driving offenses than theft. The poorer juveniles, in greater need, were more likely to turn to economically remunerative crimes. Leon Fannin and Marshall Clinard[7] find other types of differences between the two classes, but, again, differences that in the long run will make the middle-class delinquency pattern less persistent. The lower-class boys studied insisted on a much tougher and more brutal definition of manhood, engaged in more fights, and had less desire to do things the clever way. Such attitudes might help account for statistics showing much higher arrest rates among the lower class. Such studies would no doubt show a higher incidence of drug problems in both cases if they had been made three or four years later, but even in this offense, as noted in the previous chapter, it is more likely that the person of better socioeconomic background will limit drug use to marijuana. For him the psychic tensions that lead to drug use seem to be less severe.

Before leaving the subject of age and crime, it should be mentioned that the common view that the young years are the years of violent crime is considerably exaggerated; youthful crimes are usually of other types. In 1966, those under age eighteen (about 40 percent of the population) committed much less than their share of violent crimes: 9 percent of the criminal homicides, 19 percent of the rape cases, and 17 percent of aggravated assault cases. In auto theft they were vastly overrepresented, accounting for 63 percent of the cases; they also accounted for 50 percent of burglary and larceny cases.[8] Most of the auto theft cases are one-time affairs.

Does your community have a Big Brother program or any other plan for helping delinquent youth? For those interested in juvenile work, trying to aid boys and girls in juvenile homes or on probation will be a very helpful experience.

---

[6]Ronald J. Chilton, "Middle-Class Delinquency and Specific Offense Analysis," Edmund W. Vas (ed.), *Middle-Class Juvenile Delinquency*, Harper & Row, Publishers, Incorporated, 1967, pp. 91–101.
[7]Leon F. Fannin and Marshall B. Clinard, "Differences in the Conception of Self as a Male among Lower and Middle Class Delinquents," *Social Problems*, vol. 13, pp. 205–214, Fall 1965.
[8]Gresham M. Sykes, *Crime and Society*, Random House, Inc., New York, 1967, pp. 90–91.

Often the same is true for burglary and larceny, although those who become involved at an early age are the ones most likely to repeat. There is a large amount of juvenile crime just because there are so many juveniles, reflecting the baby boom of the 1950s.

If parents wish to avoid arrests among their offspring, they would be well advised to have all girls, assuming they had the know-how for such a biological trick. The male-female arrest ratio is about 8 to 1. No doubt much of the reason is the difference in roles assigned to the two sexes by society. The very fact that boys are expected to be aggressive and adventuresome almost guarantees that many will be arrested. Where less differentiation of role is evident, as in the impoverished ghetto, the male-female rate of involvement in delinquency becomes more even. In countries where women are sheltered much more than in the United States, the sex ratio becomes greater. A traditional Moslem woman, for example, always kept at home under a veil and watched carefully, would have little chance to commit delinquent acts. A girl of the impoverished slums, fighting for a living in a criminogenic environment, would be much more likely to get involved with the law. The majority of American girls are somewhere between these extremes.

CRIME: POVERTY AND RACE Poverty is associated with crime in many cases, but not always. The poorest countries do not necessarily have high crime rates. It seems more likely that the association between poverty and crime occurs in a case where poverty is so close to riches as to cause a strong feeling of relative deprivation. Another possible explanation of why crime is often associated with poverty in an affluent society but not in impoverished countries is accounted for by a special use of the sociologist's concept of anomie—a strain within the norms. Merton has characterized our society as one that sets a universal achievement goal for all people and judges people by their success, or more bluntly, by how much money they make. If ours were a society that gave high honors to the honest poor or that looked askance at all people who have made wealth in a crafty manner, then there would be no compulsion to get ahead by fair or foul means. We *do* expect success of everyone, however, so the temptation to dishonest means is unusually great, especially since people do not have equal access to honest means for success. Poor family background, race discrimination, and various other factors guarantee inequality in respect to achievement by honest means. It must not be forgotten, too, that the offenses of the poor are more likely

---

Make a survey of juvenile crime in your community (usually the police will give you the needed information). Chart high delinquency areas on a map, then travel through them and study their physical characteristics.

to lead to arrest and conviction than are the types of fraud and graft sometimes practiced by the well-to-do.

Whatever the reason, poverty, especially urban poverty, is closely associated with high crime rates in the United States. Urban poverty areas are usually areas of high unemployment rates, few opportunities, ready access to drugs, petty theft patterns to imitate, family disorganization, and hostility toward police and authorities.

Race has been included along with crime and poverty because racial differences in crime rate are mainly a reflection of greater poverty and emotional tensions for the black and brown than for the white. There are probably secondary causes as well. Negroes, for example, are strongly overrepresented in arrests for "suspicion." Since suspicion is defined in the Uniform Crime Reports as arrest for no particular offense, it implies a coverup for an error by the police.[9] It is just more evidence that more blacks than whites are arrested for trivial causes, and this could help to make their crime rate look higher than it really is. Even for solid causes, though, the arrest rate is higher, as is inevitable for a people highly concentrated in urban poverty areas and suffering the hostile feelings that often go with minority status.

CRIME AND CRIMINAL TYPES   Years ago there were many efforts to describe a "criminal type" as a human type somehow physically or mentally or emotionally inferior by birth. Such early attempts have been discredited, but there have been more creditable attempts to describe psychological types—particular types created by their environments. Sociologists do not deny the possibility of character types with far more hostility than others, nor can they deny that individuals adjust differently to the same circumstances. However, the sociological approach is usually one of analyzing environments rather than isolating personality types. In sociological theory, the right set of social circumstances will call forth a considerable percentage of people who will be lawbreakers. Over a period of years, similar city areas have produced similar amounts of juvenile delinquency, even though the ethnic groups inhabiting them and the particular personalities have changed.

The future may cause us to take new looks at physical causes. There have been a few isolated cases of brain tumors or concussions associated with berserk behavior. Recently courts have listened to arguments about XYY chromosome patterns but have generally ruled against them as being actual causes of crime. We may eventually prove that some types of crime are associated with brain damage from accidents, drugs, or faulty chromosomes. Even if such cases should acquire plausibility, however, they could not be assumed to account for any but a tiny part of crime. In sociology, we are more impressed with the degree to which crime rates relate to deteriorated city cores, poverty, faulty types of success drives, value conflicts, and inability to succeed by legitimate means. It is much easier to show that such factors are associated with rising crime rates than it would be to prove that some strange type of physical

[9]Savitz, *op. cit.*, p. 27.

or mental deterioration has afflicted vast numbers of people in modern America. Furthermore, there are types of crimes closely associated with the most reputable elements of society—people of high intelligence, good education, and enviable position.

WHITE-COLLAR CRIME

A large amount of crime is committed by respectable, well-placed members of society. This is the type of crime referred to as "white-collar crime." The analysis of white-collar crime was first started by Edwin H. Sutherland, who defined it as "crime committed by a person of respectability and high social status in the course of his occupation."[10] Bribery and graft are types of white-collar crime, and so are most of the means of beating the consumer discussed in Chapter 4. Sutherland used many examples from the days of the nineteenth-century robber barons, who were generally willing to admit that they could not carry on business if they had to stay strictly within the law. Since Sutherland's book was written many years ago, more timely examples will be used, but his analysis of the distinction between white-collar crime and common crime is still completely valid.

First of all, Sutherland finds considerable fault with the type of analysis that shows a concentration of crime mainly in areas of poverty. Certainly there is such a concentration, but it is of particular types of crime: burglary, petty larceny, auto theft, and aggravated assault. Violation of labor laws, cheating the government out of income-tax money, milking insurance companies, conspiracy in restraint of trade, illegal contributions to political parties and candidates, illegal fixing of weights and measures, and disguising true interest rates are all examples of crimes that have no connection with poverty areas, deprived home backgrounds, or personal pathologies. Furthermore, although they are all defined as crimes, they are treated differently. One reason for different treatment is that such crimes are perpetrated by people in a position of influence who can usually escape arrest and publicity. Second, even if people are arrested, their crimes are often treated as civil offenses. Furthermore, as Sutherland shows, the public has little awareness of such crime, usually does not understand it, and does not get excited about it. The small-time thief or narcotics agent excites public fury. Probably the loss to the public through white-collar crime is many times greater than through common larceny. Sutherland mentions, for example, the dramatic case of the suicide of Ivar Kreuger, who had finally trapped himself in financial manipulations that resulted in losses of more than 550 million dollars for stockholders.

With the passing of time, new differences in the types of crime have become apparent. The dividing line between crime and noncrime in the white-collar world is often indistinct. If a man robs a service station, there is no question that he has committed a crime. But what are we to say when we learn that in 1968 there were twenty-

---

[10]Edwin H. Sutherland, *White Collar Crime*, Holt, Rinehart and Winston, Inc., New York, 1961, p. 9. (The book was written in 1948, republished with slight revisions in 1961.)

one cases of people with incomes of over 1 million dollars who managed to get by without paying any income tax whatever?[11] There were 381 Americans with incomes of over $100,000 who paid no federal income tax. The irony is that these people were not even lawbreakers. They had committed no crime. They had found legal loopholes — no doubt helped to persuade Congress to leave legal loopholes — so that they could evade taxes legally.

We also read in the daily press that firms providing supplies, consultations, and technical assistance to the OEO are growing rich on the war on poverty. Contracts worth over 11½ million dollars were awarded to companies that have thirty-five former OEO officials working for them.[12] Somehow the whole idea of profits out of the war on poverty sounds a little immoral. But is it illegal? No. Tie-ins between all kinds of business and agencies of the government are inevitable; we even have to admit they are necessary. At what point does the tie-in become too close and make the profiteer or the influence peddler a lawbreaker? It has happened frequently, even at high levels of government, and we do not have to go back to such graft-ridden administrations as those of Grant and Harding to find examples. Bobby Baker, a friend of former President Johnson and one-time Senate secretary, was convicted of fraud through income-tax evasion, pocketing campaign contributions, and illegal influence peddling. The earlier Eisenhower administration had been embarrassed by improper dealings by the White House Secretary Sherman Adams. In 1968 Senator Thomas Dodd, a man of solid accomplishment and believed to be of unimpeachable reputation, was censured by the United States Senate for diverting $203,000 of campaign contributions to his own personal use and also evading income tax on the amount.[13] In a previous chapter it was mentioned that the former mayor of Newark, New Jersey, and several of his friends were sentenced to prison for embezzlement. In 1963, Billie Sol Estes, a young multimillionaire friend of many Texas politicians and a man who seemed to have the King Midas touch, was found guilty of various counts of fraud, totaling about 22 million dollars.[14] Among his tricks had been borrowing vast amounts of money against assets he did not actually hold. He had managed to establish credit mainly by showing what enormous loans he had already secured. Indebtedness was interpreted as a sign of wealth.

The Armed Forces have not been immune to white-collar crime. While Paul Douglas was Senator from Illinois, he conducted investigations of the military purchasing systems, whose costs could be explained only by colossal inefficiency or by corruption. Several years later, an odor of corruption was detected in the Army post exchange system, and by the spring of 1971 it became an unmistakable stench, rousing a Senate investigating committee to action. There was a disclosure of special

[11]Philip M. Stern, "How 381 Super-Rich Americans Managed Not to Pay a Cent in Taxes Last Year," *New York Times Magazine*, pp. 30–31+, April 13, 1969.
[12]"Firms Get Rich in War on Poverty," *Los Angeles Times*, November 30, 1970, Part I, page 2.
[13]Fred C. Cook, "Large Questions about Our Times," *Saturday Review*, vol. 51, pp. 31–32, March 16, 1968.
[14]"Silent Partners of Billie Sol Estes," *The Nation*, vol. 196, pp. 485–495, June 1, 1963.

favors, avoidance of tariff laws, swindling of noncommissioned officers clubs, deals for the operation of slot machines, and kickbacks for favors to officials ranging in rank from sergeant to general.

White-collar crime is not always spectacular, and it is often suspected but hard to prove. After each election, political parties accuse each other of having accepted illegal contributions; there are threats of official investigations and tighter laws, but little happens. Sometimes there are strong efforts to enforce antitrust laws, and sometimes not.

THE ELECTRICAL EQUIPMENT CASE   Although the above examples have been mainly political and military, Sutherland contends that the majority of white-collar crime is in the business world. One of the spectacular cases of prosecution for the business-man's type of white-collar crime occurred in 1961, when the Tennessee Valley Authority found itself getting identical bids from the majority of competing companies for the production of technical electrical equipment. This occurred in spite of the fact that all bids had to be submitted in sealed envelopes and were supposed to be highly secret. It developed that arrangements had been made whereby one company was allowed to be low bidder on one contract and the next one on another contract, so the territory was divided to the profit of all companies concerned. The higher bidders often submitted identical bids. Eventually twenty-nine companies and forty-five individuals were indicted and nearly 2 million dollars in fines was levied, the heaviest fines being against General Electric and Westinghouse.[15] In the electrical equipment case there was violation of the law with unquestioned intent. Seven officials, four of them vice presidents, were sent to jail for thirty days.

There are several features of the electrical equipment case that are significant in the study of white-collar crime. Most important was the origin of the criminal behavior. In most cases the officials who were found guilty had been trained into the system, just as surely as many young people in high delinquency areas are trained by their friends into thieving. They had found price-fixing agreements to be part of policy and common practice. They tend to validate Sutherland's thesis that crime is essentially learned behavior.

A second notable fact in the case is that the public was amazed, not at the existence of white-collar crime, but at seeing people actually arrested and convicted. There is little public confidence that white-collar crime will be punished. A third noteworthy observation is of the nature of a corporation as a defendant. Over $1\frac{1}{2}$ million dollars in fines was paid by corporations, which actually means a cost sustained by large numbers of stockholders. This points to a special problem in the prosecution of white-collar crime. A corporation is "a body without a soul." It is usually hard to pin the blame at any particular place in the corporation or to punish

---

[15]Stuart L. Hills, *Crime, Power, and Morality: The Criminal-Law Process in the United States*, Chandler Publishing Company, San Francisco, 1971, pp. 162–166.

Crime touches the respectable: Bobby Baker, Secretary of the Senate and friend of former President Johnson, convicted of several counts of fraud.

particular individuals. The electrical equipment case was more clear cut than the usual case in this respect.

EMBEZZLEMENT The electrical equipment violations were cases of lawbreaking encouraged by company policy. Such is not the case with embezzlement. In both cases, however, the crimes are committed by supposedly respectable men in positions of trust, and in both cases the violators find rationalizations to preserve their self-image as good, honest citizens. In the first case, one's self-image can be preserved in terms of complying with the policies of a respectable corporation and associates. In the case of embezzlement the rationalization is more difficult, but it is accomplished.

Donald Cressey[16] summarized the process of becoming an embezzler after studying a number of cases. The most typical case of appropriating funds occurs when a man in a position of trust finds himself in serious need of money. The need is

[16]Donald Cressey, "The Criminal Violation of Financial Trust," *American Sociological Review*, pp. 738–743, December 1950.

usually occasioned by an incident that would be embarrassing to have to admit—gambling debt, extramarital affair, or other situations of possible blackmail. In practically all cases, the violator of financial trust takes the money, telling himself that it is really a loan, a loan that he will eventually pay back. Serious need, plus opportunity, plus a means of rationalization makes this type of white-collar crime possible.

Other types of white-collar crime are numerous: public office holders receiving kickbacks from public employees, padding of expense accounts, acceptance of bribes by politicians, giving of bribes by businessmen, overcharging of patients or health insurance companies by doctors, beating of fair labor laws, black marketeering, false advertising, and the adulteration of foods. All these practices are carried on by the respectable world. As is the case with commonly indexed crime, the acts are committed when the need is considerable, when restraints are not too strong, when opportunity presents itself, and usually when a pattern of law violation is already established by which others can learn.

Below the level of white-collar crime, but operating in fields that tie the respectable world to the underworld—the law makers with the lawbreakers and the victims with their exploiters—is the world of organized crime. Like white-collar crime, much organized crime has been overlooked in the crime statistics and in the outcry against criminality. The organization is nevertheless there, growing, spreading, and corrupting—the "syndicate," the "family," the Mafia, Cosa Nostra, or whatever its name, the organization is a pervasive part of the Troubled Land.

ORGANIZED CRIME: COSA NOSTRA

Organized crime differs from other types of crime not only in its level of organization but also in its relationship to the legitimate world. The white-collar criminal is typically a legitimate businessman, politician, or professional. The blue-collar criminal is outside the law and not connected with the legitimate world except in the relationship of predator to its prey. Organized crime, on the other hand, although a creature of the underworld, is closely connected to the legitimate world. It provides gambling and night life for the ordinary citizen, it caters to his vices by providing houses of prostitution and various kinds of pornographic entertainment, and for a usurious sum, it will lend him money to get him out of a tight spot. Organized crime also supplies the vast and growing narcotics market, which is by no means legitimate, but has the same characteristic as so much of the business of organized crime—meeting a need not met by legitimate business by catering to the desires of people who are otherwise not criminalistic.

For many years there has been the feeling that there is tight organization within the world of crime. Even in the writings of such late nineteenth-century muckrakers as Lincoln Steffens there was reference to the growing degree of underworld organization. References to the Mafia and the Black Hand have been made for generations, but the period of a virtual monopoly in the world of organized crime is fairly recent in America's history.

FROM GODFATHER TO CHAIRMAN OF THE BOARD   There has long been the feeling that reference to an American Mafia partakes more of melodrama than of reality. Even J. Edgar Hoover has avoided the word Mafia, although since about 1961 he has used the name Cosa Nostra, the modern name of the organization.[17]

The Mafia as it existed in Sicily was an underground organization whose members were considered one big family, linked together by close kinship loyalty. Just as in Mario Puzo's recent novel *The Godfather*, important members were often referred to as godparents and the institution of godparenthood (*compradazo*) made it possible to extend a kinship organization past the ties of actual blood relationship. There were also initiation rites for joining Mafia families and becoming fictive kinsmen. The American underworld character Joseph Valachi underwent such an initiation into Mafia kinship in New York in 1930.[18] Just as fictive kinsmen could be adopted into the organization by initiation, actual kinsmen could be excluded if they were not good at criminal activities.

Apologists for the Mafia say that in Sicily it sometimes had the function of supplying measures of government where government was nonexistent or of supplying opposition to tyrannical government. However, such secret organizations, whatever their function, are easily given to terrorism, and many common Sicilian peasants and shopkeepers were victimized by the Mafia.

The organization was headed by a *capomafia* (Mafia head), and subdivided into *setta* (cells). All members of the organization were treated as kinsmen unless they failed in their loyalty to the group, in which case they were likely to be murdered. There was little formality or structure within the organization in the nineteenth century; in recent years the formality has increased somewhat, but the old familial characteristics are still preserved.[19]

Small groups of Mafialike gangs have existed in American cities since the late nineteenth century, but they were not organized into one great syndicate. In fact, strong rivalries for leadership existed, resulting in a war between Italian and Sicilian groups in 1930. Giuseppi Masseria, leader of one gang, passed a death sentence on prominent members of the opposition. In a period of two or three days, forty leaders of the older organization of the Mafia were killed, and later Masseria, who had started the war, was also killed. Eventually Charles "Lucky" Luciano became the head of the organization and expanded the leadership to a commission of nine to twelve men. Sometimes the organization is still called the Mafia; sometimes it is called Cosa

[17]Donald R. Cressey, *The Theft of the Nation*, Harper & Row, Publishers, Incorporated, New York, 1969, pp. 22–23.
[18]Robert T. Anderson, "From Mafia to Cosa Nostra," *American Journal of Sociology*, vol. 71, pp. 302–310, November 1965.
[19]*Ibid.*

Nostra (Our Thing), or the Outfit, or the Syndicate, or simply the Organization. Whatever it is called, it now combines the old close-kinship ideal of brothers-in-crime with many of the characteristics of modern, bureaucratic organization.[20] It has all the loyalty and secrecy of the former and the efficiency of the latter.

COSA NOSTRA TODAY The syndicate has flourished. According to the President's Commission on Law Enforcement and Administration of Justice, the core of organized crime consists of twenty four families operating in all the biggest cities of the United States.[21] Five families are located in New York City. The term Cosa Nostra is a little misleading because it is such a purely Sicilian name. Many people can therefore deal with non-Sicilian associates of Cosa Nostra and have no idea they are part of the Syndicate. However, the inner core of the families remains Italian- and Sicilian-American. So great are the rewards of their well-organized business that they have another trait in common: they are all rich; most are millionaires.[22] Outside the inner circle there are thousands of poorer people of all ethnic stocks working for Cosa Nostra. Crime knows no class or ethnic barriers as long as it pays.

The fact of the Sicilian- and Italian-American leadership and organization of Cosa Nostra is a source of embarrassment to the millions of honest Italian-Americans in the United States, who outnumber the Cosa Nostra members 1,000 to 1. A very good statement of the attitude of the honest Italian-American was made by Ralph Salerno of the New York City police and author of *The Crime Confederation*. A member of the mob accused him of being against "his own people":

> I'm not your kind, and you're not my kind. My manners, morals, and mores are not yours. The only thing we have in common is that we both spring from a common Italian heritage and culture — and you are the traitor to that heritage and culture of which I am proud . . . .[23]

The commission that heads the syndicate continues as it was founded by Lucky Luciano, still consisting of nine to twelve members. The twenty four families range in membership from 20 to as many as 700, with several specialized positions. Most sinister of the specialties is that of "enforcer," whose duty is to maim or kill those members who fail to cooperate.

THE FIELDS OF OPERATIONS Organized crime once made most of its profits from bootlegging liquor. After the repeal of the Eighteenth Amendment, other lucrative activities had to be found. The most profitable field of operations of the underworld today is gambling. Very few gambling houses are independent of the organization, although

---

[20]Ralph Salerno and John S. Tompkins, *The Crime Federation*, Doubleday and Company, Inc., Garden City, N.Y., 1969, pp. 85–88.
[21]Winslow, *op. cit.*, pp. 191–209.
[22]Cressey, *op. cit.*, p. 84.
[23]Winslow, *op. cit.*, p. 205.

A lucrative field for organized crime,
often leading the victim to gambling
bankruptcy and to the loansharks of
the underworld.

the network leading from the bottom to the top of the organization is so complex that many people have no knowledge of who makes the final profit. A conservative estimate is that the net profit per year to the Syndicate from the gambling interests is about 7 billion dollars.[24]

Because of its tragic consequences, the narcotics trade is more in the public mind than gambling. It is estimated that heroin alone nets 350 million dollars annually for the Syndicate. There is no area in which the chain or organization is more apparent to the person with even the most casual knowledge. The user becomes a dealer in order to earn money for his addiction, and he buys from an agent closer to the organization, who knows a wholesale supplier yet nearer to the top of the pyramid. Those who sit at the top are isolated by such a long chain of command as to be invulnerable to arrest unless they make a mistake. The best legal advisors available are hired to make sure there are no mistakes.

Prostitution, which was once important in the profits of organized crime, is much more difficult to organize than many other enterprises. It has declined to relatively little importance.

Various forms of labor racketeering have become a major source of profits to organized crime. Infiltration into unions has resulted in the raiding of union retirement funds. Sometimes Syndicate members accept pay from companies to prevent unions from striking or otherwise pressing for more benefits. Sometimes they extract funds from management by threatening to stir up labor sentiments and force a strike.

USURY AND THE PENETRATION OF LEGITIMATE BUSINESS There are no reliable figures on the total profit of the loan-shark business, but it is one of the most profitable rackets of the Syndicate. Cressey tells of one man who increased his fortune from $500,000 to $7,500,000 in four years in the usury business. Interest rates vary, but a common charge on short-term loans is "six-for-five." The loan shark lends $500 and demands repayment of $600 at the end of the week. If the debtor is as much as one hour late, he owes another $100. Longer-term loans range from about 10 to 250 percent per year. The loan shark closest to gambling joints usually charges 10 percent per day.

People are most frequently driven to such loans when financial reverses destroy their credit ratings or when a possible blackmail situation prevents their going to legitimate sources of loans.

The loan sharks working for the Syndicate seem unusually generous about making loans, but leniency ends on payday. One man who borrowed from a California loan shark to buy some jewelry introduced two friends to the money lender. They also took out loans. When they were unable to repay, the original borrower was held responsible for their debts. When he refused to pay, he was met by four goons who beat him with a blackjack, knocked out two of his teeth, and tied him to an overhead pipe

 [24]*Ibid.*, p. 196.

and took turns punching him in the stomach. They also stole his car and phoned a threatening message to his girlfriend. After his release from the hospital he was given a brief "stop-the-clock" period for raising the money.[25]

It is unusual for the Syndicate to kill a debtor, although they occasionally do so to set an example. More likely, a stop-the-clock period will be called, meaning a brief halt in the interest rate while a person tries to work all his friends and relatives for the money to pay his debts. To kill him would be too much like killing the goose that laid the golden egg. He is kept alive and bled as long as possible. A favorite device is to bring him into the organization, if his only possible way of paying off the debt is to commit a crime for the Syndicate. After that he can easily be blackmailed into committing more crimes. He is hooked.

Another serious result of the loan-shark business is the invasion of legitimate business. Often, if a businessman has borrowed and cannot repay, he is forced into accepting "partners" in his business. Sometimes the Syndicate becomes the complete owner. If the business does not pay well, the Syndicate is as clever at disposing of it as at acquiring it. The procedure is to sell all the inventory and then declare bankruptcy, always through a man who fronts for the organization, often the original owner himself.

THE TIE-IN As we have seen, organized crime bilks the public of billions of dollars. It adds immeasurably to the other costs of crime. It furnishes the narcotics that destroy so many lives; it wrecks legitimate business and corrupts labor unions. Even more sinister, organized crime corrupts our court system and gains control over many of the political and economic institutions of our metropolitan areas. In Donald Cressey's words:

> The danger of organized crime arises because the vast profits acquired from the sale of illicit goods and services are being invested in licit enterprises, in both the economic sphere and the political sphere. It is when criminal syndicates start to undermine basic economic and political traditions and institutions that the real trouble begins. And the real trouble has begun in the United States.[26]

CRIME THEORY AND PRACTICE

There are many theories of crime, not contradictory, but stressing different aspects of the phenomenon. Some are interested primarily in explaining juvenile gangs, others in more remunerative crime, and yet others in crimes of violence. Two well-known theories of crime that are particularly apt for explaining the types of crime just discussed are those of Merton and Sutherland. Merton's is the more comprehensive theory, aiming first at an explanation of why America has a high crime rate, and second at explaining different types of crime.

[25]Cressey, *op. cit.*, p. 83.
[26]Cressey, *op. cit.*, p. 1.

Merton's[27] theory is basically one that stresses a strain between societal goals and access to those goals. Our cultural norms, says Merton, are unusually strong in expecting a good measure of material success from everyone, and they stress the success goal more strongly than the honest means to the goal. Moreover, insufficient attention is given to making sure that all people have access to the goal. Four possibilities result from the situation:

1. One can conform to both success goals and honest means, in which case he will win the highest applause of the society.

2. The second-best adjustment is to win the success goals by deviant means, especially if the means are clever and one gets by with them. Society's tendency to admire the clever scoundrel helps to cause less-clever people to also try deviant means. People with unequal access to the goals (those born poor and culturally deprived) are almost forced into deviance or to give up pursuit of the goal.

3. The third possibility is to remain poor but honest. If goals were stressed less, and means more, this adjustment would be greatly admired but, says Merton, it receives little praise.

4. The fourth possibility is to reject both means and goals and become a vagrant or an addict.

5. There is even a fifth possibility—accept some of the social norms and reject others, in the name of a new order. This is the rebellion adjustment.

For our purposes, Merton's second adjustment will be stressed, although his fourth point has a bearing on the previous chapter. Merton attempts to explain why there is so much crime in society, and his explanation certainly covers many cases. It would have to be stretched a little, however, to account for all the types of white-collar crime discussed by Sutherland, especially cases of crime committed by people who are already quite successful but desire more, or those born into wealthy Mafia families. In one respect, though, there is perfect harmony between the two theories: they both point out the desire to succeed by fair or foul means.

Sutherland sees deviant behavior as the result of an interplay of forces, with both legally supportive norms and deviant ways being learned by all people. Those for whom illicit learning is stronger than legal learning would be most likely to commit crimes. For the person reared in a Mafia family there is little ambivalence about entering a life of crime. For the perpetrator of most kinds of white-collar crime, on the other hand, there must usually be a gradual process of unlearning many of the normative attitudes he has acquired and a means of rationalizing the change in attitudes.

[27]Robert K. Merton, *Social Theory and Social Structure*, The Free Press, Glencoe, Ill., 1959, chap. 5.

The internalizing of deviant means usually depends upon group influences. Albert Cohen and James Short have sought to demonstrate that the delinquent gang is able to accept antisocial ways by creating a subculture of its own that defines rights and wrongs for its own members in opposition to the rights and wrongs of the larger society. Such a redefinition is easiest in a subculture that is hostile toward authorities. Sutherland showed, though, that a similar type of redefinition of norms was at work for a young businessman learning the used car business or learning the arts of disguising accounts. He learned such practices as standard operating procedure, supported by the actions and rationalizations of the rest of the crowd. The Cosa Nostra members, similarly, hold deviant-group norms, supported by the family, and able to make them feel right about themselves as long as they remain loyal to the organization. Cressey found that for the embezzler there was no similar group support; therefore, the task of rationalization tended to be more protracted and more ingenious.

THE REWARDS OF CRIME   The rewards of crime differ from the mere chance to show hostility and "blow off steam," as in the case of certain types of juvenile gangs, all the way to the millions of dollars made by white-collar crime and organized crime. Sometimes the rewards of crime could be best described in terms of Merton's theory, discussed earlier in this chapter, of trying to reach success goals by illegal means. For a few, especially for the organized-crime world, the goals are reached and it is impossible to preach in such cases that crime does not pay. For most ordinary thieves, however, crime is an unrewarding way of life, interrupted by years in prison and strewn with broken resolutions to go straight. Why, then, is there so little success in dealing with crime?

If we believed, as people once did, that crime occurs mainly because "bad blood" flows in the veins of certain families, the obvious solution to the crime problem would be a eugenics program to stop such families from breeding. We now know that such an explanation is nonsense. If we believe that crime is essentially learned behavior, tempered by normative conflict, group support, inducement, and a failure of access to more legitimate opportunities, we at least have a basis for judging the methods of control that are now applied and for attempting new methods of control. Obviously, the desirable attack would be to remove opportunities for learning crime, make its inducements unattractive by catching a much larger proportion of offenders, and widen opportunities for legitimate roads to success for the culturally deprived. We would also have to try to resolve some of the cultural conflict within our society in order to arrive at laws that would be more uniformly accepted.

Judging by the annual statistics on crime, and knowing as we do that a majority of all crime is hidden, we cannot be very optimistic about present methods. None of the above objectives is being achieved to any great degree. What is even more troublesome is that although our theoretical knowledge suggests many improvements for dealing with the crime problem among the poor, the problem of control of white-collar crime and of the great crime syndicates is much more baffling. It is in these areas that crime pays best. Are there any ways of removing the profit?

THE FRAMING OF LAW Part of the problem of white-collar crime is a matter of clearer definition. Although the man who presents false claims to an insurance company might gather more in ill-gotten gains than the man who robs a service station, neither the public nor the authorities consider the crime as serious. False advertising is even less clearly defined, although it can have serious consequences. Cressey's conclusion in his study on embezzlement is that any law that forces people to conceptualize their acts as crime rather than as clever tricks has a beneficial effect. What is true for the embezzler is probably true for many people who commit white-collar crimes. How the public looks upon their acts is important. In war years, black marketeering can be rampant or virtually nonexistent, depending upon whether the public sees it as a necessary act or as something akin to treason. In the case of much white-collar crime, where the difference between legal and illegal is a very thin line, it would not seem wise to impose heavy criminal penalties. Fortunately, though, the white-collar crime area is one in which even small penalties have a strong deterrent effect. The man of respectable reputation is seriously injured by having his name before the courts, and even a short sentence can be devastating. Besides careful framing of the law, then, a problem for white-collar crime is to arrive at legal sanctions that are more than a mere slap on the wrist, but that do not ruin one man's career for doing almost exactly what his more clever competitor has done without quite transgressing the law.

DILEMMAS OF DETERRENCE The whole problem of deterrence needs more investigation. It is a rather fundamental principle of learning theory that desired behavior should be awarded and undesirable behavior punished, but the kind and degree of reward or punishment is questionable. Most people are familiar with contradictory statistics as to the effect of capital punishment. In a few cases the removal of capital punishment has been followed by a slight increase in homicide rates; in other cases it has actually been followed by a decrease. The conclusion seems to be that the murder rate is influenced more by such factors as urbanization and geographical mobility than by capital punishment.[28] One reason is that murder is usually a crime of desperation rather than one of cool calculation.

A psychiatrist, Dr. David G. Hubbard, has arrived at an amazing conclusion about the failure of deterrence in another type of crime of desperation, hijacking airplanes.[29] His conclusion is that the typical hijacker is neither a confirmed criminal nor a Communist. He is usually a man of serious psychological problems, with feelings of inadequacy and fantasies of suicide. He identifies with the astronauts

[28]Thorsten Sellin, "Experiments with Abolition," in *Capital Punishment*, Thorsten Sellin (ed.), Harper & Row, Publishers, Incorporated, New York, 1967, pp. 122–125.
[29]Fletcher Knebel, "The Skyjacker," *Look*, vol. 35, pp. 23–26, February 9, 1971.

New York State undermines a major source of profit for the Syndicate by legalized, state-controlled gambling.

and dreams of achieving a manly glory that will wash away his pitiful inadequacy. The desperate venture of hijacking a plane excites his imagination. The more publicity such ventures receive, and the more frightening the promised punishment becomes, the more it appeals to his sense of adventure. The fear of capital punishment seems to be no deterrent, since the man's fevered dream is to die anyway. If Hubbard is right, the skyjacker is a better-than-average case of the misfit between reasons for crime and common assumptions about deterrence.

In turning to organized crime, however, we are returning to a case of calculation for profit, not mental illness or desperation. Is there any possible deterrence to the Syndicate?

FIGHTING THE SYNDICATE Nothing in the field of crime is more discouraging than the struggle against Cosa Nostra. If laws become more severe, the organization becomes more cautious and devotes more of its funds to the search for loopholes. In the field of narcotics, few top men are ever caught. In the case of illegal gambling, the Syndicate receives little opposition from public opinion, for the public does not regard gambling as a major evil.

Most evils of gambling are secondary evils, not of the act itself but of its corrupting influence under our present legal system. Judge John Murtagh[30] shows how gambling has been able to corrupt police forces more easily than any other kind of crime. Probably part of the reason is that police, like the general public, do not think of gambling as a very serious crime. If a police force allowed a payoff for murder, the whole nation would be outraged, but for gambling little interest is shown. Members of the gambling underworld are let off easily; records are falsified so that they all seem to be first offenders. Such covering up of gambling, Murtagh says, has been going on in New York for over a century. In our time, the profit is generally made by Cosa Nostra.

Murtagh suggests cutting out the gambling profit by legalizing gambling, believing that it could dry up the money source for the underworld almost as effectively as the repeal of the Prohibition Amendment did years ago. Cressey, although not much opposed in principle to legalized gambling, is a little dubious as to its success. He contends that the present operators make gambling more glamorous and attractive than do state lotteries and other public gambling enterprises. Nevertheless, he sees the solution to the problem of enriching the Syndicate in much the same way as Murtagh. Perhaps reputable business concerns could run gambling for the government. He also suggests that the states institute loan agencies to help people in desperate straits. Such an enterprise would probably lose money, but the cost would be far less than the present cost of enriching organized crime. Cutting the profits of crime would cut its power, which is now spreading over both legitimate business and government.

Discuss and debate the case for and against legalized gambling.

---

[30]John M. Murtagh, *Atlantic Monthly*, vol. 206, pp. 49–53, November 1960.

SUGGESTED READINGS

Cressey, Donald R.: *The Theft of the Nation*, Harper & Row, Publishers, Incorporated, New York, 1969.

A treatment of organized crime by a well-known criminologist and member of the President's

Commission on Law Enforcement and the Administration of Justice. The author, deeply concerned over the growth of organized crime, conveys a sense of urgency throughout.

Hills, Stuart L.: *Crime, Power, and Morality: The Criminal-Law Process in the United States*, Chandler Publishing Company, San Francisco, 1971.

Hills presents the problem of crime in a new perspective: why society defines criminal law as it does, and why it stigmatizes some types of criminals more than others. In this perspective he examines marijuana and the law, Cosa Nostra and organized crime, and white-collar occupational crime.

Sykes, Gresham M.: *Crime and Society*, Random House, Inc., New York, 1967.

A very popular book on crime, recently revised. Fairly traditional in approach, but clear, well balanced, and good at pointing out the dilemmas of law and justice.

Winslow, Robert W.: *Crime in a Free Society: Selections from the President's Commission on Law Enforcement and the Administration of Justice*, Dickenson Publishing Company, Belmont, Calif., 1968.

An authoritative study of many aspects of crime, well edited. Covers also police, courts, and corrections.

Yablonsky, Lewis: *The Violent Gang*, Penguin Books, Inc., Baltimore, 1967.

Based on firsthand study of violent juvenile gangs, Yablonsky's book attempts to explain their rise and to look into possibilities for control. Much of the account is told in the words of gang members.

 **QUESTIONS**

1. What are some of the social-class differences in type of juvenile crime and likelihood of persistence?

2. Explain the meaning of white-collar crime and give some examples.

3. What are the major sources of profit for Cosa Nostra? Would there be any way to cut out their profits?

4. Show how the occurrence of crime tends to fit the Sutherland theory of crime as learned behavior.

5. Under what conditions does punishment seem to be a real deterrent to crime, and when is it uncertain or of little value?

14 What is the theory behind systems of justice — revenge, deterrence, or rehabilitation? The process of criminal justice must start, obviously, with catching the criminal, a task assigned usually to the policeman. Why is the policeman's role so difficult and such a subject of bitter debate? Do age, race, and social-class differences influence the handling of justice? Why do we hear increasing complaints about delay in justice, about the unevenness of bail systems, and about detention without trial? What is military justice like? Are modern jails and prisons so organized as to be centers of reform and rehabilitation, or are they still schools for crime? Is the whole subject of justice keeping pace with psychological and sociological knowledge and changing norms, or does it reflect earlier views and attitudes? What new ideas are being tried?

In attempting to answer these questions, we shall have to admit there are great difficulties in the way of improvement. Although there is considerable upgrading of police training and selection in many communities, police power is still easily subject to abuse. Efforts are needed to speed up the court system, but it must also be remembered that part of the reason for a slow process of justice is protection of the innocent. Prisons are regarded as necessary evils, and the public likes to think about them as little as possible, yet there must be increasing public interest in all aspects of justice if significant changes are to be made. We shall see that there are reasons for increased public interest at present and, therefore, hope for a better system of justice.

IN THE NAME OF JUSTICE

The concept of justice is so important to social systems that the magistrate has occupied a position close to the throne since ancient times. In fact, in many archaic systems magistrate and king were one and the same. The givers of law have been lauded in history and tradition — Moses, Hammurabi, Solomon, Solon — and often their laws have been attributed to God. The time-honored philosopher Plato made the concept of justice the central accomplishment of his visionary Republic, and Immanuel Kant saw the craving for justice as one evidence of a divine order. However, in spite of the great intellectual effort that has gone into defining justice, justice systems have a tendency to revert to the harsh and futile principle of *lex talionis*, the law of revenge, found in Hammurabi's code and in Deuteronomy:

> And thine eye shall not pity, but life shall go for life, eye for eye, tooth for tooth, hand for hand, foot for foot.

> Deuteronomy 19:21

Even in a modern society in which the principle of an eye for an eye is outmoded and systems for processing criminals are called agencies of reform, the ancient attitudes continue to appear. A court system overburdened with a backlog of cases that grows more staggering every year finds it impossible to ponder the meaning of justice; it strives only to get cases off the books. Arrests are made by a much vilified and underpaid police force, recruited from very ordinary men, and expected to exemplify a judgment, moderation, and detachment rare in the human species.

The system of punishment is a system repellent to most people, so they think about it as little as possible. The federal prisons and a few state prisons attempt to bring humane treatment into institutions that make no provisions for most of the psychological needs of the human being. Many other prisons do not make such attempts at modern enlightenment and are understaffed, overcrowded, and essentially brutal. Whatever the ills of federal and state prisons, however, they are often summer camps compared with the thousands of county and city jails — the pestholes most frequently encountered by the first offender.

All three major links in the system of justice are being subjected to increasing criticism by a society that claims to believe more in reform than in revenge. The first link, the most criticized but not necessarily the weakest, is the police force.

THE POLICE

An organized police force is newer to American experience than the courts or the jails and prisons, but an encounter with the police is usually the first step in the modern process of justice. The first metropolitan police force was established in New York City in 1841. Previously, arrests had been made by ordinary citizens, hired guards, or deputized agents of the sheriff's office.[1] New, official police forces were looked upon as possible concentrations of power that would threaten the citizen and lead to a diminution of his rights to due process of law. After well over a century of institutionalized police forces, and the general feeling that such forces are indispensable, there is still the same concern. There is even greater feeling of concern about the growth of an all-seeing federal force, so that in the majority of cases the exercise of police power remains in the hands of the county, city, and state governments. However police power is exercised, it is an inevitable center of controversy, part of which stems from the contradictory roles of the policeman.

CONFLICTING DEMANDS Many of the policeman's routine assignments are of a community-service type, such as answering emergency calls, looking for lost children, giving escort for emergency trips to the hospital, and helping in cases of natural disaster. In such cases there is little ambiguity about his position; he is the friend of the public.

When the policeman's activities are involved in the pursuit of crime, however, greater difficulties arise. His job is that of catching the guilty, but it is just as important that he protect the innocent. He is in a position where he must exert strong force occasionally and react to situations of danger, but he must be expected to use restraint even in such cases and must not develop hostility and suspicion toward the very citizens he is hired to protect. Ideally, his position calls for a rare combination of courage, judiciousness, and self-control, and a moral resistance to all corrupting temptations to which police departments are subject. Obviously, not all policemen can live up to all these requirements, nor is the public willing to pay the price that would be necessary for recruiting and training such a model force.

The nature of a policeman's job results in certain characteristics and attitudes of personality that Jerome Skolnick[2] analyzed in a study of two large city police forces. The position of the policeman combines authority with considerable threat of danger. Judging by the number of policemen who prefer criminal investigation to other types of work, it could be said that the policeman tends to welcome the more dangerous role. His work trains him to search for all suspicious characters and situations — to take a second glance at loiterers, at occupied cars parked near children's playgrounds, at eccentric people, at the oddly dressed, the unusual, the person with poor motor control, and leather-jacketed juvenile crowds. Suspiciousness becomes part

---

Interview or invite a well-informed police official to explain the problems of the job of policeman and also to answer questions from the class.

---

[1]Gresham M. Sykes, *Crime and Society*, Random House, Inc., New York, 1967, pp. 144–145.
[2]Jerome H. Skolnick, *Justice without Trial*, John Wiley & Sons, Inc., New York, 1966, pp. 42–70.

**Role expectation for the police: the
friendly protector, guardian of the innocent.**

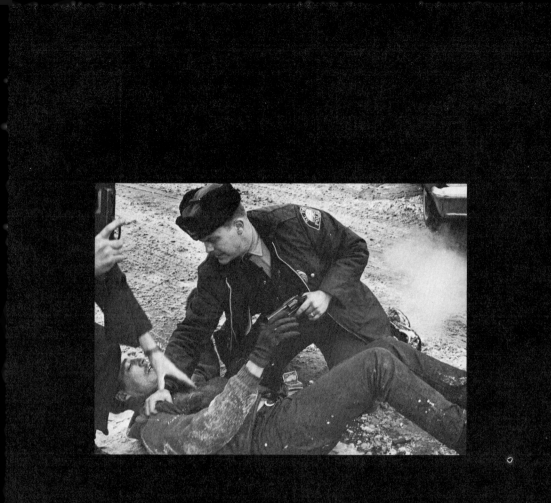

The policeman's other role: the forceful
agent of the state, reacting (and
sometimes overreacting) to danger.

of his personality. At the same time, he finds that other people are a little uncomfortable around a policeman; he therefore makes friends in his own circle and the policeman's world becomes isolated. Sometimes there is even a slight antagonism toward the general public, who, in police experience, will simply stand by in an emergency, expecting the police to do everything. The policeman is also charged with upholding the morality laws of a puritanical society, although such puritanism is not necessarily associated with the person willing to risk danger and assert authority. In the course of his work, the policeman is often assigned to ghetto areas, which he finds threatening. He is therefore accused of racial bias by a society that itself displays just as much racial bias—otherwise, why would blacks be segregated into ghettos? He is more pragmatic than philosophical in his attitude toward the law and sees little reason for court decisions that restrict his right to search and interrogate and that insist he follow constitutional procedures.

POLICE PERSONNEL AND THE PUBLIC IMAGE American policemen are predominantly Caucasians. Although slight changes have occurred in many cities as a result of riots and subsequent attempts to improve relationships within the ghetto area, as recently as 1960 city police forces were 96.5 percent white, and only 0.2 percent of state police officers were black.[3] Applications for police jobs come most frequently from low-paid, white-collar, manufacturing, or service workers, and from ex-servicemen. Pay and conditions of employment do not recruit enough manpower. A Presidential commission estimated in 1967 that there was a national shortage of at least 50,000 positions.

The police have their difficulties with public image, and insults have been hurled back and forth between police and demonstrators of various kinds. A survey in the 1960s showed that 70 percent of policemen considered their prestige to be only fair to poor. Actually, opinion surveys cited by the President's Commission on Law Enforcement indicated higher respect for the police than police officers seemed to believe existed. Only 9 percent of the public said the police do a poor job; 76 percent rated them as good or excellent.

The exposure of cases of corruption has had a much stronger negative effect on the public image of the police than have actions in demonstrations. In the 1950s several cases of tie-ins between police forces and the underworld were disclosed. In 1961 it became apparent that the Denver police force had been operating a criminal ring for more than fifteen years and had stolen more than $250,000 in cash and much more in merchandise.[4] The President's Commission on Law Enforcement found many cases of police acceptance of pay for protection of underworld activities. In recent years however, the major charges against the police have been more about

[3]*Crime in a Free Society: Selections from the President's Commission on Law Enforcement and the Administration of Justice*, Robert W. Winslow (ed.), Dickenson Publishing Company, Belmont, Calif., 1968, p. 259.
[4]Sykes, *op. cit.*, p. 149.

police brutality than about corruption, and such charges have come more from the poor, the young, the black, and the Chicano than from other elements of the population.

RACE AND THE POLICE In answer to the question "Are police often conscienceless and brutal in performing their duties?" 11 percent of Los Angeles whites said yes; 38 percent of Negroes said yes, and 44 percent of Mexicans said yes.[5] Such a statement is a matter of opinion, obviously, but it is probably opinion based either on personal experience or on known or rumored experiences of others in the social group to which the respondent belongs. The term "police brutality" lacks a consistent definition. The Wickersham Commission of the 1930s described many conditions of unquestionable brutality used in trying to extort confessions from suspects. Partly because of Supreme Court rulings, such offenses are much less common today. Often in the ghetto area the complaint referred to as brutality is more correctly called harassment. People are stopped for questioning more frequently in the ghetto than elsewhere, there are more insults, and there is greater feeling of mutual hostility between citizen and police. A Presidential commission, reporting in 1968,[6] found far less brutality than in earlier days but still enough unjustified interrogation and enough abusive language to explain part of the negative feelings. Interracial couples were particularly subject to being stopped and interrogated, and so were youths. Although the commission was extremely critical of racism in American life, it felt that the main reason for so much singling out of the police forces is that they are the front line of contact between the ghetto and the outside world. The evil was seen as essentially racism, not just police racism.

For the Mexican-Americans, mistreatment at the hands of local sheriff's offices was found in case after case of the testimony before the Senate committee investigating migrant labor (see Chapter 10). In Los Angeles, which has made great efforts in recent years to achieve a well-trained, well-paid, professionalized police force, there are still strong complaints within the Mexican neighborhoods, especially about the great shortage of Mexican-Americans on the police force.

It was also in Los Angeles that an experiment was tried to determine what effect Black Panther stickers on cars would have on arrest rates. Fifteen California State College students — five Mexican, five white, and five black, and all with perfect driving records — agreed to test the results of such signs. Within seventeen days they received a total of thirty three traffic citations.[7] The feelings of police were stronger than usual on the subject of Black Panthers, as there had been some recent deaths in encounters with them. Nevertheless, the experiment indicates that feelings have a strong influence on perception of law violations.

[5]Winslow, *op. cit.*, p. 273.
[6]*Report of the National Advisory Commission on Civil Disorders*, Bantam Books, Inc., New York, 1968, pp. 203–204.
[7]F. K. Heussenstamm, "Bumper Stickers and the Cops," *Transaction*, vol. 8, pp. 32–33, February 1971.

POLICE AND POVERTY   Part of the grounds for complaint against police is not so much a matter of racism as of social-class discrimination. A Michigan study conducted by Edward Green found that arrest rates bore a close relation to social class, unemployment, migration from rural to urban areas, and to the attitudes associated with lower-class position, regardless of race.[8] In fact, it was found that the black contribution to the arrest rate was declining slightly, but that the contribution of the unemployed was showing considerable increase, regardless of race.

Albert J. Reiss, Jr.,[9] in a study aimed more directly at the problem of police brutality, found quite a number of cases of the use of excessive force in connection with arrest and interrogation. Because the study of police actions was done under the known observation of sociological investigators, one cannot help but wonder if the situation is not worse when unobserved. On the subject of race and poverty, however, it is interesting to note that 67 percent of the cases of excessive force were of white officers against white suspects. Those who were obviously poor were much more subject to abusive language and to being hit or shoved than the others. The defiant and the deviants were especially subject to excessive force. The worst aspect of excessive force, according to Reiss, is that much of it took place in police stations after the suspect was already under control. There were also thirty seven cases of excessive force used on the streets in the process of arrest, but only one witness complained.

Reiss draws two other important conclusions. Sometimes the poor white is even more vulnerable to abuse than members of minority groups, which are now developing organizations to protest cases of mistreatment. He says that such organizations once existed among white ethnic groups—and sometimes still do—but for the rootless and unknown white there is little recourse. His other conclusion is that investigations into complaints carried on by police forces themselves have all the faults of an army self-investigation. What little is discovered is not made known to the public so that the organization can appear clean. The New Orleans police force, for example, received 268 complaints in a recent year, investigated 106, dismissed 14 officers, and took other disciplinary action against 72 others, but no details were given as to what violations had been committed.

Whatever other conclusion is valid, it is obvious that one should not be poor and isolated.

JUVENILES AND THE POLICE   Although the stigma against wearing long hair is probably wearing off with the passing of time, most longhaired male juveniles have felt themselves to be the subject of social discrimination and negative appraisal by much of the adult world, including the police. Do such antagonistic appearances really matter

---

[8]Edward Green, "Race, Social Class, and Criminal Arrest," *American Sociological Review*, vol. 35, pp. 478–489, June 1970.

[9]Albert J. Reiss, Jr., "How Common is Police Brutality," *Transaction*, vol. 5, pp. 10–17, July–August 1968.

To what extent are such traits as color, age, dress,
and far-out appearance accepted by
the police as clues to character?

in actual arrest rate? A study by Irving Piliavin and Scott Briar,[10] although done before long hair was much of an issue, would indicate that such matters as appearance are very important. Their study was conducted in an American city of about 500,000 population. The policy of the police department allowed considerable choice as to the kind of work the policeman might do, so that juvenile work had generally attracted a rather select group of those interested especially in the young. The juvenile workers on the force were given considerable discrimination in handling cases, and they tried to use their discretion in ways that would help boys they considered to be basically good, and perhaps in trouble for the first time. None had any confidence in the correctional process—of which more will be said later—and they were reluctant to stigmatize boys by giving them a police record. In their intent, they could certainly not be characterized as ill-willed, brutal, or even indifferent.

In using their discretion as to who to bring into court, the police admitted using many cues to character—age (the younger ones were more likely to be perceived as innocent), race (blacks and foreigners were perceived as more incorrigible than native whites), grooming and dress, and demeanor. Apparently, then, a young, white, good-looking, well-dressed, polite boy was almost sure to receive only a good talking to. The same could happen to a person failing in one of the other criteria—color, age, or even appearance; but the one failing in demeanor or a combination of the other traits was in serious trouble.

The police attitude toward demeanor, however, is understandable. In an interaction situation, rudeness on one side provokes hostility from the other side. Teachers and others working with the young also find it easy to be antagonized—even infuriated—by rude or surly manners, even though there may be plausible psychological and sociological explanations for such behavior.

THE CASE OF COLLEGE MILITANTS In demonstrations that have taken place in the last several years, there is no question that the police have often been provoked in ways that it is hard for people in authority to tolerate. There are cases in which the feeling of danger or the anger of the moment has led to overreaction, which is at least understandable. What is impossible to condone is the violence that has sometimes taken place with people who are already subdued. An example from Berkeley will illustrate the point. The violence of the guards at Santa Rita Prison was much worse than that of the police, but in both cases the action was excessive and of the type that further radicalizes the students.[11]

There had been a series of demonstrations in Berkeley over the demand to use some University of California land for a people's park, and demonstrations and ill-will had been mounting. Finally, on May 22, 1969, the police decided to make an example.

[10]Irving Piliavin and Scott Briar, "Police Encounters with Juveniles," *American Journal of Sociology*, vol. 70, pp. 206–212, September 1970.
[11]Jesse P. Ritter, Jr., "Nightmare for the Innocent in a California Jail," *Life*, vol. 76, pp. 51–54, August 15, 1969.

They arrested people indiscriminantly on the streets of Berkeley, catching a large number of nonstudents as well as students. No rowdy demonstration was in progress, but it was suspected that something was about to start. One of the men arrested, and the one who wrote the story for *Life* magazine, was a professor from San Francisco State College who happened to be in Berkeley in connection with an environmental project. He and his friends were arrested and put in a paddy wagon. They could not explain their business in Berkeley because they were threatened with beatings if they opened their mouths. The treatment was rough and terrifying. They were hauled off to Santa Rita Rehabilitation Center and Prison Farm, where they, along with more than 400 others, were made to lie face down on the concrete and remain silent. They were cursed, prodded, clubbed, and kicked. One diabetic who complained of his condition was unmercifully beaten. Those with long hair were particularly subject to beating and abuse and were called addicts, perverts, and reds. For hours no one was allowed to contact a lawyer. They were told that the other prisoners hated them and wanted to get at them and that they were going to be turned over to hardened criminals and sex perverts.

Finally, after a long night of intermittent torture, all the prisoners were released. For all 480, charges were dropped; there had been no evidence against them in the first place. The sheriff explained that maybe his guards had been "a little improper." Several, he said, were just back from the war and felt that any prisoners could be treated as Viet Cong. Twelve guards were dismissed. The incident was an unusually bad case, but it is the type of experience that proves the need for constant vigilance over the strong arm of police power.

JUSTICE WITHOUT TRIAL The power of the police to decide, within certain limits, how to dispose of a case is the main theme of Skolnick's book, *Justice without Trial*.[12] He shows that too much authority beyond the arrest level devolves upon the police. Part of the reason is that the courts are already so badly overcrowded that they require a certain amount of police disposal of cases. As in the previously cited case of the juveniles, the policeman has the power to decide whether to bring a boy in and make his case one of record or to dismiss him with a scolding and warning.

Other cases of "justice without trial" are more serious. In criminal cases having to do with narcotics, the police often find it expedient to bargain with suspects in return for information that might net several suspects or someone higher up the narcotics ladder. When possible penalties are high, the policeman's bargaining power is greatly increased, and he can decide whether to report a man caught in the act or to use him as an informer. The city police are usually placed under great pressure to "clear" cases, which sometimes results in a further police decision of a judicial nature. Sometimes an arrest is made of a person who readily confesses to a number of previous offenses, so they all get "cleared" from the books at once. Skolnick tells of

[12]Skolnick, *op. cit.*

one case in which a burglar, James, confessed to over 400 previous cases that had not yet been cleared by arrest. James was so cooperative in confessing to so many baffling cases and in helping to implicate several other people that he got off almost completely free. Other minor offenders, whose thefts had been uncovered by James' testimony, received stiff sentences.[13]

The police are assigned very difficult roles in society, roles often performed by people of minimal training. Although there have been improvements in the quality of police work in recent years, there are still numerous complaints. One complaint — that of police judgment being substituted for court judgment — is also a complaint against the next stage of the justice system, the courts.

BREAKDOWN IN THE JUSTICE MACHINE

We like to look upon such instruments of American justice as judges, juries, attorneys, and constitutional guarantees as an achievement of modern enlightenment. The American child, while still too young to really understand, starts to study some of the basic principles of justice. He learns of the right to a speedy trial by a jury of his peers, of the presumption of innocence until guilt is proved, of the need for warrants for search and seizure, and of the right to a writ of habeas corpus, which his teacher tells him guarantees the American that he cannot, without trial, be held in jail for long periods of time.

Partly because of the crowded conditions of our courts, and occasionally because of corruption, there are innumerable exceptions to all the above rules. The situation of overcrowding has reached such a state that the Chief Justice of the United States Supreme Court has been moved to speak of the crisis of our courts. Justice Burger delivered the first "State of the Judiciary" address in August 1970. He referred to a famous statement by Roscoe Pound sixty four years before, in which the eminent professor of jurisprudence stated that surely the twentieth-century courts of justice would not be run by the methods and machinery of the nineteenth century. Roscoe Pound was wrong, Burger continued, "We are still trying to operate the courts with fundamentally the same basic methods, procedures, and machinery he said were not good enough in 1906."[14] Burger expressed fear that the sense of confidence in the courts, so necessary for a system combining liberty and order, could be destroyed if people come to believe that inefficiency and delay are rendering justice ineffective, or if the law cannot protect the safety of the people or save them from exploitation and fraud.

THE INEFFICIENT MACHINE Sykes[15] has likened our total handling of law violations to an inefficient machine or a conveyer belt that keeps dropping part of its load at vari-

---

[13]Skolnick, op. cit., pp. 176–179.
[14]Chief Justice Warren E. Burger, "Burger on the Courts, Improvements Long Overdue," Los Angeles Times, August 16, 1970, Section G, pp. 2, 3.
[15]Sykes, op. cit., pp. 143–164.

ous places along the way. The original load on the conveyer belt could be thought of as the total number of crimes committed and known to the police. The second stage is the number of crimes cleared by arrest, a very much smaller number in nearly all cases. The load is further diminished by the number of people found innocent, whose cases are dismissed for lack of evidence, or who are paroled and never actually punished. Finally, there is a small minority left who are actually sentenced to pay their "debt to society."

Sykes says, quite correctly, that a justice machine in a democratic society with strong feelings against punishment of the innocent has to be somewhat inefficient. A justice system that always caught every offense and always punished everyone to the limit of the law would be impossible and can be dreamed of only in a nightmare of totalitarianism. Although Sykes' reasoning is perfectly correct, the present situation is beginning to overload the machine with a burden it was never meant to carry and is forcing its inefficiency so far as to render it almost totally ineffective.

Other disturbing pictures come to mind as one tries to conceptualize a justice conveyer belt. Conveyer belts in mineral processing always carry the essential load to the refinery, dropping out only what is irrelevant to the process. The justice belt, on the other hand, tends to drop all the big, well-connected criminals and convey to prison mainly the less relevant cases. Furthermore, there is frequent slippage in the gears, so that parts of the process are omitted, or even reversed. In *Alice in Wonderland*, the queen cries "First the verdict, then the trial." In some of our cases the cry becomes "First the punishment, then the verdict." Suspects have been known to wait in jail for months (in a few cases even years) before trial, then, after having received their punishment, been dismissed for lack of evidence.

There is yet another breakdown in the machine. The old saying "The mills of the gods grind slow, but they grind exceeding fine" implies great thoroughness and accuracy about a slowness of process. In the case of the courts, the slower they grind, the less likely they are to grind at all. "Delay is my best weapon. Time will beat any case if you have enough of it," says a defense attorney from Dallas.[16]

THE LAW'S DELAY In most big cities both population and crime rates increase much faster than court facilities, and simultaneously the length of time required for a major

---

> Visit a local courtroom, preferably hearing a criminal case. Is the suspect well represented by an attorney? Was he released on bail while awaiting trial? Was the court so overloaded with cases that it had to postpone his trial?

---

[16]Dale Wittner, "Logjam in Our Courts," *Life*, vol. 69, p. 19, August 7, 1970.

case lengthens — partly for the commendable purpose of giving the accused every legal protection afforded him, especially if he can hire a good lawyer.

The result of the vast increase in numbers of people and numbers of crimes is an overtaxing of the big city courts. The biggest city of all is New York, and its dilemma illustrates the court problem extremely well, although it is by no means unique. The pace of the courts is so slow that the backlog of cases constantly grows. In 1969 there were 75,000 felony arrests, but only 608 felony trials were completed.

> The criminal court began 1969 with a backlog estimated at more than half a million cases. During the year, twenty new judges were added to alleviate the congestion. Yet at the start of 1970, the backlog had risen to almost 700,000 cases and was increasing each month. . . .[17]

One result of the overcrowding of the courts is the serious injustice, previously mentioned, of keeping people who cannot pay bail behind bars awaiting trial for months. Of the 14,000 inmates of New York jails in 1969, 8,000 had been convicted of nothing; they were simply awaiting trial. Not only are jails crowded pestholes, but commitment to jail causes loss of job and often family breakup. Although the legal system speaks of innocence until proven guilty, the handling given the suspects is not that of presumably innocent citizens. The accompanying fact that bail is provided for members of Cosa Nostra so that they await trial in freedom (freedom to commit more crimes) is a hard reality that embitters the nonprofessional suspects.

Another disillusioning practice for those who retain a mental picture of the dignity of the law is the "plea bargaining" process that goes on. In plea bargaining, the suspect is given a promise of a light sentence if he'll plead guilty so his case can clear the courts; even more likely he will be given a sentence for a lesser offense than the one he has committed. The practice saves many hours of time, but it ensures that justice will be only approximated. The alternative is likely to be one of waiting for months for the case to be tried — months during which witnesses' memories grow dim and a "reasonable doubt" begins to arise. To condemn such a system is not to accuse courts of deliberate dishonor; they have no alternative. The real problem is that it reduces justice to a joke, to a process of making a deal. Occasionally even the innocent are caught up in the system, feeling it is better to plead guilty to a small offense than to antagonize the court.

LOS ANGELES "Authorities sometimes remark that the only thing worse than not catching a criminal is catching him."[18] The present situation in Los Angeles County is also one of delayed justice and of a county jail system that is overloaded, but the overloading is only starting. Using a computer fed with crime rates and court and jail

[17]*Ibid.,* p. 20.
[18]William J. Drummond, "L. A. Crime Rate Could Collapse Justice System," *Los Angeles Times*, September 13, 1970, Sec. B, pp. 1, 7.

captivity, a USC team concludes that in six or seven years Los Angeles authorities will have to have a telephone answering service programmed to say, "Sorry, we cannot accept any more crime or civil complaints. We are full to capacity."

In California, even more so than in other states, a vast amount of court crime is taken up with cases involving auto accidents and damages. There are proposals for either doing away with jury trials in such cases or reducing the size of the jury in order to save time.

THE MACHINERY OF MILITARY JUSTICE   The military justice machine is much more efficient than the civilian machine, if conviction rate is taken as a measurement of efficiency. Again it must be stated, though, that total efficiency sounds suspiciously totalitarian. The military conviction rate is 94 percent, compared to only 81 percent in civilian courts.[19] Military justice, admittedly, can have problems not faced by civilian justice. Especially under combat conditions, military forces must submit to a discipline not encountered in ordinary civilian life, and some of the amenities of freedom are difficult to maintain. A democracy has for its servant a regimented, disciplined, authoritarian organization, which includes between 3 and 4 million men and women who have been brought up to believe in the principles of civilian justice. Consequently, the military justice system comes under increasing attack, as it did at the end of World War II.

Military justice in the early days of our republic had none of the amenities of civilian justice — no bail, no defense lawyers, no indictments, no impartial judges or due process — and both branding and flogging were permitted until 1861. In 1950 more reforms were made, creating a Court of Military Appeals and providing for lawyer representation in both special and general courts-martial. Legal representation is not provided in the simple summary court martial, which can only impose a penalty of 30 days or less. In spite of reforms, there are remaining grounds for criticism. The commanding officer selects members of the court martial, his junior officers, who have a stake in staying on good terms with him. Although there are cases in which an enlisted man on trial can call for an enlisted member of the court martial, such an enlisted representative is selected by the officers and is likely to be the first sergeant, a man very close to the commanding officer. One has to have served in a low-ranking position in the Armed Forces to understand the feeling of insurmountable social distance that separates the enlisted man from a group of officers sitting as his trial board. Fortunately, a Court of Military Appeals has been created so that unreasonable decisions can be overruled and progress made in the direction of uniformity of sentencing. The progress, however, remains very slow. Twenty two defendants who protested conditions at the Presidio guard house in San Francisco were prosecuted for mutiny — a tremendous overstatement of their offense. They were sentenced to many years in prison, but the sentences were drastically reduced by

[19]Editors of *Newsweek*, "U.S. Military Justice on Trial," *Newsweek*, pp. 18–23, April 31, 1970.

the appeals court. Sentences still remain grossly inconsistent. Refusal to obey orders has in recent years brought punishment ranging from a mere reprimand to sixteen years in prison.[20]

MILITARY JUSTICE AND INTERNATIONAL LAW   The much larger question of military justice involves the problem of war guilt. If a man carries out orders contrary to the rules of so-called civilized warfare and shoots women and children, is he guilty of murder? Or is he innocent because he only followed orders? Or is he guilty along with whoever issued the orders? For that matter, can the whole military command be guilty if an atmosphere of callous brutality that gives everyone at least the implied order to kill without discrimination is allowed? These are moral questions that go beyond the scope of a brief study of the administration of justice, but they are issues that will undoubtedly haunt military establishments for all time. The Nuremberg Trials following World War II sought to establish the principle that even a disciplined soldier has the duty of disobeying orders that would require him to commit atrocities.

THE PRISON

The principle of an eye for an eye sounds savage in the twentieth century, and yet it is hardly as savage as some of the punishment prescribed. In the American system of justice men are frequently sentenced to prisons for terms of 100 to 200 years or more, and the prisons are by no means places of merciful treatment. Louis Wolfson charges that in a Florida prison one inmate was stomped to death by three guards; two asthmatics were denied treatment and died; a convicted forger with a wounded hand was denied treatment until gangrene set in and his hand had to be cut off.[21]

To another federal prison was sentenced a feeble-minded, impoverished Negro girl, not for causing loss of life or even property, but for having pasted a canceled stamp on a letter she had mailed.[22] Elsewhere a man sentenced for a $70 robbery of a gasoline station served eleven years, over seven in solitary. His hostile behavior caused a constant lengthening of his sentence. Finally he murdered a guard and was

---

Have a member or two of the class visit the local jail or a state prison if one is nearby. If you visit a prison, try to find out what sort of rehabilitation program is in progress, if any. Are modern improvements being tried? Is the institution overcrowded?

---

[20]*Ibid.,* p. 22.
[21]Jack Anderson, "What It's Like to Be in Prison," Bell McClure syndicated dispatch of June 24, 1970.
[22]James V. Bennett, "A Cool Look at the Crime Crisis," *Harper's,* vol. 228, pp. 123–127, April 1964.

sentenced to give life for life.[23] No less an authority than James V. Bennett, longtime director of the U.S. Bureau of Prisons, says of our prison system:

> Except possibly for "enemies of the state" in countries where people are sent to prison for political reasons, the American criminal on the average serves several times as long a sentence as his counterpart anywhere else in the world.[24]

In the popular mind the reason for long and severe punishment is deterrence, although there is little evidence that prisons work to this purpose. As Durkheim analyzed punishment, it served largely as a societal ritual for preserving the sense of righteousness of the law-abiding (or those who manage not to get caught). As Karl Menninger sees it in *The Crime of Punishment*, we secretly identify with the lawbreaker, but we expiate our sense of guilt by punishing him. Whatever the case, there is constant public clamor for longer sentences, and it seems to be good politics to cry for blood — eye for eye, tooth for tooth, and life for life.

THE PLACE OF FORGETTING   One reason that well-run prisons are rare, in spite of frequent agitation for reform, is that they house a forgotten segment of the population. The stocks and the pillory were brutal, but at least people saw them and knew what took place. Cruelty was always present, but it was limited to what public opinion could countenance. In the prison, public opinion is generally inoperative because the life of the prisoner is not known. In the prisons of medieval France was a deep dungeon known as *l'oublière*, or "the place of forgetting." Men in the dungeons were shut out of the minds and memories of their fellow men, there to live in dampness and filth, and there eventually to sicken and die. Although many state and federal prisons have made wholesome reforms, there are still in twentieth-century America places of confinement that can be called nothing but *les oublières*. They are places of double tragedy, not only bringing misery, but failing in their purpose of curing crime as well.

THEORIES OF CRIME VERSUS THE PRISON   In the previous chapter, two theories of crime were emphasized: crime as the latent function of too strong a success requirement, and crime as learned behavior. Hostility resulting from deprived conditions, of course, plays its part, and so does a disorganized family background. A prison system temporarily protects the public from some types of criminals and has at least some deterrent effect. At the same time, especially as seen from the point of view of crime theory, the prison has certain latent functions that promote crime. If crime is a consequence of too strong a desire for success even by deviant means, then the prison serves the latent function of being a place for discussing such means and planning how to succeed better next time. If crime is thought of as mainly learned behavior, then the prison can be seen as an excellent teacher. If crime is a result of hostilities, there is

[23]"The State of the Prisons," *Time*, vol. 97, p. 54, January 18, 1971.
[24]Bennett, *op. cit.*

What effect does the "steel-bound coffin
of a cell" have on the prison inmate?

little doubt that hostilities are increased in the majority of prisons. If crime is partly a consequence of family disorganization, certainly imprisonment adds to the problem, for it drives family relationships further apart.

If we add to these characteristics of the prison the tendency for the most hardened, old-line criminals to become kingpins in an informal organization that helps the system to function, then we will have added almost the finishing touch to a description of the perfect school for crime. The informal social system that grows up within the prison even permits crime within the prison walls — blackmail, loan-sharking, beatings, and homosexual attacks.

In short, there is little about the analysis of causes of crime that seems to mesh with the manner of running prisons. If one did not know better, he would assume that the purpose of imprisonment is to ensure the continuance of crime.

THE INMATE WORLD OF THE TOTAL INSTITUTION The "total institution," as described by Goffman, is any institution that takes complete control of the individual, leaving him no will of his own and no direction of his own life. Most prisons closely approach the following description, based largely on Goffman's work,[25] although some are making real improvements.

In the inmate world there is no such thing as a separation between time on the job and time devoted to one's own purposes; one has no purposes of his own. The total life is part of the inmate world. Antagonisms are developed between the inmate world and the guards, and also between the total institution and the outside world. For the inmate, one of the most important processes, described with great feeling by Goffman, is the process of mortification. Previous roles are eliminated, obedience tests are forced upon the inmate, and a will-breaking contest takes place. One not only dares not speak back, but he dares not defend his sense of pride even with facial expressions or gestures; he must be abject, a total slave, or face further punishment. He must be dispossessed of any property that sets him off from others or gives him special personality or dignity. He must be stripped of any personal characteristics of appearance; he must be personally disfigured through inmate clothing and hair-cut, and this very disfigurement marks him for inmate status and makes him subject to disciplinary methods. No face saving is possible to help him retain his sense of self; no privacy is possible, either in one's letters to the outside world, or in his body, his idiosyncrasies, his natural functions, or his sex nature. If he submits to the system for enough years, he may become an institutionalized type who can no longer stand life on the outside.

Within the inmate world a privilege system develops, but there are no rights. Privileges can be obtained only in terms of the rules of the system. Such simple matters as how one wants his coffee, when he can talk, when he can take a moment's

[25]Erving Goffman, "On the Characteristics of Total Institutions: The Inmate World," in Donald R. Cressey (ed.), *The Prison*, Holt, Rinehart and Winston, Inc., New York, 1961, pp. 15–45.

rest, whether he can smoke a cigarette or a cigar—all the little details that seem a part of a person's vital self become special privileges to be won in the inmate system. Even the privilege of "release-binge fantasy," of talking to someone about what one will do when he is out, is a revocable privilege. Punishment by a silent system or by solitary confinement is always possible.

There is also the problem of learning the informal rules within the inmate system, of knowing who can be trusted and who is a "stoolie." There are various possible adaptations to the situation, mentioned by Goffman, sometimes that of withdrawal or being uncooperative and intransigent. Sometimes "colonization" takes place—the acquiring of what privileges and amenities are possible within the system and forgetting the outside world. This is the type of adjustment made by a man who after many years finds a home and usually returns to the prison, almost willingly, soon after release. One might adopt a "conversion" attitude, taking on the ways of the guards, identifying with authority. Most frequently, though, the idea is to "play it cool," meeting the rules well enough and relating to one's fellow inmates well enough to speed the process of getting out physically undamaged.

THE CASE OF THE CONSCIENTIOUS OBJECTORS Conscientious objectors, draft dodgers, and war opponents are special cases within a prison. They are people of unusually strong conscientious scruples lodged among others who fall below the usual societal norm in this respect. They are political prisoners who, contrary to the quotation from Bennett, exist in fairly large numbers in our prisons.

In 1969, more than 1,700 men were tried on various violations of the Selective Service Act; 900 were convicted, and 545 were actually sentenced to prison for an average of three years. Naturally, such men are profoundly affected by the experience but generally adhere to their principles and do not regret having refused service. Two changes that take place in their thinking are, however, indicative of the influence of prison upon men and are illustrated by the following excerpts from an article by Robert Rawitch:

> Probably the most serious change in many resisters was a fear regarding their own capacity for violence, according to Merklin (the prison psychiatrist). "All of them hated more intensely than they ever had before in their lives," he explained.
>
> The prison code, which dictates that each man "does his own time and does not see anything that happens around him," is strictly adhered to by most resisters, regardless of their earlier moral convictions.
>
> An inmate told of seeing a man lying on the floor with blood streaming from his head and another man running away. He just walked on as though he had not seen a thing.[26]

[26]Robert Rawitch, "Resisters: Problems in Prison," *Los Angeles Times*, August 16, 1970, Sec. G., pp. 1, 2. Copyright, 1970, *Los Angeles Times*. Quoted by permission.

Time served in prison makes the young idealists more radical and antiestablishment. It also causes an erosion of some of their traditional moral values. Quoting Merklin again in the same article by Rawitch:

> Many feel they would think twice about stealing something when they are back on the streets. Previously they never would have considered it. The idea of theft was now something possible, he said. All have learned to be dishonest in prison.

Prison, apparently, can have powerful effects on even the most idealistic people. Some draft resisters expressed regret that they hadn't simply gotten busted for narcotics and escaped the draft in that manner.

SEX AND THE PRISON Not only does prison deprive a man of freedom, the ability to make decisions, a feeling of purpose in life, and most of what makes human existence tolerable, but it deprives him of any normal outlet for his sexual nature. In earlier times entire families were sometimes kept in English gaols or workhouses (the distinction was not too great), and, bad as the system was, it allowed for a degree of normality. Many Mexican jails allow wives to visit for periods other than short, observed daylight hours. Mexico's jails are generally dreaded like the plague, and yet La Mesa Prison in Tijuana is an interesting experimental institution making a certain amount of family life possible and also encouraging gainful employment.[27] In Sweden, where the average prison sentence is for only five months and the repeater rate is only 15 percent, men are allowed regular furloughs for family visiting. North Carolina has recently started experiments with such a system, and so have several California prisons.[28] In the majority of state and federal penitentiaries, however, normal relations are impossible.

For years there has been an awareness of homosexuality in prisons, but it was little talked about. Hayner and Ash stated the matter rather delicately years ago: "Love your fellow man gets a new definition in the prisoner community . . . for perversions are regarded as inevitable."[29] Hayner and Ash give the impression that homosexual relationships within the prison are a matter of mutual consent. Such was not the case in the Philadelphia prison system, according to a thorough investigation by the Philadelphia District Attorney's office and the police department, completed in September 1968.[30] The report is a horror story in which the young man new to the prison system is the victim of gang rapes and of severe beatings if he resists. Sometimes his complaints are ignored by guards, who wish not to be bothered or have such

[27]Charles Hillinger, "Tijuana Prison: There's No Place Like It," *Los Angeles Times*, December 27, 1970, Part I, pp. 1, 24.
[28]*Time, op. cit.*, pp. 53–54.
[29]Norman S. Hayner and Ellis Ash, "The Prisoner Community as a Social Group," *American Sociological Review*, vol. 4, pp. 362–369, June 1939.
[30]Alan J. Davis, "Sexual Assaults in the Philadelphia Prison System and Sheriff's Vans," *Transaction*, vol. 6, pp. 8–16, December 1968.

contempt for prisoners as not to care. Sometimes those who complain are placed in solitary "for their own protection," until they finally realize that the only way out is a homosexual relationship with a hardened criminal. The cases of homosexual assault are by no means unusual. The District Attorney's office estimated that 2,000 such cases occurred during the twenty six months of the study.

THE PROBLEM OF PUBLIC AWARENESS   There are several reasons why reports of homosexual attacks and other types of irregularities within prisons are seldom published. For one thing, people are little interested in prisoners who are "only getting what they deserve." Another problem is that credibility is low and reports are often not believed until such an official investigation as that of the Philadelphia system is conducted. It was surprising in the late summer of 1970 to read newspaper accounts of a group of judges visiting a prison in Nevada, in fact, spending a night there. They were shocked at the conditions. What could easily be more shocking to the public was the implication that a group of men who had spent their lives sentencing suspects apparently had little knowledge of what the typical prison is like.

In recent years there has been one note of encouragement. There are more protests than ever before about the condition of America's prisons, and several states are working in the direction of reform. It is to be hoped that the protests will not die. In 1917, John Laffin, a British subject imprisoned for his pacifist activities, wrote his protest of the "burial alive" that has been so typical of prisons:

> Mourn not the dead that in the cool earth lie—
> Dust unto dust—
> The calm, sweet earth that mothers all who die
> As all men must;
>
> Mourn not your captive comrades who must dwell—
> too strong to strive—
> Each in his steel-bound coffin of a cell,
> Buried alive;
>
> But rather mourn the apathetic throng—
> The cowed and the meek—
> Who see the world's great anguish and its wrong
> And dare not speak.

The greatest hope for rehabilitation is with the young (see Chapter 13, suggestion on page 351). There is also an organization called Friends Outside, which tries to help the wives and children of men in prison. For information write to Mrs. Rosemary Goodenough, FRIENDS OUTSIDE, 1041 Mundale Court, Los Altos, California.

THE QUALITY OF MERCY

Obviously, some serious rethinking about our system of justice is needed. Such thinking might start with Shakespeare's observation

> That in the course of justice, none of us
> Should see salvation.

In Piliavin's study, the policemen who were concerned with saving the delinquent boys they perceived as essentially worthwhile were acting in the interests of mercy. An evenhanded justice would not have permitted such leniency. The difficulty is, though, that for the policemen the quality of mercy extended only to certain types of people. This, we noted in the previous chapter, is also true of certain categories of lawbreakers. Those in the white-collar category are more apt to know the blessings of mercy than those in the Uniform Crime Reports. Since mercy is a concept more common to religion and poetry than to jurisprudence, it can only be approximated in the great legal systems of the gigantic society, but it is approached. In some of the best systems of juvenile courts the interest of the young offender is primary, rather than the interest of retributory justice. In police work, much of the same quality has been present at times in the history of American cities.

In the old days of Tammany Hall, in spite of the notorious corruption of the organization, little acts of kindness were extended by the ward boss and the police. The police were part of the neighborhood, knew the people, and related to them. If we could have similar types of community relations without having the graft of the old-time political machine, there would be considerable restoration of respect for the law.

COMMUNITY AND POLICE Arthur Waskow[31] suggests that there are three possible ways of improving community relations with the police and preventing frequent charges of police harassment. The first approach would be to restructure metropolitan police forces into neighborhood police forces, with local elections of commissioners. The second possibility would be to create countervailing power by organizations able to hear grievances and to protest injustices. Actually, some minority group organizations are approximating this solution at present. The third possibility is fairly well implied within the second: break down the barriers that separate policemen from citizens to avoid the social isolation of the police. For several years the thinking about police forces has been of a development of greater professionalization, the creation of elite forces with more sophisticated knowledge of all the detection devices of today. Certainly such knowledge is needed, but perhaps it belongs only to special units of the police forces. Otherwise the separation of citizen and police is intensified.

[31] Arthur I. Waskow, "Community Control of the Police," *Transaction*, vol. 7, pp. 4–7, December 1969.

Police and the sense of community.

In spite of the need for local control and local involvement with the police, at the time of the Presidential commission's report on law enforcement, only about ten percent of the cities had participating citizens' groups. Where they have been instituted they have been helpful in closing the gap that has increasingly isolated the police from the communities they serve.

The other major recommendation of nearly every commission that has investigated ghetto problems is to encourage a larger participation of nonwhites on police forces. Sometimes the very antagonism of the ghetto toward the police makes it difficult to recruit many black policemen, but there are cities where the policy is succeeding.

IMPROVING THE COURT SYSTEM As noted, there are inevitable incongruities between efficiency and justice. A police system completely unrestrained by any of the niceties of constitutional rights could be much more efficient than at present, but at a cost a democracy could not afford to pay. What is true of the police system is equally true of the courts. Burger notes that criminal cases now take twice as long to prosecute as they did ten years ago, and part of the reason is our commitment to "values higher than pure efficiency." There are other areas, however, in which Burger sees possibilities for improving the pace of justice. He strongly believes that long periods of delay and uncertainty do much to keep the crime rate high, and that some administrative details of the court could be rendered more efficient so that the process of justice could be speeded. Several suggestions of Burger are:

> Increase the number of courts, and also establish a judiciary council that would advise Congress of the probable impact of new legislation upon the court system.
> More administrative efficiency within the courts. The Institute for Court Management, opened in Aspen, Colorado, is viewed by Burger as the most encouraging recent development.
> Administrative rather than court handling of several minor categories of crime, including vagrancy, drunkenness, and prostitution, as well as traffic violations.
> A great reduction in our adversary system of justice. American court trials are prolonged partly because of our desire for courtroom showmanship of conflicting attorneys playing before a jury, a system that has sometimes been called "trial by combat."[32]

Burger elaborates on the final point because at first glance it might seem to run counter to constitutional guarantees. His contention is that many countries of Western Europe are able to dispense justice in a manner every bit as sure as ours and much more swift, without being abusive to peoples' rights. The swift handling of justice, however, is followed by careful and humane treatment of the offender, with a far better record of rehabilitation than we have made.

Burger sees little possibility of a reduction in plea bargaining; he considers such procedures indispensable. On this point the President's Commission on Law Enforcement is much more critical, noting cases of "excessive leniency for habitual criminals who generally have expert legal advice and are best able to take full advantage of the bargaining opportunity."[33] Both Burger and the Commission agree that some uniformity of standards in plea bargaining is needed.

There are, unfortunately, certain barriers in the way of court reform. One problem is that the public is not particularly interested, not knowing the danger of the fire until burned. Another problem is that many lawyers have a vested interest in the present system. The following set of statistics illustrates their vested interest: the Department of Transportation estimated that in accident suits settled in 1968,

[32]The Views of the Chief Justice," *Life*, vol. 69, p. 26, August 7, 1970. Also, Justice Burger in *Los Angeles Times, op. cit.*
[33]Winston, *op. cit.*, p. 295.

victims collected a total of 700 million dollars and lawyers collected 600 million dollars. The California State Legislature in 1971 defeated a bill for no-fault insurance. To no one's surprise, much of the opposition came from lawyers.

Yet another problem in the way of judicial reform is that of correlation between police work, court systems, and systems for dealing with those convicted. Clark,[34] among others, makes suggestions for a system in which detection, conviction, and disposition of cases are correlated. Too often the right hand doesn't know what the left hand is doing.

THE TREATMENT OF OFFENDERS   Certainly there is need for the courts to know more of the disposition of cases, and there is need for the public to know more about this as well. The Scandinavian countries can show their prisons with pride; we can show most of ours only with profound embarrassment. To quote Burger again:

> In part the terrible price we pay in crime is because we tend, once the drama of the trial is over, to regard all criminals as human rubbish. It would make more sense, from a coldly logical viewpoint, to put all this "rubbish" into a vast incinerator instead of storing it in warehouses for a time only to have most of the subjects come out of prison and return to their old ways.[35]

Actually, many of our juvenile courts try to treat the offender rather than merely punish him. The juvenile court system is subject to criticism, however, because since it attempts to deal with the individual case rather than with general legalistic principles it is only as good as the authorities handling the case. Such a statement points to a need for a great improvement in the personnel placed in charge of offenders, whether juvenile or adult.

The adult treatment, in spite of all that has been written about rehabilitation, still tends to be only custodial care. And it should be noted that correctional facilities are so crowded that by no means all minors are sent to special institutions. More than 100,000 minors are now housed in our state prisons, learning the attitudes and the techniques of the world of crime. Obviously, a first step toward reform would be to spend a little more money to create the needed facilities for separating minors from adults.

NEW DIRECTIONS IN REHABILITATION   There are some observable areas of progress in the American prison systems. California has at least tried new techniques, although they are not always successful. The California prisons are considered the nation's best and are oriented toward a philosophy of correction. The courts give indeter-

---

[34]Ramsay Clark, "Criminal Justice in Times of Turbulence," *Saturday Review*, vol. 53, pp. 21–24, 51, September 19, 1970.

[35]Burger, in *Life, op. cit.*

minate sentences, with the understanding that the offender can be imprisoned or not, depending on his own behavior. Very recently, a policy of allowing overnight visits for wives has been instituted in some California prisons. Two-thirds of convicted offenders are given probation, and a small number work in forestry crews under minimum security. Only 13.5 percent actually go to prison.[36] Nevertheless, the situation is far from satisfactory. The recidivist rate is high, and the much-lauded training program serves only a small percentage of the inmates. Jessica Mitford calls the whole subject of reform of the California prisons a vast hoax.[37] She does not give enough mention to the large numbers of men placed on probation, but she does have some disturbing statistics for those actually serving time. Under the California indeterminate sentence system, allegedly merciful, the average first sentence is longer than in any other state in the union. There are the same complaints over filth, overcrowding, bad food, and homosexual problems as elsewhere, but the greatest hatred of the inmate is leveled against the indeterminate sentence. The system gives vast judicial power to prison officials; they can decide whether a sentence of one to fifteen years will actually be one year or the maximum of fifteen.

Kansas, following the advice of Menninger, has set up a diagnostic clinic similar to those found in Swedish prisons. The result has been probation for far more men than in the past and a reduction in the percentage of men who break probation. North Carolina has pioneered in a work-release program that allows prisoners on good behavior to go to regular jobs during the day or to take courses in school. Senator Mansfield has introduced a bill to try to handle cases of criminal negligence by providing for working off debts to the victim or his family rather than spending idle years in prison.

Probation is a reform measure that is being used more and more, and further study is underway to achieve a degree of predictability as to who will or will not break the terms of probation. The problems of city jails can be solved partly by releasing more people on their own recognizance, if they are unable to put up bail. Experiments in this direction in Los Angeles indicate that no more people fail to appear for trial if released on their own recognizance than if they have posted bail.[38] Such a system does not discriminate against the poor as a bond system does.

What is probably more important than any of the reform measures so far attempted is a new explosive potential within the prison system itself. The prisons have received a considerable number of college students and selective service resisters whose literacy and plausibility are high and who know how to fight through the courts. More court cases than ever before are challenging the autocratic power of prison officials. An Arkansas court recently ruled that conditions within the prison constituted cruel and unusual punishment and were in violation of the Constitution. Legislatures and the mass media are taking an interest in prison conditions. The

[36]*Time, op. cit.*, p. 50.
[37]Jessica Mitford, "Kind and Usual Punishment in California," *Atlantic*, vol. 227, pp. 45–52, March 1971.
[38]Robert Waitch, "Jail Releases without Bond," *Los Angeles Times*, January 4, 1971, Part I, p. 1.

present inmates, especially members of ethnic minorities, view their situation differently than did previous inmates and make common voice with the other minority-group protesters. They are indoctrinated in the protest ideas of today and see their situation as largely the result of social injustice rather than purely of their own personal inadequacy.[39] Young lawyers now graduating from law school are also of a new breed, more interested in social causes than in working for corporations, according to a recent Gallup poll. They are increasingly involved in cases of legal challenges to prison policies. The future may see far fewer of the "apathetic throng . . . who dare not speak." We know that our traditional methods are a failure, and we know that new experiments here and abroad are finding better alternatives in the search for justice than an eye for an eye and a tooth for a tooth.

SUGGESTED READINGS

Cressey, Donald R. (ed.): *Crime and Criminal Justice*, Quadrangle Books, Inc., Chicago, 1970.

> *In his introductory essay Cressey points out that the enforcement of law and administration of justice are more complex than merely following rules. Discretion must be used to maintain the consent of the governed. Particularly authoritative in the field of organized crime.*

Gibbons, Don C.: *Changing the Lawbreaker: The Treatment of Delinquents and Criminals*, Prentice-Hall, Inc., Englewood Cliffs, N.J., 1965.

> *A basic book in the sociology of correction. Examines research material in the field, classifications, and treatments of different types of offenders. Also contains a discussion of obstacles in the way of helpful treatment.*

Finn, James (Ed.): *Conscience and Command: Justice and Discipline in the Military*, Vintage Books, Random House, Inc., New York, 1971.

> *The essays in this book deal with the differences between civilian rights and military justice and also with the dangers of a blind following of orders. Contains essays by experts and testimony by military men.*

Menninger, Karl: *The Crime of Punishment*, The Viking Press, Inc., New York, 1969.

> *Although Menninger gives credit to men of good will who have worked hard to improve the treatment of offenders, he sees most of our penitentiaries as pestholes, lagging far behind our knowledge of reform possibilities. He is strongly condemnatory in his attitude toward the concept of revenge, which he contends still permeates the prison system.*

Sellin, Thorsten (ed.): *Capital Punishment*, Harper & Row, Publishers, Incorporated, 1967.

> *A well-structured book of readings on one of the punishment problems constantly debated in American society. Especially good on the question of deterrence, with several articles written by Sellin himself.*

[39]Mitford, *op. cit.*, p. 50.

 QUESTIONS

1. Why is the role of policeman difficult and subject to conflicting demands?

2. What types of people are often treated with undue severity by the police?

3. Give some examples of and explanations for the long delays in the justice system.

4. How does military justice—in spite of recent reforms—still fall short of consitutional guarantees for the person accused of a crime?

5. What are some of the abuses found in the worst of our jails and prisons? What problems remain even in the best of our prisons?

6. What attempted reforms and further suggestions are being made for improving police forces, courts, and the prison system?

PART FOUR

THE ULTIMATE PROBLEM:
SOCIAL NATURE AND SURVIVAL

War and aggression have been part of human history for thousands of years. Although many primitive peoples fight minor skirmishes, organized warfare seems to have started with the growth of urban civilizations. Many early wars destroyed great cities and empires, but it is only in recent times that wars have had a potential for killing the entire human race.

WHAT IS NEW

What is overwhelmingly different about the problem of war today is that its menace has been intensified by the developments of science. Two great antagonists in the world now have the destructive capacity to kill every human being in existence many times over. They work busily at the building of an even greater capacity for overkill and try in vain to find some way to protect themselves. Much of the previous history of warfare has been of a fairly close standoff between the instruments of defense and those of attack. Presently the instruments of attack are so powerful that the world provides no refuge or hiding place. It is for this reason that the present generation has had to mature into a world that could conceivably destroy itself. This is a very unpleasant possibility to face, but it must be faced with a determination to survive. The research methods of science must be concentrated on ensuring the triumph of man's constructive intelligence over his destructive capacity. The weapons that pose a unique threat are also a unique deterrent that may cause major powers always to stop short of the brink.

MEETING THE SOCIAL PROBLEMS CRITERIA

No one would question that the possibility of war is a social problem except, possibly, on the basis of one criterion: some regard war as inevitable in the nature of man. From this viewpoint we shall examine some ideas about the nature of man, and question whether his aggressiveness has been an intelligent reaction to threat or whether it is some kind of berserk force that will prove his undoing. Certainly man has a tragic record of bloodshed behind him, and the world at present is not free from war. At the same time it is obvious that many countries do not go to war, and many men in warring nations do not want to serve. Arguments regarding the nature of man, although fascinating, do not point consistently to the same conclusion.

In asking whether the problems of war and aggression are amenable to solution, we can also ask whether social institutions and agencies of control might be the answer, even if mankind is seen as basically aggressive. Past wars have ended when former antagonists have been united under one government as in the United Kingdom. If such institutionalized arrangements can be seen to make peace a possibility, then warfare meets the criterion of other social problems—a danger amenable to solution.

INTERRELATIONSHIPS

The interrelationships of the problems of war and aggression with technical change may seem so obvious as to need little further comment, but there are complications that should be recognized. The titanic power developed by modern nuclear weapons is so excessive as to be dysfunctional in the limited wars that have been fought since World War II; consequently, it cannot be said for certain that the industrial giants will win all wars. Another aspect of social change—the ability to mobilize around an ideology—has a great bearing on the problems of war and peace. When underdeveloped countries begin to adopt the techniques of the Western world and succeed also in mobilizing their people, the balance is in doubt. Consequently, the United States was stalled for years in Korea, France had to give up her struggle in Indochina, and the war of the United States in the same region threatens to be a military and political failure.

War is, by nature, deeply involved in moral issues. Students of the sociology of conflict have pointed out that, although norms are usually violated during conflict, the violation is seldom total. People usually perceive themselves as fighting for a great and good cause, regardless of how badly the methods of achieving that cause violate their own norms. In the Vietnam War, however, many American soldiers are unable to see any great cause being served, and the result is a fight without conviction and spirit. As mentioned, incongruities are often seen more clearly as the educational level of a population increases. To reconcile a belief in peace with a defensive war is quite easy even for the educated; to reconcile the image of a peace-loving nation with a war far across the world, on behalf of a government that is far from democratic, places a heavy strain on the rationalizing process. As we shall see, there are conceivable grounds for rationalizing such a war, but they have not been made clear to the American public, nor are they the types of arguments that have very great appeal.

PERSPECTIVE ON THE SOCIAL NATURE OF MAN

Implied in the emphasis on war as the "ultimate problem" is the idea that the solutions to many other problems depend upon the prevention of war. Scientific genius is concentrated in the services of war and defense more than in any other area; equally great genius is needed elsewhere. War and the preparation for war and other war-related expenses take up nearly half the federal budget; the money is needed elsewhere.

In our perspective on the problems of war, human societies will be viewed as capable of living at peace, even though they have about pursuing military careers. Attempts have been made before now to develop international organizations capable of resolving disputes between major powers. Such organizations have proved very helpful in minor disputes and have also developed agencies for international cooperation in such areas as health, food supply, and air-sea rescue. There are also cases of countries joining together economically until they may eventually be linked so securely as to make war an impossibility. Such a development now includes two old enemies, France and Germany, and all the Common Market countries realize that modern boundary lines that interfere with trade are cultural lags.

Since political and international organization involves the resolution of many factors—economic rivalry, pride in full national sovereignty, and many age-old ethnocentric attitudes—it is not surprising that such an organization as the United Nations could not achieve the objective of an international legal order all at once. We have seen examples, though, of the gradual growth of

15

Is there something basic and inborn about the nature of man that, under the right circumstances, makes him a killer? Or is the aggressive nature of man something that is generally subordinate to his intelligence? Do societies, including the United States, socialize their children into patterns of violence? If socialization patterns are the explanation for the majority of human violence, then does it follow that proper socialization can make all people peace loving?

Since human beings cannot be understood in isolation, these questions should also be asked in an interactionist perspective. Are there certain characteristics of social interaction that are sure to lead to occasional conflict? If so, can these interaction problems be avoided by the abandonment of ethnocentrism, national rivalries, and economic vested interest in expansionism and war industries?

In an attempt to answer some questions about human aggressiveness, we shall examine the common assertion that the United States is a violent society. Some events, present and historical, will attest to our violence, but other events will seem to point in the opposite direction. What is the significance of such a development as public disillusionment with a war? This chapter, more than any other, will raise more questions than it answers; but if it accomplishes its purpose, it will demonstrate that man is a very dangerous type of ape, but not beyond hope.

THE KILLER APE

The world of man and beast has never been a peaceable kingdom, and the lion and the lamb have not yet lain down together. Mammals of nearly all species fight fairly frequently. Sometimes they fight against intruders of other species, but more often they fight against their own kind, for dominance, for territory, or for mates. Rarely, however, are contests of will continued to the death; in most species there is some kind of built-in mechanism that prevents the dominant from killing his antagonist if the antagonist will but yield. The instinct seems to be stronger in such dangerous animals as the wolf than in those that rarely fight.[1]

The only species of animal that seems to display no instinctive controls which would prevent the total destruction of his kind is Homo sapiens, or "thinking man." Man is fond of telling himself that he is unique among the animals, a creature ruled by intelligence rather than instinct, a creature of keen perceptions, of imagination and foresight, and of linguistic ability for conveying thoughts and feelings and warnings based on past experience. Yet this creature is also unique in his tremendous capacity to kill. Raymond Dart, discoverer of the first of the early South African skulls that have cast so much light on man's remote origins, believes that man's ancestor was unlike the other great apes. He was carnivorous; he learned to club his prey with the lethal blows of clubs made from the bones of antelopes. He was the killer ape.[2]

There is no uniformity of opinion among anthropologists as to who was the direct ancestor of man or as to what significance it would have if man's remote ancestor were a prowling, meat-eating animal rather than a harmless herbivore. Of one thing there is no doubt, however: man has generally behaved as though his ancestors were killers. His history is drowned in blood, the blood of his own species, sometimes even of his own kinsmen.

We would be doing an injustice to the killer ape if we denied that his descendants have sometimes overcome their aggressive tendencies. Sometimes even their conflicts are sporadic and limited by various types of rules, as are the conflicts of many other types of animals. Before we give up hope for the killer ape, we must ask under what conditions he lives at peace with his kind and whether the aggressive tendency can be manipulated by man.

CONFLICTING IMAGES OF MAN

There has always been a philosophical argument as to whether human nature is essentially good, but corrupted by the problems of existence, or whether human nature is essentially brutal and controlled only by firm social regulations. The third alternative—that suggested by John Locke—is that the human being is simply a blank slate to be written on by cultural and social experience. The first point seems plausible

[1]Konrad Lorenz, *King Solomon's Ring*, Thomas Y. Crowell Company, New York, 1952.
[2]Raymond A. Dart, *Adventures with the Missing Link*, Harper & Row, Publishers, Incorporated, New York, 1959, pp. 112–114.

because man is capable of close cooperation and even noble self-sacrifice. The second viewpoint is supported by other types of evidence, because man is capable of aggression, pillage, and cruelty. The third viewpoint, although perhaps exaggerated, has the advantage of seeing mankind as variable, with different cultures helping to determine whether he becomes kindly and cooperative or violent and aggressive. The idea of man as purely the product of socialization has become very prominent in sociological thinking, by implication, if not by explicit statement. Two prominent sociologists, however (Dennis Wrong[3] and Amitai Etzioni[4]), have criticized this as an "over-socialized" concept, and suggest taking a new look at basic human needs and predispositions. Other writers go further and agree with Dart that we already have good clues to the basic predispositions of man. Such a writer is Robert Ardrey.

THE TERRITORIAL IMPERATIVE Originally a playwright, Ardrey has become deeply engrossed in the scientific questions about the nature and origins of man. A popularizer of knowledge rather than a researcher, Ardrey is subject to criticism for exaggerating his point of view. However, his attitude toward the human species is interesting and worth discussion here, especially his view of human nature and instinct. For years instinct has been thrown into the refuse heap as far as human behavior is concerned. Ardrey brings back the idea of instinct in modified form, contending that it applies to territoriality. The human being, as he sees him, is inclined to defend territory, and should therefore be called a territorial species. Instinct may be a completely set pattern, as with bees, ants, and termites, or it may be an open pattern, as for territoriality with many forms of animals. Of the latter, Ardrey says "The disposition to possess a territory is innate. The command to defend it is likewise innate. But its position and borders will be learned. If the animal is of the herding type, the predisposition to be with the herd is innate; the membership of the herd will be learned, and the territory will be learned."[5]

Ardrey, in his point of view, attempts to follow the thinking of certain animal ethnologists and anthropologists, including Lorenz and Desmond Morris. Lorenz also speaks of the nature of territorial defense. "In every individual the readiness to fight is greatest in the most familiar place, that is, in the middle of his territory."[6] Lorenz also adds some comments about animal behavior that almost make the distinction between human learning and animal instinct disappear. He reminds us of the presence of social rank or "pecking order" in many animal groups and of how similar human behavior is to animal behavior in this respect. He also says that in animal bands antagonism is greatest between individuals who are only slightly different in

[3]Dennis Wrong, "The Oversocialized Conception of Man in Modern Sociology," *American Sociological Review*, vol. 26, pp. 183–193, April 1961.
[4]Amitai Etzioni, "Basic Human Needs, Alienation and Inauthenticity," *American Sociological Review*, vol. 33, pp. 870–883, December 1968.
[5]Robert Ardrey, *The Territorial Imperative*, Atheneum Publishers, New York, 1966, p. 23.
[6]Konrad Lorenz, *On Aggression*, Bantam Books, Inc., New York, 1967, p. 32.

social rank, and fairly benevolent feelings often exist toward those whose social position differs greatly. In his social-class studies, W. Lloyd Warner could have made the statement in almost the same words.

LORENZ ON AGGRESSION   Lorenz has the advantage over Ardrey of being a lifelong student of animal ethnology and one of the world's widely read scientists. In *On Aggression* he investigates aggressive behavior, rather than the merely defensive behavior that is part of territoriality. He shows that aggressive behavior has two or three minor functions: (1) outcompeting another species for a barely adequate food supply; (2) "mobbing" a potential enemy, as crows have been known to mob a fox when they are numerous enough to have the upper hand; and (3) fighting when cornered. Occasionally aggressive behavior has the function of territorial competition, but overwhelmingly it serves the purpose of sexual competition and it functions for the strengthening of the species. Since adult males often fight over mates, aggressive instincts guarantee that the strongest males will get the largest number of mates and sire the largest number of offspring. The consequence will be the development of a species with males capable of enough fighting behavior to protect the herd.[7]

Occasionally, however, there will be a strange result of mate competition. In a few bird species, mates have been won most easily by males with the brightest and largest feathers, rather than those with the greatest strength. The result has been the development of a species in which the females make the choice of mates, and the male birds of gay plumage develop their attractive trait until it becomes dysfunctional for fighting and sometimes even for flight.

Similarly with the human being, the aggressive behavior that may have developed among males in competition for females has eventually resulted in an aggressiveness which has become dysfunctional. The ambition to reach for positions of prestige has been helpful to a degree in organizing and controlling all animal groups, but it may have been carried too far in a species that can devise deadly weapons. Aggression can be turned not to its primary biological purpose of strengthening the species, but to species destruction. It might be objected that man has the mental capacity to straighten himself out from such a tendency, since man is governed so much by reason. But all the inconsistencies between man's reasoning capacity and his ability to act irrationally in groups, says Lorenz, begin to make sense when it is realized that man "is still subject to all the laws prevailing in all phylogenetically adapted instinctive behavior."[8] He even goes on to say that the social organization of humans is similar to that of rats, who are generally peaceful within their clans, "but are veritable devils toward all fellow members of their species not belonging to their own community."[9]

[7]*Ibid.*, pp. 20–45.
[8]*Ibid.*, p. 229.
[9]*Ibid.*, p. 230.

412

THE COMMON PRIMATE PATTERNS Many physical anthropologists engaged in the study of primate behavior see their study as not only of theoretical importance but of practical importance because of the light it sheds on human behavior. They say that we may best find ourselves by first finding our relatives and learning their ways. David Hamburg[10] summarizes some recent evidence on aggression in the higher primates, especially chimpanzees, gorillas, and baboons. Expectedly, the chimpanzee behavior (based on Jane Goodall's years of observation in Tanzania), comes closer to that of humans than does the behavior of other primates. There is competition and occasional conflict over food, over maternal defense of infants, and competition for females. There is also conflict over dominance and the prerogatives that go with social rank. There are two particularly disturbing types of aggression that are repeated in human behavior. One is the redirection of aggression down the hierarchy, that is, "taking it out" on those of lower rank for the abuses caused by those of higher rank. This characteristic is terribly reminiscent of the behavior of boys' gangs, of social-classes, and of races, especially where one group outranks another.

The other human trait among the chimpanzees that we would wish were not human is aggression toward the strange-looking individual, what we humans would call the stigmatized or the foreigner. The baboons, a little more aggressive by nature, fight for all the same reasons, a little more frequently for desired goods or desired places, and more easily on contact with a strange group of their kind. Many of these behaviors undoubtedly have a functional importance in some situations, but all can be carried to a point of destructiveness, especially by a more advanced relative of the chimpanzees and baboons. The disposition to draw boundary lines and to attack the strange and unusual provide limitless possibilities for both protection and mass slaughter.

A REFUTATION There is considerable difference of opinion in the social sciences. Even those familiar with the field of biology may have interpretations very different from those of Lorenz. Ashley Montagu, an anthropologist with a thorough background in biology and medicine, is vehement in his opposition to any explanation of human nature that even comes close to the concept of instinct. Primate instinctual drives have been suppressed, he says, and replaced by the much more adaptive mechanism of human intelligence. "If there are any residues of instincts, they amount only to such insignificant matters as a natural fear reaction to loud noises or to falling. For the rest, man has no instincts."[11]

As Montagu sees aggression, it will have to be accounted for in other ways. It can, of course, be an intelligent force of adjustment for driving away potential foes. It is also possible that aggression is instilled in people by particular socialization

[10]David Hamburg, "Recent Evidence on the Evolution of Aggressive Behavior," *Engineering and Science*, vol. 33, pp. 15–23, April 1970.
[11]Ashley Montagu, *Culture and the Evolution of Man*, Oxford University Press, New York, 1962, Introduction.

Learning the violence pattern, at play,
in the movies, in folk tales, on TV, and
in public attitudes.

patterns and values of the culture in which they live. Geoffrey Gorer,[12] an anthropologist with views similar to those of Montagu, feels that the idea of basic human aggression is refuted by the presence of a few tribes of people who seem to display no aggression whatever (the Arapesh of New Guinea, the Lychas of the Himalayas, and the Pygmies of the Ituri Forest). His conclusion about all these pacifist tribes is that they have one trait in common: a cultural pattern that lacks any "cult of manhood," based on fighting and dominance. In all the pacifist tribes he mentions, boys and girls grow up with similar character trait expectations.

We shall later refer to pacifist societies whose peacefulness has broken down on occasion, but we shall have to agree with Gorer at least to some degree. Certainly socialization patterns are important. Just as certainly there is no universal urge that causes all young men of all societies at all times to go marching off to war, even though human history has been, admittedly, bloody.

VIOLENCE STUDIES   A study about the effects of observing violence on television succeeded in demonstrating that subjects were more prone to violence for several hours after watching the program than before. They could be roused to greater anger over an argument than would normally be the case. The disposition to violence was particularly strong when a program was observed that showed righteousness triumphant, but only at the cost of resorting to violence.[13] The author of the study did not agree with the often-stated opinion that observation of violence is useful because it "drains off" aggressive tendencies. His study would indicate it does more to build them up.

A similar study showing cartoons of violence to children resulted in approximately twice as many acts of aggression against toys and other objects as for a control group that had not witnessed the violent cartoons.[14]

It would be a mistake to conclude from such studies that television or motion pictures are the *cause* of violence. The reason so many pictures are of violence is

How many of our people use a socialization process that encourages an aggressive cult of masculinity? See how many members of the parental generation would agree with the statement, "Boys should be taught never to run from a fight," and how many would say the opposite, "You can never settle anything by fighting."

[12]Geoffrey Gorer, "Man Has No Killer Instinct," in Herman K. Bleibtreu and James F. Downs (eds.), *Human Variation*, Glencoe Press, Beverly Hills, Calif., 1971, pp. 119–126.
[13]Leonard Berkowitz, "The Effects of Observing Violence," *Scientific American*, vol. 210, pp. 35–41, February 1964.
[14]Albert Bandura et al., "Imitation of Film-mediated Aggressive Models," *Journal of Abnormal and Social Psychology*, vol. 66, pp. 3–11, January 1963.

that the total story-telling tradition of the Western world is full of violence. Children's fairy tales are violent—when they involve baking the old witch in an oven (Hansel and Gretel), or slicing open giants (Jack the Giant Killer), or merely boiling a wolf alive in a stew pot (The Three Little Pigs). Myths and legends of the European tradition are also violent—the Niebelungenlied, the Homeric tales, Icelandic sagas, the legends of King Arthur, the *Chanson de Roland*, and *El Cid*. More recently, Western stories have replaced the older tales but have continued the dual function of entertaining and defining manliness.

The most obvious conclusion of studies of television and movie violence is that they seem to temporarily raise the level of adrenalin in the blood. The studies also lead to speculation as to whether all types of violent stories can do the same thing, and whether a tradition of recounting such stories helps to forward the violent tradition.

A SUMMARY OF AGGRESSION-LEARNING THEORY Alberta E. Siegel[15] presents a summary of the case for considering violence controllable through proper socialization. Her major points, drawn from very creditable psychological experiment and authority, are that aggressive behavior is learned largely through observation and even through rewards. Boys in particular are rewarded by the plaudits of others for being scrappy, for not "taking it lying down." Aggressiveness runs in families but, she says, not for reasons of heredity, but of socialization. There is a correlation between parental punitiveness and a child's tendency to be aggressive. The aggressive families, tending to be lower class, are likely to award aggression more in word and deed than do well-placed middle-class families. Aggression and violence can also be interpreted as attempts to cope with a difficult environment, sometimes arising out of frustration and reaction against frustration and sometimes arising among gangs of boys who find no way to status except through successful fights.

On another point Siegel comes fairly close to agreement with the animal ethnologists mentioned previously. She speaks of man as being "primed" to learn aggressive behavior, especially the young male. Man is primed to learn speech, but he will learn it only under conditions of interaction with others who speak. Similarly, man is primed to learn aggression, but he may or may not actually learn it, depending upon whether situations rouse him to great anger, whether aggressive behavior can be effective, and whether his culture condones violence.

VIOLENCE AND CULTURAL PATTERN In the United States we vacillate between praising our peace-loving qualities and sounding the alarm over our proneness to violence. Actually, a majority of societies show an ambivalence regarding violence. Occasionally, however, societies have made a fetish of all things military and have unblushingly

[15]Alberta E. Siegel, "Violence and Aggression are not Inevitable," in Michael Wertheimer (ed.), *Confrontation: Psychology and the Problems of Today*, Scott, Foresman and Company, Glenview, Ill., 1970, pp. 196–199.

glorified the virtues of combat above those of peace. Ancient Sparta is an interesting example, tending to prove that if the individual is primed for aggression under the right circumstances, society is capable of finding those circumstances. Another example is that of the Danes and Vikings and of the old English prayer "From the fury of the Northmen, Lord God protect us all."

That many cultures have specialized in warfare is so well known that further examples are unnecessary. It should be noted too, however, that the pattern of violence has not continued forever in all violent societies. The descendants of the Northmen — the Norse, the Swedes, and the Danes — seem infinitely far removed from the berserk fury of their ancestors, and Sparta is but a peaceful town in the Peloponnesus. There seems to be some reason for saying that as cultures change, the character of the killer ape changes. Can we find a culture in which his nature has always been serene and where he seems headed for the Peaceable Kingdom?

THE NONVIOLENT SOCIETY   There are nations that have not gone to war for many decades, but the reasons are various. By careful diplomacy the Swiss have avoided war for long periods of time, and so have the Swedes, but a question remains as to whether the reason is the successful building of a distinct personality. Such people seem much like the other Europeans around them, all of whom profess to be peace loving but often go to war.

In the primitive world there are several tribes who have completely peaceful ways of life, but sometimes because they are isolated from possible enemies. One tribe that is not isolated from potential enemies, but that has nevertheless been an outstanding example of nonviolence is the Semai tribe of the bamboo jungles of the Malay Penninsula, described by Robert K. Dentan.[16] The Semai believe in a complex type of taboo called *punan*. *Punan* is a restriction against doing injury to any other person, and it is also the consequence of such an injury. To hurt another person or to make him unhappy will result in his becoming accident prone, and he may injure himself severely. A violent people might say, "Good, I will injure you, and then you will become accident prone; so much the better." The Semai do not think this way. They say anger is bad, and to injure anyone is bad. Their neighbors think of them as timid or weak; they think of themselves as good people, as proper Semai, and therefore better than the outside "barbarians." They are appalled that the Malays hit their children and they ask themselves "What if you hit a child and he died!" Good people just don't hit anyone.

Even with the Semai, of course, disputes arise. Sometimes one accidentally offends another, and in this case the offended person complains of feeling ill and of having bad luck and accidents. He and his relatives look for apology and compensation, and usually receive it. If the offender is unwilling to concede, a kind of unofficial

---

[16]Robert K. Dentan, *The Semai: A Non-Violent People of Malaya,* Holt, Rinehart & Winston, Inc., New York, 1962, pp. 55–64.

court manages to bring him into line. The greatest threat that exists for the accused is that of having to suffer the ill will of the people around him; that is too much to endure.

What happens to such people, then, when a situation of war arises? During the Communist uprising in Malaya in the 1950s, the British managed to recruit Semai into the army. At first it did not dawn on the Semai that soldiers were expected to kill, but the day came when Communist terrorists killed some of their kinsmen, and suddenly the nonviolent society was ready to kill. Dentan says:

> A typical veteran's story runs like this. "We killed, killed, killed! The Malays would stop and go through people's pockets and take their watches and money. We did not think of watches or money. We thought only of killing. Wah, truly we were drunk with blood!" One man even told me he had drunk the blood of a man he had killed.[17]

The killer ape is not easily tamed!

To those who might attribute the latent violence to a suppressed childhood, it should be added that the Semai are quite permissive with their children. The only thing Dentan discusses that a psychologist might grasp as an explanation for latent hostility is the practice of frightening children about strangers and the supernatural. They tell children that if they are bad, the pale people (English) might stick hypodermic needles in them. The *Nyani* (evil spirits) might eat children, and if boys are bad their testicles will swell enormously. Fear is strongly instilled, and even adults are frightened by their own teachings. Since thunder and lightning are forms of violence, they are frightening to children and adults alike.

NEITHER APE NOR ANGEL The Semai are an unusual people, and it is not the intent here to imply that violence on the part of people of nonviolent training proves that man's aggressive nature is not amenable to modification. It is considered important, though, to show the persistence of violence, and to emphasize that, despite the growth of the behavioral sciences, there is much that is mystifying about the pattern of violence. Of course, any psychologist would find fault with the rearing pattern of the Semai children, with its use of fear, and with the insistence on a great amount of restraint. Certain other strongly restrained people have been able to show greater-than-average aggressiveness once the controls are released. Ruth Benedict concluded that the early repression of Japanese children made them particularly prone to violence in times of war.[18] Mead interpreted the fascination of the Balinese people with violent witch-and-dragon plays as a dramatization of aggressive impulses that had always been thoroughly suppressed.[19] At least one study reported for the Na-

[17]*Ibid.*, pp. 58–59.
[18]Ruth Benedict, *The Chrysanthemum and the Sword*, Houghton Mifflin Company, Boston, 1941.
[19]Margaret Mead, "Children and Ritual in Bali," in Margaret Mead and Martha Wolfenstein, *Childhood in Contemporary Cultures*, University of Chicago Press, Chicago, 1955, pp. 40–51.

tional Commission on the Causes and Prevention of Violence[20] implies that psychic tensions mount in a strongly suppressed childhood, even if the means of suppression are not physical punishment. To keep their separate integrity, certain Indian tribes have maintained internal discipline at the cost of tensions that produce irritability and constant charges of witchcraft.

It seems theoretically possible that there is a middle course between encouragement of aggression on the one hand and too much repression on the other and that such a course would achieve a relatively peaceful personality. Psychologists note how much more common violence is in families that are violent in their disciplinary methods. Sociologists note the same of subcultures that teach and condone violence or that are so suppressed and antagonized by society as to form a reaction against it. Although it is impossible to make an angel of man, the killer ape impulses can be modified. Whether they can be eliminated is still questionable.

INTERACTION AND CONFLICT

Neither inborn tendencies nor socialization patterns can explain human violence and warfare entirely. Even the most hostile creature would not fight if nothing ever occurred to provoke him. An inquiry into the nature of violence and aggression, then, must also be an inquiry into the characteristics of human interaction.

TORTS, INSULTS, AND REVENGE It is not possible even for the peace-loving Semai to get along together day after day without certain frictions arising. Within their tribe they settle such friction without violence, but in many other tribes people resort to violence in such cases, fighting over women, property, or insults. Often the fight is for direct revenge by the injured party. In better organized states the problem of revenge is left up to the state and its police force. The state itself has been defined by anarchists as "organized violence," and the expression makes sense at least to the point of describing an organization that takes over the problem of violence for injured parties.

In primitive nonstate systems, revenge usually becomes the duty of family or clan. Sometimes the problems of revenge lead to incessant quarrels between groups of families until definitions of "good people" and "bad people" arise. There is probably no better description of the situation than that given by Jules Henry in his study of the Kaingang Indians[21] As seen by the outside observer, each band is precisely the same as all the others. They seem to be kind, friendly people, with very strong affection for each other. Yet each band thinks of the others as monsters, committing

---

[20]Bernard J. Siegel, "Defensive Cultural Adaptation," in Hugh Davis Graham and Ted Robert Gurr (eds.), *The History of Violence in America: A Report to the National Commission on the Causes and Prevention of Violence*, Bantam Books, Inc., New York, 1969, pp. 764–787.

[21]Jules Henry, "The Personality of the Kaingang Indians," in Yehudi Cohen, *Social Structure and Personality*, Holt, Rinehart, and Winston, Inc., New York, 1961, pp. 12–23.

murder, incest, and all other horrendous crimes with complete abandon. Each Kaingang Indian develops the attitude that his own group is morally superior to all others, that his people are the good people, the only ones that are completely human. In this type of thinking, called ethnocentrism, all human beings are Kaingangs.

ETHNOCENTRISM AND CONFLICT Ethnocentrism is characteristic of all societies. There are, however, differing degrees of ethnocentrism. United States citizens are ethnocentric about their country, and Canadians are ethnocentric about Canada, but the attitudes are not dwelt upon to the extent of becoming dangerous. One reason is that the two countries have similar values and customs, but there is also the fact that they have a long tradition of peace with each other. Animosities have never been strong. Ethnocentrism tends to grow strong in cases of struggle for survival—a point not always noted in discussions of the topic. Ethnocentrism and conflict bear a hen-and-egg relationship to each other. It is hard to say which is the prior cause, but there is no doubt that the two reinforce each other and help to account for the process of escalation.

ESCALATION OF CONFLICT Conflicts, whether they are within a society or between societies, have a tendency to escalate. William Westley[22] has an interesting analysis of the three-step process of escalation. Whether the conflict is a matter of mob or riot, police action, or war, there is a tendency for the participants to be organized on three levels of increasing violence. The mass of observers of a mob or riot condone a certain degree of violence just by the act of watching; similarly, the public, in hiring a police force or an army, is asking for a force ready to use violence to an acceptable degree. Within the leadership, however, whether it is the mob or the official forces, there are some who are ready to take on the real action. Within the action group, too, even though it is more violent than the general public, there are limiting rules that the majority adhere to fairly well. It is only in times of real crisis that the third step is condoned. Within the group primed for violence there are always some who love violence, who are actually sadistic. These are the people who are remembered in the long-continued and bitter wars between Turk and Greek, between English and Irish, between German and French, between black man and white man.

The United States in Vietnam has been caught in a trap of escalation. The Viet Cong are cruel. In return, the South Vietnamese and the Americans become increasingly cruel. In a few cases the final acts of atrocity have been left to a handful of sadistic men, but their actions have been kept secret, almost condoned. The best known episode is that at My Lai, but news reports and rumors mention many more cases. In regard to My Lai, the officer convicted of multiple murders may be a man who belongs to the third level of escalation, possibly a man who enjoys killing; but

[22]William A. Westley, "The Escalation of Violence through Legitimation," *The Annals of the American Academy of Political and Social Science*, vol. 364, pp. 120–126, March 1966.

the other two levels of escalation have prepared the way. The longer a war lasts, the more tendency there is to condone the sadists and simply let them have their way. The killer ape emerges in a form that would cause all his simian relatives to turn away in revulsion.

POWER, CONTROL, AND TERRORISM Sometimes terroristic violence is not merely a matter of passions and hatreds getting out of hand. Sometimes it is a matter of policy. Ghenghis Khan and his followers used terrorism as a tactic, boasting of the carnage that would take place in cities that refused to surrender. The ancient Assyrians and Hittites did the same, and so did Joshua at Jericho. In modern times terrorism as a tactic has been associated with totalitarianism, especially with Hitler, Mussolini, and Stalin, but it was by no means confined to totalitarian lands or regimes. Hiroshima was bombed, after Japan attacked Pearl Harbor, to terrify Japan into surrender.

Sometimes terrorism arises without real intent. A foreign army attempts to patrol a territory, but the task becomes increasingly difficult as acts of defiance occur. Under such circumstances entire civilian populations are punished for such actions. Any such punishment leveled against whole populations is terroristic. Sometimes it is limited to fairly mild measures, but under conditions of escalation it can become sadistically cruel. Terrorism is a constant possibility wherever occupying armies are stationed.

ECONOMIC AND TERRITORIAL CONFLICT The conservative founders of the discipline of economics viewed man as a primarily economic animal. The radical opponent of the early economists, Marx, agreed completely with the idea of economic man, and even went so far as to interpret all history as an economic struggle between classes. The completely economic picture of man is an exaggeration, of course, for man does not live by bread alone. However, much of the cause of warfare has been basically economic, sometimes rather subtly so. When the white man drove the Indian off his territory in America, he was essentially depriving him of his economic means of existence, and improving his own economic opportunities. An economic explanation of war in such a case is certainly more plausible than Ardrey's idea of a territoriality instinct, and much simpler.

Economic rivalries over the materials and markets of the world helped to bring about World War I. In the case of World War II the economic motivations were hidden behind a veil of racist ideology, but Hitler's very word *lebensraum* (living space) was an announcement of his intent to take the lands and resources of other people. Such recent historical experiences have given plausibility to the Dart-Ardrey interpretation of human nature.

ECONOMIC PROMOTION OF WAR In the 1930s there were a number of books addressed to the proposition that war was caused largely by the "merchants of death" — salesmen involved in the enormous profits of the munitions industry, persuading all countries that they must arm more and more heavily. Senator Gerald Nye was strongly convinced that economic vested interest was the primary reason for war. The view was undoubtedly exaggerated, but he gave several convincing examples of how good salesmanship had helped to sow the seeds of suspicion between countries and increase the likelihood of conflict.

Recently there has been a reawakened interest in the economic promotion of war. Bernt Englemann[23] relates how weapons have been illegally smuggled into both sides in several of today's chronic conflict situations—India and Pakistan, Israel and Egypt, and to revolutionary and counterrevolutionary forces in Cuba. The operations of the munitions salesmen make it impossible to bring danger spots of the world under international arms supervision.

If we had only the sinister merchants of death to worry about, however, we might be able to handle the situation. The much greater problem that has received increasing amounts of publicity in recent times is the tendency for the entire population to develop a vested interest in munitions. Industrialists and the military brass receive most of the blame, but the fact is that much of the public is worried about the cancelation of any military contracts, not because of a known strategic need for the weapons, but because of jobs and prosperity. Colonel James Donovan states the matter well:

> In addition to satisfying the Strangeloves of military technology and the Pentagon careerists, it (the arms race) offers a livelihood to millions of Americans, in and out of uniform, whose primary concern is merely to earn a living for their families. The industries and businesses which fill military orders have become the largest single producer of goods and services in the United States and the armed services the largest single consumer organization.[24]

To accuse a rather idealistic nation of deliberately promoting militarism for the sake of prosperity would be going too far, but it is possible for vested interest to interfere with judgment. It is an unusual congressman who is willing to turn down a

---

What percent of local jobs are dependent on defense contracts? (The U.S. Statistical Abstract of the Census Bureau gives statistics on miliary contracts and employment for each state. More detailed information is available from the Office of the Secretary of Defense, Records Management Branch, Correspondence and Corrective Branch, OASD (A) Pentagon, Washington, D.C. 20301. There is a charge of $1 to $5 for the latter.)

---

[23]Bernt Englemann, *The Weapons Merchants,* Crown Publishers, Inc., New York, 1968.
[24]Colonel James A. Donovan, *Militarism USA,* Charles Scribner's Sons, New York, 1970, p. 44.

lucrative, profit-yielding, and employment-creating military project for his own district, regardless of how superfluous he might believe it to be.

CONFLICT AND IDEOLOGY Those who would find economic rivalry as the single root of war should look also at the ideational side of the argument. The ethnocentrism discussed previously is to quite an extent ideational. There is, of course, such a thing as racial ethnocentrism, derived mainly from the different appearance of the out group, but essentially ethnocentrism is a cultural matter. When a very strongly held religion or ideology becomes so basic to a culture that the outsider is a "dog of an unbeliever," then the religion or ideology can help to promote war. The Crusades of the Christians against the Moslems are the best-known historical examples, but the utterly devastating Thirty Years War was also largely religious, with two types of devout Christians slaughtering each other madly, until Europe was exhausted, starved, and to a great degree depopulated.

The economic determinist can argue that there were subtle undertones of economic rivalry and power struggle about the religious wars of long ago, and there certainly were economic implications to the largely ideological World War II, but belief systems cannot be omitted from the study of war. When the war in Vietnam is discussed by political radicals, it is often pictured as a war of United States imperialism, fought for economic advantage. Yet most of its proponents have seen it as a noble struggle to preserve a nonexistent democracy from the inroads of communism. It also has to be interpreted as a matter of jockeying for position in a frightening world balance of power, in which two great ideological systems stare at each other across a chasm of mutual ignorance.

CONFLICT, FEAR, AND GAME THEORY Fear is always a component in war. The problem would be simple if fear could be dismissed as pure nonsense, but throughout history man has given his fellow man adequate reason for fear. Yet, tragically, there is mounting evidence that people cannot think clearly under conditions of fear. What fear seems to do, physically, is to rush adrenalin into the system in preparation for fight or flight, but not for prolonged rational reflection. Certain types of experimental evidence point out the problem.

Game simulation of the conditions leading to World War I found the players making the same mistakes as the statesmen did in the actual events leading up to the war.[25] Mounting anxieties make people oblivious to various alternatives and make them settle on the one possibility of fighting like trapped animals. Other research on fear reactions found people increasingly willing to accept the judgment of the leader and to follow orders without reflection. In the conditions of teamwork, so important in warfare, independent judgment was foregone and "group think" became part of the process.

[25] John R. Rasor, "The Failure of Failsafe," *Transaction*, vol. 6, pp. 11–19, January 1969.

Stanley Milgram[26] found that even under ordinary conditions of the experimental laboratory, large numbers of subjects would obey the researcher unthinkingly and administer to experimental subjects what they were led to believe were extremely dangerous electrical shocks. When judgment is impaired by fear and great need for following orders, unintelligent orders can be followed even further. In "The Charge of the Light Brigade," Tennyson expressed the idea before the age of psychological experimentation:

> Not 'though the soldiers knew
>   Someone had blundered;
> Theirs not to make reply,
> Theirs not to question why,
> Theirs but to do and die.

There are, then, compulsions toward the diminution of intelligence in some cases under conditions of fear and combat. The case is so bad that Rasor[27] argues that our present fail-safe systems, aimed at preventing the accidental precipitation of war, are not really safe. The intelligence of the human diminishes, and basic emotional reactions come to the fore, fed by fear and rage at the enemy and dependence on the leader.

This long list, far from exhaustive, of the interaction situations that can lead to war is not very encouraging, and yet the picture is not hopeless. There are probably ways of dealing with all the problems mentioned. Certainly a beginning step would be the development of societies that place a high value on peace and orderliness, and statesmen who see their duty as the highest art of man. Restraint and diplomacy are needed, but do the societies of today produce them? The greatest need for calm rationality is in the United States, which has for many years assumed the role of leader of the free world. Although the United States might have to cope with military affairs, the safety of the world depends upon facing military problems in a spirit of rationality and calm. In some periods of our history we were thought of as a country of considerable calm and detachment in our international position. More recently even our friends have worried about our political turbulence and unpredictability. Recent events have even caused us to be thought of as a violent society. Is the charge actually true?

Try to recall personal experiences or look up articles on collective behavior showing how fear impairs sound judgment.

---

[26]Stanley Milgram, "Some Conditions of Obedience and Disobedience to Authority," *Human Relations*, vol. 18, pp. 57–76, February 1965.
[27]Rasor, *op. cit.*

THE VIOLENT SOCIETY?

It was pleasant to believe, as most Americans once did, that we had never fought an unjust war, had never lost a war, and were distinctively civilized. After a recent series of political assassination, large numbers of city riots, student uprisings, and incessant protests over our most unpopular war, we have put an end to that blissful myth. Possibly we have even gone overboard in our reaction against it. Elliott Currie[28] argues that the myth of a peaceful America has been supplanted with the myth of a uniquely violent society. He objects to what he calls the new myth on various grounds, but one of his most important objections is that it sometimes seems to produce a fatalistic consequence, viz., we are violent, all of us, we always have been, and we might as well get used to it. The new myth also leads us to miss what is perhaps the biggest issue in internal violence — the matter of suppression and resistance to suppression. Except for occasional official violence on the part of the police, there were times in the early days of Hitler's power when Germany had a high degree of internal order — no riots, no strikes, no protests, no open strife of any kind. Did that mean Germany was a nonviolent society? There is always a need to ask what kind of violence? Violence by whom? Is the violence accepted or resisted?

Examination of these questions will reveal that the United States has certain specialty traits in violence, but that they fall well within the normal range for Homo sapiens.

INTERNAL VIOLENCE It is hard to deny that the United States has had an uncommon amount of internal violence. The disturbing prevalence of political assassination caused the appointment of the last presidential commission on violence. In its reports the commission added details to what was already known. We have a high homicide rate, and high rates of crimes of violence in general. The report on the history of violence[29] discusses various kinds of collective violence, which has also been common in the United States. There are sections about vigilantism, labor violence, racial violence, Southern violence, and Western frontier violence. The very mention of types of violence reminds us that the history of the United States is very different from the histories of the countries of Western Europe in the last few centuries, and it has therefore produced different patterns of violence. Frontier traditions, heterogeneity, and the history of slavery and racism are explanations, but not excuses. In a comparative study of violence in the 1960s, one of the writers for the commission reports that the United States ranks first in violence among the seventeen democratic nations of Western Europe and the British Commonwealth, but only slightly ahead of France, Italy, and Belgium.[30] Violence is serious in the United States, but by no means unique.

[28]Elliott Currie, "Repressive Violence," *Transaction*, vol. 8, pp. 12–15, February 1971.
[29]National Commission on the Causes and Prevention of Violence, *op. cit.*
[30]*Ibid.*, p. 579.

EXTERNAL VIOLENCE If by external violence we include violence against any group perceived as an outside enemy, then the history of the United States in regards to the American Indian would have to be included. Most Americans are now familiar with the story of unprovoked aggression, treaty breaking, and general swindling relative to the American Indians. There is less willingness to think about several other aggressive episodes in our history. The war against Mexico in the 1840s can be defended only on the basis of fussy legalisms; there is no question as to who was the actual aggressor. The "splendid little war" (as Teddy Roosevelt called the war against Spain) could have been avoided. Recently, Stuart Miller has compared a portion of that war with the Vietnam War.[31] The war in the Philippines was characterized by corruption, brutality, and one general's order, "Kill everyone over ten." The parallels to Vietnam are striking, even down to the rumors, the confirmations, and the reactions to statements about torture. One soldier confessed to torturing 106 Filipinos, all but 26 of whom died in the process. The only redeeming fact was that the "splendid little war" became more and more unpopular, especially when it turned to the suppression of the Filipinos themselves. Protests ranged all the way from the Senate building, college campuses, and the press to industrialist Andrew Carnegie.

As bad as the record of the United States was in the suppression of the Filipino insurrection, it could be duplicated by the record of almost any country of the modern world in its contacts with what we now call the underdeveloped world. England, Russia, France, Germany, Belgium, Italy, and Japan have been involved in actions ranging from Africa to China. Industrial societies, in their incredible ethnocentrism, hardly looked upon "natives" as members of the human race.

THE GUN TRADITION One of the difficulties in recent years that has made the United States seem more violent than most comparable countries has been the tradition of carrying a gun. It is interesting to recall how strong the outrage was against free access to guns by practically the entire American public after the Robert Kennedy assassination. Nevertheless, almost nothing was done, in spite of one or two years of very serious talk. Certain strongly antigun members of Congress were defeated, including Senator Tydings of Maryland.

A result of the gun tradition has been far more deaths when riots occur in the United States than when they occur in most other countries. Japanese students and radical demonstrators can mount impressive, raging demonstrations. Very few deaths occur, however, because no one ever told Japan it was everyone's God-given right to bear arms.

HOW HARD ARE THE HARD HATS? It has been assumed that the less-educated working class of the American public is strong for war, and the attacks of "hard hats" against student peace demonstrators has been considered the final proof. There is some

[31]Stuart C. Miller, "Our Mylai of 1900: Americans in the Philippine Insurrection," *Transaction*, vol. 7, pp. 19–26, September 1970.

STOCK NO. 5543

LITTLE BURP®
GUERRILLA GUN T.M.
BY MATTEL

BAP!
BRRP!
BAP!
BURP!

RAPID FIRE MACHINE GUN BURST ● SINGLE SHOT TRIGGER FIRE ● SMOKING BARREL
AUTHENTIC CAMOUFLAGE ● WIRE STOCK ● FIRES GREENIE® PERFORATED ROLL CAP

Guns from cradle to grave.

question, though, about whether working-class America is particularly warlike. In many European countries, labor parties have been peace and anti-imperialist oriented for many years. Must we assume that Americans are entirely different? There is some reason for believing that attacks of the hard hats against peace demonstrators are more an attack on a young student counterculture than on pacifists as such. The working-class man has usually been only through high school, where he has been taught rather rigidly in the sacredness of patriotic traditions. To protest openly, to make slurring remarks against his country, and, especially to show disrespect for the flag is, he believes, the ultimate in sacrilege.[32] Long hair also excites his animosity as something at best weird, and at worst degenerate, although this attitude may be changing.

Dr. Harlan Hahn[33] of the University of California at Riverside made an election analysis that casts doubt on whether labor-class people are actually hawkish. In

[32]Robert E. Lane and Michael Lerner, "Why Hard Hats Hate Hairs," *Psychology Today*, pp. 45–48, 104–105, November 1970.
[33]Tom Paegel, "Hard Hats Tend to Be Dovish, Study Finds," *Los Angeles Times*, November 12, 1970, Section I, pp. 3, 28.

analyzing voting precincts in three California cities and one Eastern city that had voted on withdrawing from the Vietnam War, Hahn found working districts to be strongly antiwar. In his interviews with representative samples of the population, he found great awareness of the fact that their sons serve in much larger numbers than the sons of the upper-middle class. Nearly all knew at least one person who had been killed or seriously wounded in Vietnam. Many resented college students, but more because they considered them draft dodgers than for opposition to the war in principle.

RELUCTANT SOLDIERS If America is indeed a particularly violent nation, the violence does not show up in the form of eagerness to serve in the armed forces. It could possibly be argued that those from poorer home backgrounds are reared with more physical violence, therefore have more violent dispositions than the middle class and are therefore more willing to serve. Even if the argument has a grain of validity, though, it needs supplementing. The more obvious explanation of a social-class difference in recruiting is that the college-bound middle class is better at getting exemptions than are the school dropouts or those who stop at the end of high school. Whereas nearly 40 percent of college-age men go to some kind of college at least for a while, only 10 percent of those drafted have had any college experience.[34]

It could be said of those who were sent to Vietnam a few years ago that most absorbed the fighting attitudes they were supposed to acquire. Now, a real dedication to the work of slaughter is rarely encountered. The dedication is primarily to getting out alive. The catch word has changed from a rather fatalistic "Sorry about that" to "You owe it to yourself." The high brass still takes great care to convince reporters that all is under control, that our men are great fighters, that they are dedicated. The statement begins to ring as hollow as did the earlier statements that there was no drug problem among our fighting men. By the standards of most armies the pay is acceptable; food and conditions are made about as good as possible under combat conditions, the brass is less overbearing than in the past, and there are GI benefits to be derived from the service, but none of these inducements attracts many recruits.[35] The boredom increases, the drug problem grows worse, there are more

---

Do you have a draft counseling service on your campus? If not, write to
Central Committee for Conscientious Objectors, 437 Market Street, San
Francisco, Calif. 94105 to see about getting one started. Know your rights.
Another helpful address is Beacon Press, 25 Beacon St., Boston, Mass. 02108

---

[34]Ward Just, "Soldiers," *Atlantic Monthly*, vol. 226, p. 75, October 1970.
[35]Editors of *Newsweek*, "The Troubled U.S. Army in Vietnam," *Newsweek*, vol. 77, pp. 29–37, January 11, 1971.

Reluctant soldiers; no urge for battle.

reported incidents of failure to obey orders, and more threats to "frag" officers who are too overbearing. Fragging refers to lobbing a fragmentation grenade at such an officer. Only a few cases of such an action have been verified, but the rumors and talk are incessant.[36]

The college students who are drafted are particularly difficult for the traditional army, and animosity exists between them and the career men, the "lifers." Many others begin to grow increasingly discontented and disillusioned with the war. Actually very few Americans have taken readily to military life, and the fact of complaint, boredom, insubordination, and even the floating of rumors about fragging or its equivalent are not entirely new. But the heart of the problem today is that "many young men feel no particular obligation to serve the nation in its armed forces."[37] Furthermore, those who refuse to serve find that they are honored by many of their countrymen.

[36]*Ibid.*, p. 34.
[37]Just, *op. cit.*, p. 77.

The army's greatest difficulty is with those who are young and fairly well educated. There are, especially since the armed forces have relaxed on their mental tests, large numbers of dull soldiers, those with IQs of about 80. "There is no radicalization of the dull. . . . The army keeps them out of trouble by sending them to war."[38]

There is a much more surprising quarter from which military disenchantment seems to be on the increase—at West Point itself. Chaplain James Ford of West Point is quoted as saying "There are two boats which are sinking today, the military and the church, and I have got a foot in both."[39] There is much discontent on the part of old officers about the young. The young do not show the dedication expected. Many state their intention of finishing their education and then resigning. There is no admiration for the grand tradition, no glory. "There are no heroes anymore," said one disillusioned cadet.[40]

THE SIGNIFICANCE OF RELUCTANCE Does the reluctance to serve in the Vietnam War have any real significance to the consideration of a violent society? Certainly there are some aspects of the present war that make it a special case—the very fact of a long stalemate, the presence of American forces without much to do, the lack of support from home, a few well-documented and many rumored cases of extreme atrocities, the growing hatred of our troops by the very people we are supposed to be helping, and a disillusionment with the "democratic" state of South Vietnam Perhaps it is only a passing episode and the attitude of people toward war will return to tradition in later years. Whatever else the present mood demonstrates, it is clear that under some conditions a very large segment of America can take a stand against war. It is hardly necessary to say more. Even if man is a kind of killer ape, the right conditions can cause him to reflect and reason.

It is time to return to the opening theme of this chapter and to previous quotations from Lorenz. Although he speaks of man as being subject to the instinctive drives of his phylum, he ends his book on a note of optimism. Man also has intelligence, and the very drives that have worked him woe are subject to redirection into harmless channels. At present, after years of stalemate and living in the valley of the shadow of the bomb, America and much of the rest of the world are looking for new directions in the search for survival.

[38]*Ibid.*
[39]*Ibid.*, p. 71.
[40]*Ibid.*, p. 68.

SUGGESTED READINGS

Atlantic Monthly, vol. 226, October 1970, contains an article, "Soldiers," by Ward Just, giving special-issue treatment.

Examines changing attitudes of soldiers, decline of the military hero tradition even at West Point.

Graham, Hugh Davis, and Ted Robert Gurr (eds.): *The History of Violence in America: A Report to the National Commission on the Causes and Prevention of Violence*, Bantam Books, Inc., New York, 1969.

An excellent anthology of articles on internal violence—immigration, the Western tradition, racial violence, labor violence, and violent crime. A few articles deal with the theoretical question of whether the United States is an unusually violent society.

Lorenz, Konrad: *On Aggression*, Bantam Books, Inc., New York, 1967.

Pictures man as a clearly recognizable part of the animal kingdom with many of the same mechanisms of aggression found in other species. In the conclusions of Lorenz, this does not mean man is beyond hope for a peaceful existence, but he needs to be well warned of his essential nature and provide harmless outlets for his emotions.

Morris, Desmond: *The Naked Ape*, Dell Publishing Co., Inc., New York, 1967.

An entertaining book, but one that gives attention to the dangerous potential of man (the naked ape). Man's ancestors had to develop ferocity to drive off enemies, says Morris, and he now frequently turns that ferocity against his own kind.

Donovan, Colonel James A.: *Militarism USA*, Charles Scribner's Sons, New York, 1970.

Colonel Donovan fears a growing fascination with the military in American life, brought on by both necessary and unnecessary wars of recent times, the entanglement of the military in government and industry, and the vested interest of too many people in keeping up defense spending.

 **QUESTIONS**

1. What is the evidence pro and con for looking upon man as a naturally aggressive species?

2. What are some of the ways in which our society may be socializing children into a pattern of violence?

3. Why can we not be certain that even a peaceful socialization pattern will create an entirely nonviolent personality type?

4. What is the relationship between ethnocentrism and conflict?

5. How can economic considerations become a factor in war?

6. Is the United States a particularly violent society? Give evidence pro and con.

The staring eyes of a bomb-test manikin reflect the
horror of nuclear war.

The Roman peace, whose glories are somewhat romanticized in the above passage, was won by the expansion of empire and by the gradual conquest of all rivals. Greece had been incorporated into the system, the Ptolemaic and Seleucid Empires had fallen, Carthage was defeated, and long ago Hannibal, broken and defeated, unable to find asylum, had taken his life.

Whatever the ills of Rome, there was a legend not only of grandeur but of peace. Small wonder that many attempts were made to reconstitute the Roman Empire. When Charlemagne of France succeeded in carving out a large empire in Western Europe, he declared himself the successor to Rome. A later manifestation of the dream of unity was called the Holy Roman Empire. Apparently a well-chosen name was expected to help restore the order that had existed in European affairs. Over the centuries the Holy Roman Empire declined to the state of the ludicrous — "neither holy, nor Roman, nor yet an empire," in Voltaire's famous phrase.

OTHER PAX ROMANAS   A Roman peace is possible only when one social system gains complete ascendancy over all those around it. When the civilizations of the circum Mediterranean were all united, they constituted an advance in technology and organization that was beyond the power of outside enemies to overthrow. There have been times in history when China has held a similar type of supremacy in the Far East, benevolent emperors have ruled the "Middle Kingdom," and the Temple of Divine Harmony has seemed well named.

The expression Pax Britannica has sometimes been used to describe much of the nineteenth century, for England, not by size but by productivity and naval power, was able to control much of the world. "Britannia Rules the Waves" was more than just a song. Although the rise of Germany under Bismarck toward the end of the century was causing a degree of anxiety, the nineteenth century was, generally speaking, a British century. Well could Kipling say of Queen Victoria (in "The Widow at Windsor"):

For kings must come down
And emperors frown,
When the Widow at Windsor says, "Stop."

PAX AMERICANA   The end of World War I left the United States in a remarkably strong position in relation to the rest of the world. The only major participating power not left exhausted by the war, the United States became the financial and industrial capital of the world, but public sentiments of isolationism and the able political maneuverings of the isolationists in the Senate caused us to stop short of a role of world leadership. World War II was very different, however, and the United States assumed the leadership role eagerly. For a brief moment in history we alone had the bomb, and the wreckage of Hiroshima warned all rivals against any direct confrontation with the United States. Vast amounts were spent on postwar reconstruction, revitalizing economies and purchasing gratitude. Old enemies were quick to scramble to the side of

The clouds that started at Alamagordo and exterminated Hiroshima now proliferate in the deadly testing games of the United States, France, Russia, and China.

the United States, and Russia and her satellites felt the cold chill of diplomatic isolation.

There were limitations to the Pax Americana, however. For one thing, the atomic weapon was excessive for the new international situations that were to arise. One does not rid his house of roaches by leveling it with a steam roller; neither does he crush peasant uprising with nuclear bombs. There were strong possibilities that the hegemony of the United States would be nibbled away by uprisings here and there and by stealthy acts of aggression too limited to call for the utlimate deterrent. Finally, there was the realization that a monopoly of power could not last indefinitely, and it did not. Within a few years new clouds were gathering in the sky, and they were mushroom clouds, billowing out of Russia and China, and joining in the deadly game the United States had started at Alamagordo and Hiroshima and Nagasaki. Challenges to the unilateral leadership of the United States had been anticipated, however. American leadership had never really expected to achieve a new type of Roman peace in the world that moves so rapidly and had, instead, placed great hope in other methods of seeking peace—international systems.

UNIVERSAL SYSTEMS

Pax Romana systems, as we have seen, are rare occurrences in the world, and can exist only when superior technology and power make one state supreme over all others. So rapid is the spread of scientific and technical skills and knowledge today that it would be madness to expect any one country to long remain the arbiter of world affairs. There are other situations in world history that have called for a different type of imposed system of peace. The eighteenth century ended with the French Revolution, and before the beginning of the nineteenth century Napoleon was learning to manipulate the forces of revolution and French nationalism to his will. By the time of his downfall, nearly all parts of Europe had heard the roar of his cannon and the cry of *Liberté, egalité, fraternité*. Kingly heads had rolled, and there had been fear for all the aristocracies of Europe, a fear of general revolution and the triumph of the masses. Although Napoleon had changed a republic into an empire and had subdued the radicalism of earlier days, he had, in the minds of the kings, only spread the infection of revolution more widely. When they closed their eyes and listened they could hear "the tumbrils toiling up the terrible way" to the *Place du Guillotine* and could almost feel the blade. Consequently, upon the fall of Napoleon, a great international system was formed to keep the peace and to make the world safe for monarchy.

THE QUADRUPLE ALLIANCE   The Congress of Vienna, in 1815, under the guidance of Prince Metternich of Austria, defined the borders of Europe, placed a crowned head on each throne, and swore to maintain the status quo forever. Students of United States history know that our ancestors saw the reactionary Metternich as a threat to us and to the independence movements of the restive countries of Latin America and that we reacted with the Monroe Doctrine. Great Britain, ever distrustful of the continental powers, soon disassociated herself from the alliance, and even the Czar of Russia showed disappointment, having expected something more idealistic along the line of a League of Nations. Nevertheless, the Metternich system had its day, and from 1815 until 1848 revolutions, nationalistic stirrings, and potential wars were blocked. By 1848, however, everyone was ready to rebel, and almost everyone did. Most of the uprisings in various countries of Europe were suppressed, but the old alliance of Metternich drew to a close, never to be revived.

The most valid generalization to be drawn from the period of the Quadruple Alliance is that a modern age was being born, in which aspirations for national independence and rule by the people were becoming impossible to suppress indefinitely.   439

There were also gaps in the system, for it never did have the enthusiastic support of Great Britain, the colossus of the nineteenth century.

THE LEAGUE OF NATIONS The nineteenth century was ushered in by what amounted to, but was never called, a world war. The twentieth century began with the diplomatic maneuverings that were eventually to fail and bring on the first great conflict to be so called—World War I. In one important respect the war was very different from that of the age of Napoleon—the victors considered themselves to be the champions of freedom and democracy, although they had been joined by such strange allies as the Czar of Russia and the Emperor of Japan. In spite of a claim for liberalism and enlightened internationalism, the allies were much more severe with their defeated enemies than the Quadruple Alliance had been with France. Germany was partly dismembered, and the old empires of Austria and Turkey were pulverized. Even Russia, which had been one of the allies in the first part of the war, suffered the loss of her western territories and was treated as an enemy because she had gone Communist. The reaction against communism was an almost perfect parallel to the reaction against republics in the days of Metternich.

The second great international system collapsed because it started in a spirit of bitterness and recrimination, allowed Germany and Russia to join only after it was already moribund, and was never joined by the United States, for reasons only an expert in the mysteries of American politics could explain. The League of Nations, however, had been founded in a dream, a dream of a truly united world. Its failure was manifest early in its life, but the hope did not die. Perhaps there would be another chance.

THE UNITED NATIONS Another chance did occur, and the United Nations was born. This time great care was taken to learn the lessons of history and not to duplicate previous mistakes, but historical predicaments are never precisely the same, and what might have worked in the 1920s did not work in the post-World War II period. The great lesson learned was not to exclude the vanquished enemy or other potential antagonists. The defeated powers were all eligible for membership in the United Nations without signing a document admitting their guilt. Russia was included from the first, with the eminently reasonable explanation that it was better to meet a rival across the conference table than across the battlefield.

To many knowledgeable diplomats there was never a real expectation that the United Nations would serve the purpose of stopping potential wars between the great powers,[2] but to many idealists and to many common men, this was the expectation. The UN has been a success or a failure, depending on what one expects of such an organization. Like the League of Nations, it has provided a forum for discussion, and has promoted many helpful international projects: the aid of refugees, prevention

[2]Eugene Rostow, *Law, Power, and the Pursuit of Peace*, University of Nebraska Press, Lincoln, 1965, p. 4.

The United Nations, whatever its
weaknesses, represents another attempt
to substitute the conference table for
the battleground.

of famine, improvement of world agriculture and health, care of war orphans, and cooperation in air-sea rescue. It should not be forgotten, either, that the UN has helped to settle disputes between minor powers, such as Greece and Turkey, and in the past between India and Pakistan. At times the UN has been helpful in cooling down the long, intermittent war between Arabs and Israelis, although at present more traditional forms of diplomacy are being attempted. For those who dreamed of an international force that would make war an impossibility, however, the United Nations is a disappointment for several reasons.

One or two weaknesses of the United Nations are simply matters of structure and organization. Like the League before it, the UN has given priority to certain "great powers," making them permanent members of the Security Council. By a fluke of history, China went Communist soon after being accepted into the big five, and therefore for years one of the "great powers" was the tiny island of Taiwan, ruled over by the aged General Chiang Kai-shek. Insufficient allowance is made for the fact that the great powers of one period of history are not necessarily the great powers of another age. The China issue was debated for almost twenty-five years before Red China was accepted into the United Nations.

Although there is gross inequality in the Security Council, there is a strange type of democracy in the General Assembly. Each nation has one vote, whether that one vote represents the 540 million people of India or the 500,000 people of Botswana. More important, the vote doesn't really mean anything, since no country can be compelled to comply with decisions of the United Nations. It is the general reasoning behind the creation of an international organization without teeth that is the crux of the problem. Neither the United States nor Russia wanted to join an international organization that could actually have the authority to tell its government what to do. Consequently, each, along with the other permanent members of the Security Council, was given the veto power. Russia has used the veto power on many occasions, and the other countries hardly at all, but the important point is that neither the United States nor Russia was willing to surrender national sovereignty. In fact, among right-wing elements in the United States, there has been a vehement opposition to the United Nations just for fear it might someday acquire a measure of decision-making power superior to that of the nation. The doctrine of total national sovereignty is incompatible with a strong, effective international organization. The only world union that could ensure peace would be one with the power and the means to make and

---

Do you have a local chapter of United Nations Associates? If so, attend and make a study of its work. If not, write to the United Nations for informative pamphlets about its work.

enforce decisions. At present the great powers of the world are not willing to take a step toward that degree of internationalism. In looking to the United Nations in our search for peace, we can find it to be of some help, but far from a panacea. It will probably continue to perform a number of good services for the welfare of mankind and to help settle a few disputes between minor powers. Looking forward to the future, it could be used to set up agencies for the control of oceanic and atmospheric contamination and for the prevention of world-resource depletion. In the search for control over major aggression, we must look elsewhere, unless the nature of the United Nations changes in unlikely ways.

FROM BALANCE OF POWER TO BALANCE OF TERROR

If neither a Pax Romana nor an international organization seems sufficient for ensuring world peace, there are yet other methods to be tried. Although the nineteenth century has been called a British century, Great Britain did not rely on force of arms alone for guaranteeing her position in the world. The century began with the episode of Napoleon, who was suppressed only by the gathering of a grand alliance. The century ended with the emergence of Germany as a threatening world power.

THE BRITISH BALANCE OF POWER   Great Britain faced the rise of Germany, as she had faced other problems, by trying to maintain a balance of power in Europe. If one side seemed too weak, Great Britain took action to help that side; otherwise British statesmen feared a power vacuum of weakness on one side would invite aggression from the other. When Prussia defeated Austria, Denmark, and France in rapid succession and proclaimed the German Empire, she was becoming too powerful for the comfort of Great Britain. A number of years passed before British opinion, traditionally anti-French, began to shift. Eventually Russia and France joined an alliance which seemed much weaker than the combination of Germany and Austria-Hungary. Britain, to preserve the balance, signed with France.

U.S. APPROACH TO A POWER BALANCE   The balance-of-power type of diplomatic maneuvering looked sinister to the naïve United States, and she determined to follow an independent policy of nonalignment. The time was to come, though, when balance-of-power thinking became much more prominent in America. Russia assumed control over the "shatter belt" of Eastern European countries, and the United States took the leadership of the West. The situation was not exactly the same as the earlier balance of power, for it did not involve the manipulating of a number of major powers, only confrontation between the United States and the Russian bloc. President Truman declared his intention to protect any country menaced by Communist aggression—a doctrine first applied to Greece and Turkey.

In 1949, new tension was added to the confrontation between Russia and the United States when the American monopoly on atomic power came to an end. Russia exploded her first bomb, and the balance of terror had begun.

THE BALANCE OF TERROR The new balance was not perceived in terms of juggling existing systems of alliance, but rather of simple addition and subtraction. Each side could count steel production, nuclear weapons, and allies. There were many uncommitted countries in the world, and they were the remaining stakes to be gambled for. The United States felt hurt that the Republic of India decided to walk a neutral course and remain unaligned. Some elements in America tended to regard all neutrals as secret supporters of the U.S.S.R.

In the counting of bombs, steel, and allies, the United States came in far ahead of Russia for a number of years, and it seemed the terror balance was strongly on our side. Yet there was always fear in the balance-of-terror situation, fear that communism could not be contained within its existing territorial limits. The fear became greater when China fell to the Communists, for in those days there was a certainty about the idea of monolithic unity—the idea that all Communist powers would work together in close accord, and all would be directed from the Kremlin. There was even a myth that every untoward event in the world was the consequence of a "Lenin time plan," which had to be blocked at all costs.

The first costly attempt to stop the spread of communism occurred in Korea, where the Communist North started an invasion of the non-Communist South. The United States was able to turn the defense of South Korea into a United Nations action. To its strongest supporters the Korean action was seen at first as a vindication of trust in the United Nations, because the General Assembly had called upon member nations to assist in the resistance against aggression. Actually, most of the fighting and the final decision about peace was left to the United States and the Republic of Korea. The total action became more a matter of maintaining balance of power than of building the United Nations into an international police force.

THE ARMS RACE A balance of power depends upon weapons as much as upon allies. Whenever the level of weapons development increases on one side, the other side must react. In recent times, an arms race has occurred that dwarfs all the arms races that have ever taken place before. The American military budget is about 80 billion dollars per year and for many years has never been less than 7 or 8 percent of Gross National Product. Bruce Russell[3] presents figures to show that, typically, there is not only a reduction in consumer spending as arms expenses increase, but there is also a negative impact on investment in capital goods. Investment in capital goods is closely related to economic growth and prosperity. War investment could be one of several reasons for the slow growth rate of the American economy in the last five years. The international balance of payments, according to Russell, is another serious casualty of the arms race, occasionally resulting in a worrisome gold drain. In Russia, investment in industry continues despite arms costs, but consumer goods production bears the brunt of the cost.

444 [3]Bruce M. Russell, "The Price of War," *Transaction*, vol. 6, pp. 28–35, October 1969.

A much more serious problem is the fact that no amount of weaponry brings security. If terror is in balance, the world is probably safer than if it is not, but there are differences between the balance of today and that of the nineteenth century. In earlier times, additional weapons seemed to make sense, but once there are enough weapons to destroy the enemy many times over, further accumulation makes no sense. Another difference is well stated by foreign affairs expert Hans J. Morgenthau:

> It has often been said that throughout history each new weapon has called forth a defense against it. That may have been correct for conventional weapons. It is certainly incorrect for nuclear weapons; for the destructiveness of nuclear weapons is so enormous that it dwarfs all possible defense.[4]

Despite Morgenthau's comment, we all know there are antiballistic missiles. Why do they not constitute the required defense?

ABM AND MIRV As the years go by, the names of war devices and their levels of sophistication change, but the present arguments about ABM and MIRV illustrate the self-defeating nature of the balance of terror. After the two colossal powers, the United States and the U.S.S.R., acquired stockpiles of nuclear weapons, their next step was the development of delivery possibilities, first by heavy bombers then by intercontinental ballistic missiles (ICBMs). By mid-1970 the statistics in the balance were approximately as in the table below.[5]

The statistics showed the two countries to be approximately even, the situation generally regarded as safest. Too uneven a situation calls for the weaker side to accelerate production to gain the advantage, to seek new allies and strategic positions, or conceivably to seek the advantage of surprise attack.[6] By 1970 forces were already at work to upset the fairly even balance. Each country was aware that its rival was studying the possibility of improved antimissile missiles. If one country could make itself secure against missiles, then its advantage would be very great,

[4]Professor Hans J. Morgenthau, in Erwin Knoll (ed.), *American Militarism 1970*, The Viking Press, Inc., New York, 1969, p. 67.
[5]"The Real Issue in the ABM Showdown," *US News & World Report*, vol. 69, pp. 19–21, August 17, 1970.
[6]George W. Rathjens, "The Dynamics of the Arms Race," *Scientific American*, vol. 220, pp. 15–25, April 1969. See also, Herbert F. York, "ABM, MIRV, and the Arms Race," *Science*, vol. 169, pp. 257–260, July 17, 1970.

	U.S.	Russia
ICBMs	1,054	1,250
Submarine-based missiles	656	200
Long-range bombers	500	150

Peace now, or at least the containment
of conflict, or the whole world could
become a scene of moonlike desolation.

until the other reached the same state of preparedness. Even then there would be another phase of development, the MIRV (multiple independently targeted reentry vehicle). An ABM intercepts a missile in flight, exploding the atomic warhead before it reaches its destination. A MIRV seeks out the bases of enemy ICBMs. The effect of clear superiority in these two classes of weapons would be to make the unthinkable war seem thinkable, with the hope the enemy could be destroyed without the attacker facing destruction—an unlikely event. When one country makes advances in such systems, the other feels compelled to keep full parity. Since neither is sure what the other is planning, each feels compelled to develop more than a sufficiency. Hence, we now have overkill in ICBMs and ABMs and will eventually have overkill in MIRVs. Rathjens suggests[7] a policy of frank disclosure of developments and intentions, not just as a warning to Russia, but also to lessen the uncertainty and the chance of overreaction on their part. He also advocates strategic arms limitation agreements. The present administration in Washington also favors arms limitations but seeks to use more ABMs to pressure Russia into bargaining. Russia frequently expresses a desire for arms limitation, too, but each side is so suspicious of the other that little or no progress has been made.

It is obvious that there is no safety in a race that causes the continued production of bombs, missiles, antimissiles, and anti-antimissiles, ad infinitum. George Wald[8] estimates that Russia and the United States now have enough nuclear explosives to deliver the equivalent of 15 tons of TNT for every man, woman, and child. Their only way of grappling with the dread of such a situation is to build more bombs and outrace each other in the potential to deliver them.

A BOMB FOR ALL SEASONS At present the most influential American international relations expert is Henry A. Kissinger, a man reportedly closer to the White House than the Secretary of State. There is no question as to his knowledge of the field of foreign affairs. In his writings he shows a grasp of the unthinkable nature of allout thermonuclear war.[9] He is also brilliantly aware of all nonlethal channels of international influence—moral persuasion, economic pressure, and threat and bluff. He speaks also of the advantages of a strategic system that poses less absolute sanctions than allout war and that sees the possibility of limited, "contained" wars. During the nineteenth century there were a number of minor wars, which were not allowed to get out of hand, and Kissinger considers such situations possible today. He would like to prevent the present tendency to turn all conflicts into a part of the great East-West confrontation. Such a strategy, if followed, would represent progress over the all-embracing balance of nuclear terror.

[7]*Ibid.*
[8]George Wald, "A Generation in Search of a Future," MIT Address, March 1968, in Lloyd Sexton and Walter Kaufmann (eds.), *The American Scene,* Wadsworth Publishing Company, Belmont, Calif., 1971, pp. 261–268.
[9]Henry A. Kissinger, *Nuclear Weapons and Foreign Policy,* W. W. Norton & Company, Inc., New York, 1969, chap. 5.

There are two or three disturbing problems about the Kissinger philosophy, however. In his major book on weapons (*Nuclear Weapons and Foreign Policy*), Kissinger wrote in favor of tactical use of nuclear weapons: "With proper tactics, nuclear war need not be as destructive as it appears when we think of it in terms of traditional warfare."[10] The first edition of the book appeared in 1957, and his more recent *American Foreign Policy* (1969) implies a great change of opinion as to the possibility of tactical use of nuclear weapons.[11] Nevertheless, it is disturbing to read Hans Morgenthau's accusation that official Washington has considered a nuclear threat in Vietnam in very recent years.[12] According to Nora Beloff,[13] a British foreign affairs expert, Kissinger has daring points of view about playing a risky game in the international balance of power. Kissinger greatly admires Bismarck's statesmanship of an earlier period. His view of his task, says Beloff, is similar to that of Bismarck's—juggling many balls at once and taking calculated risks. In his recent book, Kissinger makes remarks that seem to call for a policy of "brinkmanship"—using bluffs and threats that could take the country to the brink of war, but without going over the cliff.

> For purposes of deterrence, the opponent's calculations are decisive. A bluff taken seriously is more useful than a serious threat interpreted as a bluff. . . . Psychological criteria vie in importance with strategic doctrine.[14]

What if someone uses a threat that is meant as a bluff, and it is interpreted as a bluff, and the bluff is called? In an age of nuclear terror, psychological gamesmanship is not reassuring.

FALSE ASSUMPTIONS

As we have seen, there is little possibility of making the world safe by any of the methods now in use. There are a number of other false assumptions that still linger, although the first of the following is finally being recognized as unreal.

Public pressure on foreign policy decisions is difficult, but Senate Committees are powerful in this field, and there are strong disagreements among senators. Find out the voting records and stands of your senators. Be sure to make your opinion known with letters of support or criticism.

---

[10] Kissinger, *op. cit.,* p. 152.

[11] Henry A. Kissinger, *American Foreign Policy: Three Essays,* W. W. Norton & Company, Inc., New York, 1969, pp. 65–78.

[12] Hans J. Morgenthau, "What Price Victory," *The New Republic,* vol. 164, pp. 21–23, February 20, 1971.

[13] Nora Beloff, "Professor Bismarck Goes to Washington," *Atlantic Monthly,* vol. 224, pp. 77–84, December 1969.

[14] Henry A. Kissinger, *American Foreign Policy: Three Essays,* W. W. Norton & Company, Inc., New York, 1969, p. 14.

MONOLITHIC UNITY The theory that the Communist world possesses "monolithic unity" has led to much confusion in the United States. Not all Americans have followed the assumption. Even as long ago as the Truman administration, financial aid was extended to the Communist regime of Yugoslavia, hoping to win its government over to a position of reconciliation with the West. Over the years, apparently, Yugoslavia has been won over to a position more friendly to the West. Attempted defections from the Communist bloc by Czechoslovakia and Hungary, on the other hand, have not worked. The latter countries were contiguous to Russia or of great strategic importance to her, and so important that their defection could not be tolerated. The obvious conclusion is that different strategic situations will help to determine whether a policy of monolithic unity can be maintained.

To view Russia simply as an ambitious country following its own self-interests may be more realistic than to interpret it as the center of a great, unified effort to subvert the entire world. Historically, Russia has always sought buffer states to her west and has reached toward warm-water ports. For Russia to give ground in a dispute over Yugoslavia or Cuba is understandable in these terms, and her stubbornness about Hungary and Czechoslovakia is equally understandable.

It is finally becoming clear to almost everyone that Red China is a potential enemy of the U.S.S.R. and has shattered what little unity existed in the Communist world. There are historical reasons for hostility between the two red giants. Russia in the eighteenth and nineteenth centuries spread eastward, occupying lands that had once been considered part of the Empire of China. In the 1920s Russia helped Mongolia against China to gain "independence"—a euphemism for making her a Russian rather than a Chinese satellite.

Probably more important than historical incidents in the antagonism between the two great powers is the simple fact that both Russia and Red China are colossal nations sharing the world's longest border, a border that is hard to defend. Their interests clash along most of that border, with each occupying land the other looks upon hungrily. Russia, with her relatively sparse and slow-growing population, must also be disturbed at the very multitude of her Chinese neighbors. The rift between the two countries first became obvious when Khrushchev started talking about peaceful coexistence with the West, indicating a declining zeal for being the missionary of world communism. China has also been incensed at Russia's partiality for neutralist nations.[15]

The diplomacy of the past has called for exploitation of such potential conflicts as that between Russia and Red China, playing one off against the other. Such a strategy is at least as old as Rome and was once known as *divide et impera* (divide and rule). This is not to suggest that the two red giants could be so completely separated as to make the policy of the United States simple and easy, but our policy

---

[15]Chow Shu-Kai, "Significance of the Rift between the Chinese Communist Regime and the Soviet Union," *The Annals of the American Academy of Political and Social Science,* vol. 372, pp. 64–71, July 1967.

of recent years could have profited from letting them drift apart, rather than taking actions that have tended to give them a common cause. Recent changes in policy toward China indicate a belated official awareness of new diplomatic possibilities.

As long as the idea of monolithic unity held, it seemed logical to assume that every Communist revolution or act of aggression could be interpreted as a whittling away at the non-Communist world. It seems possible, in retrospect, to interpret some of the "whittling" actions as the work of one or the other of the two great Communist powers against the other, not their concerted effort against the West. Jealousies over Southeast Asia could possibly have been exploited, but no such attempt seems to have been made. Instead, the United States followed the domino theory.

THE DOMINO THEORY   The late President Eisenhower once compared the countries of Southeast Asia with a row of dominoes. If you knocked over one of them, he said, the others would fall. Even before his time, work had been started on forming an organization called the Southeast Asia Treaty Organization (SEATO) to prevent the incursion of communism into that area of the world.

A portion of Southeast Asia had been carved out of the old Empire of China by France in the nineteenth century—a region then called French Indochina. At the end of World War II French Indochina was divided into its component parts: Laos, Cambodia, and Vietnam. France attempted to maintain control over Vietnam through the puppet emperor Bao Dai or at least to prevent Vietnam from becoming a Communist state. France fought a long, hard war but was finally defeated at the battle of Dien Bien Phu. The war was becoming too costly in money and lives to be worth continuing, and the French forces withdrew. The Red regime of Ho Chi Minh was recognized in the North, and Ngo Dinh Diem emerged as ruler in the South.

The northern regime seemed much more powerful and better organized than the south, and the United States saw yet another threat to the power balance. Many Americans assumed that any anti-Communist regime must be democratic and good and that its people must be desperately intent on being rescued by the United States.

THE RESCUE THEORY   In its attitudes, the United States is reminiscent of an old Oriental tale of the monkey and the fish, recounted by Don Adams.[16] A monkey was caught in a shallow stream just as a flood arose, and the stream became dangerous and threatening. The monkey managed to save himself by scrambling up a tree, but as he looked down he saw a fish in the water below him, hovering on the downstream side of the tree, seemingly afraid of being washed away by the flood. The monkey went to the rescue of the fish, lifted him out of the water, and brought him up to the safety of the tree. In a similar way the United States has sought to lift Southeast Asia out of the troubled waters of domestic turmoil.

[16]Don Adams, "The Monkey and the Fish: Cultural Pitfalls of an Educational Advisor," *International Developmental Review*, vol. 2, pp. 22–24, 1960.

Even the explanation for the intervention in Southeast Asia was never stated in terms meaningful to international relations experts or to interactionist sociology. The official pronouncements have described an attempt to save a freedom-loving people from dictatorship, even though it has been hard to disguise the regime in Vietnam as particularly freedom loving. It is a land where political opposition candidates disappear and political prisoners are held in tiger cages. The war would have had far more plausibility if it had been explained from the first as an attempt to maintain a power balance in the world. The explanation would have been less heroic than the idea of saving an infant democracy, but it would have been a little more credible. As it is, the credibility gap regarding everything Southeast Asian has grown steadily during two administrations.

THE IMMINENT COLLAPSE THEORY Another common American assumption is that no one will willingly fight for a Communist regime and that such regimes must be on the point of imminent collapse if they face war. Since the owner class is dispossessed by a Communist revolution, there is little doubt that Communist regimes do face opposition, but they face an opposition that is by no means universal and that has no way of making itself heard. It is also likely that much of the opposition dies down in the face of a threat to national integrity. Many historians would agree that in the early days of Russian communism the one thing that saved the regime from counter-revolution was the rallying of the Russian people behind Mother Russia when it looked as though their country was faced with invasion. Similarly, the small country of North Vietnam has fought with determination, first against France and then against the United States. Both countries have been startled and taken aback by the ferocity of the fight, rather like Macauley's description of a rabbit hunt by boys who

> Come to the mouth of a darkened lair
> Where, growling low, a fierce old bear
>   Lies amidst bones and blood.

The fierce old bear has proved far more stubborn than had been thought possible.

THE MYTH OF VICTORY What is much more disturbing than the very great difficulty of winning a "minor" war is the indication that there is no end in sight. Neither side seems willing to recognize the need for a compromise that would leave both sides unsatisfied, and yet often an unsatisfactory compromise is the only hopeful solution to a war. A really major victory on the part of the United States could easily drive Hanoi into the arms of Peking, even re-create an uneasy alliance between Peking and Moscow and start the plot for revenge. A major defeat could easily make a self-fulfilling prophecy out of Eisenhower's statement about a row of dominoes.

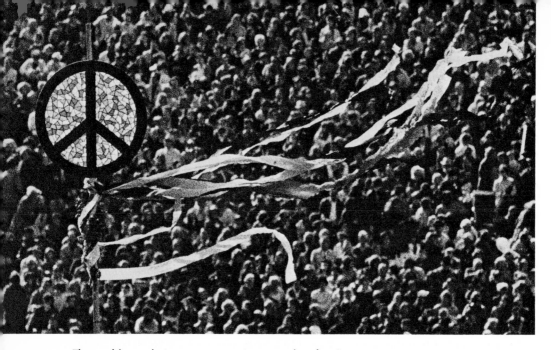

The revulsion against war—permanent, or a passing phase?

INTERDEPENDENCE AND COMMUNICATION   The trend of the world toward greater interdependence in economic matters has long been noted, and it continues to accelerate. Old enemies of Western Europe are now united in a Common Market, which is proving so successful that it would be difficult for France, Germany, Italy, and the Benelux countries to drift apart. The trend is toward economic unity, and the promise of the future is for political unity.

If one looks at Eastern Europe, the situation can be interpreted in different ways. The most pessimistic person can easily say that Europe has simply divided into two antagonistic blocs that are much larger and more dangerous than in the past. However, there have been recent talks between Germany and Eastern Europe, and the level of East-West trade is increasing. Channels of communication are kept open— the traditional diplomatic channels, trade channels, and the United Nations. The "hot line" between Washington and Moscow is a further indication of the attempt to avoid fatal miscalculations. Such a line is perhaps a desperation line, but it is better than no line at all. Charles Horton Cooley, one of the fathers of American sociology, looked upon wider channels of communication and understanding as the hope of the world. Time may prove him right. If he could but see international television via satellite, he would be sure the age of world understanding had arrived.

REVERSING THE ARMS RACE   Whatever good is accomplished by trade and communication is partly offset by the arms race. Rathjens was cited for demonstrating that any attempt of one of the great powers to get far ahead of the other in the arms race would bring greater danger rather than safety. His suggestion was to try to keep the arms race approximately in balance. Ross Stagner[17] suggests a policy, based on psychological principles, for going a step further and deescalating the arms race. His suggestion (for which he gives credit also to psychologist Charles E. Osgood) is that any reduction in arms will be seen by the opponent as a threat-reduction that may be reacted to. He does not advocate going very far with such a reduction; rather, he suggests making a series of gestures in that direction, always publicizing them to the world, and especially to Russia. For example, we could reduce our weapons bases in Spain or Turkey, advertise our action to the world, and suggest that Russia reciprocate in some way. If no response is received, we would have to stop at that point. Nothing would be lost, and a door might possibly open. Stagner also approves changing the tone of Radio Free Europe to appease Russian feelings. After all, we have made it perfectly clear that if our radio station helps to encourage insurrection in Eastern Europe we shall do nothing to help. We proved the point by nonintervention in Hungary, after our speeches had helped encourage rebellion in 1956. Why antagonize for no purpose? Stagner does not suggest we follow conciliatory policies indefinitely if there is no response, but he does ask that we give such policies several trials, especially in areas that do not immediately threaten our position.

CONVERGENT REORIENTATION   By the summer of 1970 we had spent more than 105 billion dollars on the Vietnam War, but nothing for peace research. Many millions of dollars per year are spent to sell the point of view of the Defense Department to the American people, and part of the effort includes the circulation of old hate-and-fear films dating from Stalin's time and indicating the impossibility of compromise. Fortunately, a few nongovernmental organizations are interested in how wars are ended rather than merely in how they are prepared for and how they are fought. The November 1970 issue of *The Annals of the American Academy of Political and Social Science* is devoted to a study of how wars end.

One of the interesting analyses of the termination of conflict is written by sociologist Paul Kecskemeti[18] of Brandeis University. Kecskemeti speaks of various outcomes of conflict: total defeat, a compromise acceptable to both sides, or a final desperate effort at survival when no compromise or surrender is possible. Regardless of how a war is ended, an important consideration is whether the peace treaty will last. Kecskemeti's suggestion is that peace will be fairly certain to last only if there is a "convergent reorientation," that is, a change in the original ideas of the antagonists.

[17]Ross Stagner, "An Arms Race in Reverse," in Michael Wertheimer (ed.), *Confrontation: Psychology and the Problems of Today,* Scott, Foresman and Company, Glenview, Ill., 1970, pp. 206–212.
[18]Paul Kecskemeti, "Political Rationality in Ending War," *The Annals of the American Academy of Political and Social Science,* vol. 392, November 1970, pp. 105–115.

The United States War for Independence is his first example. Following the war, Great Britain completely changed her ideology, no longer feeling it important to try to hold political possession of her former colonies. The result was continued trade and cooperation, resulting from convergent reorientation.

The question is whether such a reorientation is possible in today's ideological struggle between East and West. There are certainly indications that the two sides are more willing than previously to live and let live. The Korean War was settled, admittedly or not, on a reorientation basis—a mutual admission of the right to independent existence of the southern section of the country, along with an abandonment of any hope of eventual reunification under a non-Communist regime. So far, no such convergent reorientation has been achieved in Vietnam, and the Vietnamization of the war makes the likelihood even less. What is happening, though, is a reorientation of American thinking on the matter, with the majority of public opinion opposed to the indefinite pursuit of the war.

On the much larger issue of East-West confrontation, there is no indication of a convergence of opinion about communism and capitalism. However, there seems to be a reorientation of thinking to the extent that neither side sees the politico-economic system of the other as a threat to its existence. A convergent reorientation seems to be taking place in the direction of a doctrine of coexistence.

THE NEED FOR COLLECTIVE EFFORT   In the long run there is need for a stronger international organization than now exists. Peace alone is not enough. The world could not permanently rest with a mutual understanding between the great powers that might maintain only the peace of suppression. The Quadruple Alliance of Metternich, with which we started this discussion, brought peace, but it was too much the peace of the grave. Cases of large-scale injustice need to be heard; boundary lines and other international disputes have to be settled. The aspirations for independence of various subject peoples need to be examined by an international body. Complaints of racial oppression, cruel prisons, slavery, and other reprehensible conditions need to be exposed to the light of world opinion. The United Nations, whatever its defects of organizational structure, must be reinforced in its capacities to perform these duties.

So far, the United States, acting alone, has been unable to bring the desired reforms to the world. The nation born in a spirit of rebellion and freedom has frequently found itself supporting governments that represent old aristocracies and elite classes and that have little concern for the people. We have determinedly

---

> **Discuss and debate the possibility for eventually achieving some type of world organization powerful enough to prevent all wars.**

opposed the tyranny of communism without asking what other tyrannies have accounted for its appeal. We have known what to oppose, but not what to bring about. We have grasped the role of world leader, but have not known where to lead. A clearer understanding of the social drift of the modern world and of the aspirations of the underdeveloped countries is needed. Only by giving them a hearing in the halls of world opinion can we learn to realign ourselves with the forces of democratic change that can open the road to both peace and justice. Acting alone, we have succeeded only in sending our men to a series of foreign wars, asking them to die, unhonored and unsung, and even uncertain of their cause.

The land is troubled and the world is troubled, but the human race has survived many crises before. The menace this time is greater than ever before — so great that all comparisons pale to insignificance. Yet there are also possibilities for human existence in an abundance never before known. The crises of our times can be resolved only if the sciences of human understanding can be pursued in a spirit free of the hatreds and fears that debilitate the mind and soul of man.

SUGGESTED READINGS

Annals of the American Academy of Political and Social Science, vol. 392, November 1970.

> *The entire issue is devoted to a discussion of conflict resolution — historical, experimental, and theoretical.*

Douglas, William O.: *International Dissent: Six Steps toward World Peace*, Vintage Books, Random House, Inc., New York, 1971.

> *Justice Douglas worries over our futile attempts to establish a Pax Americana and our frequent support for entrenched upper classes in emergent nations. Then he turns to his six steps toward world peace — controversial, thought provoking.*

Deutsch, Karl W., and Stanley Hoffman (eds.): *The Relevance of International Law*, Anchor Books, Doubleday & Company, Inc., Garden City, N.Y., 1968.

> *Contains essays by such distinguished international relations experts as Hans J. Morganthau and Quincy Wright. Examines the meaning of international law, problems of colonialism and of equality among nation-states, and the possible fields for application of law among nations.*

Duffert, John (ed.): *Against the Crime of Silence: Proceedings of the International War Crimes Tribunal*, Clarion Books, Simon & Schuster, Inc., New York, 1970.

> *A shocking book, documenting a long record of war crimes, of many Songmys, torture for the interrogation of prisoners, and of the dropping of "about 200 pounds of bombs for every man, woman, and child in Vietnam" (quoted from Introduction, pp. xiv–xv).*

Kissinger, Henry A., *American Foreign Policy: Three Essays*, W. W. Norton & Company, Inc., New York, 1969.

> *Gives a good insight into the thinking of the man currently most influential in the formation of American foreign policy. Especially good on the dilemmas of deterrence and the fallacy of strictly bipolar conceptualization of international problems.*

Munves, James: *A Day in the Life of the UN: The Hundred Faces of Peace*, Washington Square Press, Simon & Schuster, Inc., New York, 1970.

> *A brief glance at the activities of a score of agencies working for international coopera-tion—Food and Agriculture Organization, International Labor Organization, UNESCO, International Bank for Reconstruction and Development, United Postal Union, and World Health Organization, among others. Also describes the work of the Security Council and the General Assembly.*

QUESTIONS

1. What is meant by Pax Romana? What similar attempts at world order have been made?

2. What historical lessons were learned from the Quadruple Alliance and the League of Nations that the United Nations tried to take into consideration?

3. Compare the old British balance of power with today's balance of terror.

4. Why does Rathjens conclude that a search for complete military supremacy is self-defeating?

5. What evidence can be raised against the theory of monolithic unity?

6. What proposals have been suggested for ending conflict and bringing about world peace?

A

ABMs (antiballistic missiles), 445, 447
Abortion, 8, 177, 220, 223, 224, 229, 230, 278, 280
Abrams, Charles, 40
Accommodation, 188, 190–192
Achievement ethic, 237, 251, 352
  (See also Protestant ethic)
Activists (see Student activists)
Adams, Don, 450
Adams, Sherman, 355
Addiction, 328, 337, 340, 343, 349
Adult education, 143
Advertising, 72, 83, 87, 89, 124, 342, 366
Aerospace industry, 23, 24, 126, 127
AFDC (Aid to Families with Dependent Children), 30, 251–252, 255
Affluence, 20, 278
AFL-CIO, 255
  (See also Labor unions)
Age-graded society, 157–164
Age sets, 157, 158, 159, 161
Aged, 149, 162, 163, 243, 295, 302
  homes for, 164, 248
  and poverty, 242
  and social security, 251
  welfare aid to, 240
Aggression, 7, 404, 405, 410, 411, 413, 415, 438, 443
  and human interaction, 419–430
  as learned behavior, 416
  Lorenz on, 412
Agnew, Spiro T., 113
Agriculture, 8, 17, 47, 126
  employment in, 129, 136
  and pollution, 59, 65
Aiken, Michael, 38
Air pollution, 15, 17, 51, 56
  and automobiles, 61, 64
  and city governments, 37
  control problem, 60
  and steel industry, 61
  (See also Pollution; Smog)
Air Quality Act (1967), 67
Alcatraz, 202

Alcohol, 9, 99, 161, 288, 322–330, 336, 337, 341, 349
  consumption of, 333
  drunk drivers, 83
  and group controls, 323–324
Alcoholics Anonymous, 340
Alcoholism, 306, 310, 323, 328, 333, 340
  and broken homes, 155
Alford, Robert R., 38
Alienation, 16, 107, 108, 116, 176, 218, 224, 343
  and poverty, 240
  and work, 138–139
  (See also Counterculture)
American Heart Association, 76
American Medical Association (AMA), 76, 294, 297, 303, 338
  and medicare, 302
Amphetamines, 329, 331, 336, 340
Anderson, Jack, 331
Anderson, Martin, 26
Andosterone, 315
Anomie, 11, 225, 290–291, 335, 352
Antisemitism, 203
Appalachia, 236, 239
  poverty in, 241, 244–245
Arabs, 442, 452
Arapesh society, 225, 415
Ardrey, Robert, 411
Ariès, Philippe, 149
Arkansas prisons, 399
Armed Forces:
  black officers in, 194
  drug abuse in, 330–332, 428
  military justice, 387–388
  Vietnam draftees, 428–430
  and white-collar crime, 355
Arms race, 444, 455
Ash, Ellis, 393
Assassination, 190, 425, 426
Assault, 349, 351, 354
Assembly line jobs, 130, 131, 134, 136
Atomic Energy Commission (AEC), 51
Atomic fallout, 275
Atomic power, 51, 62, 64
Atomic radiation, 7, 51, 52

International law, 388
IQ tests, 198, 199, 273
Isla Vista, California, 112
Israel, 422, 442, 453
Italian-Americans, 27, 360
Italy, 426, 454
  alcoholism in, 325
  welfare expenditures, 238

J

Jackson State College, 110
Jacobs, Jane, 26
Jails, 348, 374, 386, 393, 399
Japan, 64, 426, 440
  and mercury pollution, 56
  population stability, 283
Japanese, 183, 187, 203, 326
  relocation centers, 184
Jews, 184–186, 322, 323
Jim Crow laws, 9, 190–192
Jones, Victor, 37, 39, 226
Junior high schools, 98, 330
Juries, 384
Justice, 5, 7, 289, 291, 348, 373–400
  in Armed Forces, 387–388
  breakdown in, 384–388
  President's Commission on, 239, 360, 396,
    397
  without trial, 383–384
Justice Department, 87
Juvenile courts, 239, 395, 398
Juvenile crime, 239, 348, 352, 363
Juvenile delinquency, 4, 7, 16, 156, 290, 351,
    353, 365
  and divorce, 155
  and police, 380, 382
  and poverty, 255

K

Kaingang Indians, 419
Kansas prisons, 399
Kant, Immanuel, 374
Kecskemeti, Paul, 455
Kelsey, Frances, 75
Kelso, Louis L., 258

470

Keniston, Kenneth, 107, 108, 109
Kennedy, Edward, 303
Kennedy, Robert, 426
Kent State University, 110, 112, 113
Kenyatta, Jomo, 157
Kerner Report, 31, 175, 379
Kerr, Clark, 110
Keyserling, Leon, 257
Khrushchev, Nikita, 449
Kibbutz, 165, 168
Killer ape, 10, 410
Killingsworth, Charles, 136
Kindergarten, 96, 158
King, Martin Luther, Jr., 5, 190
Kinsey, Alfred E., 212, 316
Kirk, Dudley, 278, 282, 283
Kissinger, Henry A., 447, 448
Knauer, Virginia, 87
Kolko, Gabriel, 186
Komarovsky, Mirra, 153
Korea, 282, 283, 405, 444, 456
Kramer, John, 339
Kretschmar, Robert, 82
Kreuger, Ivar, 354
Ku Klux Klan, 187
Kwashiorkor, 239, 250

L

Labor, 17, 100, 124, 427
  alienation of, 138–139
  and black Americans, 188
  and Family Assistance Program, 255
  hours of work, 137
  and immigrants, 183, 185
  and middle class, 130
  problems of, 130–138
  in technological society, 140
  (*See also* Blue-collar workers; Farm workers;
    Migratory farm labor)
Labor unions, 124, 130, 175
  and organized crime, 362, 363
  and safety regulations, 133
  and women, 226
Laffin, John, 394
La Follette, Robert M., 201

O

P

R

Racial discrimination, 174, 352
  in employment, 30, 193–194
Racial inequality, 5, 7, 9, 107, 108, 112, 174
Racial problems, 25, 175
Racism, 32, 105, 110, 181, 190, 379, 425
  and Chicanos, 199
  institutions of, 193–195
  and police, 378
Radin, Paul, 323
Radio Free Europe, 455
Radioactive wastes, 51, 59, 62
Railroads, 180, 183–185
Rape, 349, 351
Rapid transport, 24
Rasor, John R., 424
Rathjens, George W., 447, 455
Rats, 270, 412
Rawitch, Robert, 392
Reagan, Ronald, 253
Recidivism, 399
Recreation, 23, 138, 166
Recycling, 65
Red Power, 203
Redevelopment, 39, 41
Redlich, Frederick C., 305, 306
Reds (see Barbiturates)
Regional government, 38, 41
Regional planning, 38
Rehabilitation, 397–399
Reiss, Albert J., Jr., 380
Religion, 10, 46, 162
Relocation in urban renewal, 26
Relocation centers, 184
Research, 103–105, 128, 140
Reshetylo, T. J., 309
Rest homes, 164, 258
Retirement, 137, 162, 251
Revolutionary technique, 112
Rex, Robert, 64
Riesman, David, 218
Riessman, Frank, 132
Riots, 30, 188, 190, 240, 348, 378, 420, 425, 426
Robbery, 349

Role expectations, 10
Role failure, 9, 290–291
Roles, 7, 16, 288
  and anomie, 225
  of father, 218
  of men, 175, 215, 216, 218, 225, 227, 229, 352
  occupational, 148, 159, 215
  of patient, 304
  of police, 383
  sexual, 213, 215, 218
  training for, 158
  of women, 175, 210–214, 225, 227, 229, 231, 352
Roman Empre, 436
Romano, Octavio, 198
Romantic love, 6, 10, 148, 152
Roosevelt, Theodore, 72, 174, 277, 426
Rosen, Bernard, 185
Roszak, Theodore, 108, 112
Rough Rock, 203
Ruitenbeek, Hendrick, 215, 218, 224
Russell, Bruce, 444
Russia, 47, 281, 426, 438–440, 443, 455
  and arms race, 444
  and balance of power, 443
  and balance of terror, 444
  child-care centers, 220
  and China, 449
  nuclear weapons, 445, 447
  psychiatry in, 305
  in United Nations, 442
Rustin, Bayard, 137, 255, 257

S

Saccharin, 76
Safety:
  of automobiles, 80, 81
  and working conditions, 132–133
St. Louis, 38, 58
Salerno, Ralph, 360
Salmonellosis, 74, 76, 249
San Francisco, 36, 38
San Francisco State College, 107, 143
Sanchez, George I., 197

476